Agriculture
in the
Global Economy

HUNGER 2003
13th Annual Report on the
State of World Hunger

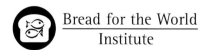

Bread for the World
Institute

50 F Street, NW, Suite 500
Washington, DC 20001
USA

© 2003 by Bread for the World Institute
50 F Street NW, Suite 500
Washington, DC 20001
Telephone: (202) 639-9400   Fax: (202) 639-9401
E-mail: institute@bread.org
Web site: www.bread.org

Printer: HBP, Hagerstown, Md.

Cover photos: PhotoDisc, Jim Stipe, FAO, Margaret Nea

Manufactured in the United States of America
First Edition Published in March 2003
ISBN 1-884361-11-0

Table of Contents

Table of Contents

Foreword

Rick Reinhard

Many people will face uncertainty this year. A worldwide economic slowdown means that hundreds of millions of poor families find it even more difficult than usual to provide food for their children. Wars and natural calamities threaten the very survival of millions of people.

While the number of undernourished people in the world has been gradually declining for several decades, the number may be increasing right now. Hunger crises have struck many countries.

One bright spot is the Bush administration's proposal to increase development assistance by $5 billion annually for poor countries that demonstrate their ability to use the money well. Funding would be channeled through a new Millennium Challenge Account, with the money increasing to the new level between 2004 and 2006. This could be a significant step forward in the fight against global poverty and hunger. Bread for the World's main campaign in 2003, *Rise to the Challenge: End World Hunger,* aims to win funding for the Millennium Challenge Account and keep it focused on reducing hunger and poverty.

While more development assistance is needed, hungry and poor people also must be able to earn a living on an ongoing basis. Most hungry people in developing countries live in farming communities. They work hard to grow their crops, but protectionism keeps some of their products out of the world's biggest markets. The prices they receive for their crops locally are sometimes depressed by imports of subsidized crops from industrialized countries.

The 2003 Hunger Report, *Agriculture in the Global Economy,* urges the United States and other industrialized countries to live up to their free-trade rhetoric and work to eliminate trade-distorting farm policies. That would open opportunities for millions of struggling families to work their way out of hunger and poverty.

Many Bread for the World members live in farm states. In preparation for this report, Bread for the World Institute staff visited California, Minnesota and North Carolina to talk with farmers and rural community leaders. While these people expressed concern about the severe hunger in poor countries, they also expressed anxiety about what the reduction of government subsidies might do to small farmers and rural communities in this country.

In fact, *Hunger 2003* finds that the current system subsidizes a small minority of farmers, and a few wealthy farmers and farm corporations receive huge payments. But most farmers get no help. Some of the money could be better spent on rural development, conservation programs and assistance to poor people in rural communities. These approaches help rural America without hurting poor farmers in developing countries.

U.S. agriculture also could draw some benefit from progress against hunger and poverty worldwide. Hungry families typically spend about three-fourths of their income on food. So when their incomes increase, they mainly buy more food, including some imported food. Take Southeast Asia: As it reduced hunger and poverty, it became a dynamic market for U.S. agricultural exports.

The book of Proverbs in the Old Testament says, "A poor person's field may produce abundant food, but injustice sweeps it away."

The world's richest nations need to reform their farm policies to serve the needs of rural America and, at the same time, give hungry farmers in poor countries a fighting chance to improve their livelihoods.

David Beckmann
President
Bread for the World and
Bread for the World Institute

Executive Summary

The world today produces enough food to feed everyone. Yet when farmers in Mozambique sink their hoes into dark red soil, most toil not knowing whether they and their children will go to sleep hungry that night. They face hunger despite hard work because they do not produce everything they need and often receive low prices for what they produce. This state of affairs happens partly because the United States and other developed countries flood Mozambique's markets with cheaper products – subsidized by taxpayer dollars.

Of the 840 million people in the world who are undernourished, nearly three-fourths live in rural farming communities and will continue to do so for generations. Agriculture is central to their ability to earn a living and feed their families. But for developing countries to build their economic potential, the 2003 Hunger Report, *Agriculture in the Global Economy,* finds that industrial-

…industrialized countries like the United States and European Union members should live up to their free-trade rhetoric and work together to eliminate trade-distorting subsidies and tariffs.

ized countries like the United States and European Union members should live up to their free-trade rhetoric and work together to eliminate trade-distorting subsidies and tariffs. As structured, the global agricultural system is stacked against poorer countries.

Many Americans believe the old saying, "Give a man a fish, and you feed him for a day. Teach him how to fish, and you feed him for a lifetime." They want U.S. foreign policy and development assistance to reflect this truism. According to a 2002 survey commissioned by the Alliance to End Hunger, nearly 40 percent of Americans polled say the most effective way to fight world hunger is to help farmers in poor countries produce more food. The second most popular solution is to promote more open markets and economic development in poor countries.

Yet the United States and other developed countries continue to protect their agriculture by paying some farmers more than $300 billion in subsidies annually – six times what they give in development aid. Because these payments encourage farmers to produce more, world agricultural markets are glutted with subsidized crops like corn, cotton, sugar and wheat, ultimately leading to lower prices for all farmers.

Current U.S. farm policy enables it to export certain commodities at prices well below production costs; corn, for example, is priced at 20 percent below costs. Though many developing countries have the advantage of cheap land and labor, their farmers cannot compete with these subsidized prices. Unable to sell their products even in national and local markets, poor farmers and rural communities are condemned to a cycle of poverty and hunger.

The current system of agricultural subsidies is not the best way to deal with poverty and economic decline in rural America either. Less than half of U.S. farmers receive subsidies. Economically stressed communities in rural areas would be better served through economic development initiatives, business promotion, job training, infrastructure development and direct assistance to poor families. Subsidies have been in place for generations, and some farmers would need time and help to adjust without them. But a better path must be found that supports America's rural economies and provides U.S. farmers with feasible options without distorting global markets.

Marty Lueders

Marty Lueders

important to developing countries, but reforms in North America and Japan also are needed. The impact of liberalization would vary among developing countries, and some low-income food-importing countries would need help in coping with less food aid and higher food prices. But over time, nearly all developing countries, especially poor rural populations, would benefit from the liberalization of agriculture.

In fact, liberalizing agriculture is in the interest of rich and poor alike. The estimated gains to all countries from the elimination of trade-distorting subsidies and tariffs in developed countries would be $100 billion, according to the International Monetary Fund. Most of the gain would go to consumers in industrialized countries themselves.

Reducing world hunger also would contribute to peace and security. And it would increase demand for agricultural products. Poor, hungry families spend most of any increase in income on food, including food imports. As East Asia reduced poverty and hunger in recent decades, it became a dynamic market for U.S. agricultural exports.

Of course, trade alone cannot solve the many complex problems facing poorer countries. Developing countries themselves must support agricultural and rural development with research and agriculture extension, roads and communication networks, credit, and storage facilities. Property rights and involving poor people in decision-making processes, especially women, also are important. Industrialized countries can help by increasing poverty-focused development assistance. But reforming global agriculture would raise farm prices and improve export prospects, so that hungry rural people have more opportunity to work their way out of poverty.

The many powerful interests at stake in global agriculture will make reform difficult. But unless the reform process begins, farmers and their families in Mozambique and other poor countries will not escape the grip of poverty and food insecurity. Farmers and communities in rural America will face continuing economic decline as well.

The farm policies of industrialized countries are contributing to the persistence of world hunger. Yet an agricultural system that really works to sustain rural communities and feed the world is within reach.

Last year, the Bush administration took a significant step forward in the fight against global poverty and hunger by proposing to increase development aid by $5 billion annually for poor countries that demonstrate their ability to use the money well. Funding would be channeled through a new Millennium Challenge Account, with the money increasing to the new level between 2004 and 2006. If achieved, this increase should include important new funding for agriculture and rural development. But poor countries also need access to U.S. and other developed country markets for their agricultural products.

New research released in this report indicates that the elimination of subsidies and protection in industrialized countries would allow developing countries to triple their annual net agricultural trade (exports minus imports), from $20 billion to $60 billion. That is about two-thirds the value of all development and humanitarian aid provided by industrialized countries. Getting European countries to liberalize agriculture is especially

Wisdom is like a baobob tree;
no one individual can embrace it.

Akan and Ewe Proverb

March marks the peak of the dry season in Mali. The fields are brown and – to an unknowing eye – appear as vast desert plains dotted with an occasional baobob tree reaching to the sky. It can be hard to imagine that the land produces enough millet and other cereals to feed nearby villagers; some years, it doesn't.

Still, Baro Toure – a 36-year-old farmer who lives in Garna, a village outside of Segou – normally is optimistic at this time of year. March is a good, steady month during which she earns extra money selling tomatoes or onions at the weekly village market, and the grain supply remains ample. But this March is more difficult than most. The past couple of seasons have been drier than normal, and harvests have been thin. Although Baro usually has enough millet and extra income from making soap and selling vegetables to feed her family until the next harvest, this year she may not.

In her region of Mali – part of the sahel – the "hunger season" begins and ends with the summer rains. July marks a month when many families run out of millet or rice and switch to peanuts or other groundnuts for food. Cruelly, this happens just as the planting of fields begins, and everyone needs as much energy as possible. It's also the height of malaria season. Some people – especially young children and *koroches* and *koromusos*, old men and women – die before the year's end because of sickness aggravated by hunger.

In past years of low millet yields, Baro's family has purchased extra grain with money that her husband, Nyemey, gains from selling the peanuts he grows as a cash crop. But this year, few people are buying his peanuts. Modibo Koulibaly – a cotton farmer from Sikasso – typically buys much of Nyemey's peanut crop to sell along with his cotton. However, this year Modibo will receive 2 cents less a pound for his cotton. World cotton prices have dropped to their most unprofitable level in three decades. Meanwhile, he also must pay 2 cents more a pound for fertilizer.[1] He can barely cover the costs of his harvest, much less buy Nyemey's peanuts. As Baro gathers firewood to prepare the after-

noon *toh* (millet porridge) she ponders the uncertainty of this year's rains and wonders how she will feed her family when July comes.[2]

Baro and her family are just a few of the 840 million people who live and work not knowing whether tomorrow they will have enough food to eat. [3] One in five people who are hungry is a child. In a poor country like Mali, even more children go hungry – two out of five – and nearly a fourth of all children die of hunger or related causes before they reach their fifth birthday.

Wages of Hunger

Every day, hunger eats away at our world's future. Yet hunger persists. It continues despite the fact that the world produces enough food to feed everyone (see Figure I.2). In 2002 farmers produced 2,800 calories of food per person, enough to adequately nourish everyone everywhere.

Hunger persists because people either do not have access to food, as in Maharashtra, India, where 800 children reportedly died of starvation in 2002 despite the fact that the government was spending some 350 million rupees daily ($7,000) to stockpile food, a third of which ending up rotting,[4] or they cannot afford to buy the food available to them.

In the United States – one of the richest countries in the world – the number of poor and hungry people is on the rise, with farming communities in the South and West experiencing large increases (see Figure I.1).[5]

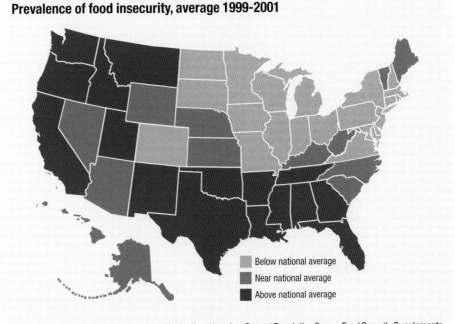

Figure I.1: Hunger Affects the U.S. South and West Most Severely
Prevalence of food insecurity, average 1999-2001

Below national average
Near national average
Above national average

Source: Calculated by U.S. Department of Agriculture based on Current Population Survey Food Security Supplements

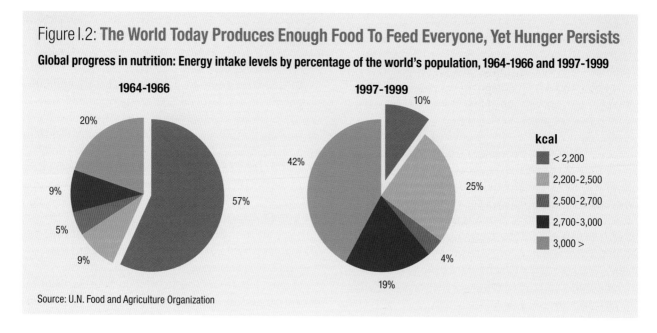

Figure I.2: The World Today Produces Enough Food To Feed Everyone, Yet Hunger Persists

Global progress in nutrition: Energy intake levels by percentage of the world's population, 1964-1966 and 1997-1999

1964-1966

20%
9%
5%
9%
57%

1997-1999

10%
42%
25%
4%
19%

kcal
■ < 2,200
■ 2,200-2,500
■ 2,500-2,700
■ 2,700-3,000
■ 3,000 >

Source: U.N. Food and Agriculture Organization

Although hunger also is a problem in cities, three-fourths of the world's poor people live and work in rural communities and will continue to do so for many decades. Their employment and income usually derive from agricultural activities. They have little land, schooling or other assets and opportunities, and thus face many barriers to escaping poverty.[6]

The agricultural productivity and sustainability of these communities, as well as agriculture's role as an income source for them, must be considered when addressing long-term food security strategies.

Feeding Today's World

For decades, nations have professed their desire to end hunger. At the last World Food Summit, they even set a deadline for cutting hunger in half: 2015. Food security initiatives now are considered hand-in-hand with most poverty-reduction efforts, which are receiving more attention in the post-Sept. 11 campaign against terrorism. Yet governments' actions usually fall short of their rhetoric.

The 2003 Hunger Report, *Agriculture in the Global Economy,* argues that the current international trading system is unfair. Commodity dumping and market protection practices undermine developing countries' ability to improve their agriculture. As long as industrialized countries like the United States continue to protect their agriculture markets with trade-distorting subsidies and tariffs, developing countries' rural areas cannot realize their full potential. *Hunger 2003* finds that U.S. subsidies are not the best way to deal with poverty and economic decline in rural America either.

Despite efforts by the World Trade Organization to liberalize agricultural trade and phase out developed country market protections, the United States, European Union, Japan and other developed regions continue to maintain trade-distorting policies that artificially depress world prices for some key agricultural commodities like corn, cotton, rice and wheat – commodities that many poor people rely on for their livelihoods.

In 2001 these protections totaled 30 percent of gross farm income in industrialized countries at a cost of $300 billion. This amount represents six times what industrialized countries are spending on overseas development assistance. This level of agricultural protection costs developing countries $2.5 billion a year in lost revenue.[7] At the same time, foreign aid levels are near their lowest levels since the 1970s (see Table I.1)

In a country like Mali, the world's third-largest cotton producer, cotton's potential to enhance the economy and help alleviate poverty for Mali's 8.2 million people who live on less than $1 a day is unquestionable. Instead, the United States and other industrialized countries subsidize their cotton farmers. An overabundance of subsidized cotton on the world market undercuts Mali's competitiveness and reduces its options for moving from poverty to self-reliance.

The 2002 U.S. farm bill, the Farm Security and Rural Investment Act, provides $180 billion to American farmers over the next 10 years in the form of subsidies, conservation and other agriculture-related payments – nearly $84 billion more than they received in the previous bill.

Farm subsidies are a controversial and complex issue. But clearly, eliminating farm subsidies in industrialized countries would benefit agriculture in developing countries. Eliminating subsidies would benefit industrialized countries as well.

Still, subsidies continue.

Subsidies Ease U.S. Farming Changes

For smaller American farmers, like Tom Briggs, subsidies serve a vital purpose. Every year, alterations in the world economy coupled with advances in agricultural research and technology trigger changes in his farming methods and way of life. The subsidies help ease the difficult and often-costly transitions such change may require.

Tom has worked as a peanut farmer in south-central Georgia for 33 years. Like Nyemey and other farmers worldwide, he struggles daily to balance too much rain with too little, sweltering summer heat that arrives at the wrong time, market prices that plunge below production costs, insects and diseases that undercut his labor, increasing international competition and evolving consumer demands.

In 2002 dry weather and disease during the growing months and wet weather during harvesting curbed the production of Georgia peanut farmers by 730 pounds per acre compared to the year before. Tom will be the first to tell you that farmers need dry conditions for the best crop yield, and too much rain disrupts harvesting. Sometimes, peanut vines can get so damaged that the peanuts can't be picked.

During a year like this, Tom must consider whether his yield will make the crop profitable. Will crop quality be a problem? Will the market price change between now and harvest? Will he need more fertilizer or pesticides than normal? These factors and others affect his bottom line.

Farming's ups and downs are not new to Tom. Between 1989 and 1995, peanut consumption in the United States decreased by 18 percent, threatening the viability of Georgia's peanut industry. News stories linking peanut consumption with obesity and cardiac disease fueled some of this decline. Fortunately for Tom and other peanut farmers, later research debunked these reports, and helped reverse the negative trend.[8]

More recently the 2002 farm bill scrapped the peanut quota system, which had been in place since 1935 to control supply and prop up market prices. A new subsidy program was established that pays farmers $610 per ton less than they made under the old system. While Tom admits that these subsidies are better than none, over the long run he likely will have to reduce his acreage or settle on earning less money per ton of peanuts that he did before. Short-term, the U.S. government will pay him 11 cents per pound ($220 per ton) per year through 2006.

Common Struggles

At first glance, Tom's and Nyemey's struggles are not so far apart. Both farmers grow peanuts, and they always have; both battle the weather, and they always will; and both continue to grow peanuts even though the market no longer pays them enough to cover costs.

However, unlike Nyemey struggling on his own, Tom has the U.S. government to help cover financial losses. He also has access to groundbreaking research, time-saving (although expensive) technologies and, to a certain extent, credit should he decide to change crops or quit farming altogether. When world peanut prices tumble, his family does not go hungry. The average U.S. farm household now earns $64,117 annually, nearly $6,000 more than the average American family.

Nyemey, on the other hand, still grows peanuts not only because that's what he knows, but also because during lean times they help feed his family. Larger Malian farmers – mostly cotton growers like Modibo – have

Table I.1: Developing Countries Are Receiving Less Help From Richer Neighbors

Foreign assistance to developing countries has declined steadily during the 1990s, from $103 billion to $84 billion. The share of assistance for agriculture and rural development activities also has declined, from 13 percent in 1990 to 11 percent in 1999.

Total Official Development Assistance (ODA) from Industrialized Countries in Billion Dollars*

Year	1990	1991	1992	1993	1994	1995	1996	1997	1998	1999
Total ODA commitments	**$103**	**$94**	**$82**	**$85**	**$85**	**$79**	**$80**	**$76**	**$83**	**$84**
Total agriculture and rural development commitments	$13	$10	$11	$8	$9	$9	$9	$11	$10	$9
Share of agriculture and rural development assistance in total ODA	12.6%	10.6%	13.4%	9.4%	10.6%	11.3%	11.3%	14.5%	12.0%	10.7%

* Expressed in terms of 1995 U.S. dollars.

Source: U.N. Food and Agriculture Organization

better access to buyers and ports and can participate in the larger national and international markets. Smaller farmers, like Nyemey, often sell some of their peanuts to these middlemen to earn needed cash.

But when Modibo no longer can make enough money from his cotton because dumped product from industrialized countries is crushing world cotton prices, then Modibo no longer can buy Nyemey's peanuts. His purchase of other people's goods and services in Mali, Burkina Faso and Senegal also decline. Without Modibo as a buyer, Nyemey, like many other small farmers, no longer has access to a market. As a result, his family's chances of becoming food insecure multiply.

Poverty Claims Many

Poverty and hunger are a fact of life in many countries and many communities; the United States is no exception. Despite being one of the richest countries in the world, its poverty rate has held steady for the past 20 years at slightly more than 12 percent.

Although urban centers traditionally have been associated with the highest rates – a trend that continues – hunger and poverty in suburban and rural areas are increasing. The communities with the fastest growing rates are found in the farming areas of the rural South and West.[9]

In Georgia, overall rural poverty rates are about the same as the national average, slightly more than one in 10 people lives below the poverty line. However, in many rural areas – especially the southern part of the state – one in three people lives in poverty. In Tom's Washington County, poverty afflicts one in five people.

As Congress debated the 2002 farm bill and whether to increase subsidies, many of its discussions focused on rural poverty's connection to the rising number of small farms being lost to agriculture's growing consolidation. "We have witnessed and are experiencing the failure of recent farm programs that have driven farm families off the land that their parents and grandparents settled, causing rural poverty and decline of rural communities," according to the National Family Farm Coalition in testimony submitted to the House of Representatives as part of 2001 hearings on the commodity title of the farm bill. "Lack of net farm income is the fundamental reason for this ongoing rural crisis."

Georgia's peanut and cotton growers – and spokespeople for other agriculture sectors – used these U.S. rural poverty numbers and concerns about the loss of small family farms to bolster their argument that subsidies must continue because rural America's survival depends on them.

However, employment numbers tell a different story. Agriculture now provides less than 8 percent of the jobs in rural America. Moreover, farm subsidies reach barely more than a third of all farmers. Most farmers of fruits, livestock, poultry and vegetables receive no direct support from the government.

Remembering a Past...

Although Tom cannot imagine himself farming without quotas or subsidies, his father and grandfather coped with little to no support from the U.S. government.

Tom's father would tell his son that as a young boy he had witnessed Tom's grandfather hitching up the plow to

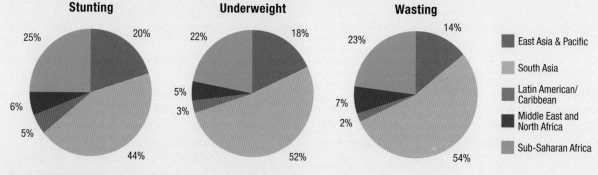

Figure I.3: Undernourished Children Suffer Severe Health Effects

An alarmingly high number of children in developing countries suffer serious health effects because they are chronically hungry. Nearly 200 million children have stunted growth; close to 150 million children are underweight. And almost 50 million children are seriously underweight, a condition known as wasting.

Every year, 6 million children die before their fifth birthday because of chronic hunger and related diseases like diarrhea.

Undernutrition-related Conditions Affecting Children Younger Than 5 in Developing Countries, by Region

Stunting
- 25%
- 20%
- 6%
- 5%
- 44%

Underweight
- 22%
- 18%
- 5%
- 3%
- 52%

Wasting
- 14%
- 23%
- 7%
- 2%
- 54%

Legend:
- East Asia & Pacific
- South Asia
- Latin American/Caribbean
- Middle East and North Africa
- Sub-Saharan Africa

Source: UNICEF State of the World's Children 2002

a mule on the family's one-acre farm. Dressed in overalls and hat, the grandfather would plod behind his mule with his homemade plow, up and down the rows, working sometimes more than 75 hours a week to produce a mere acre of peanuts, which as a tenant farmer he had to share with his landlord.

The tenant farmer lifestyle was the backbone of southern agriculture during the 1930s and 1940s. It is what many Americans still think of when they hear the words "farming" and "rural America."

What they soon forget – or never know – is that farmers traded in their mules for Model 8N Ford tractors that could produce the same acre of crop in just six or seven hours. Still, life was hard and farming was uncertain. Many farmers grabbed any chance they could to make life easier. As they grew more productive, their numbers declined and farms grew larger.

This change did not happen overnight. Public investment in agricultural research and technology as well as rural roads, schools and health care led to healthier, better educated, more productive farmers who had the choice to trade in the farm for a job in the city or suburb.

Some people look at the changing face of rural America and see the disappearance of an era, a lifestyle, a natural resource; some see growing suburbs, increasing congestion, pollution and urban sprawl. Others see sharecroppers' children who now have options and enjoy a quality of life that their parents and grandparents worked hard to secure.

Imagining a Future...

The strength and diversity of people living in rural America today highlights the need for agricultural programs that go beyond commodity programs and instead focus on reducing poverty and developing rural areas both in the United States and worldwide. But how do we build an agricultural system that works for the benefit of poor and hungry farmers like Baro, Nyemey, Modibo and Tom's poorer Georgian neighbors? A system that works for the poor but does not undermine Tom's and other U.S. farmers' well-being in the process?

The 2003 Hunger Report, *Agriculture in the Global Economy*, seeks to answer these questions by first understanding how the current agricultural system works, who is benefitting from it, who is losing because of it and what likely is the best path for moving forward.

Chapter 1 describes the relationships that characterize agriculture worldwide, such as the those between consumers and producers, rural and urban communities, and domestic and international policies. It explores the varied roles agriculture plays, focusing on the potential of agricultural development for promoting economic growth and reducing poverty and hunger in developing

Marty Lueders

The intensification of war and conflict in the Middle East and worldwide, rising rates of HIV/AIDS and other diseases, and weather-related disasters mean that record numbers of vulnerable people – especially women and children – are facing hunger.

countries. It also examines the roles farmers, consumers, governments and corporations play in agriculture's evolving complexity as a business.

The chapter then turns to North-South tensions over agriculture, mostly stemming from trade concerns. It explains the lopsidedness of current market protections and their impact on developing countries.

Chapter 2 focuses on U.S. agriculture and the role U.S. farm policy plays in sustaining U.S. farmers' income and rural development. The chapter shows that continued efforts to tweak farm subsidy and other farm programs have failed to support the smaller, family farm. Indeed, farm programs appear to have sped the disappearance of mid-level farmers who, unlike their smaller counterparts, work full time in agriculture, but unlike their larger counterparts, often operate at a loss.

The challenge is to create a comprehensive U.S. farm program that promotes sustainable agriculture, assists those farmers most in need and encourages rural economic development.

Similar matters are explored in Chapter 3, but on a global scale. This chapter finds that while the system technically should work to balance the uneven nature of today's global trade – while promoting sustainable development for poor countries – the reality is that the rich and powerful gain. To correct this imbalance, developing countries must gain access to trade negotiations, especially those related to agriculture, to ensure that their voices are heard and their interests are protected.

This need is nowhere more apparent than in sub-Saharan Africa, where rates of hunger and poverty

U.S. Farm Policy: The First 200 Years[1]

By Anne B. W. Effland

Passage of the 2002 farm bill stirred much debate about the direction U.S. farm policy should be taking. Reflection on the precedents and origins of today's policy can help frame this debate.

Since the founding of the national government more than 200 years ago, U.S. farmers have been supported by markedly different approaches, which roughly coincide with four overlapping periods of debate and transition. Although conflicting interests have marked each period, one remarkably consistent public consensus has remained: The problems inherent in farming warrant public support.

Promoting Agriculture in a New Nation (1785 – 1890)

For the first five or six decades after the United States became a nation, the focus of national government was expansion and development.

Early federal land policy favored the sale of large amounts of land at relatively high prices to increase government revenues and transfer public lands to private hands. Slow sales, however, and pressure from interests that favored transfer of public lands to small, independent farmers led to progressively more liberal laws governing sales, culminating in the Homestead Act of 1862, which provided for the free distribution of land to anyone who would settle and farm it. Land distribution on these terms continued in unsettled areas into the 20th century, but the bulk of American farmland had been claimed and the traditional American frontier considered closed by 1890.

Two political-economic philosophies dominated debate over land distribution issues during this period: (1) those who argued that public land was an asset to be sold with most revenues going to the government, reducing the need for taxes; and (2) those who argued that public land should be used to foster settlement by small, independent farmers.

This latter group believed that widespread settlement would support further development by increasing population in new areas, fueling economic growth and, in the earliest years, securing the nation's territorial claims. Such settlement also would assure development in the new territories of a reliable independent citizenry not beholden to the politically or economically powerful. These citizens would own their land and depend only on the labor of their families for their well-being, exemplifying the agrarian ideal.

With the passage of the Homestead Act, this group succeeded in embedding this agrarian ideal in federal land policy, setting a precedent for national support of independent family farm systems that continues to influence farm policy today.

Moving Agriculture Toward Efficiency (1830 – 1914)

In the 1820s, many progressive farmers, journalists, educators and producers of commercial farm inputs began to look for ways to improve farmers' productivity and quality of life. Farmers began to organize into state and county agricultural societies, promoting the need for specialized training and scientific research to advance the industry's productivity and professionalism.

Much support for these ideas came from older farming regions in the East and South, which had begun to suffer from competition with newly opened lands in the West. The availability of extensive, fertile lands on which staples like cotton, wheat and livestock could be produced more cheaply forced farmers in older, settled regions to evaluate their production methods. Years of cultivation without attention to preserving soil fertility had led to falling yields and even land abandonment, particularly in areas growing cotton and tobacco. Some of these farmers saw potential for greater competitiveness through, for example, improved fertilizers and better methods of preparing soil for planting.

The United States also was maturing as a nation and experiencing rapid urban and industrial growth in cities along the eastern seaboard. Improving agriculture productivity would support other industries' development by releasing labor, producing raw materials for these industries and feeding the growing urban population. Agricultural leaders looked to government for support of the research and education programs such productivity growth would require. Arguments for public support of such programs centered on the belief that to be effective, advancements in agricultural productivity needed to be broadly accessible to the large population of independent farmers on whom the nation depended.

Federally supported agricultural education and scientific research eventually took four major forms: establishment of the U.S. Department of Agriculture (USDA) (1862), authorization of a national system of agricultural colleges (1862), appropriation of federal funds to support agricultural science research at state agricultural experiment stations (1887), and organization of an adult education system, USDA's Cooperative Extension Service (1914).

In May 1932, workers plodded behind mules tied to plows, cultivating cotton on a farm in Eastover, S.C.

Agrarianism Clashes with Industrialism (1870 – 1933)

As agriculture, manufacturing and other industries continued to expand, the increasing consolidation and wealth of urban-based industries began to contrast with the relative poverty and unconsolidated nature of agriculture. Between 1870 and 1890, chronic national surpluses of farm products depressed prices, while regionally repeated droughts, grasshopper infestations and other natural disasters compounded problems for farmers in the Great Plains and Far West. Repeated national financial panics throughout the period made credit scarce and expensive.

Most farmers had moved beyond self-sufficient frontier farming and were becoming increasingly dependent on markets. As farmers saw their incomes falter, they watched the rising revenues and increasing political influence of railroads, processors and urban financial interests.

Primarily in the South and West, farmers organized to demand federal assistance. Eventually forming the Populist Party in the 1890s, they advocated national government control of an expanded money supply, government ownership of transportation (railroads) and communication (telegraph) systems, an income tax to replace high tariffs as a source of federal revenue, and continued government support for land distribution to small, independent farmers.

Other farm organizations proposed expanding education and research programs to help individual farmers compete in free markets. During the 1910s and 1920s, several such programs were administered through the Cooperative Extension Service and USDA's new Bureau of Agricultural Economics. Farmers gained other assistance as well that improved their ability to compete, such as agricultural cooperatives, market information services and infrastructure development.

Tackling Economic Depression & Chronic Overproduction (1924 to Present)

Between 1910 and 1914, the rise in population migration from rural areas to cities and the end of a continual expansion of acreage in agricultural production led to slower growth in food production. With increased demand for food from growing U.S. urban populations and, during the second half of the 1910s, from a world embroiled in war, food prices reached levels at which farmers could achieve incomes on par with other industries.

Soon after the war ended, however, demand for U.S. food exports plummeted as European production started to recover, and U.S. farm prices fell accordingly. In response, farm leaders began discussing a proposal for a national program to support farm prices by controlling domestic supplies and using exports to absorb surpluses.

Although presidential vetoes held off the program during the 1920s, Congress twice passed measures providing for direct government intervention to lift farm prices by controlling supplies. But it took a Depression to get the price supports farmers wanted.

USDA Photo/Russell Lee

Pea pickers work under the hot sun of June 1941, unloading buckets of peas collected on a Nampa, Idaho, farm.

Farmers' demands for an equal share of prosperity were swept up in a much broader package of direct federal interventions as the overall economy faltered. Beginning with Franklin Roosevelt's New Deal in 1933, the solution to rapidly falling farm incomes was primarily price supports, achieved through dramatic reductions in supply available to the market. Supply controls for staple commodities included payments for reduced planting and government storage of market-depressing surpluses when prices fell below a predetermined level.

> **Congress twice passed measures providing for direct government intervention to lift farm prices by controlling supplies. But it took a Depression to get the price supports farmers wanted.**

The combination of price supports and supply management functioned as the essential outline of federal farm policy through 1996, although the mechanisms and relative weights of the policies' components were modified by successive farm legislation. In some years, notably during World War II and postwar reconstruction, and again during the early 1970s and mid-1990s, global supplies tightened sharply, sending demand and prices soaring above farm price supports and rendering acreage reduction programs unnecessary. But repeated cycles of above-average production and/or reduced global demand put downward pressure on prices, keeping the programs popular and well-funded.

Nonetheless, intense debate continued between proponents of high price supports and those who believed farm prices should be allowed to fluctuate according to market forces of supply and demand. During the mid-1950s to the mid-1960s, the Eisenhower administration fought to return the U.S. economy and government bureaucracy to pre-New Deal, pre-World War II structures. Out of the debate came a compromise for farm policy, the Food and Agriculture Act of 1965, which made most production controls voluntary and set price supports in relation to world market prices, abandoning the "parity" levels intended to support farm income at 1910 levels. A system of direct income support ("deficiency") payments compensated farmers for lower support prices.

During the 1980s farm financial crisis, the debate over price supports and supply control recurred. The Reagan presidency sought to end "big government" and place the American farm economy on free-market footing. This time, with steadily increasing government program commodity stocks and record-level federal budget deficits, the argument against continuing expensive government support of the farm economy gained support.

The farm crisis also eroded some of the farm sector's confidence that domestic price supports and production controls were an effective way to secure U.S. farm income in a global economy. Supported U.S. prices reduced international marketing opportunities, and increasing global supplies undercut domestic production control efforts.

Farm legislation passed in 1985 and 1990 maintained the traditional combination of price supports, supply controls and income support payments, but introduced changes that moved farmers toward greater market orientation (i.e., lower price supports, greater planting flexibility and more attention to developing export opportunities for farm products).

By the time of the Federal Agriculture Improvement and Reform Act (FAIR) of 1996, which legislated a dramatic shift in the character of federal assistance to farmers, farm policy seemed again to be passing into a new period. The policy consensus behind the 1996 legislation held that farmers would be better equipped to compete in global markets under a system that allowed nearly complete planting flexibility and that promised continued government efforts to enhance access to international markets.

Another Transition at Hand?

The Farm Security and Rural Investment Act of 2002 continued two of these key directions, the separation of some income support payments from production and planting flexibility, while increasing support for conservation-related programs. The chronic low prices of the late 1990s led to the addition of new counter-cyclical income supports under the 2002 Act, but developments in agriculture over the past several decades have led to a changed context for farm policy that works against wholesale return to past policies.

Increasing productivity, consolidation in the agricultural industry, movements toward more open global trade, an increasing emphasis on market-driven production decisions and attention to environmental costs of agricultural production appear to be gaining influence on current policy discussions. Public debate surrounding the 2002 farm bill suggests some have begun even to question the long-held consensus that farmers should receive government assistance, at least in the form of direct payments. The level of support provided in the new farm legislation, however, indicates public support for payments to farmers remains strong for now.

Transitions are never clear while they are ongoing. But given the continued scrutiny of commodity programs and the advancement of conservation programs in the 1996 and 2002 farm bills, it appears that a new type of agricultural policy may be emerging.

Anne B. W. Effland, holds a Ph.D. in agricultural history and rural studies from Iowa State University. She has been a historian and social science analyst with the Economic Research Service of the U.S. Department of Agriculture for more than 10 years.

In October 1928, Reuben Manning (right) and his three sons, Arnold, Nathaniel and Myron (right to left) readied for evening chores on their family farm in New London County, Conn.

[1] This article is a condensed version of "U.S. Farm Policy: The First 200 Years," which appeared in the March 2000 issue of *Agricultural Outlook* published by the Economic Research Service of the U.S. Department of Agriculture.

continue to climb. Although Africa faces many political, social and economic challenges, its progress in the fight against hunger and poverty has been hindered by specific constraints to agriculture, which is the lifeline of most African economies. Chapter 4 explores some of these constraints as well as how the choice to refocus investments in agriculture would benefit the majority of poor people. Increasing market access for and eliminating unfair competition against African products by reducing agricultural tariffs and removing industrialized country farm subsidies are not a panacea to the complex problems that African nations face. However, such steps would speed African agriculture along the road to economic development and improved welfare for its people.

When discussing improved welfare for people around the world, one cannot ignore the continuing slump in the U.S. and world economies, the intensification of war and conflicts in the Middle East and other parts of the world, the scourge of HIV/AIDS and other diseases, and the reality of drought, flooding and other natural disasters. Because of such troubles, record numbers of people are facing hunger and, in some parts of the world, starvation. Chapter 5 reports on these hunger hotspots, including the looming famine in Southern Africa, and efforts being made to avert such international disasters.

In Chapter 6, Bread for the World Institute outlines policies to move agriculture and trade in a fairer and more just direction and accelerate progress against hunger both internationally and in the United States. It urges rural economic growth that includes poor people and focuses on sound, sustainable agricultural policies, including the elimination of trade-distorting subsidies to developed country agriculture. The quantity and quality of development and financial assistance to poor countries also must be improved, and reforms should focus on empowering poor people, especially women.

Finally, Chapter 7 shows what you can do to help reform agriculture and trade – and help end hunger in our lifetimes. Reforming agricultural policies in the United States and other industrialized countries would open opportunities for millions of hungry families in the rural areas of developing countries to get higher prices for what they produce. That would encourage them and their governments to invest in ways that would raise their productivity.

But reforms will not take place until the damage that the current system is doing is more widely understood. Also, reforms should be designed in ways that would minimize hardship among farmers and communities in industrialized countries. In fact, reforms could channel more assistance to rural families and communities that really need help. But the shape and process of reform is complicated (see related story, p. 10).

So one of the first things you can do to help is to read this report. It will take you through the economic and political complexities, so that you can help others understand how the global agricultural system slows progress against hunger, and become an active and informed agent for change.

This report ends with data tables on hunger and related issues internationally and in U.S. states.

The Road Ahead

Although trade alone will not solve the many complex problems that poorer countries face, it can play a crucial role in developing their economies and improving their ability to help themselves (see related story, p. 14). In fact, creating a more equitable trading structure for agriculture is in the interest of all countries, rich and poor. The International Monetary Fund estimates that if all countries removed their agricultural protections – tariffs and both export and domestic subsidies – the world would gain $128 billion annually, with about three-fourths of the gain going to industrialized nations and the rest benefiting developing countries.[10] This figure does not include other "dynamic" gains that likely would result, such as countries adopting new technologies, increasing investment and improving productivity – gains that could double or triple this benefit.

Even if industrialized countries acted alone in liberalizing agriculture, they would increase their own real income by about 0.4 percent of gross domestic product. Using 1997 figures, that would amount to nearly $92 billion more for these nations. If just a fraction of that money was targeted at long-term development initiatives in poor countries, that would further accelerate progress against hunger and poverty worldwide.

Despite these clear benefits, changing today's agricultural system will not be easy. And no one knows that better than farmers like Baro and Nyemey, who deal with seemingly impossible challenges every day, challenges like feeding their families, caring for the sick and finding enough money to send their children to school.

• • •

Evening has fallen in Baro's village, and as she hears the Iman's call to prayer and begins to head back toward the village with a 15-pound drum of water perched on her head, she pauses, looks out toward the horizon and soaks in the dark silhouette of a boabob tree drenched in silky yellow, orange, red.

She's reminded of an old saying, Wisdom is like a baobab tree: No one individual can embrace it.

Changing today's agricultural system is possible, but it will require both wisdom and courage, the wisdom of people like Baro and the courage of national leaders to take the right path.

Enabling Rural Poor People to Overcome Poverty

By Lennart Båge

The world's poor people are hard-working experts in their survival. We can enable them to pursue their aspirations and overcome poverty by providing development assistance that is both responsive to their needs and strengths, and linked with opportunities to prosper.

This path firmly establishes poor people as the leaders in poverty reduction and constitutes the basic objective of the International Fund for Agricultural Development (IFAD), a specialized agency of the United Nations that has spent its 25 years empowering rural poor people to change their lives by linking them with assets, finance, technology, institutions and markets.

Why Focus on Rural Poverty?

Confronting rural poverty is central to overall poverty reduction. Why? Three-quarters of the 1.2 billion poor people living under the income equivalent of less than $1 a day are found in rural areas where livings are made through agriculture and related activities.[1]

Life is hard for rural poor people, most often women and indigenous peoples. Hunger, disease, lack of education and discrimination often prevent them from building a better future for themselves and their families.

Ventorina Odur at her farm in Alela, Uganda.

IFAD Photo/Robert Grossman

IFAD projects foster improved links between the rural poor and the basic tools they need to succeed as family farmers, farm laborers, herders, fisher folk and traders. Making their livings primarily from natural resources, like land and water, rural poor people need secure access to these resources. This provides them with a reliable economic base and the incentive to manage it sustainably. To enhance their capacity as producers and stewards of the environment, rural poor people also need:

- technologies (such as fertilizers, irrigation equipment and crop processing facilities) and training so that their businesses can become more efficient and competitive;

- financial services and markets, so that investment capital to increase the productivity and sales of their businesses is available, either in the form of savings or credit; and

- their own institutions, such as farmer co-operatives and water-use management associations, that are empowered to engage governmental bodies and make decisions related to their access to these tools.

Improved access to these resources helps rural poor people increase their incomes through hard work and ingenuity. Over time, poor rural households are able to provide for their basic needs and, ultimately, thrive.

Ugandan Partners in Development: A Case Study

In 1998 IFAD and Uganda began an eight-year partnership through the Vegetable Oil Development Project. The project helps poor Ugandan farmers, like Ventorina Odur, increase and diversify their incomes by growing sunflower and palm seeds to produce cooking oil, a product used by most Ugandan people.

The ongoing project:

- trains farmers in sunflower and palm seed cultivation;

- provides credit to farmers so they may invest in production and seed processing implements;

- establishes farmer associations that manage mills to process the sunflower and palm seed crops into cooking oil;

- builds roads in remote communities so the cooking oil that they produce can be shipped to meet consumer demand; and

- consolidates cooking oil producer associations within the Uganda Oil Palm Co., in which 7,500 smallholder families will own 10 percent of total shares.

With the credit and training Ventorina received through this project, and after significant amounts of work, basics like salt and soap are no longer luxuries. She has used the profits of a single year's sunflower seed crop to diversify her farm's assets. Although she still produces traditional crops, such as cotton, sesame, sweet potatoes and groundnuts, she has purchased chickens, goats, and a cow. She also has saved enough money to send her children to school and buy them new clothes.

Ventorina's success shows how community-based rural and agricultural development can make a real difference in the lives of poor people by pairing productivity improvements with market access. Such applications of development assistance drive broader economic growth linkages throughout national economies, opening new opportunities for poor rural people to prosper. Higher incomes from agriculture fuel greater demand for goods and services from the rural nonfarm sector as well, such as in agricultural inputs, machinery repair, crop processing and transportation. In sub-Saharan African countries, for example, each $1 increase in agricultural production generates more than $2 for the national economy.[2] Moreover, each 1 percent increase in agricultural productivity reduces poverty by 0.6 percent.[3]

Markets and Rural Poverty Reduction

Powerful, community-driven economic growth by itself cannot eradicate poverty over the long term. For farmers like Ventorina, continued prosperity will depend on their ability to enter and compete in the larger national, regional and global markets.

In developing countries, improved farmer-to-market linkages have been constrained by overly restrictive legal frameworks concerning the registration of farmer institutions, the lack of effective

Ventorina (middle) harvesting her sunflower crop with her daughter Joan (left) and mother Flora (right).

legal frameworks for contract enforcement and by excessive licensing requirements for traders. Differing standards and inspection systems for crop quality and safety, as well as bureaucratic bottlenecks, also have been obstacles.

Developed countries now spend $300 billion in agricultural subsidies to some farmers each year. These subsidies result in large crop surpluses that, when traded, lower prices received by poor farmers in developing countries.[4]

In nearly all countries, agricultural goods face trade barriers and tariff systems that increase the rate of import taxes proportionately to processing levels that increase product value. These make the cost of imported agricultural goods artificially expensive and less desirable to consumers who subsequently purchase cheaper goods from domestic producers.

The cumulative effect of these agricultural and trade policies are distortions in markets, which stifle trade in agricultural products and, subsequently, the expansion of commerce in the poorest countries where agriculture is the basis of the economy. Because most poor people in these countries make their livings through agriculture, these distortions effectively reduce the potential of development assistance to reduce poverty.

In view of the risks associated with farming – such as drought, floods, pests and price fluctuations – and the need for a reliable food supply, the existence of these protections around the world is not surprising. Yet by liberalizing trade in agricultural products, rich gains can be shared broadly. If all countries were to remove their systems of protection in agricultural trade, the International Monetary Fund and the World Bank estimate that world export revenues could expand by $378 billion. The majority of these revenues would go to developed countries. About $122 billion would be shared among developing countries.[5]

With ongoing negotiations aiming to liberalize trade in agriculture through the so-called Development Round of the World Trade Organization (WTO), the international community has a chance to create new opportunities for the rural poor to prosper while pursuing broadened economic integration. Still, liberalizing trade in

agricultural products is only part of the task before us. Other entrenched obstacles will prevent rural poor people's access to markets. Increased, targeted aid has a crucial role to play in helping the poor overcome these obstacles.

Today, roads linking the poor rural communities with larger markets often are seasonal, badly maintained or nonexistent, making transportation of products expensive and difficult. Farmers' ability to transport goods to markets often depends on what they and their animals can carry. And in the absence of crop storage technologies and facilities, many perishables do not survive the journey to market. Additionally, poor communication infrastructure makes access to reliable and up-to-date information about prices, products and potential business partners difficult, if not impossible.[6]

Translating liberalized agricultural trade into an engine for poverty reduction ultimately requires effective rural community development and initiatives that broaden market access. Big challenges lie ahead. Fortunately, world leaders have expressed the

We possess a historic opportunity to support millions of poor people struggling to build lives of dignity instead of deprivation.

resolve to surmount them by pledging at the U.N. Millennium Summit to cut poverty in half by 2015. Vested with the ability to achieve this goal, we possess a historic opportunity to support millions of poor people struggling to build lives of dignity instead of deprivation.

Lennart Båge is president of the International Fund for Agricultural Development.

[1] International Fund for Agricultural Development (IFAD), *Rural Poverty Report 2001: The Challenge of Ending Rural Poverty*, IV and 1.

[2] Per Pinstup-Andersen, Mattias Lundberg and James L. Garret, *Foreign Assistance to Agriculture: A Win-Win Proposition.* International Food Policy Research Institute, Food Policy Statement Number 20, July 1995, *http://www.ifpri.org.*

[3] C. Thirtle and J. Piesse Lin, "The Impact of Research-Led Agricultural Productivity Growth on Poverty in Africa, Asia and Latin America," Working paper, Department of Environmental Science and Technology, Imperial College of Science, Technology and Medicine, London, United Kingdom, 2001, 17.

[4] Organization for Economic Cooperation and Development (OECD), "Agricultural Policies in OECD Countries: Monitoring and Evaluation 2002," 4, *http://www.oecd.org/pdf/M00030000/M00030609.pdf.*

[5] International Monetary Fund and the World Bank, "Market Access for Developing Country Exports: Selected Issues." Approved by Timothy Geithner and Gobind Nankani, Sept. 26, 2002, 32, *http://www.worldbank.org/research/trade/marketaccess.pdf.*

[6] IFAD, 163-164.

Poorer Countries Would Gain from Open Agriculture Markets

By Xinshen Diao, Eugenio Diaz-Bonilla and Sherman Robinson

Global agricultural trade could help poor and hungry people in developing countries help themselves. But to do so, rich countries like the United States and European Union nations must eliminate their trade-distorting agricultural protections.

New research by the International Food Policy Research Institute (IFPRI) finds that liberalizing industrialized country agriculture would triple developing countries' agriculture net trade – agricultural exports minus imports – from about $20 billion to $60 billion (see Table 1). This net gain would result from an increase in exports of about $37 billion and a reduction in imports of about $3 billion (see Table A.1, p.123).

Moreover, farmers and agro-industries would see an estimated $26 billion more in annual income (see Table 2).[1] And this figure does not include additional economic growth that would be stimulated in the rest of the economy from expanded agriculture, which would double or triple rural incomes.[2]

For the nearly 3 billion mostly poor people living in developing countries' rural areas, this additional income would help them lift themselves out of poverty. In sub-Saharan Africa – where one in three people are undernourished and most (80 percent) live on less than $2 per day – incomes from primary agriculture and food processing could increase by $2 billion a year.

Because of the complexities of agricultural trade, liberalization's overall impact on specific countries would vary, with some countries importing and exporting more or less than others. Still, the results suggest that most developing country farmers would produce more food domestically, leading to expanded employment and incomes not only in the agricultural sector, but also in the rest of the economy, which ultimately would decrease hunger.

Regional Divide

Agriculture is highly protected in many industrialized countries, especially in Japan and member countries of the European Union. The average tariff rate for bulk agricultural commodities – one indicator of agricultural protection – is more than 50 percent in Japan and more than 23 percent in the European Union.

Because developing countries' export markets are concentrated among a small group of industrialized countries – such as European Union nations and the United States – agricultural liberalization among these countries would create export opportunities for many, if not most, developing countries.

These benefits would be distributed based on regional trading patterns. For sub-Saharan Africa, nearly two-thirds of its increase in exports ($2 billion of $3 billion) would stem from trade liberalization in the European Union. For Asia's developing countries, the results would be more balanced, with the United States, European Union and Japan-Korea each contributing a third to their overall gain. Meanwhile, for many Latin American countries, such as Mexico and Colombia, most of their increase in agricultural exports would be due to opening E.U. and U.S. markets.

As the largest market in world agricultural trade, the European Union's agricultural policies have important effects on developing countries. While the majority of developing countries share a common interest in calling for more open E.U. trade, more open Japanese, Korean and U.S. markets also are in the interest of developing countries, especially those located in Asia and the Western Hemisphere.

Food Prices and Incomes

Eliminating agricultural tariffs, domestic support and export subsidies worldwide also would cause different agricultural prices to fall or rise, depending on current levels of market protection and subsidies. Oilseeds, sugar and wheat would experience the greatest price hikes, with the elimination of E.U. protections appearing to have the largest effect on world prices (see Table A.2, p.123).

While higher prices help farmers both in developed and developing countries, higher prices could hurt some consumers – especially poor urban consumers – and net food-importing countries. Better farm incomes and related employment benefits to rural communities from higher prices of traditional crops, greater access to global markets for other products, such as fruits, sugar and vegetables, and the multiplier effects on employment and income for the rest of the economy resulting from a more vibrant agricultural sector, likely would more than compensate these vulnerable populations, thereby not harming overall food security.

Still, steps would need to be taken to ensure that vulnerable populations are compensated and food security is not compro-

By opening industrialized countries' agricultural trade, poor small farmers in developing countries would benefit from greater productivity, expanded employment and higher incomes.

Jim Stipe

Table 1: Developing Country Net Agricultural Trade
(Exports Minus Imports)

| Developing Country Regions | 1997 Trade Levels | Agricultural Trade Liberalization of | | | | Percent Gain |
		United States only	European Union only	Japan, Korea only	All Industrialized Countries	All Industrialized Countries
		Trade in Billion Dollars				
Sub-Saharan Africa	$7.4	$8.1	$9.6	$7.6	$10.7	45%
Asia	$12.3	$15.6	$15.6	$15.7	$22.8	85%
Latin America and Caribbean	$31.7	$37.1	$39.3	$32.5	$46.4	47%
Other Developing Countries*	−$31.0	−$29.4	−$21.9	−$30.1	−$19.1	38%
All Developing Countries	$20.4	$31.4	$42.6	$25.7	$60.8	198%

Table 2: Annual Income Increase of Farmers and Agro-industries from Trade Liberalization

| Developing Country Regions | Agricultural Trade Liberalization of | | | | Percent Income Gain per GDP |
	United States only	European Union only	Japan, Korea only	All Industrialized Countries	All Industrialized Countries
	Income Gain in Billion Dollars				
Sub-Saharan Africa	$0.5	$1.5	$0.2	$2.0	3.6%
Excluding Republic of South Africa	$0.2	$0.9	$0.1	$1.1	5.1%
Asia	$3.3	$2.9	$2.3	$7.4	2.0%
Latin America and Caribbean	$3.9	$5.1	$0.6	$8.9	3.2%
Other Developing Countries*	$1.5	$6.5	$0.3	$7.5	3.6%
All Developing Countries	$9.2	$15.9	$3.4	$25.9	2.8%

*Other developing and transition economies.

Note: Simulations for the European Union, United States and Japan consider each country/region only. Simulations for all industrialized countries include the three countries/regions at the same time, plus other developed countries, such as Canada and Australia. Because of the complexities of agricultural trade and countries' trading practices, the effects of liberalization will change depending on which markets are being liberalized. Consequently, the individual scenarios depicted in the model simulations may not add up.

mised. Fortunately, poverty-focused assistance is more effective – because it is more easily targeted – in urban communities, where some poor consumers could be harmed by higher food prices. International food aid can help in this regard if it is managed in a way that does not displace domestic production in the recipient countries.

Some food-importing developing countries with high food-import tariffs should consider reducing them progressively to cushion the impact of higher world prices on poor consumers. After all, high tariffs on imported food operate as a regressive tax on poor consumers. At the same time, all developing countries, particularly the poorest, should expand investments in rural development, poverty alleviation and health and nutrition. For this to happen, additional funding from international institutions and bilateral donors will be needed, as well as firm political commitment and good governance in the countries involved.

Xinshen Diao, Eugenio Diaz-Bonilla and Sherman Robinson are researchers at the International Food Policy Research Institute.

[1] These estimates may be conservative to the extent that overall use of land has been kept fixed in the model scenario. Further information on land uses would allow more precise estimations of the total impact of the policies considered.

[2] These results also have implications for the debate, mainly in rich countries, about the multifunctional effects of agriculture, that is the notion that additional positive results, such as beautiful landscapes or environmental protection, flow from agriculture, which would justify its subsidization and protection. It seems clear that subsidies and protection in rich countries displace agricultural production in developing countries, which, if the argument about the multifunctional nature of agriculture were true, would imply that those effects, along with the displaced production, also are negative for developing countries (see Eugenio Díaz-Bonilla and Jonathan Tin, "That Was Then But This is Now: Multifunctionality in Industry and Agriculture," Trade and Macroeconomics Division Discussion Papers Number 94, International Food Policy Research Institute, March 2002).

Global
Agriculture

Today's global agriculture system produces more than enough food to feed everyone and provides people access to a wider range of foods than ever before. Yet 840 million people remain undernourished, with most living in developing countries' rural, farming areas.

Although the world population has doubled in the past 40 years, remarkably food production has kept pace with – even exceeded – this increase, permitting a steady if slow rise in average food intake per person. Between 1969 and 1999, the average daily amount of food available per person worldwide rose from 2,410 kcal to 2,800 kcal. In developing countries, the increase was 2,110 kcal to 2,680 kcal.[1]

Measuring caloric intake in the aggregate, however, masks the fact that not all people in all countries are eating more. Hunger affects individuals and households, and for many people, food insecurity and hunger are a part of everyday life. During the 1990s, food insecurity actually increased in the Near East, North Africa, South Asia and sub-Saharan Africa.[2] In the United States, where the rate of overweight Americans increased by 61 percent between 1991 and 2000 resulting in more than half of Americans being overweight, some 33 million people continue to live in households at risk of hunger (see related story, p. 54).[3]

The scale of food insecurity and hunger differs by region and country. The dynamics of hunger are different in Australia than in Bangladesh. But no matter where, people who are hungry usually face one or a combination of two problems: lack of food and lack of income to buy food. Mohammed Ali Indris of Ethiopia describes food insecurity this way: "We have stopped buying teff [staple starch] and edible oil. We are eating mainly corn. The children's skin is getting dry and they are showing signs of malnutrition."[4]

In some regions, notably sub-Saharan Africa, a lack of money is compounded by a physical absence of food and other problems, such as ongoing conflicts and rising HIV/AIDS rates. Degraded soils, dependence on rain and lack of fertilizer can inhibit agricultural productivity, leading to chronic food shortages. In West Africa, several countries face food supply difficulties because of localized unfavorable weather (Chad, Ghana), or past or ongoing conflict and population displacements (Guinea, Liberia, Sierra Leone). Weather catastrophes can cause the failure of a year's staple crop, like the 2002 Southern African drought, which decimated the corn crop, leaving 14 million people confronting starvation. Even in countries that produce enough food, weak distribution systems and isolated populations can cause local food shortages.

Unless people can grow their food and/or earn enough money to buy it (assuming it is locally available), all the food in the world will not alleviate hunger. Both rural and agricultural development play crucial roles in helping to address this predicament.

Figure 1.1: Global Hunger: Widespread, Persistent and Unacceptable

Today 840 million people are undernourished and nearly all of them – 800 million people – live in developing countries. While great strides have been made in the fight against hunger, unless decisive action is taken, the number of people undernourished and hungry will rise again in regions like East Asia and sub-Saharan Africa.

Hunger in the Developing World

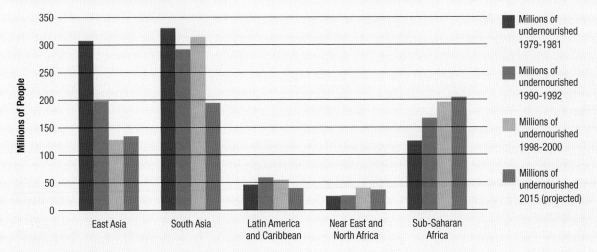

Source: Food and Agriculture Organization of the United Nations

Key Hunger Terms

Key Terms	Definition
Hunger	A condition in which people do not get enough food to provide the nutrients (carbohydrates, fats, proteins, vitamins, minerals and water) for active and healthy lives.
Malnutrition	A condition resulting from inadequate consumption (undernutrition) or excessive consumption of one or more nutrients that can impair physical and mental health, and cause or be the consequence of infectious disease.
Undernutrition	A condition resulting from inadequate consumption of calories, protein and/or nutrients to meet the basic physical requirements for an active and healthy life.
Food Insecurity	A condition of uncertain availability of or ability to acquire safe, nutritious food in a socially acceptable way.
Food Security	Assured access for every person to enough nutritious food to sustain an active and healthy life, including: food availability (adequate food supply); food access (people can get to food); and appropriate food utilization (bodies can absorb essential nutrients).

Rural, Agricultural Development

Nearly three-fourths of poor people who live on less than $1 a day are found in developing countries' rural areas.[5] Moreover, the U.N. International Fund for Agricultural Development (IFAD) projects that most poor people will continue to live in rural areas until at least 2035.[6] As such, rural agricultural development is key to increasing poor people's access to both food and income.

Agriculture accounts for an average 14 percent of developing country gross domestic product (GDP). In 2000 more than half (55 percent) of workers in developing countries labored in agriculture. The average for sub-Saharan Africa, South Asia and East Asia was 64 percent.[7]

These statistics not only highlight agriculture's economic significance in developing countries, but also a way for small farmers and their families to win the fight against hunger and poverty: by earning a sufficient living from agriculture and its related activities. As stated by Abt Associates President John Mellor, "It is only with rising farm incomes that poverty can be reduced."[8] Increasing farmers' incomes, even by small amounts, increases demand for services in local communities, providing income sources for others living in rural areas as well. Rural development also helps ease urban poverty by slowing migration from the countryside.[9]

Evidence suggests that in developing countries, agricultural growth nearly always benefits poor people,[10] with the greatest gains going to those most in need.[11] Empirical work points to a "strong relationship between agricultural productivity and poverty," associating a 1 percent yield increase with a 1 percent drop in the severest poverty, people living on less than $1 per day.[12]

In most countries, agricultural growth also is more likely to reduce poverty than industrial growth. In India,

a project assessing poverty reduction through household surveys during the past 50 years found: "Fostering the conditions for growth in the rural economy… must be considered central to an effective strategy for poverty reduction in India."[13]

In industrialized countries, the relationship between agriculture and rural development is less direct. Although some of rural America's poorest people are landless laborers and indigenous people who rely on agricultural employment, a greater number of rural poor people depend on other industries, such as service, mining and manufacturing, for their livelihoods.

Whether in developed or developing countries, for agricultural and rural development to succeed, a sustainable approach must be pursued, stressing effective use of labor and environmental conservation. Concurrent progress also must be made in infrastructure, rural institutions, health and education.

Although agriculture's poverty-fighting potential in developing countries is gaining wider recognition, national policies and funding trends have yet to reflect its promise.[14] The United States and other developed countries continue to protect their agricultural industries in ways that undermine poorer countries' trade opportunities. Moreover, agriculture continues to receive low levels of aid and investment from both donor institutions and developing country governments. Agriculture's share of total official development assistance (ODA) averaged a mere 12 percent during the 1990s, while developing regions themselves spent only an average of slightly more than 4 percent of total expenditure on agriculture. Such trends must be reversed.

But these trends are tangled in a net of complex relationships, some of which are impeding progress. As such, it is necessary to understand the modern role of producers; consumers; local, national and international markets; rural and urban constituencies; developed and developing countries; and domestic and international politics and how they interact to shape agriculture in the global economy.

Farmers' Vital Role

Most of the world's farmers live in developing countries and are poor. Farmers' activities fall between subsistence (producing only enough for personal consumption) and commercial (producing solely for sale). In developing countries, most farmers grow crops both to eat and sell, whereas in industrialized countries, most farmers grow crops primarily for commercial markets.

Sixty percent to 80 percent of farmers are women. As families' primary caretakers, rural women in developing countries grow and harvest most staple crops that feed their families. In sub-Saharan Africa, women account for 75 percent of household food production. Food security throughout the developing world depends primarily on women. Yet they own only a fraction of the world's farmland and receive only a fraction of agricultural extension delivery (less than 10 percent) and agricultural loans (see related story, p. 22).

Most women and other developing country farmers operate in what is called the informal economy. In Peru, 90 percent of the agrarian sector is informal, meaning official institutions do not legally register it. These farmers do not have legal ownership of their possessions.[15] In India, only 1.39 million people officially are recognized as being employed in agriculture even though the Washington, D.C.-based Indian Embassy estimates that two-thirds of Indians – approximately 660 million people – derive their livelihoods from agriculture.[16]

Despite geographic and economic differences, farmers share similar needs – productive land, water and capital – and struggles. At the beginning of the growing season, they need at the very least seeds and tools, although many also rely on machinery, pesticides, herbicides and fertilizer to boost yields. At harvest time, most farmers need somewhere to sell their produce, a market. And if a farmer does not earn enough from selling his produce to cover the cost of next year's seeds, fertilizer and other inputs, he will need to borrow money, a credit source.

Of course, these general necessities manifest themselves differently in various countries, reflecting great variety in farming size, structure, production methods and complexity. The average farm in Africa is roughly three acres. In the U.S. Midwest, it is more than 1,000 acres. A U.N. Food and Agriculture Organization (FAO) study identifies eight broad categories of farming systems, each which can be subdivided further. In Latin America alone, no fewer than 16 different systems operate. Vast differences exist among regions and within countries as well. Legal and political systems, labor markets, standards, available resources, and transportation networks also color farmers' experiences.

In South America, land ownership is highly concentrated, with a few landowners possessing the most fertile lands while most farmers are relegated to ecologically fragile lands. In Brazil, 19th century parceling of land into large holdings precluded the development of a viable family-farm system. Largely as a result of this policy, Brazil today is a highly urban country with one of the most unequal income distribution rates in the world. In some countries, such as Mozambique, the government officially owns all land; private citizens live on and work certain plots, but do not hold formal title. While this policy ensures that every family has a place to live, it also precludes Mozambicans from using their land as a productive asset. Without title to land as collateral, farmers often find it difficult to receive credit for investment. In the United States, secure land tenure is assured, but high land values support farm consolidation and serve as a barrier to young farmers looking to enter agriculture.

Water is another necessity. Though drought affects farmers worldwide, in Africa less than 10 percent of the cultivated land is irrigated, meaning African farmers depend much more on variable rainfall than European farmers. Moreover, rural poor people in developing countries increasingly are concentrated in arid, semi-arid and unreliably watered areas,[17] making chronic water shortages more common for poor farmers.

BFWI Photo/S. Bunch

In the United States, while agriculture remains important to rural economies, the majority of rural people depend on other industries for their livelihoods.

Women Can Lead the Way in Trade

By Marceline White

Edline Normil, a Haitian rice trader at a mill in the Artibonite valley, says that when the markets in Port-au-Prince are awash with imported rice, many buyers do not make the journey to the valley to purchase domestic rice. On two or three occasions every month she is left with rice she cannot sell. "When this happens, either I have to pay additional transport costs to take the rice home to store it, or I have to sell it at an even lower price just to get rid of it," she explains.[1]

Edline is one of thousands of women farmers and farm workers around the world struggling to succeed in the global economy. While some have gained new opportunities, many others are struggling to make ends meet.

In Edline's case, the problems began in 1995 when trade liberalization policies eliminated import restrictions on agricultural goods and reduced tariffs from 40 percent and 50 percent to between zero and 15 percent. As a result, Haiti's rice production has dropped from 180,000 tons of rice to slightly more than 100,000 tons. Meanwhile, within a decade, imported rice from the United States has grown from 79,000 tons to more than 215,000 tons. Haitians have given up eating traditional crops in favor of cheaper, imported rice, further increasing the country's vulnerability to world price fluctuations for rice.

Edline's story is similar to many others. Although the locales vary, women play an important role in farming and food production around the world. In 1990 women subsistence farmers accounted for 62 percent of total female employment in low-income countries.[2] In Africa, women farmers are responsible for 80 percent to 90 percent of domestic food crops.[3]

Despite these important contributions, women constitute more than 70 percent of the worlds' poorest citizens, according to the United Nations. Trade liberalization and trade agreements affect women differently than men for myriad reasons.

- Women are disproportionately poor due to social and cultural discrimination, which limits their access to education, technological training, credit and land.

- Women are not hired for many jobs for which they qualify because the jobs are considered "male" jobs. Moreover, women often are considered secondary wage earners, often earning lower wages than men for the same or similar types of jobs. They also usually are the last workers hired and the first fired.

- Women still do the bulk of reproductive work – caring for their families, preparing meals, and keeping the household clean and functioning. This invisible work means that women have less time to gain new job skills, seek new jobs or rest.

- Finally, race, class, ethnicity and geography affect the ways in which women can or cannot participate in the local, national or global economy.[4]

Women are clearing land to help build an artificial lake in one of Haiti's arid zones. This is an important step in increasing their farm productivity.

These factors affect women farmers' ability to reap benefits from the global economy. For example:

- Formal laws and customary rules govern women's access to and control of land in many cultures. As a result, women often possess marginal land that is difficult to farm, and their right to land often is precarious.

- Social and cultural discrimination means that women farmers are less likely to receive agricultural extension services, credit or training.[5]

- In developing countries, men and women often cultivate different crops. Sociocultural norms typically dictate that women produce staple crops for domestic production while men engage in cash crop production.

- While both men and women engage in agricultural production, women are solely responsible for household food production, household maintenance and family care provision. Time use studies of women in Tanzania found that on average a woman worked between 12 hours and 16 hours a day in agricultural and household work.

Trade Liberalization and Women Farmers

Trade policies often encourage countries to shift their agricultural production from staple foods for domestic consumption to products for export. To promote export-oriented agriculture, governments often cut subsidies to farmers that grow traditional crops. At the same time, tariff reductions can make it cheaper to import lower-cost fruits and vegetables that compete with domestic products. For example, in Guyana fruit juice from France and Thailand displaced domestically produced juices.[6]

Although these imports mean that cheaper foods are available for urban markets, they also mean that small farmers receive less income. One result is the increased consolidation of farms, often at the expense of small farmers and their communities.[7] Export-led agriculture subjects basic commodities to the will of the market. This change can lead to wild price fluctuations and devastatingly low prices on basic crops if there is a glut in the market, and small farmers may lose money on crops if their input costs are too high compared to the prices they get for the crops.

For women farmers, this shift has several implications. As farmers move toward cash crop production, the amount of land being allocated to domestic crops has decreased and food security has diminished in many countries, notably in parts of Africa. Susan Joekes' research in Africa has shown that as families have shifted women's and children's labor toward more labor-intensive cash crop production, the production of household crops has declined and nutritional status has fallen for women and children.[8]

Because women are in charge of household and staple crops, women farmers often fail to gain from export-oriented agriculture. In Ghana, men control cash crops like pineapples. Women may work on family farms or as itinerant farm workers to grow pineapples but they do not receive the cash income from the produce. At the same time, many of the crops that women produce, such as rice, maize and cotton, are the ones hit hardest by imported-crop competition. Ghanian women have had trouble diversifying their crops because they have difficulty garnering the credit and land needed to shift to other nontraditional exports.[9]

When credit and other support is available for growing cash crops, some women farmers have benefited from trade liberalization. In Kenya, women farmers who own small plots of land have succeeded in exporting green beans to Europe and other regions. The profit margin on green beans is high. Most importantly for women, green beans can be grown on a family farm, which provides women the flexibility to care for their families while cultivating cash crops. In addition, green beans require specialized skills that women already possess from growing their family garden crops.[10]

Small farmers who cannot compete with commercial, monocrop farms or the influx of cheaper imports have developed new coping strategies to meet basic needs. As a family's income falls, many women take new jobs on large, monocrop farms as seasonal farm workers or food processors. While this work is an improvement over unpaid labor, these seasonal jobs can be poorly paid and precarious.

Colombia, for example, is the second largest source of flower exports in the world. One out of every two flowers sold in the United States originates in Colombia where more than 80,000 women work in greenhouses earning less than $2 per day. The flower plantations use harsh pesticides and rarely provide safety gloves or other equipment for workers. National health and safety regulations are rarely followed on these plantations. Medical surveys have shown that flower workers have illnesses ranging from nausea, asthma, rashes and headaches, to miscarriages. Such flora culture costs affect entire rural communities. Environmentally, the flower boom has huge costs as well. Water tables are shrinking, and high levels of toxins have been found in the groundwater.

In sum, more needs to be done to help women farmers gain new opportunities in the global economy, both to increase their families' incomes and their families' food security. Internationally, trade agreements should include provisions that protect people who may go hungry because of trade liberalization. Trade negotiations should allow the continuation of policies that protect food security. The United States should provide development aid to:

- support traditional and nontraditional agricultural exports in which women control the proceeds.

- work with women's groups in low-income countries to increase women's entitlement to land and access to credit.

- retrain women farmers who have been displaced.

- provide legal support and health care assistance to workers who are exposed to pesticides and other harmful chemicals.

- ensure that American companies, contractors and subcontractors that produce agricultural products abroad abide by U.S. labor standards and observe U.S. health and safety protocols for their workers.

Marceline White is director of the global trade program of Women's EDGE, a coalition for women's economic development and global equality.

1 Mark Curtis, *Trade for Life: Making Trade Work for Poor People.* (London: Christian Aid) 2001, 156.

2 Rekha Mehra and Sarah Gammage, "Trends, Countertrends and Gaps in Women's Employment." *World Development* Vol. 27 No. 3, 1999, 538.

3 U.N. Development Program statistics, 1999.

4 Marceline White, "Making Trade Work for Women: Opportunities and Obstacles," Women's EDGE, May 2000.

5 Sarah Gammage, Helene Jorgensen, Eugenia McGill and Marceline White, "Framework for Gender Assessments of Trade and Investment Agreements," Women's EDGE, Oct. 15, 2002.

6 "Agriculture, Trade and Food Security Issues and Options in the WTO Negotiations from the Perspective of Developing Countries – Volume I." Food and Agriculture Organization (FAO) of the United Nations Symposium at Geneva, Sept. 23-24, 1999. Available from http://www.fao.org/docrep/003/X4829e/X4829e00.htm.

7 "Agriculture, Trade and Food: Country Case Studies – Volume II." FAO, July 2000. Available from http://www.fao.org/DOCREP/003/X8731e/x8731e00.htm.

8 Susan Joekes and Ann Weston, *Women and the New Trade Agenda.* (New York: UNIFEM) 1994, 54.

9 Myriam Van Stichele, "Ghana Case Study." International Coalition for Development Action, 2000.

10 Office of Women in Development, U.S. Agency for International Development, Information Bulletin No. 7, December 1999.

Farmers' Declining Value

Because of their direct relationship to food, land and water, farmers have the most influence on food quality and land stewardship. Yet they are the "weakest link in the chain."[18]

Many of the corporations involved in agriculture have gone global. The opportunities presented by the global marketplace are vast. But international marketing – especially commodity dumping – can limit small farmers' opportunities to sell their products in local markets, making it difficult for them to earn wages and buy food. Generally, input costs have risen and commodity prices have fallen during the past few decades, with small farmers worldwide earning ever less money.

Farmers' share of food revenue also has declined because of the trend toward food processing. If a consumer purchases an ear of corn at a farmer's market or roadside stand, he knows that corn probably came straight from the farm and that most, if not all, of the money goes to the farmer. On the other hand, a bag of tortilla chips bought at the grocery store is the result of a much longer chain of events – few of which involve a farmer. Although the farmer still grows the corn, the corn is sold not to a consumer, but a trading company or processor, which then grinds it and adds it to other ingredients to make tortilla chips. These chips then are packaged and sold to a grocery store where companies like Tostitos and Frito Lay vie for shelf space to display their brand. Only then can a mother buy a bag for her family.

With each processing level, value is "added" to the corn – now in the form of a bag of corn chips – and its price increases, while the original farmer's role in creating the final product shrinks as does his share of the profit. If a marketing campaign accompanies the product, as in most cases, consumers' prices increase while farmers' consumer-dollar share decreases further (see Table 1.1).

On average U.S. farmers receive approximately 20 cents per dollar spent on food.[19] The other 80 cents pays for marketing – including processing, transportation and distribution – involving myriad middlemen and other players. Of the $619 billion Americans spent on domestically grown food in 1999, approximately $498 billion was spent on marketing.[20] Only $121 billion went to farmers.

At least most U.S. and other developed country farmers are assured a market by their governments. Not all farmers have that luxury. In many developing regions, farmers face the practical problem of physically reaching a market. Often, roads connecting rural areas with urban centers, if they exist at all, are poorly maintained and may be impassable in wet weather. Without good roads, rural populations remain isolated and likely poor.

This difference highlights the most fundamental difference between developed and developing country farmers: choice. Whereas most industrialized country farmers farm because they want to – and their governments help assure that option through market protection measures – poorer country farmers farm because they have to in order to survive (see related story, p. 27).

Strength of Local Markets

In developing countries, many farmers sell most of what they grow at local markets. A small farmer in Bolivia likely takes his rice to the village market, where various local people can purchase it. If farmers can sell their produce locally and directly to consumers, they save on processing, marketing and other middlemen costs. In industrialized countries, too, farmers may do best by catering to local markets. More often, farmers in

Table 1.1: More Processed Foods Leave U.S. Farmers Shortchanged

Food	2000		
	Retail Price	Farm Value	Farmer % of Retail Cost
Eggs – Grade A large, 1 doz.	$0.91	$0.48	53%
Apples, red delicious, 1 lb.	$0.92	$0.19	21%
Potatoes, 10 lbs.	$3.80	$0.66	17%
Peanut butter, 1 lb.	$1.89	$0.42	22%
Corn flakes, 18-oz. box	$2.14	$0.09	4%

Source: U.S. Department of Agriculture food marketing and price spreads: farm-to-retail price spreads for individual food items
http://www.ers.usda.gov/briefing/foodpricespreads/spreads/table1.htm

Consumers: Primary Players in the Global Food System

Consumers are the ultimate participants in the food system. Everything that takes place on the food-production ladder has the consumer dollar, euro, peso, rand or rupee in mind. Food companies spend vast amounts of money on marketing and advertising each year to make their products appealing to consumers. Consumer preferences, therefore, can be a powerful force in the food system.

For example, American demand for beef that looks, tastes and costs the same every day, every week of the year has led to arguably a more efficient beef industry. As the beef and other food industries strive for consistent product at cheaper prices, they are becoming larger and more consolidated in order to take advantage of economies of scale.

Consumer preferences in how foods are produced also can shape the industry. The organic market has developed and prospered in many industrialized countries because some consumers increasingly prefer to buy bread or other food items made from

Consumer demand for a variety of consistent, inexpensive food influences how foods are produced and can shape how the industry does business.

chemical-free, pesticide-free ingredients. Consumers who desire their meat or poultry raised under specific conditions can buy "free-range" products. Whereas "fair trade" items, like coffee, allow consumers to choose having more of their consumer dollars filter back to farmers.

Consumer preferences also can affect global agricultural production and trade. For example, Europeans' rejection of beef from cows given hormone injections led to a serious trade dispute between the United States and European Union, resulting in significant losses to the U.S. beef industry. (World Trade Organization arbitrators awarded the United States the right to suspend tariff concessions to the European Union in the amount of $117 million per year to make up for the damages caused by the ban, which it

ruled to be illegal.) In another case, European unease in consuming foods grown from genetically modified (GM) seeds has caused rising concern for African growers who are considering using GM seed to increase productivity, but need Europeans to buy their agricultural exports.

Moreover, consumer demand is not static. It changes over time, and with it the market for certain foods. A 2002 study of world agriculture by the Food and Agriculture Organization (FAO) of the United Nations found that diets worldwide slowly are converging on a North American model, with higher-protein and more expensive foods like meat and dairy becoming popular. People moving to urban areas also find a wider choice of foods in markets and changes in lifestyle that make time-saving processed foods more attractive.[1]

In developing countries, consumption of milk and dairy products has risen from roughly 61 pounds per person per year in 1964-1966 to 99 pounds today. By 2030, it could reach 145 pounds per year. According to the FAO, "These changes in diet have had an impact on the global demand for agricultural products and will go on doing so."[2] For example, global meat production has increased by almost a third since 1990, with most of the consumption growth in developing countries.[3]

Consumers' Changing Relationship to Food

Over the past several decades, consumers' relationship to food has changed considerably, especially in richer countries where most consumers no longer live on or near farms and rarely see food in its original form. Most food now eaten has been processed, packaged and transported many miles before it is pulled off the grocery store shelf and taken home. How often do city-dwellers pick apples off a tree, milk a cow or see it slaughtered? Consider even how much food the average American purchases at farmers' markets as opposed to grocery stores? Consequently, consumers are further removed from food sources than ever before.

Because of the complexity and invisibility of the many processing steps that occur as food leaves the farm and arrives on a supermarket shelf, consumers increasingly find it difficult to make informed choices and exercise their power as purchasers. To a certain extent, consumer preferences also are shapeable. Recent cases filed against major fast food companies charge that false advertising led consumers to eat more fast food than was healthy. While the legal merits of this argument might be doubtful, it does highlight the power of marketing to influence consumer behavior.

Still, the power of consumers to change today's agricultural system is high.

1 International Food Policy Research Institute, "Future Consumption Patterns in Developing Countries: From Rural to Urban, Malnutrition to Obesity, Sorghum to McDonald's." Available from http://www.ifpri.cgiar.org/2020/backgrnd/consump.htm.

2 FAO, *World Agriculture: Towards 2015/2030*, 2002. Available from http://www.fao.org/docrep/004/y3557e/y3557e00.htm.

3 Calculated from FAOSTAT data.

Rural poor people in developing countries increasingly are concentrated in arid and semi-arid areas with unreliable rainfall, making chronic water shortages more common for poor farmers.

industrialized countries cater to national and international markets. They typically take their produce to the local elevator or clearinghouse, which then sells to a trading company that may operate worldwide.

The Minnesota corn farmer gets paid at the local grain elevator, but the price is set on the Chicago commodity exchange and reflects global supply and demand.

Food and International Trade

Most food still is consumed in the country in which it is grown. In 2000 trade in agricultural products made up 9 percent of total world merchandise trade (compared to 74.9 percent for manufacturers), down from 12.2 percent in 1990.[21] Trade in food, valued at $442 billion, accounts for 7.2 percent of world trade.[22]

Only 6 percent of global rice production is traded, 17 percent of wheat production and 30 percent of soybeans.[23] Coffee and cocoa are examples of the few agricultural products raised primarily for export. Even so, agricultural products are the main source, sometimes only source, of foreign exchange for many developing countries.

It is important to remember that countries do not trade; companies trade. When 6.5 percent of 2000 world agricultural exports are attributed to France, it means that 6.5 percent of total world agricultural exports were grown in France. Grain trading companies – which may or may not have been French – in fact traded these products. To a certain extent, the profits earned by these companies are transferred to the rest of the economy

through job creation, rising share value (if publicly traded) or via the government through taxes that are used to finance government programs.

When it is said that the United States is pushing via the World Trade Organization (WTO) to open new overseas markets for agricultural goods, in fact U.S. trade representatives are negotiating greater opportunities for their corporations to move agricultural products internationally and do business in other countries – again, with potential benefits to the entire economy. The extent to which these benefits are distributed, though, depends on many factors, including agricultural policy.

Agricultural Policy

Certain features of agriculture make it fundamentally different from other industries. Agriculture is dependent on weather and other environmental factors, such as disease and pests, beyond a producer's control. Variation in temperature or rainfall can lead to lower crop yield. Severe drought or flooding can wipe out an entire year's harvest.

The fact that food is essential to human survival makes agriculture more likely than other industries to need government intervention to correct market failures and cope with natural disasters. People can survive without airplanes or telephones, but not without food and water.

Only recently has the industrialized world shifted from primarily agrarian to urban societies. Yet this agrarian heritage still greatly influences modern farm policy. In Japan, though little economic reason exists for growing rice, the country views its rice farmers as essential to its history and culture, and rice paddies as integral to the countryside. In the words of Kazuhito Morimoto, former president of Japan's National Council of Agricultural Cooperatives Youth Associations, "Rice, indeed, is our national identity, an identity that our nation has developed with wisdom and efforts over the last 2000 years."[24]

Governments usually cite three reasons for supporting and protecting agriculture, to: ensure sufficient food production for a country's needs; shield farmers from weather effects and world price swings; and preserve rural society.[25] Most developed countries use agricultural policy to help protect farmers and the agriculture industry, support agriculture research, and build rural communities. Of course, agriculture also has different functions in different countries. Industrialized countries' maintenance of rural landscapes to preserve scenic vistas for urban dwellers, for example, does not have an obvious equivalent in poorer countries.[26]

If industrialized countries tend to support their farm sectors, developing countries rather do not. In the past

Central American Drought Reveals Complexities of Food Insecurity

By Liz Fox

The community of Las Ovejas, Guatemala, is located within 200 yards of a flowing river. Yet persistent water shortages have destroyed three consecutive corn harvests. The 250-family community depends on rain for its subsistence crops, but richer landowners on the riverbank continually deny them access. Moreover, without adequate employment for day laborers, farmers lack money to buy food and drought-tolerant seed.

"It's all we can do" to survive, Las Ovejas resident Niomi Cruz says. "There is no hope. It all depends on the rain."

Fortunately, Las Ovejas' dry spell is an exception this year. For the most part, rain has returned to Central America after last year's devastating drought. Although most subsistence farmers in El Salvador, Honduras, Nicaragua and Guatemala can expect to fill their families' bellies till the next harvest, the underlying causes of food insecurity and endemic malnutrition remain. According to the World Food Program, more than 8.6 million people live in Central America's "drought corridor," with many people going hungry every year. Moreover, natural disasters will be the norm in this region for the foreseeable future.

Still, Mother Nature can be only partially blamed for these crises. Even during the driest months, local markets reportedly brimmed with fresh fruits and vegetables, meats and grains. "It wasn't that there wasn't food here," says an international agricultural researcher in Guatemala. "The food was here, but nobody could afford it."

Even when people can afford to buy food, bountiful markets can be a mixed blessing. Cheaper agriculture imports from the United States and Mexico mean local farmers must sell their products at lower prices. Unable to fetch profitable or break-even prices, many farmers have given up trying to produce more food than they can consume. And so, a perilous cycle ensues of farmers planting only what they can eat. If half their crop is destroyed by weather, they are left with little to live on.

Years of decaying governmental agriculture programs and export markets – largely in response to International Monetary Fund loan conditions to reduce bureaucracy and create smaller, more efficient states – further complicate matters. Agriculture funding and research no longer continue on the "same magnitude as before because there has been a restructuring of the economy and politics," says Manuel Osorio, a corn engineer at El Salvador's Center for Agricultural Technology. Although many government programs have been downsized, agriculture is the lowest priority, he adds.

In Guatemala, a government-run storage program that once housed surplus grain – and which could have helped feed the hungry – shut down shortly before the drought as part of government reforms. Likewise, El Salvador's agriculture ministry once played a crucial role in introducing higher-yielding and drought-resistant hybrid seeds, but Osorio says politicians have switched gears regarding the country's food production, and he is worried about the country's future food security. "They are thinking about the markets and cash crops, not about food security," Osorio says.

"If we continue this situation, if there is another period of these same politics, I don't know what people are going to do."

Until a few years ago, cash crops provided a reliable alternative income for farmers by enabling them to purchase seed and food, supplementing their subsistence diets. But Central America's role as primary exporter to the United States has suffered from the ebb and flow of international markets. As more countries develop export industries, global prices increasingly fluctuate, sometimes hurting small farmers well positioned to change with them.

World coffee prices are at an all-time low for the third consecutive year. According to the World Bank, some 600,000 coffee labor jobs have been lost in the past two years. Many Central

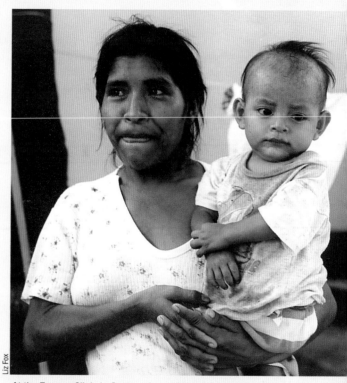

At the Zacapa Clinic in Guatemala, a mother brings her 1-year-old son for a checkup. Says Azucena Corado, a nutritionist at the clinic, "You can't tell from the outside, but when you weigh [the children], there is something wrong."

American coffee farmers have given up on the bitter bean and begun to replant their fields with less labor-intensive fruits and vegetables. The Central American melon market also has soured, eliminating the need for day workers who need these meager earnings.

"Before there was cane and coffee to give seasonal work," Osorio says. "There were subsidies for farmers. Now these are gone, and credit is harder to get, so people are cultivating less."

Liz Fox is a Mickey Leland International fellow with the Congressional Hunger Center.

40 years, developing countries generally have emphasized expanding industry over agriculture. In the race to build an industrial base – long considered the sign of a developed, prosperous state – many developing country governments either ignored agriculture or discouraged and exploited it. Governments often have taxed agricultural exports or maintained overvalued exchange rates, both which make agriculture exports more expensive and difficult. In India, government policy has suppressed agricultural prices to ensure cheap food for industrial workers.

The results have included persistent and entrenched poverty and hunger among rural people. Without a policy environment that supports agricultural productivity or at least removes the policy bias against rural concerns, rural poverty cannot decline.

Protecting Markets

Although most food is consumed in the country in which it is grown, one country's agricultural policy can – and does – have powerful effects on farmers and consumers worldwide. Its effects are transmitted both privately, via trade, and publicly, via the international institutions that attempt to manage today's increasingly global economy, notably the WTO.

Once demand at home is met, producers must look outside national borders for new buyers, as in the United States and European Union, where commodity production far outstrips domestic demand. These governments' agricultural policies focus on seeking and opening foreign markets as a way to keep excess production from depressing domestic prices. Because of their economies' size, they dominate the international agricultural markets. The United States is both the leading exporter (12.7 percent) and importer (11 percent) of agricultural products in the world. The top five agricultural exporters – the United States, France, Canada, the Netherlands and Germany – account for more than a third of world agriculture exports (by value); the top 15 exporters account for nearly two-thirds.[27]

Many arguments related to agriculture, especially between the North and South, are about market access. Market access refers to the extent to which foreign producers can export products to another country without facing barriers.

A country can limit access to its market in several ways. The most common example of an access barrier is the tariff, a tax put on an imported product when it enters a country. The intent of a tariff is to protect domestic production by making imports more expensive. For example, the European Union applies a tariff to cane sugar, raising the price of imported Dominican sugar in Europe, even if it was produced for much less.

Consequently, European consumers will purchase less Dominican sugar, less cane sugar will be imported than without the tariff, and trade is distorted.

The highest tariffs in the international trading system occur in the agricultural sector. The average tariff for an industrial product is 4 percent, while that for agricultural products is 62 percent (although they are not necessarily applied at this rate). The highest tariffs, called tariff peaks, exist in developed countries and often are applied to those products of most interest to developing countries. The United States, for example, applies peak tariffs to dairy products, peanuts and sugar. Although any tariff higher than 15 percent is considered a peak, they can be much higher. The European Union's tariffs on meat products peak at 826 percent.[28]

A common criticism of tariffs is that their cost falls disproportionately on poor people. The highest tariffs in the United States are on food and textiles. These are the things most often exported by developing countries and the things that make up a large percentage of the expenditures of low-income people. As such, they are doubly harmful to poor people.

A phenomenon called "tariff escalation" refers to raising the tariff on a given commodity at every processing level. For example, the European Union allows unroasted coffee free access while roasted coffee (one-level processing) is taxed at a rate of 7.5 percent. The United States charges 7.7 cents per kilogram on almonds in the shell but 24 cents per kilogram for shelled almonds. The more value added to a product outside the United States, the more it is taxed at the border. Tariff escalation is of special concern to developing countries because it discourages their development of a processing sector, thereby

Farmers who can sell their produce locally and directly to consumers often are most successful because they save transportation, marketing and other middlemen costs.

Food Aid: Help or Hindrance to Development?

When considering how to help poor and hungry people around the world, one of the first solutions that come to mind is food aid. Although simple in concept – one country giving food to another – in some cases food aid can harm a country.

For most people, food aid is the free food shipped to countries in crisis and on the verge of mass starvation, as in the summer 2002 when famine began to advance across countries in Southern Africa. The U.N. World Food Program (WFP) appealed for donations of food from the rest of the world to hold off a humanitarian catastrophe. When people think of food aid, they often envision large sacks of grain being unloaded from flatbed trucks against a parched landscape. But this emergency assistance is only one of many programs that come under the heading of food aid.

Program food aid forms a major part of U.S. food donations. The U.S. Department of Agriculture also provides long-term food assistance through grants, concessional sales or concessional financing. An explicit goal of the long-term programs is to enhance marketing opportunities for American farmers. According to former Secretary of Agriculture Dan Glickman, food aid has "been a useful market development tool."[1]

Moreover, the impacts of these long-term programs are unclear and possibly negative because they can create dependency, discourage local production and increase poor-country indebtedness. C. Stuart Clark of the Canadian Foodgrains Bank identifies three reasons why long-term food assistance can hurt recipient countries.

- First, it discourages local economic activity and creates dependency by providing free food beyond the immediate aftermath of an emergency;

- Second, it depresses market prices for locally produced staple crops, thereby acting as a disincentive for local production; and

- Third, it encourages a change in local food preferences, thus curtailing long-term demand for locally grown food.

The effects are disturbingly similar to those caused by dumped agriculture products. The criticism that program food aid tends to be driven by supply rather than demand is backed by the fact that the food used in these programs is rarely purchased locally, and rather taken from American commodity surplus stocks, even when local supply is available. Is it just another way to keep surplus grain from depressing the domestic market?

This question remains a bone of contention between the United States and the European Union in international trade discussions. The European Union accuses the United States of using these programs in lieu of export subsidies, saying they amount to much the same thing. The United States denies these accusations and refuses to discuss it within the World Trade Organization context.

[1] Ann Pettifor, "Debt is still the lynchpin: The case of Malawi." *Jubilee Research@New Economics Foundation*, July 4, 2002. Available from http://www.jubilee2000uk.org/opinion/debt040702.htm.

keeping them in the role of basic commodities supplier – raw cotton, raw coffee, raw cocoa. According to World Bank President James Wolfensohn, "Escalating tariffs in rich countries help confine Ghana and Côte d'Ivoire to the export of unprocessed cocoa beans; Uganda and Kenya to the export of raw coffee beans; and Mali and Burkina Faso to the export of raw cotton."[29]

Nontariff barriers to trade include quotas, which limit imports of a certain commodity for a certain period of time, and voluntary export restraints, in which a country refrains from exporting as much as it normally would to a given country.

Food safety standards and labor standards – indeed any international regulatory standard – also can be misused to keep foreign products out of a domestic market and, therefore, are the subject of heated debate among countries, especially between North and South.

The most controversial aspect of the global agricultural system is the level of financial support the European Union, United States and Japan give to their farmers. The European Union spends half its annual budget of $82 billion on support to farmers under its Common Agricultural Policy. The U.S. government legislated $180 billion over the next 10 years in its most recent farm bill, the 2002 Farm Security and Rural Investment Act. Although not all of this money supports commodity production, in 2001 the U.S. Department of Agriculture spent roughly $28 billion on commodity support and export programs.[30] Low-income countries cannot afford to subsidize their farmers to anywhere near this extent, if at all.[31]

Export subsidies, the most common form of export support, are government payments to a firm, industry or producer of an agricultural product to boost export performance.[32] Payments reduce the costs of marketing agricultural exports and can include handling, processing, international transportation and freight. Export credits, another form of support, guarantee to commercial banks that they will be repaid if they help foreign banks finance the import of certain agricultural products. Export support's ultimate purpose is to move excess domestic production onto the world market, keeping domestic prices high. Consequently, much food aid (excluding emergency food aid) also belongs in this category because it can be used to manage domestic supply by promoting exports (see related story, above).

The European Union remains the primary user of export subsidies, sparking a great deal of criticism from the rest of the world. The United States, while not a user of export subsidies, has come under fire for its extensive use of export credits and unwillingness to discipline its food aid practices.

Domestic support payments are another category of subsidy, comprised of payments made directly to farmers by their governments regardless whether their produce is exported or sold in country. Such financial assistance can be either income or price support. Domestic support comes in a variety of forms, divided by the WTO into categories based on the extent to which they are deemed trade distorting, that is, the extent to which the payments are linked to production (and, therefore, the extent to which the payments interfere with normal market interactions) (see related story, this page). Because payments grow as world prices fall, farmers have no incentive to cut production when prices are low. Rather, these payments serve as an incentive to produce at the same level or higher, driving prices ever lower. According to the WTO, "When some countries subsidize and others do not, the result can be that the subsidizing countries are producing more than they normally would."[33] One study estimates that the E.U. farm policy has led to a twofold increase in dairy, grains and other crops.[34]

Dumping on Developing Countries

The result of heavy agricultural subsidies in industrialized countries is a commodity glut on world markets. Price support policies that protect E.U. and U.S. commodity farmers have stimulated overproduction of certain crops – notably corn, cotton and wheat. These policies aim to export some of the domestic market excess, dumping crops on the international market – by selling below production cost – and keeping world prices artificially low. This practice reinforces a pattern of systemic oversupply that has characterized global agricultural markets for the past three decades. Between 1997 and 2001, cotton prices fell by 39 percent and wheat prices by 20 percent, both important exports to poorer developing countries.[35] These low prices are plaguing commodity growers worldwide.[36]

Dumped products cut market opportunities for developing country farmers, even in their home markets. They cannot compete with artificially cheap imports. Whereas richer countries can protect their farmers from the depressed world market via government payments that make up the difference, poorer countries cannot (at least not to the same extent), and these farmers must make do with what the market gives them. Without substantial domestic support, developing country farmers from Jamaica to the Philippines are driven out of the market by these below-cost imports.[37]

World Trade Organization Boxes: Amber, Green, Blue

The World Trade Organization (WTO) uses different colored "boxes" to categorize different types of agricultural support; the colors (amber, green and blue) correspond to different levels of trade distortion.

Amber Box payments are those directly related to how much a grower produces. In the United States, the federally legislated price for a bushel of wheat is $2.80, which means that whatever the market price, a wheat grower will receive $2.80 per bushel. The grower sells as much of his produce as possible at the market rate. He then receives a "loan deficiency payment" from the government, for the difference between the selling price and the official price. Because the amount a farmer receives is tied directly to the amount he produces, Amber Box payments are the most distorting. Participating nations promised to reduce, "with a view to phasing out," these types of payments at the launch of the current round of WTO trade negotiations.

Green Box payments have been judged to be non- or minimally trade distorting, although critics of the Green Box have expressed serious doubts about the claims that these payments do not distort trade.

The Blue Box is an intermediate category, mostly comprising direct payments based on historical production rather than current production. A farmer must be growing something in order to receive the payments, but the actual payments do not relate directly to the quantity actually grown in the current year. It was instituted primarily to allow the European Union to continue its payments under its Common Agricultural Policy.

Nearly three-fourths of poor people who live on less than $1 a day are found in developing countries' rural areas, and most depend on agriculture for both food and income.

In Mali, where exported cotton accounts for almost half of annual export revenues, cotton growers feel the effects of subsidies paid to U.S. cotton farmers, totaling $3.4 billion in 2001. Malian farmers must make do with what they receive from the resource-poor state purchasing agency. In 2002 cotton paid 11 cents per pound after expenses. Such paltry profits leave Malian farm families with less money to invest in new equipment, pay school fees and buy medicine or food. While U.S. farmers are guaranteed 80 cents per pound for extra-long staple cotton, in Mozambique many farmers choose not to finish picking their cotton crop because the price they anticipate is not worth the effort.

According to the Cairns Group, a coalition of agricultural exporting developed and developing countries that negotiates as a bloc on many agricultural trade issues within the WTO, "Export subsidies force [developing country farmers] to compete with the richest treasuries, contributing to increased rural poverty, the swelling of overcrowded cities and the promotion of social unrest." The International Monetary Fund and World Bank maintain that if world cotton prices were not distorted by subsidies, the number of people living in poverty in Burkina Faso, where roughly 60 percent of the population lives on less than $1 per day, could be halved within six years.

Cheap Food Policy?

One can make the case that subsidies that keep world prices low for certain commodity crops are beneficial to poor countries, especially those that are net food importers. Some economists have argued that food crops for sale at below production costs act as a subsidy for developing country consumers by providing cheaper food at no government expense.

But artificially cheap imports render local production uncompetitive and depress rural incomes. They also allow and even encourage developing country governments to neglect the farm sector in favor of industrial development, which further undermines agricultural investment and growth.[38] In the past, developing countries have placed inordinate emphasis on developing the industrial sector at the expense of agriculture, a policy made possible by dumped agricultural commodities. The result has been lower farm productivity, lower farm incomes and greater reliance on imports, leaving fragile countries vulnerable to price shocks, which they may not have the resources to weather. Long term, cheap imports resulting from dumped surpluses hurt food security.[39]

Even with government payments, many commodity farmers in industrialized countries remain unprofitable. In the United States, while subsidy payments enable some farmers to stay on the land, they also push other farmers off the land.

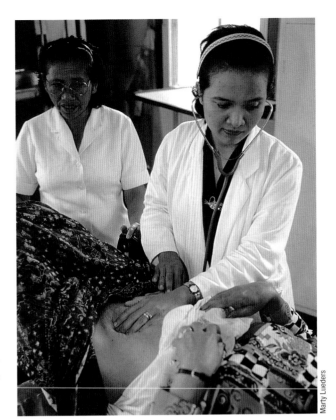

Marty Lueders

For agriculture to succeed in developing countries, health care must be improved. HIV/AIDS and other chronic diseases are devastating agriculture as more farmers become weak, sick and die.

Additional Barriers

Agriculture is inextricably tied to such seemingly unconnected factors as conflict, health crises and biodiversity. Especially in sub-Saharan Africa, decades of civil wars and the HIV/AIDS pandemic have crippled agriculture in some countries, reinforcing cycles of hunger and poverty. Farmers cannot ensure a consistent food supply if periodically they are forced to flee an advancing army. And cropland ravaged by battle is unlikely to grow much of anything.

Angola faced a famine in the summer 2002 that was almost entirely the result of the 27-year war between government forces and Jonas Savimbi's National Union for the Total Independence of Angola (UNITA) rebels. Villagers forced to hide in the bush for years could not grow adequate food. Even though a ceasefire has been signed, leftover landmines still make cropland unusable and transportation dangerous, hampering efforts to move food to the places most in need. The FAO concludes that conflict deprived Africa of roughly 30 percent of its agricultural production between 1970 and 1997.[40]

HIV/AIDS and other chronic diseases, such as malaria, have a similarly devastating effect on agriculture. When a large percentage of farmers are weak and sick, agricultural productivity suffers, strengthening the cycle of

Farmers Must Protect the Environment for Tomorrow's World

If poverty reduction and food security are to be sustainable over the long run, increased food production and natural resource management must go hand in hand. Ten percent to 20 percent of the 3.7 billion acres of land that is under cultivation worldwide suffers from some level of degradation, and roughly one quarter of the farmland in the developing world has been degraded. Agricultural reform must be sensitive to the risks of land degradation due to overcultivation, desertification, water supplies and biodiversity.

As with other aspects of farming, land degradation manifests itself differently in the developing and industrialized worlds. Researchers find that "while excessive use of fertilizers causes widespread damage to soils and waterways in wealthy nations, in the developing world farmland generally suffers from the depletion of nutrients as farmers continuously harvest crops without fertilizing or fallowing the land."[1]

Farmers operating on the edge of profitability are hampered in their ability and willingness to use conservation technologies and practices. One researcher noted, "Unless farmers, particularly those in developing countries, can anticipate an economic return commensurate with their level of investment, they will have little incentive to adopt such practices. One cannot assume that conservation investments will be attractive to farmers simply because those practices are known to protect the resource base."[2]

Concentrated ownership of land or shortages of arable land can result in the cultivation of fragile, marginal lands that yield less, accelerating land degradation and setting in motion a "downward spiral of low production and low investment."[3] In Rwanda, for example, the need for land has caused farmers to clear the vegetative cover from mountains' mid and upper slopes for intense cultivation. This practice has resulted in serious erosion problems, including landslides.

The well-being of the land is directly tied to the well-being of its inhabitants. Only when rural people and poor farmers have a way to earn sustainable, stable livelihoods will the planet's biodiversity be safe. Indeed, research at Future Harvest finds that across the tropics, "it is futile to attempt to conserve tropical forests without addressing the needs of poor local people; nor is it desirable."[4]

---

[1] The Worldwatch Institute, *Vital Signs 2002*, 102.

[2] Daniel C. Clay, "Fighting an Uphill Battle: Population Pressure and Declining Land Productivity in Rwanda." Michigan State University International Development Working Paper No. 58, 1996, 2.

[3] Ibid., 9.

[4] "Balancing Rainforest Conservation & Development," Future Harvest Alternative to Slash-and-Burn Background Paper, Aug. 23, 2002. Available from http://www.futureharvest.org/pdf/ASB-Backgrounder.pdf.

---

declining productivity. AIDS also affects other areas that contribute to agricultural development, such as education.

Clearly, peace is a prerequisite for long-term development, and real efforts to address the HIV/AIDS pandemic are crucial. Moreover, these issues must be handled with the conservation of developing countries' natural resources in mind (see related story, above).

Politics of Agriculture

The global agricultural system needs change, for the economic good of industrialized countries themselves and to give hungry and poor rural people in developing countries a fighting chance to increase their production and income. But reforming the global agricultural system is no small feat given political realities. In an increasingly connected world, national policymakers are sandwiched between domestic and international interests. On one hand, they must answer to their citizens and industries; on the other, they must participate in the international community and deal with global market realities. Often these forces pull in opposite directions. When crafting national farm policy, a government must answer to its urban and rural constituents, trading partners, and (for member nations) the WTO.

In developing countries, farmers and rural constituents often lack sufficient political power to pressure national governments to invest in agriculture and rural development. This trend is not surprising given rural poverty rates. Urban people tend to be more affluent, educated and organized, putting them in a better position to demand government policies that serve their interests. Unfortunately, "increasing urbanization may have further strengthened the political voice of urban populations and their claim on both domestic and external resources," notes the FAO.[41]

City dwellers also have the advantage of being concentrated and closer to the seat of government, making effective protest easier. As one aid worker in Africa during the 1984-1985 famine said: "Starve the city people and they riot; starve the rural people and they die. If you were an African political leader, which would you choose?"[42]

On the other hand, the agricultural sector in industrialized countries has power far beyond its size. Less than 5 percent of the U.S. population farms, yet elements within this group receive billions of dollars in federal support each year at taxpayer expense. The same is true for Europe.

Reducing long-standing agricultural subsidies could be devastating to some farmers and their communities.

Changes in farm technology and economics have put severe pressure on farmers and rural communities for decades, and millions of people have come to depend on farm subsidies. They have built their livelihoods and lives, in part, on these subsidies. As farm policies are changed, rural people and communities should be protected.

But the current system of farm support comes at a high financial cost to both governments and consumers. Industrialized countries spent nearly $300 billion supporting their commodity farmers in 2000. The European Union spends half its annual budget on agricultural support. Indeed concerns over the budgetary effects of admitting 10 new, relatively agrarian countries to the European Union were a major source of tension in expansion negotiations. The average European family of four pays roughly $25 more per week in food prices due to the European Union's Common Agricultural Policy.[43]

Similarly, the passage of the 2002 U.S. farm bill sparked a torrent of criticism over the fact that (mostly urban) taxpayers essentially are supporting a small part of the rural population. The United States spent 0.56 percent of GDP on agricultural support in 2000. While these policies support and protect the farming sector as a whole, they generally target the largest farming operations.

Agribusiness companies lobby actively and effectively for legislation supporting their interests. While some of the largest agribusinesses are large livestock operations that do not receive direct subsidies, they do benefit from – and lobby for – cheap feedgrains, such as subsidized corn and soybeans.

Some of today's farm policies began decades ago in response to circumstances that since have changed. U.S. farm policy is rooted in support programs first legislated as part of Roosevelt's New Deal. In Europe, widespread food shortages following World War II led to a policy to ensure sufficient domestic food production. While technological advances since have led to agricultural surpluses, policies do not reflect this change. Both the policy and its interests have become entrenched in national politics. In the United States, for example, domestic support is associated with "saving the small farm," even though small farms continue to disappear while the largest farms profit the most from subsidies. Although agricultural reform in fact is needed to save rural communities, larger farmers and agribusinesses prefer the status quo. Not surprisingly, little has changed.

Because of such political realities, any type of agricultural reform will be difficult. Says Kofi Annan, "Powerful interest groups within rich countries will try hard to block meaningful concessions to the developing world. They will argue that the interests of workers and farmers are being sacrificed. But there are other ways to help those groups that really need help – ways less costly to consumers and taxpayers in rich countries, and less harmful to producers in poor ones."[44] Without change, the human suffering taking place in too many places in the world will continue. Moreover, all countries have a stake in reducing global hunger and poverty, because as incomes rise, consumers spend more money on food, increasing demand for agricultural products worldwide.

In today's integrated society, countries no longer can afford to act without carefully considering their actions' impact on others. By understanding how people, businesses, governments and international systems relate to economies, the environment and each other, we move one step closer to creating a fair and just agricultural system that works to feed the world and sustain rural communities.

Agricultural subsidies to industrialized country farmers are distorting global market prices for corn and other commodities, and can undermine the ability of small farmers in developing countries to sell their produce in local markets.

… all countries have a stake in reducing global hunger and poverty, because as incomes rise, consumers spend more money on food.

CHAPTER 2

U.S. Farm Policy

U.S. farm policy is broken. It fails to support smaller U.S. farmers or adequately deal with rising hunger and poverty in rural America. Moreover, it perpetuates a system of market protections that distort agricultural production, in turn depressing global prices and ultimately hurting the nearly 600 million people who live and work in developing countries' rural areas not knowing whether tomorrow they will have enough food to eat.

Both rich and poor countries have much to gain from eliminating production-distorting subsidies and tariffs. Yet instead of moving toward subsidy reduction, the 2002 U.S. farm bill increased agricultural support to farmers by nearly $84 billion over the next 10 years, with most subsidies continuing to go to the largest, wealthiest farmers.

Farm subsidies are both complex and controversial. Most Americans support the idea that the United States should grow its own food and that farmers should be able to make a living from the land, even if they need help from taxpayers to do so. But about 80 percent of subsidy payments go to only a handful of farmers – 150,000 out of 2.2 million. The beneficiaries are primarily larger, commercial operators in the South and Midwest that grow five commodities: corn, cotton, rice, soybeans and wheat (see Figure 2.1). Approximately 60 percent of farmers receive no subsidies at all.

Today's policies also have increased the rate of farm consolidation, leading to larger but fewer farms, which has contributed to many rural communities' problems.

Fewer farmers in a rural community, such as St. Anthony, Idaho, mean fewer people shopping, eating out, visiting the dentist or getting a haircut. And as rural economies shrink, jobs disappear, people move away, schools and hospitals close and eventually, even churches shut their doors.

Paul Romrell's family has been farming near St. Anthony for 100 years. The Romrells have struggled the past few years to keep their farm going, even agreeing to put some marginal land in a wetland program. But they've been lucky. One by one, nearby farms have disappeared. "That's been a tough thing the last couple of years, watching neighbors disappear and watching the small traditional farms vanish," Paul says.[1]

Current Debate

Since U.S. farm programs were first established in 1933, their primary goals have been to stabilize markets and assure farmers' incomes, especially during difficult economic times and following weather-related disasters. Simply put, supply-control policies seek to manage crop supplies, ensuring higher prices. When prices fall too low, income-support policies seek to provide additional money to farmers so they can bridge income gaps and stay in business.

But critics argue that supply controls undermine market forces and actually depress prices. They also doubt whether commodity payments are benefiting those farmers who need them. Rather, they charge that the supports may undercut smaller farmers' efforts to stay in business by raising farmland values. Critics also argue that U.S. farm programs distort international trade and undermine poor farmers in developing countries.

In the mid-1990s, lawmakers began to respond to many of these concerns by moving to more market-driven policies. The 1996 Federal Agricultural Improvement and Reform (FAIR) Act ended supply-control measures, granted farmers greater planting flexibility and began weaning them from income-support payments. Although farmers experienced good weather and a bumper crop in 1998, the Asian financial crisis sent commodity prices plunging, and many farmers faced economic hardship. Instead of holding true to the intent of the 1996 legislation, Congress responded with several emergency measures, totaling billions in additional income-support payments.

In 2002, when the farm bill came up for reauthorization, many reforms instituted just six years earlier were abandoned. Although supply-control measures were not re-established, income supports resumed at historically high levels.

Figure 2.1: Large Farms Receive the Biggest Share of Direct Government Payments (2000)

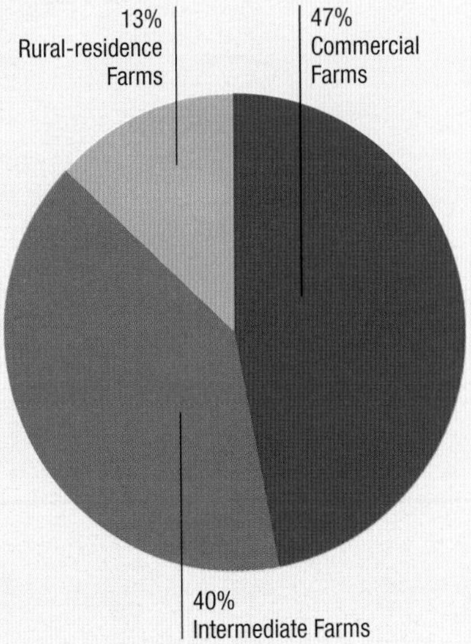

13%
Rural-residence Farms

47%
Commercial Farms

40%
Intermediate Farms

Source: U.S. Department of Agriculture

Agriculture's New Look

As the most recent farm bill debates indicate, many agricultural and political leaders appear comfortable with farm policy that is little changed from the policy of more than half a century ago. However, agriculture as a business no longer looks the same.

Farming and food production businesses have become increasingly consolidated and industrialized. Average farm size continues to grow (see Figure 2.2). Family-run hog and poultry farms have been replaced with so-called farm factories, with farmers working for larger businesses as contract suppliers. Consolidation also has occurred in agriculture's food processing, transportation and trading sectors.

Increasing productivity has reduced the number of people needed to work on farms, and because of decreased profitability, most small farms no longer can fully support a family. Many farmers have left rural areas for employment in cities; others have stayed but are relying on nonfarm employment or other farm-related businesses to supplement their incomes.

"Industrialization has separated farmers from the land, if not physically, at least psychologically," says John Ikerd, professor emeritus of agricultural economics at the University of Missouri.[2] "Most farmers don't even own the land they farm and most who own land don't have enough time or can't afford to care for it even if they do care about it."

Concerns about agriculture's impact on the environment are growing. While some advocacy groups claim that the 2002 farm bill is the most environmentally beneficial bill since the Clean Water Act, other groups maintain that more needs to be done.

The past 50 years also have seen international agricultural trade issues grow in importance to the United States as rising farm productivity has created a need for additional outlets of U.S. goods in export markets. This pursuit of export markets sometimes has led to the dumping of U.S. commodities on the global market, which has hurt poor and hungry rural people in developing countries.

Agricultural production processes and business relationships have come to resemble other industries more than the traditional agrarian model of small, independent farmers. Although most analysts maintain that these changes have increased productivity and efficiency, many disagree over whether these developments have led the United States in the right direction, especially when considering costs to rural communities both in America and abroad.

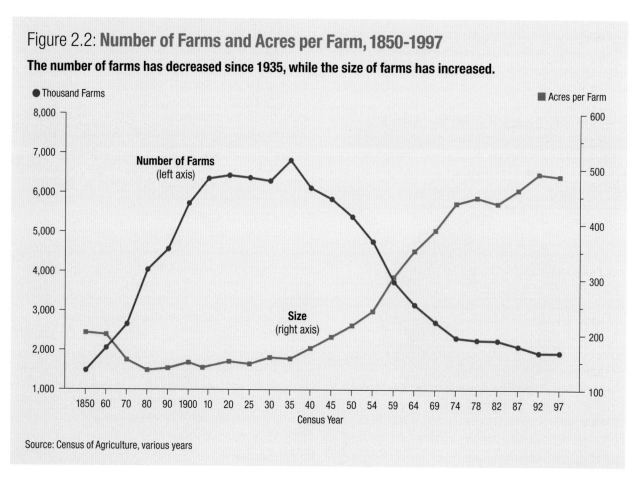

Figure 2.2: Number of Farms and Acres per Farm, 1850-1997

The number of farms has decreased since 1935, while the size of farms has increased.

Source: Census of Agriculture, various years

Rising Farm Productivity

Early supply-control programs essentially restricted farmers to planting fewer acres, which in turn would ease supply and shore up prices. But farmers responded by cultivating these acres more intensely, using new technologies, fertilizer, pesticides and management methods.[3] Any gains from land being taken out of production under these programs slipped away because of higher productivity.

While early land restrictive measures eventually were abandoned, new supply-control programs continued through 1996. Between 1948 and 1996, U.S. agricultural output grew an average 1.89 percent per year, outstripping other U.S. industries in productivity, including manufacturing (1.2 percent per year).[4] Although increasing productivity sometimes led to higher farm incomes in the short run, over the long term it continued to increase supply, lower farm prices and, ultimately, depress farm incomes. Rising costs for fertilizer, seeds, machinery and other inputs exacerbated this trend.

Although higher productivity reduced production costs for food manufacturers, little of that benefit was passed along to consumers or farmers. Increases in other costs – especially marketing costs, which reflect the value added to a product as labor, advertising, processing, transportation and packaging – not only led to higher costs for consumers but also to lower consumer-dollar share for farmers, so-called farm value. In 1970 farm value represented a third of consumer food expenditures; marketing costs were two-thirds. By 2000, farm value had declined to a fifth, a 40 percent drop in farm value in 30 years.[5]

Because of the growing gap between the prices farmers receive for their crops and retail prices, market swings on the agriculture market often cost consumers a pittance at the cash register. Rising food prices now reflect mostly increases in marketing costs, which are more closely tied to the overall economy. This disconnect between farmers' and consumers' prices grows wider the more foods are processed. For example, a farmer receives 35 cents for a 5-pound bag of wheat flour selling for $1.75; a farmer receives less than 9 cents for a similarly priced loaf of bread.[6]

Farmers' Choice: Find a Second Job or Buy More Land

Today a farm family of four living in Mechanicsburg, Ohio, needs about $45,000 a year to make ends meet. With agriculture expenses eating 80 percent of revenue, their family must generate approximately $250,000 in crop sales.[7] Because of stagnant or declining commodity prices and dwindling farm value, farmers have had to either take on other jobs or increase their acreage some every year to survive.

Marty Primus, who owns a 198-acre mostly cattle and hog farm outside of Sauk Centre, Minn., farms as part of the local Whole Food Cooperative in an effort to manage the changing rules and economics of owning a farm in today's global economy.

Income-support programs were developed to prop prices at levels that would sustain farmers in times of economic hardship. However, a review of farmers' net income in relation to good and bad agriculture years shows that the general farm economy bears little resemblance to the economic health of farmers' households.

One would assume that when crop prices are low and farmers' aggregate income falls, their household income also declines, leading to a lower living standard. However, in 1997 – generally considered a good agriculture year with aggregate net farm income reaching a record $48.6 billion – nearly one-third of farmers lacked enough income from agriculture to meet basic household needs, such as food, clothing and health care expenses.[8] At least half of small farms had net incomes of less than $6,000.[9]

Meanwhile, in 1999 – when net incomes fell almost 11 percent from the previous year to $43.4 billion – less than a fifth of farmers lacked enough income to meet their needs. In this case, most families were able to offset the average $2,000 decline in net farm income with an average $16,000 increase in off-farm income.

This reflects a trend over the past two decades of farmers increasingly relying on off-farm incomes – usually not related to agriculture – to help pay household expenses. The primary occupation of most farm households – 62 percent – is something other than farming.[10] Many of these part-time, small-scale farmers typically lose money or produce low earnings from agriculture, which covers only a fraction of their household budget.

Mazon, Ill., Farmers Share Acres to Help Others and Themselves

By Doug Harford

For 29 years, my family has made its living growing corn and soybeans in Mazon, Ill., – population 764. Most of my neighbors live on or near farms; they always have. Many of the people I worship with every Sunday at Mazon Congregational Church (UCC) still work on farms, though they're not sure how long they'll keep going.

Still, the personal satisfaction – the sense of fulfillment – that we all used to experience from working hard and bringing in a harvest has dwindled, and for some, disappeared. My first year in farming was 1973, and that year we sold corn for $3.90 per bushel; I was able to buy a new tractor for $12,500. Last year I sold corn for $1.90, and a similar new tractor cost $100,000.

No one likes to talk about our reliance on farm subsidies, but a big portion of our income now comes from government programs. There's a certain frustration that comes with the reality that you're not making it on you own.

This economic reality is becoming more and more obvious to most farmers. We're struggling to accept that farming has become more about living a certain lifestyle than making a living.

A Choice

I decided that if I'm going to make a lifestyle choice, then it should be one that serves my community, world neighbors, and God.

Norm Braksick, executive director of Foods Resource Bank, gave a sermon on world hunger at our church about a year ago. Shortly after the service, he met with me, several other farmers and community leaders to talk about how we could use our skills to help feed the hungry. Farmers have developed a certain skills set in farming, but it doesn't seem to have much value in society now. As in other industries, these skills are being replaced with technology and lower-cost foreign goods.

The world hunger program being implemented by Foods Resource Bank is unique. This program doesn't involve shipping container after container of food: it provides for people in the world's poorest villages to know the dignity and pride of feeding themselves. And as we listened to Norm's talk, we knew what that feeling was about. It was about using our God-given skills to help other people, and as Norm emphasized, it was a gift only we could give.

Ask me to write a check for a thousand dollars for world hunger… now that would be tough. But we can use our knowledge and skill to put in the crop and then harvest it with our equipment. Shoot, that's no big deal – that's what we do every day. And that's a gift only we can give! Wow!

Sharing Ownership

Within a couple of days of the "world hunger" service at our church, one of our farmers donated the use of 40 acres of his land for this year. We offered to help him farm it, but he said we'd just "screw him up," so we helped him harvest it instead. We also set out to help him find the inputs he would need.

Norm had mentioned "twinning" with an urban church. He helped us find a partner: The Congregational Church in Western Springs, Ill., a large church in a Chicago suburb with five pastors and 1,500 members. Four of us went there and met with its Mission Outreach Committee.

To grow an acre of corn today costs about $205. We brought along a line-item budget justifying these costs. That in itself was an eye-opener for our new city friends. We challenged them to offer families or groups of families the sponsorship of an acre for $205. They enthusiastically accepted the challenge. We did a similar worship service and sermon on world hunger at their church, and by 12:30 p.m. that day, 42 acres at $205/acre were "owned" by our city partners… and the people loved it!

Now they had ownership, and it was not high-level theory on what should be done on a "global level;" it was "owning an acre" and solving world hunger one village at a time!

While the suburban "owners" had provided the resources to purchase the seeds, fertilizer and other crop needs, we knew that if we worked hard to get those inputs donated, the $205 per acre would be added to the crop's cash value when we turned our mission projects profit over to Foods Resource Bank. We were amazed! Once agribusiness people knew about our project and its design to help hungry people feed themselves, almost all of our inputs were donated, and we had the urban gifts to pay for any that were not.

We celebrated God's great gifts of abundance with a harvest celebration. At 11:30 on Oct. 20, 2002, we met at the field. More than 100 people made the 50-minute trip from

Illinois farmers and parishioners from Mazon Congregational Church and The Congregational Church in Western Springs gather for a fall celebration to harvest a shared corn field. Proceeds from the effort are helping women and children in Gambia.

Foods Resource Bank

Western Springs. We had a worship service of dedication, a typical rural-community potluck, and then that afternoon we harvested the field. City kids big and small rode in combines, helped haul the grain to the elevator, and heard discussions on how we care for the land God has loaned us. As one urban person said to me, "This is wonderful. When I write a check and close the checkbook, it's all over. Now I feel like I've been involved in feeding the hungry, and I'm sure that now many young people know corn flakes don't grow in a box!"

To date, both churches have worked to raise additional money. The total project has generated $31,000 for world hunger. To put things in perspective, our total church budget is $90,000. We never would have been able to collect such an amount just through personal donations.

Partnering with Western Springs also is reaping unexpected rewards. Although the relationship is still unfolding, this project will provide an arena for the Mazon community to learn more about the "urbanization" that is sitting at our doorstep, and for Western Springs to learn about their farming neighbors. It will build that rural-urban connectedness that has been lost and that both of us desire to renew.

We are going on a mission trip! Our funds will be designated to Wider Church Ministries of the United Church of Christ, which is an implementing member of Foods Resource Bank. They select and oversee programs in developing countries through Church World Service, another member. Stephen Mbandi, director of development at Church World Service, was at our harvest festival, and with him we decided that our proceeds will go to the Gambia, where they will assist women in five villages in constructing wells and developing gardens to help reduce malnutrition in their children. A year from now a group of us want to visit that site. In a small way, we will build solidarity between the abundance in Mazon and the needs of that village… and I bet we'll learn a thing or two from them as well.

Reclaiming the Future

More than anything, this project provides an opportunity for farmers like me to do what we love to do, and it provides a rationale for doing it. People like to do good things, to feel good about what they are doing.

If we can find different ways to apply our skills, such as with this World Hunger project, we will have the opportunity to help a large number of people and reap personal rewards as well.

Times are uncertain, but farmers need to look at their future from a fresh perspective. Many of us are now in our fifties and facing retirement, so extra time is an opportunity. For me, I've decided to back off from farming a bit, and devote more energy to mission work.

I see this World Hunger project as an opportunity to renew my energy and reclaim the soul in my work.

Doug Harford is a farmer who lives near Mazon, Ill.

In most farm families, women work full time off the farm to provide additional income and benefits, such as health insurance. In addition to their full-time jobs, many women also work part time on the farm keeping records, balancing accounts and doing chores. A significant number of married farm households – 40 percent – rely on both spouses to work off the farm in addition to any agricultural work. Only one-fifth of farm couples work solely on the farm.[11]

Cheryl Anderson lives with her husband and three sons near Walcott, N.D., farming land first owned by his great-grandfather. She has worked full-time at MeritCare in Fargo for 21 years, though when she married, she never imagined working off the farm for so long. "I thought when we started having kids, I could cut back to part time and have more time dedicated to being a mom," Cheryl says. But the financial realities of farming have not allowed her this option.[12]

Farm families' diversifying their income sources rather than relying solely on farm revenue has helped insulate them from farming's financial volatility. Of course, for those still relying primarily on farming, the general farm economy has a greater bearing. In 1999 the average household income for farm-dependant families was $53,172. For households headed by operators whose primary occupation was not farming, the average was $79,726.[13]

For those farmers who want to or must farm full time, profitability usually requires making their operation bigger. Since 1935, the number of U.S. farms has decreased by two-thirds, from 6.8 million to 2.2 million, with the rate of decline slowing in recent years.[14] Meanwhile, the average acreage per farm tripled, from 155 acres to 487 acres in 1997.

Farm assistance programs have sped this decrease in farms and increase in acreage by encouraging farmers to expand their operation to acquire more base acres to attain higher guaranteed government payments. Before the 1960s, government payments accounted for less than 10 percent of a farmer's net income. Between 1960 and 1980, this percentage grew to an average of about 20 percent. Says Illinois farmer Doug Harford, "No one likes to talk about our reliance on farm subsidies, but a big portion of our income now comes from government programs. There's a certain frustration that comes with the reality that you're not making it on your own. We're struggling to… accept that farming has become more about living a certain lifestyle than making a living" (see related article, p. 38).

As government payments become a larger share of net income, the incentive to grow and consolidate strengthens. Recently, the largest farms have gained the greatest share of government support. Farms with sales of more than $500,000 a year received 22 percent of government payments in 1999, an increase from 13 percent in 1993. Farms with sales of between $250,000 and $500,000 received 21 percent of payments, compared with 18 percent in 1993.[15]

Sky-high Land Values

Feeding this consolidation and growth cycle is another unintended consequence of U.S. farm programs: escalating land values (see Figure 2.3). The value of farmland, as with most items, depends on the anticipated future earnings. Two factors increasingly contributing to expectations of higher revenue from farmland are direct government payments and urban influence.

In 2000 direct government payments totaled $22.9 billion.[16] Because these payments – most of which are tied directly to the farmland – have continued uninterrupted for more than 50 years, many investors view the farmland as a steady supply of government payments and are willing to pay now for the expected financial return on the land later.

Increasing demand for country homes, farm estates, recreational properties and other encroaching suburban developments on rural America also are impacting agriculture land prices. The U.S. Department of Agriculture (USDA) estimates that between 10 percent and 20 percent of U.S. farmland – especially land near cities – may be subject to such urban influences.[17]

Consequently, the value of agriculture land continues to rise, reaching a record high of $1,130 per acre in 2001 – a 4.6 percent increase from the year before.[18] Since the 1980s economic farm crisis, when land values plunged, farmland values have risen steadily, increasing by nearly 90 percent from the 1987 low of $599 per acre.

Arguably, farmland's increasing value may be the biggest benefit to farmers of the U.S. farm programs. As a group, farmers now have an accumulated average net worth exceeding that of the average U.S. family, with real estate accounting for more than three-fourths of farmers' assets. In 1999 farm households' net worth averaged $563,000; the average U.S. family's net worth was $283,000.[19]

However, this growing wealth does not benefit all farmers equally. Beginning

farmers face enormously high costs, primarily because of land prices. It is not surprising that the share of farmers younger than 35 years has declined from 15 percent in 1954 to 8 percent in 1997.[20]

High land values also make it more costly and, therefore, more difficult for existing farms to expand, either by purchasing or renting additional acres. According to the USDA, this trend also erodes U.S. farmers' ability to compete in a global marketplace. Because land value is a large part of farmers' overall costs, "sustained increases in land prices and rents have a decidedly adverse effect on the competitiveness of our farmers in the marketplace compared with those in other exporting countries, a cause of growing concern in recent years."[21]

Debt, Bankruptcy and Foreclosure

Given that farmers' incomes and wealth bear little relationship to the agricultural economy, it should come as no surprise that farmers' debt levels and decisions related to filing for bankruptcy protection or foreclosures also have little relationship. Contrary to most people's belief about farming, debt is not a primary source of capital for farms. At the end of 2000, only 42 percent of farmers reported debt outstanding.[22]

However, as more money is needed to expand operations or invest in new technologies, the size of this debt grows. Total farm debt in 2001 was estimated at $192.8 billion, an increase of 4.8 percent from the previous year. In 2002 total debt is expected to jump again by 1.9 percent, which will be the 10th consecutive annual rise.[23]

Despite chronically low commodity prices that continue to depress farm incomes, all major lender groups – including the Farm Services Agency, the government's lender of last resort – continue to show low levels of

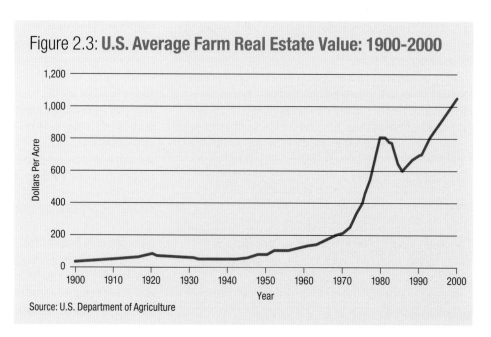

Figure 2.3: **U.S. Average Farm Real Estate Value: 1900-2000**

Dollars Per Acre / Year

Source: U.S. Department of Agriculture

USDA Photo/Ken Hammond

Most farmers' wealth is tied up in their land, often leaving them strapped for cash unless they sell or rent some of their property.

delinquencies and other loan problems. "The stability of farm loan portfolios is benefiting from large government payments and sizable amounts of off-farm income," according to the USDA's 2002 Agricultural Income and Finance Annual Lender Issue.[24] Historical trends in agricultural loan delinquency rates as reported by the Federal Reserve show that loan repayment delinquencies peaked in 1987 at 11 percent of loan volume. Since then, delinquency rates have declined, leveling off at about 3 percent of loan volume in recent years.[25]

A greater threat to farmers' solvency is the lack of cash flow. Whereas in the 1980s, farmers were strangled by too much debt, today most farmers' wealth is tied up in their land, often leaving them without cash unless they sell or rent some of their property. Like other competitive businesses, farms go out of business every year for many reasons. The American Bankers Association reports that farm foreclosure rates peaked in 1986 at 6.2 percent. Since then, these rates have leveled off at between 2 percent and 3 percent. Bankruptcy filings also peaked in 1986 (4.2 percent) and have stayed around 1 percent and 2 percent for most of the 1990s.

In fact, farms are less likely to go out of business than other businesses, primarily because new farmers incur higher start up costs and risk greater amounts of equity. The costs of closing their operations, therefore, are much higher than those of other businesses. In fact, nonfarm businesses – which average closure rates of 15 percent – are four times more likely to fail than new farm ventures.[26]

High start-up costs also present another complicating factor that feeds chronic commodity oversupply: agriculture's high capital investment. If a restaurant or manufacturing plant is no longer profitable, then the equipment, buildings and supplies (capital) can be reused or sold for another purpose. While a farmer similarly can sell his farm if he no longer is profitable, almost always a larger operation is waiting to purchase and plant the land – often with the same crop – and no net decrease in production results.[27]

Today's Farming Communities Vary Greatly...

While the aforementioned trends illustrate the shortcomings of income-support and supply-control measures of traditional farm programs and provide a sense of where agriculture stands today, they hide the variability and complexity of farming communities. For the sake of discussing farm policy's impact on the divergent types of U.S. farms, they have been grouped into three categories: large, small and mid-size (see Table 2.1).[28]

...from Large, Commercial Farms...

Generally speaking, the only farmers profiting today are those with the larger, commercial operations with sales of more than $250,000. And while they represent only 8 percent of all farms, they receive nearly half – 47 percent – of subsidy payments. Moreover, because they earn a profit, they have the cash to pay escalating farmland prices and, thus, can grow bigger.

A typical large farm is a family farm that specializes in cash grains, such as corn or soybeans, with sales between $250,000 and $500,000 annually. The average farmer is 50 years old, and although he earns at least $100,000 a year from the farm, his wife likely works in a nearby town to help supplement their income. They received about $43,000 in government payments in 2000 from commodity and other farm programs.

This category also includes larger operations, such as large corporate farms, with sales exceeding $500,000. The very large operations typically specialize in poultry or hogs, comprising approximately two-thirds of U.S. production of these animals. They also produce comparable shares of commodity crops and receive a comparable share of subsidies. Family households in this subgroup earn slightly more than $200,000 a year – more than four times the average U.S. household – with most of their income coming from the farm.

...to Small, But Not Always Traditional Farms...

On the other hand, the typical small farmer loses money from his operation and must rely on outside income to bridge the shortfall; subsidy payments are not enough to cover these losses. This farmer has gross sales

Table 2.1: The Many Definitions, Looks of Today's Farms

	Small Farm[1]	Mid-size Farm[2]	Large (Commercial) Farm[3]
Average age of farmer:	59 years	54 years	50 years
Number of Farms:	1,362,605	625,615	177,840
Share of Farms:	62%	30%	8%
Average Acreage Owned Per Farm:	110 acres	351 acres	767 acres
Average Acreage Operated Per Farm:	160 acres	605 acres	2,180 acres
Total Value of Production:	$21 billion	$62 billion	$111 billion
Share of Production Value:	11%	32%	57%
Average Farm Household Income:	$63,918	$46,205	$120,044
Average Income from Farm:	$-4,498	$2,243	$81,142
Average Income from Non-farm earnings:	$68,416	$43,962	$38,902
Average Income from Subsidies:	$1,552	$10,009	$43,379
Subsidy per acre owned:	$14	$29	$57
Share of Total Government Payments	13%	40%	47%
Average Farm Household Net Worth:	$385,029	$611,569	$1,366,124
Average Farm Household Debt:	$47,076	$78,791	$312,367
Farms by Specialization:			
Cash grain:	8%	30%	25%
Other field crops:	25%	14%	16%
High value crops:	7%	7%	15%
Beef:	43%	26%	11%
Hogs:	n/a	n/a	n/a
Dairy:	n/a	14%	11%
Other Livestock:	16%	8%	16%

Source: 2000 Agricultural Resource Management Survey (ARMS)

[1] "Small farm" is defined using USDA's ARMS category of rural-residence farm, which includes the subcategories of limited-resource, retirement and residential, with sales less than $250,000.

[2] "Mid-size farm" is defined using USDA's ARMS category of intermediate farm, which includes the subcategories of low-sales and high-sales, with sales less than $250,000.

[3] "Large (Commercial) farm" is defined using USDA's ARMS category of commercial farm, which includes the subcategories of large, very large and nonfamily.

of less than $250,000. Many small farmers (43 percent) specialize in beef cattle, which is a relatively flexible operation with low labor requirements.

As a group, small farmers represent the majority of farmers in the United States: 62 percent. Most small farmers are considered recreational or lifestyle farmers. Usually, both the husband and wife work full time off the farm – sometimes in a city – where they earn most of their income. These farmers are the only ones in the "small" category who earn an income – $83,800 in 2000 – above the average U.S. household.

Most retired farmers also fit this category. Because they are retired, they are older – averaging 69 years – and earn most of their income from unearned sources, such as Social Security and investments. Much of their land is rented to other farmers or retired to conservation programs. In 2000 retired farmers received one-fifth of all conservation program payments. These farmers' average household income is $40,600.

The remaining small farmers are among those most in need. Typically, they have sales of less than $100,000 and farm assets of less than $150,000. Their average household income is $9,500. The average farmer in this subgroup is 59 years old and does not have a high school education. Because of limited resources, education level, age and financial needs, the USDA has identified this group as the most difficult to help with today's farm programs.

...to Struggling Mid-size Farmers

The farmers hardest hit by income shortfalls resulting from depressed commodity prices are those with mid-size operations, which are not large enough to benefit from economies of scale but are too large to permit farmers to work off the land. Most of these farmers (73 percent) have sales of less than $100,000 and like their small, retired counterparts, most specialize in cattle. Many of these farmers, whose average age is 59 years, are preparing for retirement, with many receiving supplemental income from investments. Most farmers' wives still are working as well, which brings in most of the $43,000 household income.

Of the younger farmers in this group, many are struggling to stay afloat. And because their budgets are tight, most of them do not have access to the cash needed to expand their operation or rent additional land. About a quarter of mid-size farmers have sales between $100,000 and $250,000, with most specializing in cash grains and dairy. Nearly all (81 percent) receive commodity program payments. Their average household income in 2000 was $53,300.

Changing Face of Rural America

Even more diversity can be found in rural America. In the not-too-distant past, farming was nearly synonymous with rural. That is no longer true. Although farming remains important as a source of jobs and income in many rural areas – and remains the largest user of land – it is no longer the dominant rural industry.

Jon Evert, coordinator of Rural Life Outreach in Minnesota, has seen this change over the years. He remembers helping neighboring farmers survive the 1980s' economic crisis that forced many farmers to file for bankruptcy. "Farmers were begging us to find a way for them to stay on the farm," Jon says. "All of us felt that the crisis was temporary, and that just getting the farmers over the hump would allow them to regroup and carry on with their prior and comfortable way of life. Today,

farmers, tired and often hopeless, ask instead for us to help them find a way to get out of farming" (see related story, p. 44).

In the past four decades, farming-related jobs dropped from slightly less than 8 million to little more than 3 million. As the number of farms has dwindled in the past 20 years, the percentage of the rural workforce employed in farming has been cut in half, from 14.4 percent to 7.6 percent.[29]

Rural Hunger and Poverty

Many of these farm jobs have not been replaced. The USDA has classified more than 500 rural counties as "persistent-poverty" areas, meaning that they consistently have had poverty rates of 20 percent or higher during the past four decades.[30] Although the majority of food insecure people live in urban areas, their numbers are increasing in suburban and rural areas, with the fastest growth occurring in western and southern farming communities.[31] In 2000 the rate of food insecurity in rural neighborhoods (13.4 percent) outpaced the urban rate (10.8 percent) (see Figure 2.4).

Of the 33 million people in the United States who either do not always have enough to eat or regularly go hungry, 7 million live in rural communities (see Figure 2.5). Most disturbingly, at least one in five of these hungry people is a child.

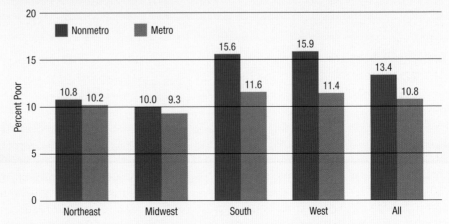

Figure 2.4: Rural Poverty Rates Exceed Urban Poverty

The number of people living in poverty in rural America reached an all-time low of 6.9 million people in 2000, according to the U.S. Department of Agriculture. Rural poverty numbers and rates improved largely because of the unprecedented economic expansion experienced throughout the United States between 1993 and 2000.

Now that this economic growth has slowed and unemployment numbers have risen, poverty rates are beginning to climb as well.

Rural poverty rates (13.4 percent) also continue to be higher than urban poverty rates, which stood at 10.8 percent in 2000 – another record low. Moreover, rural poverty is most severe in the South and West.

Source: USDA's Economic Research Service calculations based on the 2001 Current Population Survey, March Supplement

Rural Life Outreach: 'Farming Ain't What It Used To Be'

By Jon Evert

Nostalgically, many remember when farming was considered a comfortable, laid back, safe and healthy way of life. The farm was a "good place to raise kids." The hard work of farming was offset by a sense of independence, the joy of being your own boss. While the financial stresses were many, farmers often talked about the two good years in farming as "1917 and next year," always expecting that this year may well be the next year for which they had long waited.

My parents, both sets of grandparents, four sets of great-grandparents, and five sets of great-great-grandparents all farmed within 15 miles of Comstock, Minn., where I grew up. My father reluctantly welcomed me into the farming operation because he was not certain that my future should be on the farm. He knew there were much better opportunities for financial success in other pursuits.

I started farming by renting the land that my father and uncle had previously rented, while my dad farmed his own and my uncle's land. Using my father's machinery and living at home with my parents allowed me to get started. That first year, I had to borrow about $3,000 to put in my crop.

As luck would have it, I had to wait only two years for what farmers in general had waited 56 years to see. "Next year" came in 1973, following a massive Russian grain sale. What made the year so big for farmers was that it had come so unexpectedly and while prices were up, inputs and other farm costs had remained relatively low. Farmers were able to buy new machinery, tractors, trucks and tools, replacing their worn out and obsolete equipment. They also were able to buy more farmland and bid up rents for additional land, thus beginning the upward spiral that continued until the crash of 1981.

The boom lasted through the '70s, even though many people experienced crop disasters during this time. In 1975 our farm experienced the worst flood disaster we had ever seen, and in 1976, we experienced a devastating drought that literally dried up the Red River. It was inflation that kept us going through these years. While I had started with a zero net worth in 1971, my wife and I were (on paper) worth half a million dollars by the end of the decade. While others were buying land and large new machinery at greatly inflated prices, in 1980 we built a new house and purchased the seed conditioning facility where I had worked during my seminary days.

For about a year, both these investments appeared to be good decisions. But then interest rates soared to 21 percent; land prices fell by well over 50 percent, and used machinery prices weakened while inflation continued to increase input costs and the value of new machinery.

Suddenly, the banks required that each acre of cropland had to provide cash flow, where in the past they looked only at the net worth of the farmer to determine the loan viability. Bankers and input suppliers began to close down farms by shutting off credit and, in many cases, initiating foreclosure proceedings.

Over breakfast with Rural Life Outreach staff, two Minnesota farmers discuss the 2002 flooding and other weather and economic problems that threaten their ability to keep their farms afloat.

Many churches and other organizations became concerned with the number of farmers being forced off their land and organized to help them. Many groups rallied because they were aware of the lack of caregiving offered by similar groups during the Great Depression, which had been the last time that such numbers of displaced farmers were seen. Determining that the church needed to do better, I sought to find a way in which I could help the church respond to this crisis in our communities. While I continued farming and operating my seed business, I also began working for the Lutheran Church, through Lutheran Social Services, as a Rural Life advocate. Meanwhile, the Catholic Church, through Catholic Charities U.S.A., hired a farm advocate, and a local mental health center started a program called Project Reality to help care for farmers' mental health needs. Over the years, these organizations merged to become Rural Life Outreach.

What started as an organization to provide short-term crisis response has continued for 17 years. Rural Life Outreach assists farmers and other rural residents through listening, assessment and referral. Families find assistance for their emergency needs and are led through the maze of legal and financial red tape that so often paralyzes them.

While the number of farmers seeking help has not lessened during this time, their attitude has changed considerably. In the early days of the 1980s' farm crisis, farmers would beg us to find a way for them to stay on the farm. We felt that the crisis was temporary and that just getting the farmers over the hump would allow them to regroup and carry on with their way of life. Today, farmers, tired and often hopeless, ask instead for us to help them find a way out of farming.

Most farmers are still living off the earnings of the '70s. In this region, federal disaster declarations for excess rain and floods have occurred on average every other year for the past 12 years. For most of this time, commodity prices have been very low. In fact the price for wheat, which is the largest acreage crop in this region, has been lower in recent years than those my father received in the late 1940s.

Our farm operation continued, with regular help and occasional financial support from my parents, until the end of the 1997 crop year, when we decided to concentrate on other employment ventures. The hardest part of quitting farming was the fact that our son, who had always wanted to farm, would have to wait for his chance to start.

Due to a slightly increased optimism from the 2002 farm bill, we have decided that he will start farming a portion of our farm this year, while still continuing his other employment. Only time will tell if his timing is right.

And what of our 1980 net worth of half a million dollars? We still have assets worth about that much, but we also have about $350,000 in debt that we continue to try to pay off.

In private conversations with farmers, you often hear comments like: Farming isn't fun anymore. I sure hope my children don't want to farm. I should have quit farming earlier when I still had some equity. Encouraging your son to farm could get

In spite of the federal government's attempts to strengthen agriculture, one farm program after another has failed to stabilize our farms and rural economy.

you charged with child abuse. In spite of the federal government's attempts to strengthen agriculture, one farm program after another has failed to stabilize our farms and rural economy. It is still too early to know if the 2002 farm bill is any better. Many farmers see no hope for the future. The saying, Wait until next year, now is seldom heard.

One exception: The rare group of nonconventional farmers, such as organic farmers, who are discovering new ways to farm. Their methods are more sustainable by using less input and more intense management. They choose to work with the land, rather than against it, and are finding ways to make a living in the process. There seems to be a sense of that old fire in their hearts and conversations. I can only hope that my son chooses to be one of them.

Maybe yet another generation of the Evert family will call this farm home.

Jon Evert is the coordinator of Rural Life Outreach in Minnesota.

Figure 2.5: Food Security Status of U.S. Households, 2001

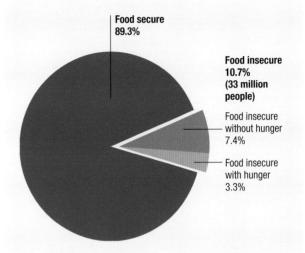

Food secure
89.3%

Food insecure
10.7%
(33 million
people)

Food insecure
without hunger
7.4%

Food insecure
with hunger
3.3%

Source: Calculated by USDA's Economic Research Service using data from the December 2001 Current Population Survey, Food Security Supplement.

The high rates of rural poverty and hunger are costing communities much more than what they pay in taxes to support needs-based services or what they donate to local churches and soup kitchens. When children receive insufficient food or must skip a meal, they become dizzy and feel faint; their learning is impaired. Hungry people are more likely to need health care, are not as productive as well-fed people, and are more likely to feel powerless to change their situation.[32]

A "Poverty Pulse" survey by The Catholic Campaign for Human Development interviewed average Americans as well as those considered low-income about what they think it means to be poor in the United States. Although most low-income respondents talked of not having a home or adequate housing or enough money to meet their basic needs, they also described poverty in terms of how they feel. According to them, being poor is depressing and degrading; they feel they are looked down upon and ignored; they feel hopeless, lonely and powerless.[33]

Even when rural jobs are replaced, it often is with lower-skilled, lower-paying jobs, such as in light manufacturing and service industries.[34] This shift means not only a loss of jobs and income for families in rural areas – and corresponding increases in poverty and hunger – but a loss of tax revenues to help communities pay for public services, such as schools, hospitals and social programs. Such losses have spiraled into long-term decline for many rural communities.

The Center for Rural Affairs reviewed the economic condition of a six-state "rural farm" region in the Great

Plains and confirmed severe population losses coupled with increasing and widespread poverty as compared to the states' more urban areas.[35] Some key findings:

- Agricultural counties lost 4 percent of their population from 1997 to 1998, while the region as a whole gained 6 percent in population;

- Poverty rates are considerably higher in rural farm areas both generally and for children. Child poverty rates in farming communities average 18 percent, compared to 12 percent in urban areas; and

- Rural farm poverty is not limited to isolated pockets. More than one-third of rural households earn less than $15,000 a year.

"When family farmers go out of business, they won't return," says Annette Dubas of Fullerton, Neb., who farms with her family, and fears the toll the loss of farms is having on her community. "Rural America needs family farmers and ranchers to drive their economy."[36]

Farm Workers and Native Americans

Some of the most at-risk populations in rural farm areas are farm workers and the original inhabitants of the land, Native Americans. Although most farm workers migrate to their jobs – whether from within the United States or across national borders – they tend to work only one agricultural job a year, earning an average $5.94

On a farm near Selma, Calif., a farm worker helps pick peaches. Despite the hard work, most farm worker households earn less than $10,000 per year.

an hour.[37] More than three-fourths of farm worker households earn less than $10,000 a year.

In the United States, farm workers primarily pick fruits, vegetables, nuts and other labor-intensive crops – all profitable, thriving areas of agriculture. Yet workers' hours have declined in the past decade, as has their pay. Since 1990, the purchasing power of farm workers' earnings has decreased by 10 percent.[38]

The contrast between farm workers' poverty and the industry's prosperity is nowhere more apparent than in California's San Joaquin Valley, home to one of the nation's most diverse and productive agricultural sectors as well as some of the nation's poorest communities. During the past decade, growers in communities such as Visalia, Fresno and Madera have experienced record revenue increases.[39] Meanwhile, farm workers struggle to house and feed their families.

During the fall harvest in California's Napa County, 6,000 vineyard workers are needed, but the community provides only 200 low-cost beds in worker dorms.[40] Many workers end up sleeping in outdoor squatter camps with makeshift tents of cardboard or plastic bags. Even if families have a place to sleep, many of the dwellings lack indoor plumbing or even kitchens.

Despite such impoverishment, few agricultural workers take advantage of services, such as Social Security and public housing. For example, in 1998 fewer than one in 100 farm workers in the United States applied for welfare, Temporary Assistance for Needy Families. Similarly, less than 3 percent of farm workers seek relief through community- and church-based services, a significant safety net for other poor U.S. groups.[41] Instead, most farm workers rely on help from friends and families. In general, relatively few food pantries are located in many rural areas. In California, for example, Tulare County's FoodLink program runs 20 food pantries countywide – less than one pantry per rural community.

More farm workers (10 percent) do take advantage of direct food-assistance programs, such as food stamps and the Special Supplemental Nutrition Program for Women, Infants and Children, and slightly more use Medicaid (13 percent). But these low numbers suggest that many families are going hungry or without other basic needs.

Hunger and poverty rates are even more dire among Native American communities. Nearly one-third of Native Americans live in poverty, and nearly a fourth of all households are considered food insecure.[42] Because many communities are fairly isolated from public services, such as food stamp and welfare offices, the USDA has created special programs designed to better meet their needs, but more needs to be done (see related story, p. 47).

Medicine Lodge Woman's Letter to America: A 'Basket of Hope' Gives Families One More Shared Meal

The Basket of Hope Food Pantry in Wolf Point, Mont., provides valuable security in this rural area because it allows families to share at least one more humble meal together.

I serve as a volunteer for this local food bank and can share, first-hand, what I see and how it feels to live in a rural, isolated community like the Fort Peck Indian reservation.

Wolf Point, the Roosevelt County seat, is the largest city in the county, with a population of 2,880. The city is located in the southeast corner of Roosevelt County in the historic Missouri River Valley and is the trade center for northeastern Montana. Wolf Point lies within the boundaries of the greater Fort Peck Indian reservation, which includes more than 2 million acres of land – nearly half of which is held under tribal control and jurisdiction.

Prairie, farmland and ranch land stretch as far as one can see. When I look across the land, the sky seems endless. It is a beautiful sight. But amid this calm, peaceful setting also resides the inner pains of hunger.

Hunger is said to be the invisible companion of poverty that strikes far too many families in this area. Unemployment rates exceed 50 percent; more than half the adults living here lack even a high school diploma. Families live in crowded housing conditions, and all too often people struggle with problems of alcohol or drugs. Federal, state and tribal programs exist to try and help families meet their basic needs. But the needs are greater than these many efforts.

I remember one young native mother – whose story is like all too many young mothers I see – who came to the food pantry with her young toddler and school-aged sister. She qualified for food stamps, the Special Supplemental Nutrition Program for Women, Infants and Children (WIC) and tribal housing. She carried the title of "single parent," but being young and lacking life skills, she came to the food bank for assistance, because she could not stretch her monthly budget to meet her needs.

The role of the volunteer is to gather the intake information – the mother's personal information – and begin to fill out a basket or box of food.

This "basket of hope" is served as an emergency measure, so only a three-day supply of food is provided. Volunteers like myself fill the box with food for toddlers and infants, such as milk supplement, canned fruit and vegetables, fruit juices and some type of meat source.

About once a month, a truck from Chicago drops off many of the food supplies that stock our food bank's shelves. State agencies and volunteer efforts, such as food drop-off boxes, also help. The local grocery store also donates bread and pastry products.

After the box or basket is weighed and documented and the mother signs for it, she is free to leave with the food to share with her children. I see many clients on a typical day.

Wolf Point has the only food bank within the county and reservation, so people have to travel fairly far to come here; some people travel by carpool. It is not uncommon for a volunteer to fill out two or more applications based on one carload of people.

Rosella Archdale is holding a braid of sweetgrass, a sacred herb used for prayer, that she harvests during the summer near her home in Wolf Point, Mont.

I realize that food banks offer a "band-aid" solution to much deeper social problems. But the assurance of food that food banks provide is welcomed and valued by those in need, even if it's a temporary solution. A mother can find peace for the moment because she knows she can feed her family on this one day.

I'm not sure how many children we've helped feed this year, but I know that I see many of their promising faces every time I volunteer. Statewide, more than 120,000 children received food from food banks and feeding programs in 2000.

They say, "It takes a village to raise a child." This statement implies that each child is born with equal opportunity and each person is responsible for his or her well-being. Can we say this holds true today?

The Native American family system is a close-knit connection for one and all. Traditional life is highly regarded and retained by those who live on the reservation. Whereas most Americans base their wealth on material accumulation, traditional Native Americans base their wealth on the shared benefit to their community.

I have chosen to relate my experience as a food bank volunteer and as a Native American who resides in rural America. As I sit down to share a meal with my family tonight, I hope to say that I've shared the benefit of my knowledge and services with my husband and children, with my Fort Peck family and with my greater American community.

mitakoyasin[1]
Rosella Archdale
Medicine Lodge Woman

---

[1] Respectfully to all of my relations

Small Farm Connection

As Nebraskan farmer Annette Dubas and other observers argue, rural America needs small farms if its economies are to survive. Historically, these communities relied primarily on agriculture for employment and income. Not just family farms, but nearly all family businesses – the grocery, grain elevator, feed store – were part of an agricultural structure that supported the community. Newly generated dollars would circulate among three of four pairs of hands before leaving the community.

Today rural America has reduced its reliance on agriculture and embraced other industries, and many economists now discount agriculture as crucial to rural economic development. Both farmers and rural communities have learned that to survive they must change and diversify. That said, Do smaller farms – including struggling mid-size farms – have an important role to play in creating a sustainable agricultural system?

Small farm advocates maintain that the get-big-or-get-out philosophy driving current farm policy fails to recognize the real costs of increasing consolidation on communities, the environment and the economy. Even for communities having success in finding new employers, the transition can be difficult and costly. It can take years for a community to attract a major new employer, much less the two or three to truly diversify its economy. During the meantime, families may be forced to commute long distances for work or survive long periods of unemployment and, often, poverty.

Dan Smalley, a poultry producer of Red Hill Farms in Guntersville, Ala., recalls the structural changes he has seen in his industry during the past few decades. In 1980 the top four chicken companies accounted for approximately one-fourth of all production, with 34 plants. By 1988, the top four firms accounted for nearly half of all production, with 70 plants.[43] Although Smalley acknowledges that growing chickens on "contract" as part of a "vertically integrated" industry is not everyone's choice, he adds, "Forming alliances may be the most palatable way for individual producers to assure themselves of market access."

In vertical integration, companies own and control various stages in the food-processing chain. It is most prevalent in livestock industries, such as poultry and hogs, but also is growing in the grain, fruit and vegetable sectors. By controlling many aspects of food production and processing – from feed to slaughterhouse packaging plants to transportation – "integrators" drive down the prices of commodities (i.e., poultry or pork), which allows them to better control the costs of final processed products, such as packaged chicken nuggets.

Companies like Virginia-based Smithfield Foods Inc. contract with farmers to raise hogs or other animals, a

In the not-too-distant past, nearly all rural family businesses – the grocery, grain elevator, feed store – were connected to agriculture. But to survive today, rural communities are learning they must diversify.

practice known as contract farming. Although the contracts offer some incentives and protection from risks, critics of such practices contend that because the companies control most segments of the operation, farmers have little leverage to negotiate better prices or better terms.

In North Carolina, traditional small family hog farms, once a staple of the economy, are a remnant of the past. The state now houses 2,200 hog "factories," 1,600 of which are owned and/or controlled by Smithfield.[44] "The same process of vertical integration has bankrupted five out of six of America's hog farmers over the past 15 years," testified Richard Dove, of the New York-based environmental group, Waterkeeper Alliance, before the Senate Committee on Government Affairs on March 13, 2002.[45]

Many small farmer advocates and others contend that such large-scale farming – concentrated animal feeding operations (CAFOs) – does not account for the full environmental consequences of concentrating a large number of animals on limited land. North Carolina's Neuse River and other waterways are struggling with nutrient pollution from CAFOs and other sources. This pollution breeds *Pfisteria piscidia*, a one-cell parasite that paralyzes fish, sloughs their skin and feeds on their blood cells.

As a result of the hog waste, North Carolina experienced severe fish kills in 1991 and 1995, when more than 10,000 dead fish were documented. Despite negative publicity and local efforts by environmental groups to hold the companies responsible, the problem continues.

Such environmental concerns bolster the argument that the loss of small and mid-size family farmers diminishes farmers' role as good stewards of the land. Small farmers manage nearly 60 percent of U.S. farmland. They also are most likely to use current environmental

North Carolina's Opportunity to Help Small Farms, Rural Communities

By Betty Bailey

Thirty-three million people worldwide farm tobacco. As a cash crop, these families – 120,000 which live and work in the southern United States – depend on tobacco and its income to feed their families.

Recent changes in the tobacco industry – reductions in the federal quota program – mean that these U.S. farm families no longer can depend primarily on tobacco income for their livelihoods. While devastating on one hand, the change presents a tremendous opportunity to help these farmers make a transition into other ventures, preserving many modest-sized American farms in the process.

Business Changes

Changes in the tobacco industry have come fast and furious. In just three years, tobacco quotas – the federally determined amount of tobacco that can be grown based on market demand – has been cut in half. Tobacco companies are buying more of their leaf from outside the United States. In just two years, the amount of tobacco grown under contract arrangements between farmers and tobacco companies has grown to 80 percent. Moreover, the old auction system is rapidly declining, with 106 tobacco warehouses going out of business in North Carolina in the past year.

A bright spot amid this upheaval is the tobacco Master Settlement Agreement (MSA), which was signed in 1998 between 46 states and the major tobacco companies to compensate tobacco-related losses. In exchange for ending state lawsuits, tobacco companies agreed to compensate states for health care costs and, in tobacco-producing states, losses to tobacco-dependent farmers and communities.

States have considerable leverage in how they use the funds. According to the Campaign for Tobacco Free Kids, few states have spent a significant portion on stopping teen smoking or in other tobacco-control efforts. In the major tobacco-growing states, eight of 14 states have targeted some funds for agricultural development. Five of the eight have allocated an average 22 percent for that purpose. But much more could be done to help farm families as well as curb youth smoking.

Life After Tobacco

Tobacco farmers know that they must change to survive. A survey of 1,236 tobacco farmers in North Carolina by Wake Forest University and the Rural Advancement Foundation International-USA (RAFI) shows that farmers see the handwriting on the wall. Most farmers:

- believe tobacco will not be grown on their farms in the future;
- would not advise their children to grow tobacco because they believe the federal tobacco program would be gone in five years; and
- are interested in diversifying their income and staying in farming.

Moreover, of the tobacco farmers surveyed, one in five no longer was in tobacco, although most were still struggling to remain in agriculture. Most farmers (96 percent) already are growing other crops, typically traditional commodity crops, but they are not making money from these ventures.

Farmers say that key barriers to their profitability are lack of capital, local processing and marketing opportunities, labor, and suitable equipment. In a marketplace where the farmer's share of the food dollar is declining as the profits of processors and distributors rise, farmers must try to tap into post-harvest markets and consider what happens to a crop after it leaves the farm.

A Golden Opportunity

States should use their tobacco-settlement money to help farmers diversify and build rural communities. Before the MSA, a few programs had been developed to help farmers make the transition out of tobacco. RAFI operated a pilot Tobacco Communities Reinvestment program, and the Commodity Growers Cooperative in Kentucky set up a similar program. Through the reinvestment program, farmers and communities were given cost-share support to test their ideas for increasing income from other enterprises. Funded projects included farmers markets, cooperative processing, farm-based services and new uses of old equipment. A number of farmers increased their income by converting tobacco greenhouses for use in off-season fruit and vegetable production. Other projects include farmers creating pick-your-own, fish-your-own and direct farmer-to-consumer markets.

North Carolina expects to receive $4.6 billion from tobacco companies over 25 years. Half goes to the Golden Long-Term Economic Advancement Foundation (LEAF) and the other half will be split between a Health and Wellness Trust and a Tobacco Trust that benefit farmers, workers and businesses. An additional Phase II fund was provided to North Carolina and the other tobacco-producing states for direct payments to farmers and quota holders. Decisions by the first Phase II board mean that only those who remain in tobacco receive payments.

Estimates are that $43 million of the $59 million spent thus far in North Carolina went to tobacco processing and marketing efforts to keep state farmers and communities competitive in the global tobacco market. North Carolina, like many other states, is experiencing state budget shortfalls. In 2002, instead of going to farmers, the $80 million in settlement funds was re-directed to plug holes in the general budget.

Yet, significant funds still are being spent on agricultural development. The Golden LEAF foundation has spent $15 million on developing alternative crops and other economic-development projects in the poorest and most tobacco-dependent counties. The Tobacco Trust just announced a $3 million round of grants for agricultural and job development, including support for RAFI's reinvestment fund and complementary projects.

The tobacco South has an unprecedented opportunity to revitalize small farms and rural communities through wise application of the settlement funds. Political tides and the downturn in the economy will place great pressures on the use of these funds. In a time of unprecedented opportunity, states should not forget that small farms are good for the region. They contribute fresh local food, employment, green fields and forests, and much more to southern communities.

Betty Bailey is executive director of Rural Advancement Foundation International-USA.

incentives. Their role as responsible managers of the country's natural resources – soil, water and wildlife – should be supported and enhanced.

These issues aside, many Americans simply believe that the culture and heritage of rural America is worth preserving. According to former Sen. Jean Carnahan (D-Mo.), "Yes, the family farm is a part of our culture... one that should be preserved and supported. Rural America reflects our values... hard work... respect for the land... neighbors helping one another. Basic virtues that are important for our personal, community and national well-being."[46]

1996 Farm Bill: Moving Closer to Market Approach

Clearly, today's system does not serve well most American farmers or the poor and hungry people in rural America. The facts highlight the need for a range of agriculture polices that, by going beyond protecting commodity programs, reduce poverty and develop rural areas in the United States – and ultimately worldwide.

In 1996 Congress attempted to remedy many of the traditional farm programs' shortcomings by adopting a more market- and export-oriented approach. Under the FAIR Act, supply controls were eliminated. Farmers were allowed to plant as much of whatever crops they wanted in exchange for a gradual reduction of government income supports by 2003. Policymakers expected farmers to manage their farming by shifting to the most profitable crop mix dictated by the market, not government programs. But these expectations were short-lived.

While policymakers anticipated an initial period of price disequilibrium, for which transition payments would be made to farmers, they expected prices and incomes to stabilize as the market corrected itself. A fundamental assumption behind these forecasts was that consumer demand would grow as a result of expanding export markets, such as in China and Southeast Asia where incomes were rising.[47]

U.S. farmers welcomed this new "freedom to farm," and between 1996 and 2000 embraced greater planting flexibility by reducing their acreage of wheat by 16.7 percent and increasing their acreage of soybeans by 16 percent. However, the 1997-1998 Asian financial crisis sent demand plummeting. Moreover, during this period other countries increased their production of key commodities, including corn, soybeans and wheat. Argentina and Brazil increased their soybean exports by 13 percent.[48] Argentina and the European Union increased wheat production by 3.7 percent and 5.8 percent, respectively.[49] As a result, U.S. exports between 1996 and 2000 fell for corn (by 8 percent) and wheat (by 11 percent), and rose only 5 percent for soybeans.

What many farmers and policymakers saw as the failure of the 1996 farm bill in reality was a reflection of changes in the global food system and market place. Many countries – especially developing countries – enjoy a comparative advantage of cheaper land and labor in comparison to the United States. As their economies grow, they are better able to exploit this competitive edge in agricultural production, which in turn affects international supply and the prices U.S. farmers receive in a global market. In Brazil, for example, cheaper land accounts for more than three-fourths of its soybean cost advantage over beans produced in the United States.[50]

U.S. efforts to move farmers into a truer market economy are complicated by another factor: the level of protection that other industrialized countries continue to give to their farmers. For these and other reasons, the 1996 FAIR Act failed to increase commodity prices or market share for U.S. farmers. Overall, the U.S. farm trade balance fell by more than half from the 1996 peak of $29.5 billion to $12.6 billion in 2000, as prices for major commodities declined. As a result of declining prices, the U.S. government responded with billions of dollars in emergency assistance, payments many farmers said were necessary to ensure that they stayed in business. Yet even with these payments, small and mid-size farms continued to disappear (see Table 2.2).

This experience colored the 2002 farm bill debate. Although many farmers lost faith in the market approach touted in the 1996 farm bill, more of them acknowledge that price subsidies serve more to undermine than sustain them. The 2002 farm bill saw more Midwest legislators calling for crop subsidy reforms, such as capping

Gary Braver, an organic farmer who lives in Minnesota, says that organic farming is a better way to protect and manage the United States' natural resources while also providing a superior product to consumers.

Table 2.2: Changes in the Distribution of Working Farms, 1993-1999

| | Farm Size Class (annual sales) | | | | |
	$500,000 or more	$250,000-499,999	$100,000-249,999	$50,000 99,999	Total
1993	45,856	70,982	224,823	212,531	554,192
1997	53,531	82,984	207,058	187,831	531,404
1999	63,422	80,917	199,012	166,208	509,559
Totals 1993-1999					
Percent change	38%	14%	-11%	-22%	-8%
Number gained or lost	17,566	9,935	-25,811	-46,323	-44,633
Number lost with gross incomes $50,000-249,999					-72,134

Source: U.S. Department of Agriculture, Farm Business Economics Briefing Room. Farm Structure Reading Room, "A Close-Up of Changes in Farm Organization": (USDA 1996a and 2000).

subsidies to the largest agribusinesses, than before. Other legislators pushed for funding increases to farmland conservation programs, which are more likely to benefit smaller farmers.

Many of these reforms survived initial rounds of congressional negotiations. The 2002 farm bill expanded programs for farmland conservation, rural development, promotion of equity and nondiscrimination among farmers and farm workers, and nutrition (see related story, p. 52). But in the end, agribusiness lobbyists proved too powerful and the payment caps did not survive. The weaknesses of past programs largely remained in the 2002 farm bill, which allows large farms to receive unlimited marketing loans, which directly affect farmers' production decisions, and a single farmer to collect up to $360,000 in payments.[51]

Moving Past Politics

Overall, the 2002 farm bill will provide nearly $84 billion more to farmers over the next decade in the form of subsidies and conservation and other payments than they received in the last bill. This increase in farm support has met with significant resistance and criticism from the international community. Says Sophia Murphy, director of trade and agriculture for the Institute for Agriculture and Trade Policy:

> The [2002] farm bill seems to have hit a sore spot with nearly everyone, but howls of protest are perhaps the loudest outside of the United States. From Brazil to Brussels to Brisbane, countries are lining up to challenge the farm bill before the WTO. The farm bill really puts U.S. trade negotiators in a bind. The U.S. can no longer pretend that the billions of dollars it was already spending, in

steadily increasing amounts since 1997, were somehow an anomaly related to emergencies.[52]

Despite the much-publicized trade setback of the 2002 farm bill, the Bush administration presented a global agricultural trade reform proposal that calls for the elimination of export subsidies over five years – though the United States does not use export subsidies – a reduction in average farm tariffs, from 62 percent to 25 percent; and a cap on trade-distorting subsidies to no more than 5 percent of total agricultural production.[53] Although this proposal would move global agricultural trade in a positive direction, it is not clear how much support it will receive in the United States or as part of the ongoing international trade negotiations in Doha, Qatar. Support seems to be coming from countries with the least to lose, such as New Zealand, which already has an efficient, liberal agriculture program. The European Union, which provides most of its agriculture protection in the form of export subsidies, has much to lose and has been quite vocal in criticizing the U.S. proposal.

Many countries question the U.S. failure to advance its own agricultural policy in the direction of this proposal. The Bush administration attributes this anomaly to the realities of U.S. politics. According to Agriculture Secretary Ann M. Veneman, who spoke before the International Policy Council on Agriculture, Food and Trade, in Ottawa, Canada, on May 3, 2002, "The farm bill that has been negotiated by the conferees represents a compromise on a very contentious process. ... But I want to make one thing perfectly clear, we remain committed to continuing to aggressively pursue trade reform in the Doha round. The farm bill does not in any way change that."[54]

2002 Farm Bill: Many Wins, Important Losses

President Bush signed the 2002 farm bill – the Farm Security and Rural Investment Act – into law on May 13, 2002, after more than a year of debate.

The bill contains more new and expanded funding for conservation than in any past farm bill, yet does little to address price distortion, commodity overproduction or family farmers' concerns on concentration and competition. The bill also significantly increases spending on farm-income payments, considered trade distorting by developing countries and others, and unfair because they mostly accrue to larger producers.

This final legislation will govern farms and shape the food system for six years. The next farm bill is scheduled for consideration in 2007. The nearly $180 billion budget for the bill will be expended over 10 years and includes baseline spending of about $97 billion, with an additional $83.8 billion added over the previous farm program budget.

Additional Spending for Next 10 Years

Title	Total ($ Billion)	Percentage of Budget
Commodities	$56.7	68%
Conservation	$17.1	20%
Nutrition	$6.6	7.9%
Trade	$1.1	1.3%
Rural Development	$1.0	1.2%
Research	$1.3	1.5%

Overall, the bill includes several positive measures for poor and hungry people and rural communities, including the following:

Nutrition (Title IV of the Farm Bill, The Food Stamp Reauthorization Act of 2002)

The nutrition title of the 2002 farm bill encompasses many programs that have the most potential to directly impact and enhance food security for low-income consumers, including farm workers, seniors and children. Food stamp victories in the 2002 farm bill include:

- restoration of food stamp benefits to legal immigrants who have been in the country for five years;

- restoration of benefits to all children and disabled persons who are legal immigrants, with no minimum residency requirements; and

- giving states incentives to reduce the red tape and bureaucracy that keeps millions of eligible people off food stamps.

A poultry farmer in Suwanee County, Florida, adds water to compost to keep the bacteria working that ultimately turns chicken waste into usable topsoil. The 2002 farm bill provides more incentives for farmers to practice such environmentally friendly methods.

The Special Supplemental Nutrition Program for Women, Infants and Children (WIC) and Seniors Farmer's Market Nutrition Program (FMNP)

These programs allow women, children and seniors who are on public assistance to purchase locally grown fresh produce from independent family farmers. This program recycles food stamp dollars into farmer' pockets, lowering the amount of tax dollars spent on food stamp and WIC programs and providing a double benefit: feeding hungry families and bolstering small farm income. The farm bill incorporates the following:

- WIC FMNP will receive an additional $15 million for fiscal year 2002 to substitute funds that were withheld from the regular WIC program; and

- Seniors FMNP became permanent, with mandatory funding at $15 million per year.

Community Food Projects

The Community Food Security Program helps pay for community food projects designed to meet the needs of low-income people and increase community nutrition. The 2002 farm bill increases mandatory funding to $5 million per year, doubling past funding levels.

Promote Buying of Locally Produced Foods

This program encourages institutions participating in the National School Lunch Program and School Breakfast Program to purchase locally grown food. The 2002 farm bill authorizes up to $400,000 to help institutions begin buying locally produced foods.

Rural Development

The 2002 farm bill increased spending for rural development and focuses on supporting independent agriculture enterprises and small business development, through the:

- Value-added Agricultural Product Market Development Program, which awards up to $500,000 to small and mid-size farms that are trying alternative ways to increase farm income; and

- Rural Business Enterprise Grant, which supports small and emerging private business enterprises in areas with fewer than 5,000 people.

Conservation

This farm bill increased conservation funding 80 percent over past spending levels, although more than half of conservation spending ($9 billion of the $17.1 billion) will go to the Environmental Quality Incentive Program (EQUIP).

- Conservation Security Program provides financial incentives to producers to implement conservation practices on their farms. As an entitlement program, it is the first conservation program to be on par with commodity programs (i.e., if a farmer or rancher qualifies, she or he can participate in the program); and

- The EQUIP program offers cost-share assistance to producers to make their farms more environmentally sustainable.

Minority Farm Outreach and Assistance Program

The 2002 farm bill significantly improves and strengthens the Minority Farm Outreach and Assistance Program, first created in 1990, which supports organizations and institutions that assist small and minority farmers in gaining access to credit, commodity, conservation and other programs through the U.S. Department of Agriculture. The 2002 bill increases funding authority from $10 million to $25 million. As this program remains discretionary, it will be essential to educate the Agriculture Appropriations subcommittees on the critical need for full funding for this program, which has never received an appropriation above $3.2 million.

Protections for Farm Workers

The farm bill includes few benefits for farm workers beyond the restoration of food stamp benefits for legal immigrants noted previously. The 2002 farm bill contains a few provisions that will benefit a small number of farm workers, including:

- Emergency Grants to Assist Low-Income Migrant and Seasonal Farm Workers, which provides emergency funding to farm workers affected by disasters; and

- up to $10 million in grants for training farm workers in new technologies and specialized skills needed for higher value crops.

Part of what makes agricultural policy reform so difficult in the United States is the divergent political pulls of various states, regions and farmers. Although trade liberalization would benefit U.S. agriculture on the whole by providing expanded markets for American products as well as giving U.S. consumers greater access to a variety of foods from U.S. trading partners, this gain would help some industry sectors and farmers more than others, with a few groups possibly being pushed out of agriculture entirely.

Practically all stakeholders in today's food system would be winners under broad agricultural trade liberalization. However, the process would not be without its negative repercussions. The shift from highly protected to highly liberalized agriculture would leave many U.S. rural communities reeling from lost jobs and resources. For others, it would entail a lifestyle change.

Those hardest hit by liberalization would be commodity farmers and farmers in specific regions of the United States whose communities rely heavily on farm subsidy programs. Although it is difficult to estimate how many farms would be lost to the curtailment of current programs, most researchers agree that farmers favored by the programs – such as sugar, peanut, wheat and cotton growers, and dairymen – and farmers in states that benefit the most from price support programs – such as the southeast and Plains states – would suffer the greatest transitions. Some research suggests that as many as 25 million acres of crops in these regions would turn to grass, trees and other noncrop uses.[55]

Farms with sales between $100,000 and $250,000 are struggling most under the current farm programs because they are not big enough to achieve economies of scale but are too large for their owners to work off the farm. For these same reasons, mid-size farmers also would suffer the most if the United States eliminates current income supports. This trend is not the same for small and larger farms, which either are profitable without the programs or rely primarily on other income sources.

Other potential losers include landowners who would experience declining farmland values. Without a system that depresses the global commodity market, prices for corn and other grains would rise. As a result, livestock and poultry feeders likely would see their costs increase, although some economists anticipate that these costs will be passed along to consumers.

Still, the overall gains to consumers and taxpayers are estimated to be higher than losses to farmers and other producers, with the United States gaining real income in the end. These net gains could be used to compensate the "losers," culminating in a system in which everyone is better off: consumers, farmers, and poor and hungry people. The challenge is to design a program that com-

Unwrapping the Paradox: Obesity and Hunger in the United States

By Sarah Farmer

In the past couple of decades Americans have become increasingly preoccupied with issues of diet and exercise. As a country, Americans have spent millions of dollars promoting and purchasing weight control books and workout videos. Americans spend more than $33 billion a year on diet and weight-loss products and services. Despite the country's growing obsession with weighing in and working out, America's incidence of overweight and obesity is spiraling out of control, reaching epidemic proportions. More than half of all American adults and more than one in 10 American youths are considered overweight or obese.

At the same time, the number of people who are food insecure or hungry in the United States is growing. One in 10 U.S. households experience food insecurity.

Because people associate the state of hunger or food insecurity with eating too little and being overweight and obese with eating too much, most people see hunger and obesity as opposite problems. But recent studies among poor populations in the United States show that widespread hunger and food insecurity actually can contribute to people being overweight and obese.

In 2001 some 33 million Americans, including 13 million children, lived in households that experienced food insecurity.[1] Food insecurity, the primary measure of hunger in the United States, occurs when access to nutritionally adequate and safe foods is either limited or uncertain or the ability to obtain foods occurs in socially unacceptable ways.

People become overweight or obese when they consume more calories than they need. Overweight and obesity are measured by a ratio of weight to height. A body mass index (BMI) of between 25 kg/m2 and 29.9 kg/m2 is an indicator of overweight status; a BMI of 30 kg/m2 or greater defines one as obese.[2] According to a 1999 Centers for Disease Control and Prevention National Health and Nutrition Examination Survey, nearly two-thirds of adults (61 percent) are overweight or obese, and 13 percent of children (ages 6 years to 11 years) and 14 percent of adolescents (ages 12 years to 19 years) are overweight.[3]

Poverty Connection?

Although being overweight and obese is not confined to any one socioeconomic or racial group, poor people, especially women, have been hit disproportionately hard, facing multiple barriers to maintaining a healthy weight. For all racial and ethnic groups combined, low-income women (income equal to or less than 130 percent of poverty threshold) are approximately 50 percent more likely to be obese than those with higher incomes (income greater than 130 percent of poverty threshold).[4] A 2001 study conducted by University of California-Davis' Nutrition Department has provided one possible explanation for this complex relationship between poverty, food insecurity and obesity.[5]

Although still in its infant stages, the study links the "food acquisition cycle" of food stamp recipients to a high prevalence of being overweight. The food acquisition cycle of food stamp recipients is characterized by a short period of involuntary food restriction at the end of the month when food stamps or money runs low, followed by a brief period of over or binge eating of highly palatable, rich foods at the beginning of the next month when the food supply is restored.

Why do food stamps tend to run low before the end of the month? In 2001 the average monthly food stamp allowance was $75 per person and $174 per household.[6] These monthly food stamp figures amount to less than $1 (83 cents) per meal per person and do not take into account geographical price differences or ages of all members in the household.[7] Most households on food stamps sometimes run out of food toward the end of the month. The adaptive response to "episodic food insufficiency" among food stamp recipients in this study proved to be a serious risk factor over time to unhealthy weight gain.

Others factors also increase low-income people's risk to obesity. Many low-income Americans more likely are consuming foods low in nutritional quality and high in calories, fats and sugars. This overconsumption of nutritionally poor foods largely results from the need to buy the cheapest foods.[8] Nutritionally beneficial foods such as fresh fruits, vegetables and whole grains often are more expensive in low-income neighborhoods than alternative junk food. Cash-strapped families increasingly rely on fast food chains, which promote oversized burgers, extra-large servings of fries and buckets of soda – all at low prices.

Furthermore, poor neighborhoods often lack large grocery stores that typically offer the lowest prices and greatest range of brands, package sizes and quality choices, and farmers markets that sell locally grown fresh fruits and vegetables. Transportation to these large grocery stores and farmers markets also often is either unavailable or expensive. Consequently, many residents of low-income neighborhoods depend on their corner convenience stores – stocked with mostly high-cost processed, pre-packaged foods – to provide them with the nutrients needed to maintain an optimal weight.[9]

Additionally, poor families, especially those living in urban areas, often do not have access to a safe space conducive to physical activity. This situation is problematic considering that burning calories or exercising is half of the weight control solution.

A diet rich in fresh fruits and vegetables is key to maintaining overall good health.

Rising Health Problem for All Americans

Overweight and obesity represent a serious health problem among all income groups. Obesity is the second leading cause of preventable death in the United States, killing an estimated 300,000 adults each year.[10] The disease burden associated with obesity includes type 2 diabetes; hypertension; cardiovascular disease; colon, breast and prostate cancer; gallstones; arthritis; complications of pregnancy; menstrual irregularities; and psychological disorders.

The total health-related costs for obesity in the United States is approximately $117 billion, including $61 billion in direct costs (treatment of related diseases), plus $56 billion in indirect costs (lost productivity due to disability, morbidity and mortality).[11] Solving the problem will require significant social change that will require serious and effective efforts by individuals. Americans also must recognize being overweight as a social problem and begin to address it through public policy, as the nation has addressed smoking.

Policies especially should target low-income Americans, who are at higher risk of becoming overweight or obese. The connection between poverty, food insecurity and obesity must be realized, and insufficiencies in our federal safety net programs, such as the often meager, monthly food stamp allowance, must be addressed. Larger grocery stores and farmers markets that offer a wide variety of highly nutritious foods also must become available in low-income neighborhoods. Cities also should make low-income neighborhoods safer and provide more sidewalks, bike paths and alternatives to cars.

Sarah Farmer was a Bill Emerson National Hunger fellow at Bread for the World Institute in spring 2002.

1   Mark Nord, Nader Kabbani, Laura Tiehen, et al, "Household Food Security in the United States 2000." Economic Research Service of the U.S. Department of Agriculture Food Assistance and Nutrition Research Report No. 21, March 2002. Available from http://www.ers.usda.gov/publications/fanrr21/.

2   U.S. Department of Health and Human Services, "Obesity and Overweight; Body Mass Index (BMI)." Available from http://www.cdc.gov/nccdphp/dnpa/obesity/bmi.htm.

3   U.S. Department of Health and Human Services, "National Health and Nutrition Examination Survey." Available from http://www.cdc.gov/nchs/data/nhanes/databriefs/overwght.pdf.

4   U.S. Department of Health and Human Services, "With Understanding and Improving Health and Objectives for Improving Health." *Healthy People 2010*, 2nd ed. Vol. 20 (Washington, DC: GPO) 2000.

5   M. Townsend, J. Peerson, B. Love, et al, "Food insecurity is positively related to overweight in women." *Journal of Nutrition*, Vol. 131, 2001, 1738-1745.

6   U.S. Department of Agriculture Food and Nutrition Service, "Food Stamp Program National Level Annual Summary 2001." Available from http://www.fns.usda.gov/pd/fssummar.htm.

7   P. Eisinger, *Towards an End to Hunger in America.* (Washington DC: Brookings Institute Press) 1998.

8   C.M. Olson, "Nutrition and Health Outcomes Associated with Food Insecurity and Hunger." *Journal of Nutrition*, Vol. 129 (2 Suppl), 1999, 521S-524S.

9   Amanda Shaffer, "The Persistence of L.A.'s Grocery Store Gap." Center for Food and Justice, Urban and Environmental Policy Institute, May 2002. Available from http://departments.oxy.edu/uepi/cfj/resources/supermarketsexecsumm.htm.

10 D.B. Allison, K.R. Fontaine, J.E. Manson, et al, "Annual Deaths Attributed to Obesity in the United States." *Journal of the American Medical Association*, Vol.282 No. 16, Oct. 27,1999, 1530-8.

11 U.S. Department of Health and Human Services, "The Surgeon General's Call to Action to Prevent and Decrease Overweight and Obesity," 2001. Available from http://www.surgeongeneral.gov/library.

prises various safety nets – but not necessarily subsidies – for farmers in transition. The first, and perhaps most difficult, step is to identify and articulate a domestic U.S. farm-policy goal that is broad enough to promote economic equity and efficiency for the well-being of people everywhere.

The Bush administration has identified several important priorities as it crafts future agricultural policy: help rural America, improve the environment and address infrastructure needs.[56] These priorities are a start, but the ultimate goal of U.S. farm programs must be to promote sustainable agriculture, reduce rural poverty and eliminate food insecurity, both in the United States and throughout the world.

Toward this end, the United States should:

- gradually eliminate tariffs on developing country agriculture exports, export subsidies and production-linked domestic support payments;

- support U.S. farmers who leave agriculture with adjustment assistance that would include counseling, job training, education reimbursement and transportation aid;

- support small and mid-size farmers with comprehensive rural development programs and technical assistance in adopting new technologies and developing greater economies of scale;

- establish provisions for farmers to help them sustain losses resulting from catastrophic weather events;

- strengthen assistance for farmers in meeting conservation goals and environmental mandates, including increased technical assistance, cost-share programs and incentive payments for use of environmentally friendly practices;

- increase research and regulation in areas, such as biotechnology, food safety, disease prevention and environmental quality;

- invest in rural communities by supporting economic development initiatives, job training, business promotion and infrastructure development; and

- reduce hunger in the United States (through nutrition and poverty reduction programs) and worldwide (through development assistance and trade opportunities), with this adding to the ongoing demand for food production.

More attention, research and investigation also needs to focus on social justice issues related to agriculture, such as whether contract agriculture needs reform and the impact of agribusiness consolidation on the food system.

CHAPTER 3

Trade and Agriculture:
Rules of the Game

The United States, European Union and other industrialized regions often profess a desire to reduce worldwide poverty and hunger by helping developing countries' economies grow. Often, the elixir of choice is free trade. They speak of a country trading its way out of poverty, of trade not aid. Yet while exhorting developing countries to dismantle their trade barriers, the United States, European Union and others continue to protect the sectors most important to developing countries' economies, notably agriculture. In the words of Thailand's Deputy Prime Minister Pitak Intrawityanunt, "The disturbing fact is that economic policies in developed countries effectively prevent poor countries from trading their way out of poverty."[1]

As in most international relationships, economic power translates into structural power. Nations with larger, more productive economies are able to exert undue influence over the terms of international agreements, even shape the global economic system itself. Meanwhile, smaller countries like Haiti or Senegal have little say about how rules are developed and little bargaining power for getting rules changed. The result: international trade rules that reflect industrialized world interests and a trading system that fails poor and hungry people in developing countries.

A stated principle of the World Trade Organization (WTO) – the body created to govern international trade – is that trade relations should be used to raise living standards.[2] Although in spirit the body recognizes that nations differ in their "respective needs and concerns in different levels of development," in practice international trade rules reflect the interests of the most powerful governments and markets, with little regard to developing countries' needs and concerns.

Consequently, the United States, members of the European Union and other industrialized countries can pursue markets abroad while using tariffs and domestic and export subsidies to protect their farmers and agricultural markets at home from global competition. These protections encourage overproduction of supported crops like corn, cotton, soybeans and wheat, and the dumping (selling at below the cost of production) of excess produce onto the world market, depressing commodity prices for all farmers.

While the United States and other rich countries have the wherewithal to help their farmers and rural communities, poorer countries do not. Poor farmers worldwide are forced to make daily decisions about what necessity their families must do without: medicine for a mother fighting malaria, tuition for a son or daughter to attend school, fertilizer to boost poor yields, or food.

According to Center for Global Development President Nancy Birdsall, "The rules of the new global

A more equitable agricultural trading system would benefit both industrialized and developing countries through economic growth and greater political and social stability.

economy are stacked against the developing countries and particularly against the poor in these countries."[3] For the players shaping the rules, the system reflects a shortsighted assessment of national self-interest. The industrialized world has real interests in promoting a more equitable agriculture system via a more equitable trading system. Such interests range from global political and social stability to economic efficiency and growth. Industrialized countries would benefit directly from reducing their subsidies and trade restrictions, and they would benefit indirectly from accelerated growth in poor countries. These countries can contribute more to the global economy as both producers and consumers.

World Bank President James Wolfenson says, "There is no wall" separating the rich world from the poor. "There are not two worlds. There is only one."

Why Trade?

Trade has been a part of human activity for as long as history has been recorded, and probably before. Whether by barter or exchange of money, trade is a way to acquire the things people need but cannot make themselves. This transfer of goods takes place among individuals and among companies, and between individuals and companies. It occurs within and among countries as well.

International trade gives people in one country access to goods produced in another. In the Middle Ages, European demand for silks and spices that could not be grown or made in Europe led explorers to India and the Far East. Today, E.U. trade with tropical countries like Costa Rica and Honduras means European consumers find bananas in grocery stores year round.

The economic theory of comparative advantage explains why countries benefit from trade. They can specialize in production areas where they have a comparative advantage and buy other products from other countries. Each trading country can benefit from an increase in affluence.

International trade also has dynamic benefits. Trade puts new competitive pressures on industries where only a few companies dominate the national market. It stimulates creativity and innovation and spreads new ideas from one country to another.

The potential economic benefits of trade liberalization are almost universally acknowledged. Yet liberalization is difficult to achieve because trade by definition is a cooperative activity. Countries can afford to import more if they export more, but they can only export more if other countries also reduce trade barriers. Therefore, countries need to reduce protection concurrently.[4]

Politics of Trade

Although trade liberalization leads to economic gains at the national level, not everyone benefits the same way. Industries that do not enjoy a comparative advantage vis-à-vis new trading partners will probably lose market share and become unprofitable without protection, while those that are efficient should gain new markets. Such variation inevitably creates domestic political tensions.

Witness the uproar over the U.S. government's 2002 imposition of tariffs on certain steel products. The relatively small yet vocal American steel industry demanded tariff protection, claiming that steel was being dumped in the United States.

Automakers and the construction industry, which had been benefiting from less-expensive imported steel, fought the move. Despite its size, the steel industry won the day, probably because its facilities are concentrated in a few electorally important states.

Most protection reductions are subject to similarly rancorous political tugs-of-war over the perceived costs and benefits of more open trade. These debates, however, are not over open trade per se, but rather liberalization's effects on a specific industry. In the 1980s, the U.S. automobile industry, which was pro-liberalization in the steel case, successfully lobbied the government to convince Japan to voluntarily suppress its car exports to the United States, another form of trade protection.

The WTO – or rather the General Agreement on Tariffs and Trade (GATT), the predecessor organization to the WTO – was created to help alleviate such inherent liberalization difficulties by providing a forum for simultaneous, binding tariff reductions. The tumultuous period between World War I and World War II, during which the global economy was characterized by conflict rather than cooperation, convinced policymakers of the need for such an institution (see related story, p. 60).

A WTO strength is that it is rules-based, meaning that agreements signed under its auspices are binding and subject to a formal dispute-settlement system. Governments can use these binding agreements to deflect the pressures of domestic interests, politically

E. Byers

Whether by barter or exchange of money, people trade to acquire things that they need but cannot make or grow themselves.

Jim Stipe

Agriculture is vital to improving the lives of poor and hungry people in developing countries because most of them derive their incomes from farming, either directly or indirectly.

powerful sectors or industries that have an interest in maintaining the status quo.

Especially important for developing countries, enforceable rules can reduce the abuse of the asymmetrical power wielded by industrialized countries and set a precedent for equal treatment that otherwise would not exist. "The rules may not be perfect, but they are better than no rules at all," according to the International Food Policy Research Institute. "When all that counts is raw power, the small and weak are likely to suffer most."[5]

Another equalizer: the WTO's dispute-settlement process, which was instituted to protect countries from unfair trading practices. India, for example, scored a victory in March 2001. The European Union had claimed that India was dumping cotton bed linens, cutting European producers' sales. The European Union imposed a tariff of 24.7 percent on the imported linens. India, insisting that the linens had not been dumped, took the case to the dispute settlement board, which found that the E.U. tariff was unfair. The Europeans revoked the duties.

Despite some success stories, the ability of developing countries to take advantage of the dispute-settlement mechanism remains quite limited. Using it effectively requires substantial financial resources and significant expertise in international trade law, both of which may be in short supply in low-income countries.

Rules also can be a double-edged sword. Once rules are set, it is difficult to change them. It is crucial, therefore, that WTO rules are appropriate, relevant and fair to

developing countries' needs. Unfortunately, the rules that govern agricultural trade today fall short of these criteria.

Agricultural Trade Rules

Agriculture is vital to improving the lives of poor and hungry people in developing countries because most citizens of those countries derive their incomes from agriculture, either directly or indirectly. Agriculture also serves as many developing countries' major – sometimes only – source of export earnings, making it crucial to their economic development.

Yet the rules governing international trade prevent many developing countries from realizing these prospects.[6] Agriculture has been singled out as a sector for special – and highly protected – treatment, dating back to the original GATT regime (1946-1994) during which it was largely exempt from normal governance. In the 1950s, GATT member countries agreed to exceptions and allowances for agriculture that permitted, most notably, the United States to continue its post-Depression protectionist policies. Price supports, export subsidies and production controls all were allowed.

Although agriculture has been highly protected for many decades, the debate over agricultural trade is a relatively new phenomenon. In the mid-1970s, a variety of factors converged to effect a massive increase in the amount of food produced worldwide. Total cereal production increased by almost a third between 1970 and 1980. Rice production rose 80 billion metric tons during the same period. By 1990, it was up 64 percent from 20 years before. Most of this increase was in developing countries, especially in Asia.[7]

When supply soared, international markets for agricultural products collapsed, sending farmers worldwide into economic crisis. A trade war ensued as countries tried to protect domestic prices by exporting excess supply. Unprecedented levels of export commodities were dumped onto already overloaded markets, driving prices even lower. Those least insulated from the market suffered the most. Some analysts argue that the domestic displacement of production caused by the dumping worsened the mid-1980s famine in the Horn of Africa, which killed more than 1 million men, women and children.

The 1994 Agreement on Agriculture (AoA), negotiated during the Uruguay Round of the GATT (1986-1994), represented the first serious attempt to respond to the dreadful state of international agricultural markets by bringing agriculture under the umbrella of the new WTO. In it, member nations agreed for the first time to accept international governance of agricultural trade. They pledged to lower tariffs on agricultural products and reduce levels of market-distorting domestic and export subsidies.

Creating a Fair System for Global Trade Governance Takes Time

The system of managing international trade today crystallized during the years between World War I and World War II, an interwar period that truly was a 20-year crisis.[1] Instability, tension and conflict characterized both national and international affairs. The international monetary system had fallen to pieces, culminating in the worldwide Great Depression.

In addition, nations began to retreat behind high tariff walls. The United States "led the way to closure" when it passed the notorious Smoot-Hawley Tariff Act in 1930, raising tariffs to their highest level in 100 years. By 1932, the average tariff on dutiable goods stood at just under 60 percent.[2] Britain followed suit the next year, and all major countries eventually adopted protectionist policies.

World trade soon disintegrated. International economic coordination essentially was dead, and a severe brand of economic nationalism replaced it. This spelled economic disaster and ended in another devastating world war.

Policymakers of the day urgently sensed the need for an international system to coordinate trade and monetary policy. U.S. Secretary of State Cordell Hull led the charge for an open, managed trading system. He was convinced that open trade would result in economic prosperity and peace among nations. In a May 1941 radio address, he said, "Unless a system of open trade becomes firmly established, there will be chronic political instability and recurrent economic collapse. There will never be peace in any real sense of the term."

As early as 1934, Hull helped pass the Reciprocal Trade Agreements Act, which authorized the president to negotiate tariff reductions with other nations. This move also signaled the United States' willingness to reengage internationally on economic matters.

Determined to avoid another period of economic turmoil after World War II, economists and policymakers met periodically to establish rules and institutions that would govern the postwar economic order. The important players in this effort were the United States and Great Britain (represented respectively by Harry Dexter White and John Maynard Keynes), the world's largest economic powers.

At a Bretton Woods, N.H., mountain resort in July 1944, representatives of 44 countries signed agreements to establish a fixed exchange rate system based on the U.S. dollar and two international governance institutions: the International Monetary Fund (IMF) and the International Bank for Reconstruction and Development, now known as the World Bank. The IMF would manage the short-term financial aspect of the new economic system by providing emergency funds to countries facing currency and balance-of-payments crises. The World Bank would undertake longer-term development projects, initially focused on Europe.[3]

Although the architects of the postwar economic order envisioned a trade regime to complement these financial institutions, they failed to agree on the details. Negotiations on trade issues began in 1943 but soon stalled, and the United States and Great

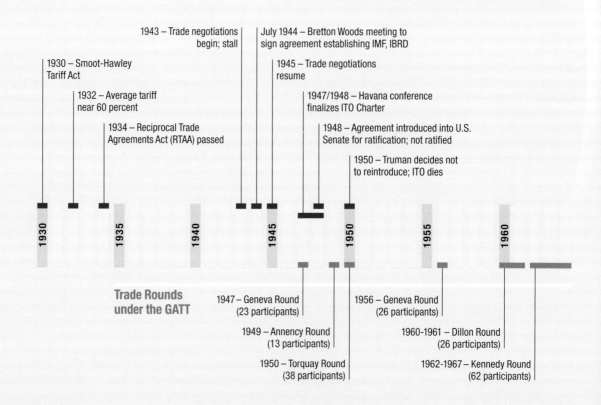

1943 – Trade negotiations begin; stall

July 1944 – Bretton Woods meeting to sign agreement establishing IMF, IBRD

1930 – Smoot-Hawley Tariff Act

1945 – Trade negotiations resume

1932 – Average tariff near 60 percent

1947/1948 – Havana conference finalizes ITO Charter

1934 – Reciprocal Trade Agreements Act (RTAA) passed

1948 – Agreement introduced into U.S. Senate for ratification; not ratified

1950 – Truman decides not to reintroduce; ITO dies

1930 1935 1940 1945 1950 1955 1960

Trade Rounds under the GATT

1947 – Geneva Round (23 participants)

1956 – Geneva Round (26 participants)

1949 – Annency Round (13 participants)

1960-1961 – Dillon Round (26 participants)

1950 – Torquay Round (38 participants)

1962-1967 – Kennedy Round (62 participants)

Britain agreed to put off discussing trade until after the war. In 1947 nations met in Cuba to draft the charter for an International Trade Organization (ITO). The product was "a complex compromise that in some ways embodied the wishes of everyone, but in the end satisfied no one."[4] Consequently, the charter never went into effect. In the United States, Republican "protectionists" felt it opened markets too much while "free-traders" and exporters felt it did not open markets enough. Knowing that the Charter faced almost certain defeat, in 1950 President Harry Truman decided against introducing the Charter to Congress to be ratified. Without American support, "the nascent ITO die[d] a quick and quiet death."[5]

The General Agreement on Tariffs and Trade (GATT) also was drafted in 1947 as a basis for ongoing tariff negotiations in Geneva. It was crafted as a temporary measure to be subsumed into the new ITO; it dealt solely with trade of and tariffs on manufactured goods. But when the ITO failed, by default the GATT – which did not need to be ratified – became the sole institution for managing international trade.

Trade rounds, where countries negotiate the conditions of trade, continued under the GATT for the next 35 years. During the eight rounds held in this period, member countries reduced tariff rates significantly (see timeline, below). By the conclusion of the Kennedy Round (1967), average tariffs on dutiable imports in industrialized countries had fallen to approximately 10 percent. By the end of the Tokyo Round (1979), U.S. average tariffs stood

at 5 percent.[6] Agricultural products, though, were exempt from this process.

By the late 1980s, it became clear that the GATT was not strong enough to deal with the changes taking place in the trading system. As tariffs fell dramatically, nontariff barriers became more common. Also, trade in services expanded greatly. These new areas needed to be addressed, but the GATT's scope was limited to manufactured goods and tariffs. Accordingly, at the last GATT trade round – known as the Uruguay Round – member countries established the World Trade Organization (WTO), expanding its mandate to include these new areas. Officially created on Jan. 1, 1995, the WTO continues to govern international trading interactions.[7]

---

[1] Beth A. Simmons, *Who Adjusts?* (Princeton, NJ: Princeton University Press), 1994, 3.

[2] U.S. Department of Commerce, *Historical Statistics of the United States: Colonial Times to 1970, Part 2.* (Washington, D.C.: U.S. Department of Commerce), 1975, 888.

[3] Today both the IMF and World Bank are referred to as the Bretton Woods institutions for their birthplace.

[4] Joan E. Spero and Jeffrey A. Hart, *The Politics of International Economic Relations.* (New York: St. Martin's Press Inc.), 1997, 52.

[5] Jeffrey A. Frieden and David A. Lake, *International Political Economy: Perspectives on Global Power and Wealth.* (Boston: Bedford/St. Martin's Press Inc.), 2000, 299.

[6] Spero and Hart, 56-7.

[7] The GATT (as GATT 1994) still exists as one of the treaties within the WTO with GATS (General Agreement on Trade in Services), TRIPS (Agreement on Trade-Related Aspects of Intellectual Property Rights) and the Agreement on Agriculture.

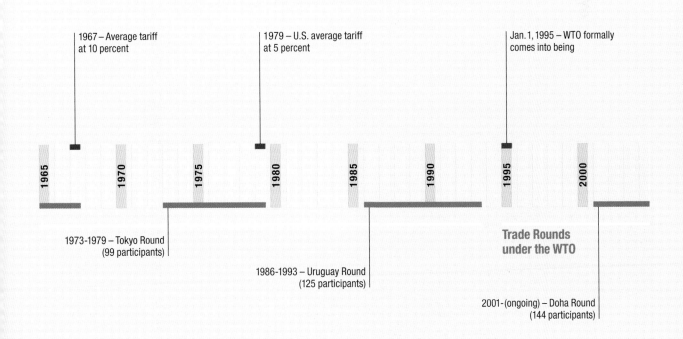

1967 – Average tariff at 10 percent

1979 – U.S. average tariff at 5 percent

Jan. 1, 1995 – WTO formally comes into being

1965 1970 1975 1980 1985 1990 1995 2000

1973-1979 – Tokyo Round (99 participants)

1986-1993 – Uruguay Round (125 participants)

Trade Rounds under the WTO

2001- (ongoing) – Doha Round (144 participants)

The AoA was meant to reduce the distortion of world agricultural markets by disciplining spending on agricultural support (which applied mainly to developed countries) and lowering tariffs on agricultural products (which applies to all countries). Some exceptions were made for developing and least developed countries, including the principle of "special and differential treatment." Under the AoA, nontariff barriers were to be converted into tariffs – a process called tariffication. Countries then agreed to begin reducing protections. Required reduction rates and implementation schedules varied by development level. Industrialized countries were given six years to cut tariffs by 36 percent; developing countries had 10 years to reduce tariffs by 24 percent. Least developed countries could not increase their tariffs, but were exempted from reduction commitments.

Pre-existing export subsidy programs were grandfathered, and reduction commitments were based on 1986-1988 subsidy levels. The agreement also prohibited any new subsidy programs. In terms of domestic support, those nations using Amber Box payments to farmers – those payments tied directly to production and judged to be trade distorting – agreed to reduce them by 20 percent.

Loopholes have allowed the members of the European Union, United States and other developed countries to obey the letter of the law without actually reducing overall trade protection appreciably.[8] For example, some countries purposely overestimated the protection value

The United States and other developed countries have committed to reducing agricultural trade protections, but legal loopholes have allowed these countries to comply without making serious changes.

of their nontariff barriers so that they can seem to reduce protection without actually doing so.

Also, because reduction commitments were not product-specific but applied to an unweighted aggregate, countries could keep tariffs high on certain products by lowering them on less sensitive ones.[9] This loophole allowed countries to maintain very high tariffs (tariff peaks or so-called megatariffs) on certain exports, usually dairy products, rice and sugar. Dealing in average tariff rates also has made it difficult to discipline tariff escalation.

Like tariffs, domestic support also has been measured as a combined total. Therefore, countries have been able to meet reduction commitments while maintaining or even increasing levels of support for certain commodities. The 2002 U.S. farm bill, for example, raised payment levels for some commodities, such as corn and cotton, and added new payments for products like lentils and honey.[10]

Moreover, because the baseline chosen as the reference point for cuts in export subsidy payments (1986-1988) was a period of relatively high support levels, countries have been able to avoid substantial subsidy reform. That the Producer Support Estimate, the measure used to quantify agricultural protection, has stayed practically unchanged since the 1986 Uruguay Round began illustrates this point.[11]

The AoA's failure to effectively discipline trade-distorting practices that adversely affect developing countries are indicative of a more fundamental weakness in the trading system: The industrialized countries dominate the WTO and manipulate trade rules in their favor.

The WTO was set up as a democratic system (one country, one vote) with enforceable rules and allowances for developing countries. But in practice, powerful countries make the rules.

One Size Does Not Fit All

Trade liberalization entails costs and difficulties for any country. But the costs may be higher and certainly less affordable for developing countries. Because of trade's potential to create wealth and higher living standards for poor countries, free-trade proponents contend that it is key to economic growth. But evidence also supports a cautious approach to trade liberalization for developing countries.

While no country has successfully developed in economic isolation, modern industrialized nations remained fairly well protected until achieving a significant level of economic development. Between 1821 and 1947, for example, U.S. tariff rates on dutiable imports averaged 39 percent; it is only in the past 55 years that tariff rates have fallen significantly.

Many developing country farmers are poor and experience periodic hunger despite hard work because they do not grow everything they need and often receive low prices for what they produce.

The U.N. Conference on Trade and Development (UNCTAD) found that the economies of least developed countries that pursued open trade policies in the 1990s fared no better than economies that remained tightly closed. "Poverty has increased unambiguously in those economies that have adopted the most open trade regime and in those that have continued with the most closed trade regime," according to UNCTAD.[12]

The East Asian tigers – Hong Kong, Singapore, South Korea and Taiwan – often are cited as exemplars and proof of the developmental benefits of trade liberalization. While it is true that these countries sought participation in the global economy and grew quickly, they did so largely without opening domestic markets to imports. In doing so, each achieved unprecedented economic success, lifting millions of people out of poverty. Between 1959 and 1999, per capita income in Singapore grew from $400 to an astonishing $24,000. The other tigers attained similar growth rates. Although these countries pursued growth by building their export industries, each tailored its export orientation to fit its cultural, political and economic realities, which often required relatively high levels of domestic market protection. In this way, the countries were able to subject their growing industries to the rigors of international competition while guarding against import surges.

It would be misleading to attribute the tigers' success exclusively to their trade policy. Many factors too complex to analyze here went into their economic accomplish-ments.[13] Their experiences do show, though, that international trade has enormous potential to drive economic growth and poverty reduction. However, developing country governments need to be able to use trade policy in ways best suited to their circumstances. Reaping the benefits of the global economy does not necessarily require deep and immediate import liberalization.

Liberalizing Deliberately

Trade's impact on poverty seems to be in part a question of how fast liberalization occurs. Mali, Nepal, Peru and Zambia have fully opened their markets, but show disappointing economic growth and poverty reduction rates. On the other hand, China, Indonesia and Vietnam – which opened their markets gradually – have succeeded in reducing poverty. In order for deep liberalization to be successful in reducing poverty, countries must be adequately prepared politically, economically and institutionally.

In the case of agriculture, researcher Eugenio Diaz-Bonilla of the International Food Policy Research Institute says that sudden tariff reductions can subject poor farmers to "drastic shocks that may undermine their survival strategies irreparably, forcing poor families to sell productive assets, increasing the possibility of illness, and so on."[14] Sudden import surges can endanger those people who lack the resources to buffer the price fluctuations of significant adjustment or transition periods.

In 1995 Haiti cut its tariff on rice, from 50 percent to 3 percent, allowing a flood of subsidized rice from the United States. By 2000, Haiti's domestic rice production had fallen by half, and many small rice growers had lost their livelihood. Without the resources to switch to other crops or other occupations, these farmers now find it nearly impossible to escape poverty.[15]

Lowering tariffs also raises budget concerns. For many developing country governments, money collected from trade taxes comprises a significant revenue source. An abrupt end to this income without a simultaneous increase in domestic taxation, which can be difficult to accomplish politically, can wreak havoc on an already strained national budget. A sudden decrease in revenue resulting from tariff elimination can harm governments' ability to buffer farmers from import shocks as well. A region like sub-Saharan Africa, which depends on tariff revenues more than any other region, would need to consider such outcomes before lowering its tariffs.

WTO member countries fall into four groups: developed, developing, least developed and net food-importing developing. These categories are intended to group countries with similar characteristics and needs for purposes of granting concessions to those who need extra help, so-called special and differential treatment. Of WTO's 144 member nations, 30 are least developed countries.[16] In addition, 32 nations are observer governments, meaning that they are not full members but are in the process of joining the organization; of these, 12 are least developed countries.

As part of special and differential treatment, developing countries are given extra time to implement certain agreements, and least developed countries are exempted from some rules.

How Rich Countries Get Their Way

The WTO nominally operates under the principle of one country, one vote. But rarely do countries formally vote. Decisions are made by consensus. Generally, negotiation continues until agreement is reached or until negotiators realize that agreement is not possible. At the November 2001 meeting of trade ministers in Doha, Qatar, for example, negotiations continued until all member nations agreed to launch a new round of trade negotiations (and on what that round would include), even though consensus was not reached until 18 hours past the original deadline. In Seattle, where ministers attempted but failed to begin a new trade round in 1999, the opposite happened. When it became clear that no amount of negotiation would bring agreement, talks were abandoned.

Because of the system's purportedly egalitarian nature, on paper every country has an equal voice in

Unfair global agricultural trade hurts poor people in developing countries, especially women and children who are most vulnerable to poverty, hunger and disease.

negotiating agreements. Theoretically, developing countries are able to take their concerns to the table in Geneva, where the WTO is headquartered. Indeed, their numerical strength ought to presage a good deal of success for them in a system based on the principle of one country, one vote. But the reality is more complex than the theory.

The WTO process is based on reciprocity. Concessions are made on a *quid pro quo* basis, meaning that concessions are traded, and this trading does not take place between equals. Relationships in the WTO reflect the world economy as a whole. Those countries with larger markets and more economic power wield more influence during negotiations. The largest trading blocs, most significantly the United States and the European Union, are able to exert pressure on weaker countries with small economies, like Bangladesh and Ghana, which depend on their larger brethren for markets and investment.

Most developing country agricultural exports go to the United States/Canada, the European Union, Japan/Korea or Australia/New Zealand. These countries as a group import almost 90 percent of Mexico's agricultural products and 80 percent of Thailand's.[17] Nearly half of Africa's total exports goes to Western Europe and another fifth goes to the United States.[18]

In other words, despite *de jure* voting equality, *de facto* the United States and the European Union have more weight. As a result, the trade rules – especially as they relate to agriculture – often profit industrialized countries at developing countries' expense.

One Kenyan Voice: Trade Talks Challenge African Negotiators

By Nicholas Sabwa

As the Agreement on Agriculture (AoA) negotiator for Kenya, my experiences participating in World Trade Organization (WTO) negotiation meetings are typical of many African trade negotiators. Sometimes we feel unprepared due to difficulties encountered in collecting information and generating clear country positions on various trade issues. Because we lack the interpersonal and political skills needed for the negotiating process, our efforts can be greatly constrained, leading more often than not to reactionary and ineffective responses.

If we are to participate well in these trade talks and achieve the goals of increasing market access and improving global trading rules, then African countries urgently need to assess their training and equip negotiators with the skills they need.

Most negotiators are government officers. Often, the private sector is left out of the process even though the negotiations greatly affect them. Governments should engage the private sector and agriculture commodity experts in these discussions to help facilitate and, where appropriate, lead negotiations.

Institutions also should be created to encourage collaboration. For example, in Kenya both government officials and private sector representatives work together as part of the country's National Committee, where they explore the full economic implications of WTO agreements. This committee examines how agreements could impact various national industries and sectors, while also reviewing Kenya's trade policy agenda and commitments in accordance with the global trading rules.

The committee is comprised of a number of subcommittees ("focal points") that deal with the different WTO agreements. In addition to developing experience and expertise, participants help implement related WTO agreement provisions and coordinate future negotiations. I relied on these committees tremendously in my work as the AoA negotiator.

Unfortunately, participating in negotiations also can be quite expensive. Most African countries have not been able to send negotiators to Geneva regularly, if at all. Even when negotiators are sent, sometimes countries can afford to send only one negotiator who cannot attend concurrent negotiating sessions. Many times, I missed key Geneva meetings due to lack of funds for travel. Fortunately, Kenya has a Geneva-based trade officer who follows up on the meetings in case no one attends from the capital. African countries that do not have diplomatic missions in Geneva are not as lucky.

High staff turnover and transfer rates – often because countries cannot afford to pay their negotiators competitive wages – also have eroded African negotiating teams' experience and consistency. African countries should review their terms of service for public employees – all negotiators are public service employees – in an effort to retain experienced trade negotiators.

Speaking with One Voice

African countries also need to fuse their interests so they can speak as one voice during negotiations. Countries could identify their arguments on key trade concerns in position papers that are shared at regional consultations prior to the negotiation meetings. These meetings then could synthesize everyone's thoughts into African positions.

In the ongoing Doha, Qatar, negotiations, Africa has decided to consolidate its negotiating proposals into one African position, making it even more crucial for African countries to participate in various procedural meetings. While this is a step in the right direction, effective participation in today's multilateral trading system will require African countries to invest and commit themselves to the process and allocate the resources needed in these negotiations.

Moreover, developed countries should assist and support African countries in such efforts, so that developing countries are better able to approach negotiations primed and focused.

Nicholas Sabwa is a Kenyan economist and trade policy analyst who also represented Kenya in the WTO Agreement on Agriculture negotiations.

Nicholas Sabwa represents Kenya's trade interests at a meeting of the Economic Commission for Africa in Addis Ababa, Ethiopia, in preparation for a meeting of The African Ministers for Trade and Regional Cooperation.

External pressure to liberalize, both from the private sector and the international financial community, also limit the ability of developing countries to maneuver within the trading system. When assessing the potential risk of investing in certain countries, investors look for policies they believe mitigate the risk involved. Trade policy is one such factor. Conventional wisdom says that a developing country that has liberalized its trade tends to attract more investment.

Similarly, conditions attached to International Monetary Fund (IMF), World Bank and regional development bank assistance often include tariff reductions. This practice was especially common as part of the structural adjustment programs used in the 1980s and 1990s. Countries that agree with the IMF or World Bank to liberalize are left with little to bring to the WTO bargaining table.

Practical factors, such as the cost of housing in Geneva and a plethora of conflicting meetings, also disadvantage smaller, poorer countries (see related story, p. 65).

Half the poor countries in the WTO have no representation in Geneva. And of those countries with representation, many lack the staff and resources needed to attend all meetings relevant to their trade interests; several important meetings may be scheduled at conflicting times. That single representative also likely covers interactions with other international bodies headquartered in Geneva, such as the International Labor Organization and UNCTAD. Furthermore, one night in Geneva can cost hundreds of dollars, a stiff price for Ethiopia, whose average per capita income in 1999 was $100.

Although effective participation in trade negotiations requires a great deal of specialized knowledge on a vast range of complex, highly technical issues, many developing countries are recent WTO members and have little experience with reciprocal negotiations. (The Uruguay Round, which ran from 1986 to 1993, often is cited as the first time many developing countries actively took part in negotiations.) These countries also may lack technical support and direction from home.

"The need for each country to do its own homework in following issues, to attend all meetings, and to have teams in capitals doing extensive background research and providing adequate instructions on all matters cannot be dismissed," according to a World Bank Group handbook on negotiating effectively.[19] A resource-poor country like Angola simply cannot match the financial resources, experience and muscle of a U.S. negotiating team.

Even in the face of these obstacles, the sheer number of developing countries in the WTO should give those countries some leverage. But to date, they have been unable to merge their varied interests into one voice strong enough to bargain for concessions from industrialized countries. This failure stems in part from developing countries' vast cultural, political and economic differences. Varying economic structures, natural resource endowments, labor markets, production profiles and political systems mean that Ecuador's primary goals likely are not at the top of Vietnam's. Indeed, it is not uncommon for one developing country to initiate a complaint against another in the WTO. Roughly half of the 27 suits brought to the dispute settlement board in 2001 were filed by a developing country against a developing country, covering everything from cigarette taxes to fresh fruit import procedures. The fact that deals often reach across issue and product areas – lower tariffs on dairy products might be conceded in exchange for an agreement on intellectual property – further complicates matters. Developing countries also compete with each other for rich country markets and investment, which further divides their positions.

Accordingly, it becomes difficult, if not impossible, to marshal a single negotiating position that fits all developing countries' needs. Nations with common interests on certain issues sometimes come together to form a negotiating bloc. For example, the Cairns Group includes a mix of mostly nonsubsidizing, agricultural-exporting developed and mostly developing countries that work together on agriculture issues. But such coalitions are few and limited in scope.

Some industrialized countries maintain very high tariffs on certain commodities, like sugar, that are key commodities for poorer countries and their small farmers.

Because developing countries – with a few exceptions like Brazil, China and India – have little leverage in trade negotiations, they often cannot protect their own trade interests, much less win developed country policy changes, such as a reduction in agriculture subsidies or an end to tariff escalation. Instead, they often sign and must implement agreements that they had no hand in writing, regardless of whether certain provisions fit their development strategies.

The so-called harmonization agreements – WTO agreements related to harmonizing domestic standards and regulation, such as intellectual property rights, customs valuation, and sanitary and phytosanitary (food safety and animal and plant health standards) measures – are good examples. Implementing these agreements have cost a typical developing country approximately $150 million, roughly a year's development budget.

While these standards might be good, or at least not anti-development, they may require many institutional reforms that would not be priorities for developing countries. They may result in funds being diverted from more pressing development needs, such as lowering child mortality rates.[20]

"It has become evident that increased participation [in the WTO] does not imply more effectiveness or, in the end, result in greater access to global markets,"[21] states the World Bank. Developing countries must be able to participate more effectively if they hope to use their WTO membership to construct a partnership for development through trade and more fully integrate into the global economy on their own terms.[22]

Current Negotiations

A new round of trade negotiations is under way. Because it was launched in Doha, Qatar, it is called the Doha Round. It is scheduled to end by January 2005, although delays are likely. So far, agriculture has figured prominently. Indeed, developing countries agreed to this round of negotiations only after industrialized countries promised, among other things, significant progress on agriculture.

For the most part, developing country governments realize that they cannot afford to isolate themselves from the globalizing trends in the world economy.[23] They understand the opportunities available in international markets. They also recognize the advantage of incorporating greater agricultural policy reform into WTO agreements. More developing countries than ever are involved in the Doha trade negotiations.

Developing countries have several general objectives in Doha. Increased access to developed country markets for their agricultural products and relief from dumping of developed country agriculture top the list. Developing

Poorer countries compete with each other for rich country markets, which can interfere with their willingness to bargain as one voice on common interests.

countries also want industrialized countries to reduce tariff peaks, end tariff escalation and bring tariffs on agricultural products more in line with those of industrial products.

When former U.S. Treasury Secretary Paul O'Neill and Bono, lead singer of the rock band U2, toured sub-Saharan Africa in May 2002, they were told that while development aid is important, market access is more important. In fact, most government officials agree that over the long run, aid is of little value without market access. "The biggest request we are making of Western countries is to open their markets," Uganda President Yoweri Museveni said.[24]

Many officials also requested an end to the use of production-linked subsidies in industrialized countries and rules to stop agricultural dumping. At the 2002 World Food Summit: Five Years Later, Sierra Leone President Ahmad Kabbah expressed the sentiments of most developing countries, "We will renew our appeal to developed countries to continue to improve on the removal of their agricultural export subsidies."[25]

Protecting Food Security

Food security concerns also play a role in agriculture negotiations. According to Botswana President Fustus Mogae, "Fair trade does have a direct influence on our ability to address the food security problem at the national level."[26]

Should Cries for a Development Box Be Heeded?

Calls for a Development Box – a series of exemptions from World Trade Organization (WTO) rules – have emerged as a significant theme in the ongoing Doha, Qatar, agricultural trade negotiations. Specifically, these exemptions would allow developing country governments to protect their poorest farmers in an effort to increase food security. Although helping developing countries attain food security should be central to Doha discussions, critics of the Development Box caution against its wholesale acceptance and question whether it would advance food security.

One difficulty in assessing a Development Box's merits is that it is not a single proposal. Rather, several different countries and groups of countries have put forth their versions of a Development Box. Even developing countries disagree on what such a box should entail. Some countries see it as a subset of special and differential treatment; others see it as a separate entity. Some countries would like to exempt certain staple food products from WTO rules; others want only certain products subject to the rules. Countries also disagree on which products should be included and which countries should qualify for the exempt status.

Another concern is the negotiation process itself. What concessions and commitments would developing countries have to make in order to get a Development Box? Should developing countries use what little bargaining power they have to earn the right to increase domestic protection if it likely means abandoning efforts to eliminate or significantly reduce industrialized country agriculture protections? Moreover, could granting a Development Box boost developed countries' legitimacy with positive press to a point where they no longer are obliged to address other development issues as part of the negotiations? Such issues must be considered.

As the rules stand, developing countries have a good deal of room to implement support programs for resource-poor farmers. They often are prevented from doing so by the terms of an International Monetary Fund loan program, bilateral pressure or simply lack of financial resources. Developing countries must avoid pushing for permission to enact policies that they cannot afford or cannot implement because of other factors.

The impact of Development Box policies also is unknown. Some research suggests that protecting certain crops could negatively affect some poor and hungry people. Tariffs tend to help the largest producers, in effect taxing poor consumers and small farmers who also purchase food. Such a situation could hurt overall food security. Some developing countries also contend that a Development Box that allows tariff barriers could stifle, instead of encourage trade between developing countries.

Perhaps the most compelling reason not to endorse a Development Box is its potential to undermine efforts to reform the overall trade structure. Concerns that the WTO needs to focus on poverty reduction and that trade rules need to protect vulnerable populations – as argued in *Hunger 2003* – should be applied to the entire institution, not just a set of exemptions. A Development Box would not be needed if the WTO were fulfilling its charter goal of improving living standards and agricultural trade rules were oriented toward development.

As a rule and not an exemption, the WTO should incorporate measures that represent and advance developing countries' interests. To separate development concerns from overall trade issues presents richer governments an excuse for dealing with poverty reduction only in the context of Development Box discussions.

To better safeguard poor people's food security, some leaders are calling for special exemptions of poorer countries, a so-called Development Box. But some critics question whether the exemptions would improve food security.

Jim Stipe

Because agricultural prices have been steered by public policy for so long, no one knows what the real market price of many commodities would be. Poor food-deficient countries probably would experience higher food prices, exacerbating poverty and hunger over the short-term and among certain populations, including poor urban and rural consumers. Similar concerns about market instability and higher food prices were expressed during talks in 1994 that preceded the AoA. As a result, member countries pledged in the Marrakesh Agreement to provide a safety net to protect least developed and net food-importing countries as they transitioned to a more liberal agricultural system.[27]

That pledge, however, was not accompanied by any resource commitments, and because it is difficult to prove that the AoA has caused increases in food insecurity, Marrakesh has not been implemented. Developing countries would like to see this agreement given some teeth in the form of operational measures and binding commitments. Such a step is key to agriculture liberalization's success, certainly to its success as a tool in reducing world hunger.

Developing countries also are seeking greater flexibility in pursuing national development strategies and protecting food security. Several developing nations and groups of developing nations – such as the Like-Minded Group, a 13-member, cross-regional developing country coalition – have made this point in the Doha negotiations. India has proposed a Food Security Box, while other countries have rallied around calls for a Development Box. While the details of neither have been fleshed out, in essence developing countries are calling for greater room within the WTO structure to adopt protectionist measures to guard food security or pursue wider development strategies.

Some analysts argue that it would be more effective for developing countries to fully explore how to use the leeway they have under the AoA rather than negotiate for further concessions, especially if winning a Development Box requires further concessions on their part to reduce tariffs or agree to more harmonization standards (see related story, p. 68).

The hypocrisy of the United States and other developed countries in protecting their agriculture while advocating liberalization for everyone else is now apparent to many people in developing countries. If industrialized countries want a well-functioning, robust global trading system, they also must reform their agricultural policies. If developing countries were not hampered by industrialized countries' subsidies and protections, they could move more rapidly to raise their living standards. The whole world would gain economically and in terms of social stability and peace.

Table 3.1: Agriculture Is Important to Developing Countries and Rural People

	Rural population as a share of total population		Agricultural labor as a share of total labor force		Share of agriculture in total gross domestic product	
	1990	2000	1990	2000	1990	2000
Developing Countries	**65%**	**60%**	**61%**	**55%**	**15%**	**14%**
Latin America and the Caribbean	29%	25%	25%	20%	8%	7%
Near East and North Africa	46%	40%	39%	33%	14%	12%
Sub-Saharan Africa	74%	67%	72%	66%	26%	31%
East and Southeast Asia	70%	65%	68%	62%	18%	18%
South Asia	75%	71%	63%	59%	28%	26%

Source: U.N. Food and Agriculture Organization

Long, Difficult Road to Reforming Europe's Common Agricultural Policy

By Matthew Griffith

The Common Agricultural Policy (CAP) has its roots at the heart of European economic and political integration. Conceived in the 1950s, it came into force in 1962 under the Treaty of Rome, the European Economic Community's founding charter.[1] Europe was a different place then, still traumatized by memories of war and hunger, and the CAP was intended to guarantee self-sufficiency in food, improved and stable living standards for farmers, and higher productivity.

These aims were pursued through a mix of mechanisms applied to what then were the principal commodities of European farmers, notably dairy products, beef and veal, and crops. As the Community expanded, new regimes were added to cover a wider range of produce, such as sheep and goats, olive oil, and fruits and vegetables.

The CAP's first decade was a great success. Agricultural production grew; Europe reached self-sufficiency and consumers could afford to buy food. But from the mid-1970s, the European Community began to produce surpluses. It propped up prices by buying and storing excess produce, giving rise to the infamous "wine lakes" and "butter mountains."

The Common Agricultural Policy (CAP) has helped Europe increase its agricultural production to a point where it can feed its people and now is one of the world's largest food exporters. But these protections are costing poorer countries their food security.

Agricultural Dumping

Since 1970, the European Union has shifted from being a net importer to one of the world's largest net exporters of beef, dairy, sugar and wheat products. The transformation has been so dramatic that the European Union now is the world's second largest exporter of agricultural products. One study estimated that because of CAP, E.U. exports of meat products are nearly 50 times higher than without support; grains, other crops and milk products are estimated at nearly a 100 times higher.[2]

This switch from importer to exporter has greatly altered world agricultural markets. Huge E.U. surpluses have created massive distortions in international agricultural trade, with profound effects on the production and trade of many countries' agricultural products. These surpluses also have led to widespread dumping on developing country markets, with serious negative effects on the agricultural sectors within developing countries, especially poor small farmers.

Research for the Catholic Agency for Oversees Development shows that in recent years, artificially cheap E.U. milk powder and sugar, which benefit from export subsidies, have caused havoc among developing world farmers. In Jamaica, annual milk production has dropped by a third since 1995 because the local market has been flooded with subsidized E.U. milk powder. Jamaican dairy processors have turned their backs to the local dairy industry, preferring instead to use cheaper milk powder from Europe. As a result, Jamaican farmers are forced to throw away thousands of litres of milk from overflowing coolers. Many have lost their jobs and their livelihoods.

According to one estimate, CAP has resulted in developing countries – excluding Latin America – decreasing milk production by nearly 50 percent and foregoing exports of: milk products by more than 90 percent; livestock by nearly 70 percent; meat by nearly 60 percent; and grains by more than 40 percent.[3]

Closed European Market

High E.U. tariff barriers also mean that many developing countries are unable to export to the European Union, costing them a valuable source of potential income. Developing countries find E.U. tariffs horrendously complex, varying from month to month for each product. The European Union also uses tariff peaks – high tariffs on particular products – and tariff escalation – tariffs that rise with the processing level.

These barriers are effective. One study by the United Kingdom found that while poultry exports from least developed countries to the rest of the world rose 87 percent between 1996 and 2001, exports to the European Union failed to increase.[4] (It should be noted that the European Union imports more agricultural products from developing countries than the United States.)

For the many developing countries that rely on agricultural exports as a key source of earnings, such changes have been devastating.

Hopes for Reform… Dashed

Although the CAP is one of the largest agricultural support systems in the world with a budget of $38.2 billion in 2001,[5] it is widely perceived to be in crisis because it is failing consumers, the environment, developing countries and the vast majority of farmers. Some 70 percent of CAP subsidies go to the largest 20 percent of farmers.

In mid-2002, Europe embarked on a process known as the CAP mid-term review, led by European Agriculture Commissioner

Franz Fischler. The mid-term review set out what was a fairly radical reform agenda for the European Union. This agenda included proposals to redirect more money into rural development, better safeguard the environment, favor small farmers and decouple payments from production. The decoupling proposals would be a significant step in breaking the link between subsidies and production and, thus, decrease the likelihood of dumping as well as provide the European Union with significant negotiating leeway at the World Trade Organization.

For developing countries, the reform proposals were seen as a small step in the right direction, inching the CAP away from its current export-oriented focus. Although nothing was

> **Although the CAP is one of the largest agricultural support systems in the world with a budget of $38.2 billion in 2001, it is widely perceived to be in crisis because it is failing consumers, the environment, developing countries and the vast majority of farmers.**

done to reduce the total CAP budget or address some of the most highly protected sectors, such as dairy and sugar, the shift to decoupled payments and greater emphasis on meeting environmental and rural development concerns was welcome.

These reform proposals, however, have been met with fierce opposition from some member governments, notably France. Seven European agriculture ministers wrote to the continent's most influential newspapers, claiming that the CAP does not cause hunger in developing countries and is "something we can be proud of." At the time of writing this report, a compromise appears to have been struck, including a rejection of the decoupling proposals. Moreover, these meagre reforms would be postponed until 2006.

Once again, politics seem to be sinking hopes for a new CAP.

Matthew Griffith is a policy analyst for the British aid agency, CAFOD, and co-authored the report, "Dumping on the Poor," with Duncan Green.

[1] The European Economic Community preceded the European Union.

[2] Brent Borrell and Lionel Hubbard, "Global Economic Effects of the E.U. Common Agricultural Policy." *Economic Affairs Journal*, June 2000.

[3] Ibid.

[4] "The Impacts of the CAP on Developing Countries," Department for International Development Workshop. (London) July 5, 2002.

[5] 43 billion euros.

Hopeful Signs

Developing countries are in a slightly better position to negotiate for change than ever before. More of them have joined the WTO and are participating in negotiations. Further liberalization of the global economy depends heavily on the participation of developing countries, and industrialized countries know it. Without a successful new agreement on agriculture, the entire round could fail, undermining WTO's legitimacy and reversing the momentum toward freer global trade. As such, it is in the interests of industrialized regions like the United States and European Union to make some agricultural concessions.

By threatening nonparticipation in Doha, developing countries already have been able to extract promises that agriculture and intellectual property rules, especially regarding drug patents, will be addressed.

As a group speaking with one voice, developing countries should seek an end to agriculture dumping, special concessions to countries with special needs and reforms that will give them a stronger voice in the WTO. These would be important victories for developing countries and, most important, poor and hungry people.

Citizens and concerned groups in industrialized countries also have a role to play. They can urge their governments to reform agricultural trade rules in ways that would be good for their people and for developing countries and rural populations. The current U.S. administration is ideologically committed to free trade and seems serious about the Doha round, so progress on this issue of importance to hungry people may be possible over the next couple of years.

As part of the current trade negotiations, developing countries are seeking greater access to E.U. and U.S. markets for their agricultural products.

CHAPTER 4

African Agriculture
A Crucial Lifeline

By Daniel D. Karanja and
Melody R. Mc Neil

Africa, specifically sub-Saharan Africa, continues to face many political, social and economic challenges, chief among them its inability to feed a rapidly increasing population. Agriculture accounts for between one-fifth and one-half of African countries' gross domestic product (GDP), employing two-thirds of the labor force and providing the main livelihood for nearly three-quarters of rural populations.

Although agriculture is the lifeline of most African economies, various domestic and international constraints prevent it from providing the food and income that African families need to survive.[1] Because most poor people in sub-Saharan Africa live in rural communities, agriculture and agricultural trade have great potential to rebuild African economies and help alleviate poverty. But industrialized countries' current trade practices are chipping away at this promise.

Today, one in three Africans are malnourished, and about half of its nearly 700 million people live on less that $1 a day; most (80 percent) live on less than $2 a day.[2] This state of affairs has not always been the case. In the not-too-distant past, Africa was in a better position to feed itself, and it contributed 4 percent of global trade. But in the past three decades, Africa's share of global trade has more than halved, and this downward trend likely will continue – together with rising hunger and poverty rates – unless the terms of agricultural trade improve.

Research by the International Food Policy Research Institute (IFPRI) finds that liberalizing industrialized country agriculture would increase sub-Saharan Africa's net agriculture trade by 45 percent, from $7.4 billion to $10.7 billion. Moreover, African farmers and food processors would see their incomes rise by $2 billion per year, a stimulus that could reap additional financial benefits for most poor African farmers and the entire economy.

By eliminating industrialized countries' trade-distorting agricultural protections, Africa would be able to stop, and likely begin to reverse, its declining share of world trade. Moreover, because Africa's trade level remains so low, even doubling or tripling its share would not largely hurt industrialized countries' footing in the global market.

While increasing global agricultural trade is important to Africa's future, agriculture itself also must be supported and developed. African poor small farmers need:

- better access to resources, such as land, credit, extension and market information;

- better roads, communication networks and other infrastructure;

African farmers can buy seeds from this farmer cooperative store in Nampula, Mozambique, that is supported by The Cooperative League of the U.S.A.

- superior agricultural production and processing technologies; and

- more stable economic and political environments.

Turning Economic Tides

Africa's economic environment has changed dramatically in the past four decades. Emerging from colonial rule, many African countries posted impressive economic and social development for a time, and were net food exporters during the 1970s. However, high population growth and stagnating agricultural productivity led to per capita food production declines. This trend was exacerbated by severe weather, falling world commodity prices for African export products, and increasing trade and nontrade barriers by developed countries.

Income growth in Africa barely has kept pace with population growth, remaining below 2.5 percent and causing Africa's share of the world's absolute poor to increase from one-fourth to nearly a third. Consequently, per capita incomes are lower and less evenly distributed now than during the 1970s. A recent U.N. Conference on Trade and Development (UNCTAD) study found that the proportion of Africans living on less that $1 a day increased steadily, from half in 1965-1969 to nearly two-thirds in 1995-1999.[3]

Meanwhile, rural populations in Africa earn half as much income as urban populations, leading to increased rural-urban migration and higher urban unemployment rates. This growing urban instability threatens countries' political and economic stability.[4] Many countries also have been weakened by inept government control of the economy, and civil strife.

As compared to other developing regions, African countries lag in primary school enrollments, improving child mortality rates and cutting incidences of endemic diseases, such as HIV/AIDS, malaria and tuberculosis. Heavy international debt only compounds the situation. In the past 25 years, grants and loans from donors amounted to more than $350 billion, increasing African debt from $60 billion to $230 billion and debt servicing from $6 billion to $11 billion.[5] While some African countries benefit from debt relief efforts, such as the World Bank's Highly Indebted Poor Countries (HIPC) program, critics maintain that current trade policies are undermining their effectiveness. "A case can be made that trade policies that seek to protect domestic producers of commodities in the developed world end up hurting countries that are receiving debt relief," says Vikram Nehru, manager of the World Bank's HIPC arm, because the debt relief is tied to a country's export levels.[6]

Unfulfilled Expectations

When most African countries gained political independence four decades ago, people anticipated rapid economic development. The immediate concern was to fight ignorance, disease and poverty that ravaged large segments of the populations. Although Africa's fight for independence also was a struggle to regain control of land and agriculture, many countries focused on industrialization to promote economic growth and fight poverty, thereby redirecting labor, raw materials and tax revenues from agriculture to industrial growth.

Many African communities lack safe drinking water. Fortunately, this community in Nampula, Mozambique, has access to a manual water pump.

However, most African economies were not prepared for industrial development. Poor infrastructure and communication networks, unskilled labor and poor marketing institutions hindered Africa's ability to compete well in an increasingly global economy. Also, many government initiatives – including governments' firm control of most service sectors – stymied private sector growth, and local and foreign investment, thwarting further development.

A few countries – such as Côte d'Ivoire, Kenya and Uganda (before Idi Amin came to power) – used their comparative advantage and invested in small agriculture, research and extension, reaping significant gains in the 1960s and early 1970s when agricultural commodity prices reached historical highs. However, the oil crises of the 1970s and a collapse of world market prices dealt a heavy blow to all developing economies, including those in Africa.

By the early 1980s, most African economies were in crisis. Frequent droughts, civil conflicts and diminishing terms of agricultural trade – largely due to industrialized countries' continued use of agricultural market protections – further undermined economic progress. The International Monetary Fund (IMF) and World Bank proposed economic austerity measures, under structural adjustment programs, whose effectiveness, so far, has been unclear. These programs sought to ease state control and open trade.

In addition to implementing the structural adjustment programs, most African countries reduced public spending on education, health care, agricultural extension and other social services. They expected the private sector to step in and provide some of these public services, but the private sector was unable to do so. Without adequate funding for social services, poverty and inequality worsened.[7]

Consequently, a new initiative, which combines debt relief and poverty reduction in a country-led process known as the Poverty Reduction Strategy process (PRSP), was proposed.[8] The PRSP encourages each country to develop its own civic-participation strategy and focus its development agenda toward poverty alleviation. Critics argue that this strategy, which is supported by the IMF and World Bank, still requires countries to implement adjustment policies. Other observers note that most of the newly articulated strategies underemphasize agriculture.

Agriculture's Many Obstacles

Agriculture and expanded trade have great potential to free rural areas and poor people from hunger and poverty. But many hurdles block the way.

Drip Irrigation in Cape Verde Makes a Big Difference, Drop by Drop

By Ray Almeida

Seldom do chronic cycles of drought loosen their grip on the Cape Verde Islands and allow farmers to produce more than a fraction of the food the country requires. In the worst times, this West African island nation must import up to 90 percent of its basic commodities. However, when the rains come in sufficient volume and at just the right intervals, Cape Verde's fertile volcanic soils produce an abundance of fruits and vegetables to feed its people and strengthen rural household incomes.

Given the island's normally limited rainfall and poor water management, Cape Verdean farmers usually are restricted to growing a few crops, such as sugar cane, cassava, and to a limited degree, tomatoes, onions and cabbages. Fortunately, with drip irrigation farmers can grow diversified horticultural crops and increase their yields, both per unit of land and per unit of water, providing rural families greater food security and allowing some farmers to expand into cash crops as well.

The Agricultural Cooperative Development International and Volunteers in Overseas Cooperative Assistance (ACDI/VOCA) has been working with small farmers in Cape Verde since 1992 to boost agricultural productivity and rural household incomes. As part of its efforts, ACDI/VOCA sells donated U.S.-grown corn, wheat and peas under a U.S. Agency for International Development Title II (Public Law 480) program to pay for its activities. Many of these proceeds help support drip irrigation projects.

Although startup costs for drip irrigation systems are more expensive than traditional methods, farmers can apply for small loans through ACDI/VOCA to finance these costs. Because drip irrigation quickly increases farmers' overall profitability, they are able to repay their loans within a few years. Many farmers who began participating in the initial program already are using their profits to expand their systems.

Since 1995, vegetable production in the country has increased more than twofold. This gradual increase in annual horticultural production also is stabilizing prices in local produce markets, ensuring farmers more reliable incomes. The increase in fruits and vegetables has enhanced the diets of Cape Verdean farmers, families and children, which only a few years ago lacked nutritional diversity.

Cape Verde may never be able to produce all its food needs. However, drip irrigation technology holds much promise for Cape Verde. In addition to improving the quality of people's diets and expanding crop diversity for farmers, the technology has led to a small, although statistically significant, reduction in the nation's reliance on commodity imports.

Looking forward, ACDI/ VOCA will continue to work with farmers and producers not only to increase horticultural production, but also develop their post-harvest handling and marketing skills. Today hundreds of small farmers are organized into producer cooperatives and marketing associations in Cape Verde, and the program is expanding because farmers see that they can make this technology work for themselves to boost production and incomes.

By working at the grassroots level through interrelated programs that reinforce and maximize all participants' contributions, ACDI/VOCA is helping to raise agricultural output, preserve natural resources, provide nutritional education and promote small business owners' access to microfinance services, while also promoting democratic governance. Most importantly, ACDI/VOCA is helping Cape Verdeans work together to find their solutions to improving the country's food security.

Ray Almeida is a policy analyst at Bread for the World.

Land: An Eroding Resource

Africa is a diverse continent that contains nearly a fourth of the world's total land area. Despite its immense size, only 430 million acres – less than one-fifth of the entire United States – are considered suitable for farming. Land degradation is a major threat to Africa's agricultural productivity growth. Pressure to feed a rapidly growing population has led to intensive working of the land and, because of inadequate soil nutrient replenishment, loss of soil fertility. The lack of appropriate soil and water conservation measures, and cultivation of previously forested and other fragile land, further compounds the problem. In Africa, two-thirds of the land is desert or dry land, and existing arable land is subjected to high degradation from overgrazing, inappropriate cultivation, deforestation and desertification.[9]

Africa's forest cover, estimated at about 1.72 billion acres in 1980, has been diminishing at a rate of about 9.14 million acres per year, and this rate is increasing. As much as half of Africa's farmland also is affected by soil degradation and erosion, and up to 80 percent of its pasture and range areas show signs of severe degradation.[10] In countries bordering the Sahara, desertification is leaving many people without land or water. If these people are unable to move – as often is the case – they face food insecurity crises, as in Djibouti and northern Mali.

Africa's inability to feed its populations is closely related to declining land quality and sluggish growth in food productivity. Although the population growth rate has declined from 2.9 percent in 1982-1990 to about 2.6 percent between 1990-1997, per capita cereal production has stagnated at about 125 kg/capita over the past

30 years. This compares to an increase from 565 kg/capita to 660 kg/capita in developed countries and from 164 kg/capita to 236 kg/capita in Asia, largely as a result of the Green Revolution.[11]

Corn – which is one of the most important staple food crops in Africa – has experienced significant declines in yield and output, mainly because of nearly no research-related productivity gains.[12] Moreover, the technological advances that characterized the past Green Revolution largely ignored crops that are significant food sources in Africa and perform well in its difficult, drought-prone environments, such as cassava, millets, pulses, roots, sorghums and tubers.[13] More research and agricultural extension education for these products can help boost Africa's food security.

Land: Farmers Need Security of Ownership and Use

Most of Africa's arable land is communally owned, which means that no one individual has property rights or ownership. This communal spirit embodies equitable treatment of villagers and the land, but it often hinders more productive use of the land or results in its overexploitation. For long-term agricultural growth to succeed in Africa, farmers need secure land ownership and user rights to increase land investments, protect the land's natural resources and promote its long-term sustainable use.

To date, most land reform efforts have involved land subdivision and redistribution to small farmers, but these efforts essentially failed to promote land tenure security, leading to numerous land-related civil conflicts. Also, past land redistributions efforts in Africa have had mixed results. After Kenya gained its political independence in 1963, the government's land reform program purchased large estates from former colonial settlers. These farms were subdivided into smaller farms and redistributed to hundreds of thousands of Kenyan farmers. The government then boosted research, agriculture extension and credit services to its small farmers, support that was nonexistent under the colonial government.[14] Almost immediately, farmers' incomes and productivity soared.

In contrast, neighboring Tanzania pursued a nationalized land program. The government, often using coercion, created large socialist land schemes or *ujamaa villages.* State-appointed managers administered these village farms, providing workers meager wages without land ownership or cultivation rights. Under this system, farm workers had little incentive to work hard, improve the land or increase productivity. Consequently, the country's agricultural growth rate declined significantly.

Recently, President Robert Mugabe of Zimbabwe initiated a fast-track land reform program in which he seized land from mostly white commercial farmers and redistributed it to black farmers who were his political supporters, according to observers. This land redistribution disrupted agricultural production and, together with one of the worst droughts in 50 years, is blamed for the current food crisis in the country.

Labor: Fewer Farm Hands

Because the majority of Africans live in rural areas where unemployment and underemployment rates are high, African agriculture tends to be characterized as

Table 4.1: Per Capita Growth in Population and Production of Major Grains

Region	Per capita cereal production (kilograms/capita)			
	1967	1982	1990	1997
Latin America	225.3	262.0	222.1	253.4
Sub-Saharan Africa	127.9	110.8	122.3	124.6
West Asia/ North Africa	255.8	231.5	245.5	245.6
All Asia	163.6	206.9	224.4	236.4
South Asia	146.0	171.3	182.1	182.6
Southeast Asia	157.8	198.8	210.1	226.3
East Asia	188.7	248.7	276.5	295.8
Developed World	564.6	670.4	680.3	660.1
Developing World	176.0	206.8	216.0	225.6

Source: International Food Policy Research Institute

African women and girls often work long hours collecting water and firewood, cooking, and caring for babies and sick family members.

labor-abundant. In fact, the opposite is true. Severe labor shortages hurt small farms, especially during peak weeding, planting and harvesting seasons.

Most small African farmers use traditional farming tools and methods that require a lot of manual labor, with most farmers relying on family labor. However, with the majority of young men and women either in school, migrating to cities or preferring to work in nonfarm activities, previously available helping hands no longer are around. In addition, HIV/AIDS is severely curtailing agricultural labor productivity (see related story, p. 80). Poor infrastructure, especially roads, also makes it difficult for extended families to travel to rural areas to help each other during the various agricultural cycles, especially in rainy seasons.

To improve agricultural productivity, countries need to improve infrastructure and reduce rural-urban migrations by creating more rural employment and boosting incomes from labor earnings, especially among poor farm households.

Women: Highly Productive But Constrained

Any effort to develop agriculture and improve household food security must include a focus on women. Most African farmers are women, and female-headed households are more prone to hunger and poverty.[15] African women generate two-thirds of Africa's agricultural production, and participate in trade and processing.

The women work long hours farming, collecting firewood and water, cooking, nursing babies, and caring for sick family members. Women increasingly run the household by themselves mostly because their husbands migrate to nearby cities and towns in search of work. Yet they confront greater barriers to improving agriculture and their livelihoods as compared to men, because they are less likely to own land and have access to credit, agricultural extension education and other support services.[16] Future reform and development policies must take into account and correct these biases.

Credit: Helps Farmers Invest, Manage Risks

Most African farmers are cash-strapped, leaving them unable to invest in their farming and often unable to purchase inputs needed for planting.[17] Seeds, fertilizer and herbicides can be expensive and beyond the reach of many small farmers. Without these farm inputs, and because of inherently low soil fertility, farmers' crop yields are relatively low.

Credit options help farmers bridge cash gaps, by providing small loans to carry them through to harvest season when they sell their crop and can repay the loan. Credit options also help small farmers better manage risks associated with farming, such as disastrous weather that can wipe out an entire crop. Better access to credit and possibilities of cash cropping allow farmers to purchase more farm inputs, leading to improved agricultural production.[18] But most African countries have few farm credit sources, many of which are run by inefficient government-controlled institutions that have poor service records. Private commercial banks, on the other hand, hardly offer any agricultural loans because they consider agriculture too risky to finance and farmers too expensive to serve.

Clearly, for agricultural development to succeed, farmers must have access to better credit so they can invest in their operations. The private sector should be encouraged to partner with governments to devise cost-effective means of disbursing to, and collecting money from, small farmers. Another option is to promote farmer groups and cooperatives, which are easier to finance and can leverage better services for farmers. The National Small Farmers Association (NASFAM) of Malawi is an example of such cooperatives.[19] It provides its members with production and marketing services, business management, marketing literacy and quality-control training (see a related story, p. 78).

The lessons of successful organizations, such as NASFAM, should be shared with other farmers and built upon. Additional help in strengthening management skills and accountability will allow such cooperatives to provide better services to farmers, so they can harness the benefits of scale economies, improve their leverage in marketing and pricing, and have greater access to agricultural services. With assistance, the cooperatives also can develop rural-based financial institutions, and

Malawi Farmers Find 'The Future Belongs to the Organized'

By the Agricultural Cooperative Development International and Volunteers in Overseas Cooperative Assistance (ACDI/VOCA)

Malawi is one of the poorest countries in Africa, regularly facing food shortages as a result of recurrent drought, limited and degraded agricultural land, and weak marketing systems. However, since 1994 ACDI/VOCA[1] has been helping small farmers organize to form village-based clubs, which work together to collectively address common agricultural production and marketing problems.

In 1997 ACDI/VOCA facilitated the formation of the National Smallholder Farmers' Association of Malawi (NASFAM), which today represents nearly 100,000 farm families in 32 self-financing agribusiness associations. NASFAM provides a range of services to its members, including transportation and input procurement contracting, domestic and exports sales, training in business management, quality control and literacy. All commercial services are paid through membership dues and fees, with external donor funds supporting training and education. In addition, NASFAM enables thousands of small farmers to engage in democratic processes, and to establish partnerships with financial service providers. Its rallying cry is: "The future belongs to the organized."

In mid-1996 ACDI/VOCA was invited to work in Mulanje with the Malawi Association of Spice and Herbs (MASH), which was experiencing serious financial and managerial problems. In light of the poor record and continuing difficulties of the association, it was decided that MASH was not a suitable partner. Local farmers, however, were eager for help in getting organized, telling ACDI/VOCA, "We know the benefits of associations. … We don't want to be left behind."

ACDI/VOCA set up a small technical support office in the area the following year and began to survey agricultural activities. It soon became evident that Malawi's fiery Birdseye chili peppers held the greatest potential for profits. Staff helped the chili growers organize into small groups, which in turn joined forces to create collection and marketing centers. They then distributed quality seed and taught the farmers how to correctly dry and grade their chilies ready for export. The farmers worked hard to overcome initial quality problems, continually improving production, drying and grading practices in order to develop a reputation of having a consistently high quality product.

Zikometso Smallholder Farmers' Association was formally admitted to NASFAM membership in 1999, having developed and adopted a set of bylaws and elected a board of directors. By that time, the association numbered more than 5,000 farmers in 239 village level clubs.

The following year, Zikometso Association marketed 62 tons of Birdseye chili peppers to Europe and Australia, making a profit of $27,000. Most of this money was returned to the members as a bonus payment. Farmers who were association members thus received 35 percent more for their chili peppers than did nonmembers. The association also was the first to graduate from ACDI/VOCA's program by recruiting its entire management and field staff, leasing two warehouses, purchasing its own computer and providing motorcycles to field employees. NASFAM acts in a field advisory capacity, and exports the chilies as a broker for a fee.

In Malawi, the Zikometso farmer association produced 77 metric tons of chili peppers for export, reaping gross revenues of $200,000.

This year, Zikometso Association's 5,700 members enjoyed another successful chili harvest, producing 80 metric tons – 77 tons of which were exported to Europe – and reaping gross revenues of $200,000. The association has opened three farm supply shops selling seed and fertilizer, and business is booming. Zikometso chairperson Byson Eruwa says, "We are having the best year ever – and this is due to strong leadership and staff at all levels of the association. Farmers are loyal to the association because we can compete strongly against traders who do not have a long-term interest in the farmer. We are getting paid a second payment from the association for the third time in four years. No trader can do that."

Zikometso Association also is sharing its newfound expertise with another NASFAM member, the Balaka Area Smallholder Farmers' Association (BASFA). High quality seeds from Zikometso have been distributed to BASFA members, and training given in seedbed preparation and transplanting. Eleven metric tons of chilies have been transferred from BASFA to Zikometso's warehouse for grading and export, and the first container of Balaka chili was exported to Europe in September 2002.

Through a commitment to quality, willingness to work together and sheer hard work, Zikometso Association members have increased their incomes and brought economic security to their communities. Like tens of thousands of other NASFAM farmers, they have proved that in Malawi, the future does belong to the organized.

---

[1] With funding from the U.S. Agency for International Development.

processing and marketing firms. Future markets and crop insurance programs also can be explored to hedge farmers against weather and market risks.

Refocusing attention and increasing investments in rural areas will create many farm and nonfarm activities that likely will increase capital flows for farming. Because farm and nonfarm economies in rural Africa are closely linked, investment in agriculture tends to reap economic benefits in other sectors as well, which boosts family incomes further – money that can be spent on family health, education and other social and economic needs.

Zainabu Msomoka, a 54-year-old Tanzanian widow, who lost her two eldest children to HIV/AIDS in 1995, gives an example of the role credit can play.[20] Unemployed and faced with caring for her orphaned grandchildren, she joined a women's micro-credit group and received a $62 loan, the most money she had ever seen.[21] With this money, she built a large kiosk restaurant and equipped it well. Business was good, and eventually she received an additional $1,238 loan to expand her business and purchase land for farming and settlement. Today, she earns a steady living for her and her grandchildren.

Agricultural Trade, Markets and Infrastructure

Historically, Africa has relied on government-controlled agricultural commodity marketing systems, which set producer and consumer prices, operated national grain silos, and managed the export and import of major foods. The 1990s' market liberalization trends, which stemmed in part from structural adjustment mandates, reduced these controls and allowed more private firms and individuals to participate in providing credit, inputs and marketing services. But the shift from controlled to freer markets has had mixed results. In extreme cases, government agencies have continued to intervene erratically in pricing and marketing, creating uncertainty for farmers and private investors.

Poor commodity pricing and limited access to markets hinder small farmers' efforts to expand their agricultural activities. Failure by many African governments to establish agricultural product standards, grading and certification methods further reduce access to regional and international trade. Not surprisingly, as most developing countries' trade and incomes grew during the 1990s at twice the rate of the previous decade, Africa's share of trade shrank and per capita income levels stagnated.

Industrialized countries' import restrictions and subsidies, meanwhile, continue to undermine Africa's agricultural growth potential. According to IFPRI, the agricultural subsidies and other developed country protections are costing African farmers at least $2 billion annually. Removal of these barriers would double sub-Saharan Africa's agricultural trade, improve incomes of poor farmers and boost entire economies. Oxfam International asserts that current global trading rules are stacked against Africa and other poor countries.[22] Moreover, poor infrastructure, costly communication and scarcity of market information increase production and marketing costs, diminishing the competitiveness of African agricultural products in regional and international markets.

HIV/AIDS: A Formidable Challenge

The rapid spread of HIV/AIDS presents major challenges for Africa. In 2002 some 70 percent of the world's 42 million people living with HIV/AIDS and 80 percent of new infections were in Africa, according to the Joint United Nation's Program on HIV/AIDS (UNAIDS).[23] This disease – which feeds on poverty, ignorance and certain cultural habits – is a major killer of African adults and children. Unless more is done to control this scourge, the infection rate and related deaths will rise and generate even greater social, political and economic costs not only to Africa, but also to the rest of the world.

The insecurity perpetuated by HIV/AIDS, such as that experienced by the Tanzanian widow and her family, is devastating Africa's rural communities. Not only must parents and grandparents worry about orphaned and/or infected children, they also must worry about declining incomes and increasing food insecurity (see sidebar on HIV/AIDS). The increasing rate of illness and death

BFWI Photo/Kimberly Burge

By stealing the lives of African farmers, teachers and leaders, the rapid spread of HIV/AIDS is creating numerous orphans and robbing this region of its future promise.

HIV/AIDS Is Increasing Hunger in Africa

By Dr. Lucy W. Karanja

Twenty-one years ago, doctors in New York and California watched helplessly as their patients succumbed to an illness they could not halt nor understand. Three years later, the illness was identified as the acquired immunodeficiency syndrome (AIDS) caused by the human immunodeficiency virus (HIV). The disease since has spread throughout the world, infecting nearly 60 million people and killing about one-third of them, making it one of the worst disease epidemics ever. The number of people living with HIV/AIDS nearly doubled in six years, from 22.6 million in 1996 to 42 million in 2002, with Africa accounting for 70 percent of those living with the disease and 80 percent of new infections.[1]

HIV/AIDS is transmitted through sexual intercourse, transfusion of infected blood, sharing needles by intravenous drug users, and from infected mothers to their newborn babies. Its infection rate and health effects are magnified in Africa by poverty, ignorance, lack of awareness, lack and high cost of antiretroviral drugs, large migrations due to wars, famine and job search, political inaction, risky sexual behavior and some cultural habits.[2]

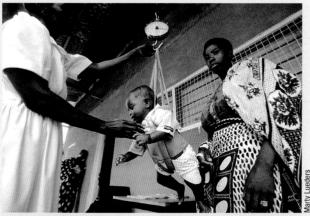

The human immunodeficiency virus (HIV) can be transmitted from infected mothers to their newborn babies. Increased education about HIV/AIDS and better health care are needed to combat this disease.

This disease initially affected primarily urban populations. But now, it has spread widely to rural Africa where it is crippling agriculture, the largest economic sector and provider of food, employment and income to two-thirds of Africa's population. African agriculture is labor intensive, and loss of labor through death and illness from HIV/AIDS is reducing food productivity and farm income thereby exacerbating hunger, poverty and food insecurity. People weakened by hunger are more likely to become infected because their bodies are less immune. The situation is aggravated further by drought, civil strife and poor economic conditions.

Women, who account for the bulk of Africa's farm labor and agricultural production, also are more prone to HIV/AIDS infection, and so are young people – ages 15 to 39 – who are sexually active. Future generations are being compromised by lower life expectancy, increased mortality and a growing dependency from orphans and children living with HIV/AIDS.

A study in Zimbabwe found that HIV/AIDS cut marketed corn output by 61 percent, cotton by half and groundnuts by one-third. In Tanzania's Kagabiro village, 29 percent of household labor was spent taking care of AIDS patients, labor that otherwise would have been used to increase food production. In coffee-banana farming systems in Kenya, research suggests that the disease also is undermining the transfer of knowledge and skills traditionally passed from parents to children, which only further exacerbates rural economic loss.

Within the next 10 years in Tanzania and Kenya, the gross domestic product (GDP) will decline by 25 percent and 14 percent, respectively.[3] Lower labor productivity and poor economic prospects will further depress Africans' ability to provide sufficient food and income to spur economic growth and development. Moreover, many governments already are constrained by rising food import bills and, therefore, cannot effectively respond to escalating public health expenses from rising HIV/AIDS rates and other opportunistic diseases.

Short-term, communities and governments must increase public awareness about HIV/AIDS and encourage voluntary testing and counseling, supply cheaper and more effective antiretroviral drugs, empower and foster social support for women, and provide education on the prevention of sexually transmitted diseases.[4] Longer-term, a vaccine is needed.

These options will require great commitment and mobilization of public and private resources, political leadership and civil participation at local, national and international levels. Uganda has shown that concerted public awareness campaigns and active participation by political leaders, religious groups and civil society can help reverse HIV-infection trends. Uganda President Yoweri Museveni takes every opportunity to address the public and caution it against the disease.

African countries need more sustained, comprehensive long-term support and commitment by their governments and foreign partners to overcome the threat and effects of HIV/AIDS. The $936 million collected so far under the U.N. Global AIDS and Health fund (of $2.1 billion pledged) is too little to meet the challenge posed by HIV/AIDS, malaria and tuberculosis. The United Nations estimates that it would need $7 billion to $10 billion annually, with half the resources needed for sub-Saharan Africa.[5] Every government and agency must step up efforts and lend support now.

---

[1] The Joint U.N. Program on HIV/AIDS, *Global Health Update*, 2002.

[2] L.W. Karanja, "Vertical Transmission of HIV/AIDS in Sub-Saharan Africa: An Epidemiological Review." (Masters' Thesis, Michigan State University) 2002.

[3] *The Economic Impact of AIDS in Africa*, The Futures Group International Inc., 2002. Available from http://www.tfgi.com/ecimaids.asp.

[4] International Center for Research on Women, "Community Involvement and the Prevention of Mother-to-Child Transmission of HIV/AIDS," 2002.

[5] United Nations, "Global AIDS, Health Fund Operational by Year End." Press Release, May 6, 2001.

associated with the disease diminishes family labor, an important resource to small-scale farmers, as family members spend more time and money caring for the sick and orphaned.

Expenses related to the disease also erode family incomes. Money that otherwise would have been used to pay for farm inputs is used to care for the sick or pay hospital bills and funeral expenses. Some families are forced to sell their livestock and farming tools. Others forego farm improvements. In some parts of Uganda, women have formed cooperatives to help each other with farm labor. They also pool cash to purchase farm inputs and food for those families suffering with the disease. In Malawi, some women farmers work communally, sharing the fruits of their labor equally among those afflicted by sickness and those who are healthy.[24] Such examples of sharing, part of Africa's communal tradition, has helped keep some communities from falling apart.

Civil Wars and Conflicts: A Heavy Burden

Conflicts and civil wars disrupt families and undercut agricultural production and economic development. One in five Africans lives in a country torn apart by war and conflict.[25] This civil and political upheaval costs countries tremendous amounts of money and human resources. Conflicts and wars lead to destruction of physical infrastructure and a loss of institutional capacity, not to mention huge losses of human life. Resources diverted from development use by conflicts are estimated at $1 billion a year in Central Africa and more than $800 million a year in West Africa, according to the World Bank, plus an additional $500 million annually for refugee assistance in Central Africa. [26]

Bad policy choices are a major cause of slow economic growth in Africa and are traced to the lack of social capital and deficient political institutions.[27] To overcome this challenge, African governments should respond to new demands for the rule of law and greater democracy. Responsible governance must be fostered and nourished, and democratic institutions strengthened to decentralize power, encouraging public participation in policymaking and promoting transparency and accountability.

Overcoming Obstacles

To overcome such obstacles, African countries must position their economies to take advantage of agricultural development and trade opportunities. Farmers and rural communities need better infrastructure, appropriate research and technologies, and greater access to local, national, regional and international markets. And to sustain these gains, African governments and the international community must confront the menace of HIV/AIDS and the ongoing wars and conflicts in the continent.

Land degradation is a major threat to Africa's agricultural productivity growth. Roads and other infrastructure also need to be improved.

Improve Infrastructure

Poor infrastructure often is cited as a major reason for Africa's low competitiveness in agricultural trade. Africa has a fair number of ports, rail lines, long-distance roads and air links, but most of these are old, inadequate or inappropriate for current markets. Agricultural products are bulky, and their profitability often depends on the efficiency and cost of transportation, which is relatively high in Africa as compared to the rest the world. For example, freight costs for East African and West African imports are 70 percent higher than for Asian countries. Similarly, air transportation costs within Africa are up to four times higher than transportation costs across the Atlantic.

Likewise, phone and Internet charges can be between 50 times and 100 times higher in Africa than in North America, partly because Africa's communication networks often are run by inefficient government monopolies. High communication costs push down agricultural profits and wages, and penalize exports. Poor access to electricity and water also can hinder agricultural development and trade, especially of value-added agricultural products. Fewer than one in five Africans has access to electricity. Nearly two-thirds of people living in rural Africa lack access to sufficient amounts of good-quality water.

Without improved infrastructure and communication networks, African countries are unlikely to become more competitive in international trade. The World Bank estimates that repairing current and constructing new

Research Holds Promise for African Agriculture

By Carl K. Eicher

The ongoing drought in Southern Africa coupled with the failure of a Green Revolution to take root has heightened concern about Africa's ability to feed itself. However, such pessimism about a continent's ability to achieve food security has been played out before – in Asia.

In the early 1960s, many experts doubted Asia's ability to feed itself because of low yields of staple food crops, devastating monsoons and the region's rapid population growth. But despite the naysayers, India responded with a long-term political commitment to coordinated investments in credit, education, extension, irrigations, research and roads. The payoff to these investments was impressive. Starting in 1965, India began its march to national food self-sufficiency, achieving its goal 16 years later. Similar efforts were made in Indonesia and Thailand and other Asian countries. By the early 1980s, Asia was awash with grain.

A bleak economic future for Africa is not certain. African countries can learn from Asia's experience. To boost agriculture, Asian countries built a strong agricultural science base, a means to deliver new technologies to farmers using extension services and a national system of state agricultural universities to train and replenish agriculture researchers.

Investing in the Agricultural Knowledge Triangle

Since the mid-1990s, agriculture has been marginalized in African nations and among many donor agencies. Currently, the World Bank's agricultural lending is less than 10 percent of total lending, an all-time low. Numerous donors have reduced their support to national research systems, citing a lack of financial sustainability. Because agricultural research is the engine of agricultural growth, it must be put back on the agenda of African political leaders and international donor agencies.

However, such a feat cannot be an idle exercise of preparing an array of donor-financed agricultural research projects. This road has been taken before. In fact, Africa's public research systems are dependent on discrete projects financed by external aid. Rather, African countries must secure research investments in three core agricultural institutions: research, agricultural extension and higher education. These three core institutions constitute what I call the agricultural knowledge triangle.

Building Research Capacity

Building a strong national agricultural science base capable of generating new technology for small-scale farmers requires seven important ingredients:

● Political Leadership

In four decades of training students and building research capacity in Africa, I have learned that the most important ingredient is African political leadership. For agriculture to succeed in Africa, its leaders must focus on creating and supporting science and technological institutions that improve the welfare of all people. Foreign assistance and increased trade can be effective

Successful development takes decades, not years, and requires long-term national and donor support.

Marty Lueders

only in countries where leaders approach agriculture with vision and commitment.

● Commitment to Long-term Development

Successful development is measured in decades, not years, and requires long-term national and donor support. It took Zimbabwe 28 years (1932-1960) of research before it released the famous SR 52 hybrid maize variety that increased farm yields 41 percent without fertilizer. The amount of time that it takes to generate new technology for small farmers varies widely. A decade is an average time period to develop new crop varieties, and 10 years to 20 years to improve livestock technologies.

● Economic Payoff

Research is an investment with a high rate of return. The pioneering study of the development of hybrid maize varieties in Kenya tallied up the costs and benefits of research in Kenya from 1955 to 1988 and found that the annual rate of return on public investment was 68 percent.[1] To be sure, other research efforts have lower rates of return, but on average research can yield favorable rates of return in Africa similar to successes in Latin America and Asia.

● Strong Networks

Africa's diversity and wide array of agroecologies require strong linkages among regional and global research systems, both public and private. The Association for Strengthening Agricultural Research in Eastern and Central Africa is a pioneering institution that links researchers in 10 countries through research networks. Because 20 percent of the agricultural researchers are in more than 35 African countries, and 80 percent are located in 13 large countries, it is difficult for smaller countries to finance major investments in buildings and research equipment. Therefore, it behooves researchers in these smaller countries to become smart borrowers of technology from neighboring countries, regional centers and public and private international research institutions.

● Public and Private Investments

Because most African countries are in an early stage of institutional development, they need the public to play a leading role in providing the funding for national research systems. Currently, about 90 percent of the agricultural research funding in Africa is from public sources, with 10 percent from private. While privatization of research and extension services are on the agenda of many international donor agencies, in the foreseeable future public investments will need to provide the bulk of research financing in Africa.[2]

● Mobilizing Universities

Many members of the academic staff of African universities have distant and tenuous relationships with researchers in national agricultural research organizations. These tenuous relationships impede the flow of knowledge from farmers back to the university curriculum and the development of research partnerships. Many international donors have pulled back from investing in African faculties of agriculture because of perceived weak performance, duplication of effort and the politicization of universities. But overseas training fellowships are drying up, and investments in African faculties and universities of agriculture are needed. National research systems are incomplete without universities to educate and train new generations of researchers.

● Positive Incentives for Scientists

Similarly, developing countries and other institutions need to hire, reward and retain gifted scientists.

Summary

The success or failure of the many community projects and farmer associations that are being formed in Africa will depend on the availability of profitable technology for small farmers. This situation harkens to some of the hard choices that Asian political leaders made in the 1960s to build agricultural knowledge triangles. Will African political leaders make the same hard choices in building strong national agricultural science bases or will they continue to rely on bottom-up, quick-fix projects and a gaggle of food aid subscriptions? Only time will tell.

Dr. Carl K. Eicher is a professor of agricultural economics at Michigan State University.

1   Daniel Karanja, "The Rate of Return to Maize Research in Kenya, 1955-1988," (Unpublished Master of Science Thesis, Michigan State University) 1990.

2   Carl K. Eicher, "Mozambique: An Analysis of the Implementation of the Extension Master Plan," Staff Paper No.2002-31, Department of Agricultural Economics, Michigan State University, 2002.

infrastructure to meet countries' needs would cost approximately $400 million, while building a more comprehensive communication network would cost approximately $18 billion a year.[28] Better roads and communication will help reduce production and marketing costs, and make African farm products more competitive in regional and international markets.

Develop Africa's Agricultural Research and Extension

Building Africa's agricultural research and extension capabilities and refocusing current efforts on increasing agricultural productivity would help nudge many rural communities toward sustainable food security. Africa's lagging agricultural productivity, coupled with rising population, poverty and unemployment in rural areas, is burdening the continent's land and water resources. Many rural areas also are battling soil erosion, deforestation and desertification in addition to serious social challenges, such as malnutrition, hunger and high child mortality rates. For African agriculture to succeed in improving the lives of rural poor people, agricultural technologies and ideas not only must accelerate food production, but also pursue more efficient and sustainable use of Africa's natural resources.

Most of Africa's agricultural research is publicly funded. Resources from government budgets – already reeling from reduced fiscal spending under structural adjustment policies – have declined since the 1980s. At the same time, foreign donors, who account for about half of agricultural research funding, have cut back on their giving. World Bank lending for agriculture also declined dramatically, from an average 31 percent of its total lending in 1979-1981 to less than 10 percent in 1999-2000. Similarly, the U.S. Agency for International Development (USAID) cut its agricultural investments to sub-Saharan Africa by 57 percent, to about $80 million.[29] By 2000, African agriculture received less U.S. development assistance than any other sector.

These funding declines must be reversed, and together with domestic public and private resources, targeted to meet specific operational and training needs of research and extension institutions. Current efforts to integrate research institutions into regional networks should be supported and strengthened to promote technology sharing, capacity building and efficient allocation of scarce resources. Renewed interest in African agriculture by the World Bank, USAID, European Union and others, should translate into additional funding that allows African scientists and policymakers to explore new technological innovations for increasing food production and quality, such as organic farming and agricultural biotechnology (see related statement, p. 84).

Agricultural Biotechnology in Africa

A Statement from Bread for the World Institute

Today, many African countries face severe hunger problems. One-third of Africans are undernourished, and per capita food production is falling. This situation demands immediate attention. As part of Bread for the World Institute's commitment to eliminating hunger and seeking justice for all people, which arises from our Christian faith, we have engaged in an evaluation of whether crop biotechnology could help reduce hunger in Africa. The year-long process involved extensive research review, stakeholder consultation and a conference attended by more than 100 people representing government agencies, nongovernmental organizations, churches, private industry, international agencies, universities and experts from several African countries.

The statement that follows represents our best thinking to date on a complex, controversial and dynamic issue. As the debate continues and circumstances change, Bread for the World Institute will review our policy in light of what we continue to learn.

Background

Most people in sub-Saharan Africa live in rural areas, and agriculture is central to the economy; it provides food, employment and income to more than two-thirds of Africa's people. Thus, one of the most effective ways to reduce hunger in Africa is to improve agricultural productivity. This improvement would raise both farm and nonfarm incomes, expand food supplies, and boost overall food access and food security. Past experience in many African countries – in addition to the lessons learned from Asia's Green Revolution – confirms that substantial progress can be made in agriculture and rural development by investing in appropriate agricultural technologies and institutions, and establishing apt policies that improve the efficiency and sustainable use of available resources, empowering women and improving their access to productive resources, and reducing regional income disparities.

Agricultural biotechnology – a term that represents a continuum of different techniques, ranging from noncontroversial tissue culture to controversial genetic engineering – potentially can increase agricultural yields; reduce yield losses from insects, diseases and drought; and enhance the nutritive value of crops crucial to poor people's health. But there is genuine concern expressed by many people about long-term negative health and environmental effects, such as those now debated in developed countries. African countries that begin to use crop biotechnology could lose exports to European consumers who broadly oppose biotechnology. In addition, because affluent farmers are more likely than others to acquire and use this technology, it might increase income inequality in rural areas.

The failure of the current discussion to resolve issues raised for and against crop biotechnology, the vast resources spent by multinational corporations lobbying and pushing the technology, and the stand-off between the United States and European Union on this issue have increased suspicion and frustration, hindering a balanced debate and objective decision making on whether the technology is useful. Moreover, the U.S. government increasingly is seen to favor biotechnology and represent the interests of the multinational corporations involved. If the U.S. government were instead seeking to strengthen the regulation of biotechnology, public confidence in its use, in the United States and abroad, would increase.

Currently, biotechnology research and development is hardly targeted toward Africa or its poor people. In 2001 only 0.2 percent of the 130 million acres of land planted worldwide with genetically modified (GM) crops was in Africa. In addition, none of the more than 50 GM crop products released in developed countries was designed to address Africa's agricultural constraints. Instead, private industry essentially controls the technology, a trend supported by intellectual property rights that favor multinational corporations. This control likely will restrict sharing and access of the technology by national, regional and international public research institutes that work largely on agricultural problems facing poor people. Hence, the ability of biotechnology to reduce hunger in Africa is severely limited.

Small farmers need access to new technologies that improve African agriculture productivity.

Because Africa has diverse cultures, economies, ecologies and politics, conclusions about the risks and benefits of biotechnology likely will differ from country to country. African views may differ from views expressed in developed countries, especially as people in each country weigh their own needs and values against perceived costs and risks. As African people debate whether agricultural biotechnology is appropriate for them, all stakeholders – including smallholder African farmers and consumers – should be included. Ultimately, the final decision on whether to use the technology must be made, and the responsibility borne, by Africans.

Guiding Principles

Bread for the World Institute supports Africa's right to choose whether to pursue the use of crop biotechnology. Therefore, we support an increase in funding to build Africa's capacity to carry out unbiased evaluations of biotechnology's benefits and risks, establish appropriate biosafety policies and institutions, and participate in related international negotiations.

We support the restructuring of the current intellectual property rights system to protect indigenous resources and ensure access to the technology and distribution of its benefits to all, including smallholder African farmers.

Any potential benefits of crop biotechnology must be weighed against potential risks and considered within a broader African agricultural and economic development framework, using benchmarks related to ending hunger and helping African countries achieve sustainable and equitable development.

Although biotechnology can play a role in enhancing agricultural productivity and food security, by itself it cannot solve the hunger problem in Africa. Agricultural improvements can also be made through organic farming, integrated pest management and conventional breeding. Agricultural development efforts must also include investments in agricultural extension, credit, marketing, infrastructure and trade.

Decisions about agricultural technologies, institutions and policies should be made by African governments with the full participation of civil society (including smallholder farmers and consumers) and without undue external influence from companies, governments or advocacy groups.

Finally, we urge the United States and other industrialized countries to increase support for efforts to reduce hunger in Africa. This will include increases in effective poverty-focused development assistance, changes in the agriculture and agricultural trade policies of the industrialized countries and more support for peacemaking in Africa. We urge development assistance agencies and African governments to adopt strategies that boost Africa's agriculture and rural development; widen access to nutritious food, water, health care and education; and improve the living standards of all Africans, especially those who are prone to hunger.

Easing Trade Reins, Improving Market Access

Expanding African agricultural exports can lead the way to fewer poor and hungry people. Although international assistance is needed to overcome barriers to agricultural development, export growth can be an efficient engine of poverty reduction because it helps put income directly into poor people's hands.[30] However, these gains for poor people are not absolute; policies and institutions that support equitable distribution of trade benefits must be put in place and enforced. Especially important, African countries must match trade's growth with food security protections, particularly for poor urban consumers.

African economies also must participate more actively in shaping the rules that govern global trade, notably international trade negotiations. Because the current rules favor industrialized countries' trade and limit African trade, African countries must demand that this bias be eliminated and international trade rules be made fair. Toward this end, African investments in greater negotiating and lobbying skills for its trade representatives at global forums, including the World Trade Organization (WTO), likely will yield significant returns and better policies for African countries.

Future Prospects for Sustainable Agriculture, Economic Growth in Africa

● Support Agriculture and Small Farmers

Because agriculture is the foundation of rural African economies and provides the main income for most poor Africans, efforts to strengthen rural economies must emphasize agricultural development. Policies must ensure that small farmers have access to markets, technologies, credit and farm inputs in a global economy. Efficient producer cooperatives can play a big role in strengthening agricultural production, processing and marketing among small farmers and rural business communities.

● Bolster Agriculture Research and Extension Services

Agricultural research and extension services can ease many of the technological constraints facing African agriculture. But to do that, these institutions must become more responsive to small farmers' needs, more efficient, and readily work within regional networks to facilitate information gathering, technology development and dissemination. Greater gains from research and extension will accrue if research organizations forge closer links with other stakeholders, including farmers and universities, as well as receive firmer support from governments and regional and international research networks.

African governments and international donors must increase budget allocations to agricultural research. They also should mobilize new funding sources through public-private sector research partnerships. Lastly, they should strengthen intracountry and regional research collaborations to minimize duplication of effort and improve technology borrowing rather than reinventing the wheel each time.

African governments also should consider enacting appropriate biosafety measures, intellectual property rights and food standards that do not alienate small farmers, either nationally or regionally. Such measures are especially important with regard to agricultural biotechnology.

Safeguard Natural Resources

Given Africa's low soil fertility and loss of natural resources, countries must make resource management a priority. Using conservation tillage and vegetative barriers to harvest water and contain soil erosion are examples of techniques that can benefit many regions without using expensive, modern inputs. Building on local knowledge for appropriate innovations also is important when managing Africa's diversity in environmental needs and resources.

Current and future land reform policies must embrace stiffer requirements for natural resource conservation. Appropriate land title and zoning regulations can guard against unwarranted destruction of forests and fragile lands, such as wetlands and indigenous flora. However, new approaches are needed that encourage

community participation, local management of common resources and civil society partnerships.[31] New policies also must consider indigenous knowledge and practices to ensure their sustainability and conformity to local traditions and expectations.

Improve Infrastructure and Communication

Because many farmers are poorly connected to roads, renewed attention and investment in rural infrastructure will help re-engage rural communities with local, national and international markets. Investments in health care, education, communication and clean water help boost agricultural productivity as well. Already, mobile telephones and Internet access in rural areas have accelerated the spread of knowledge and information among rural communities in ways not envisaged a decade ago. For example, several Ugandan women groups are using local cyber-cafes to share agricultural production information and seek target niche markets for their products.

Build Public-Private Partnerships

To fulfill its promise, African agriculture needs considerable resource investment. Because Africa's financial sources are overstretched, governments, private sector and civil society must forge new – accountable and responsible – partnerships that pool resources and address impediments to agricultural development in a comprehensive, coordinated manner.

Unlike past efforts that liberalized trade and curbed government spending at the expense of poor people, African governments must pursue sustainable strategies

Table 4.2: Public Agricultural Research Expenditures: Global Trends

Region	Expenditures (in millions)			Annual Growth Rates (percent per year)	
	1971	1981	1991	1971-1981	1981-1991
Developing Countries	$2,895	$5,535	$8,017	6.4%	3.8%
Sub-Saharan Africa	$699	$927	$968	2.5%	0.8%
China	$457	$934	$1,494	7.7%	4.7%
Asia/Pacific (excl. China)	$862	$1,922	$3,502	8.7%	6.2%
Latin America/Caribbean	$508	$1,008	$951	7.2%	-1.1%
West Asia/North Africa	$459	$738	$1,102	4.3%	4.0%
Industrialized Countries	$4,298	$5,713	$6,941	2.7%	1.7%
Total*	$7,283	$11,248	$14,958	4.4%	2.8%

Source: P.G. Pardey, J. Rosebroom and B.J. Craig, "Agricultural R&D Investments and Impact." Chapter in J.M. Alston, P.G. Pardey and V.H. Smith, *Paying for Agricultural Productivity*. (Baltimore: Johns Hopkins University Press) 1998.

*Total excludes Cuba and the Russian Federation

African countries should invest in their people by supporting employment training, education and health care.

that empower people, especially rural people. Such strategies can invigorate natural resource management and stimulate greater participation in local decision-making processes. The private sector also can contribute to rural development by investing capital in rural areas and partnering with farmers and farm cooperatives to ensure quality production, market outlets and sustained economic growth. But here, appropriate regulations will be needed to avoid exploitation of one group by the other.

Participate in International Negotiations

African countries should participate more effectively in the ongoing WTO negotiations, pressing for issues that are of interest to African countries' international trade. African participants must take advantage of the negotiations and demand agricultural liberalization by industrialized countries and other concessions that will strengthen their agriculture. Key trade issues should be protecting African countries' ability to diversify their agriculture from primary agricultural commodities, negotiating for better markets of raw and value-added agricultural products, and getting compensatory programs for low-income food-importing African countries that might be hurt by industrialized countries' agricultural liberalization.[32]

The political and economic realignments caused by regional and international trading blocs offer new opportunities for growth in agricultural trade. Such opportunities include the Africa Growth and Opportunity Act (AGOA), a legislative pledge made by the United States in 2000 to expand market access for specified African products. Although progress has been made in new access for

apparel industries and the elimination of many tariffs, it fails to cover the agricultural products most important to building agricultural trade in Africa. AGOA also has helped U.S. and African officials and business communities to focus more on U.S.-Africa trade possibilities; however, liberalizing agricultural trade under the WTO would be better for African countries than an expanded AGOA.

Other opportunities are the newly formed New Partnership for African Development (NEPAD) initiative, a detailed plan to meet the economic, political and social challenges of Africa's people. Both the African Union and the G-8 group of industrialized countries have endorsed NEPAD.

Encourage Regional Trade

African countries could gain considerable power and leverage by strengthening regional trading blocs. Such collaboration also would provide pooled critical mass in human capacity and resources for promoting regional research, development and peace. Several country blocs already have formed market unions while others are negotiating various forms of market and political integrations. Such groupings allow African countries to speak with a greater voice, especially in multilateral negotiations. As trading blocs, they also can better coordinate their trade, minimize trade barriers among themselves, and promote regional trade, with good implications for international trade, such as with the European Union.

Promote Rural Development

Farm and rural nonfarm activities are synergistic. Therefore, the broad development of institutions, infrastructure and facilities in rural areas must be seen in light of how they affect agricultural production and competitiveness. Countries also must invest in their people by supporting employment training, education and health care, and creating institutions and policies that make ending hunger and poverty an explicit and measurable goal. In this regard, strategies for improving agriculture must be cognizant of the broader rural development objectives and careful assessments done to ensure addressing one constraint does not create harm for the other, especially relating to environmental sustainability.

Notably, each African country or region will have specific needs and constraints. Thus, a cookie-cutter approach to development policy will not work. Thoughtful, innovative ways of tapping into, and intelligently using, local information and experience about local soil conditions, drought cycles, pests and diseases should be sought when formulating region-specific agricultural innovations and support services.

Community-Based Nutrition Programs Make a Difference in Southern Ethiopia

By Ashley Aakesson

Life is getting harder for some 265,000 people, mostly pastoralists, who are living in the rugged, semi-arid region of southern Ethiopia called Liben and Filtu districts. Droughts are more frequent and severe. Water and pasture resources are disappearing. More than half of children younger than 5 are stunted, a result of chronic hunger compounded by diseases like diarrhea, malaria, HIV/AIDS and pneumonia.

Save the Children has been working in Liben and Filtu to address the root causes of poverty and hunger for these people. The group helps pastoralists make a better living from their livestock, find new income sources and manage natural resources. It also helps educate more girls and boys, and empower mothers to better care for their children, in part through food distribution, and food-for-work and nutritional education activities.

Liben and Filtu people have several means for helping themselves confront these challenges. Traditional leaders help mobilize community members to solve problems cooperatively. Traditional healers (both for livestock and people) are respected and trusted educators in the community. Save the Children enlists the help of these men and women to implement programs and boost resources in their communities.

Food and Nutrition Programs

Women face formidable barriers to changing the way they feed and care for their infants and children, including local beliefs and staggering workloads. Direct, targeted distributions of food to children and pregnant and breastfeeding mothers helps to meet immediate nutritional needs while preventing the physical and cognitive stunting that results from chronic hunger. Food-for-work projects provide incentives to community members to build and maintain community resources like ponds, hand pumps and grazing land, while further closing the food gap. Traditional birth

A community worker poses with children near a newly installed hand water pump paid for by the community through food-for-work activities.

attendants are trained in safe birthing practices and help mothers start breastfeeding immediately after birth. Community health workers teach mothers that exclusive breastfeeding is best for their babies for six months, and teach better nutrition practices for older infants and children. Mothers who, despite the odds, keep their children healthy are asked to share recipes and teach cooking methods to other mothers.

Despite two years of severe drought, these programs have helped improve nutrition and food security in southern Ethiopia. Between 1998 and 2001, the stunting rate among children in Liben and Filtu fell from 53 percent to 28 percent. Nearly 10,000 households, including 70,000 livestock, benefit from ponds that have been expanded through food-for-work activities. Some 225 people in 14 communities have opened savings accounts, a new asset diversification strategy for the pastoralists, which help them survive crises like drought or disease.

Save the Children plans to continue working with communities in Liben and Filtu over the next five years. During this time, 19,080 families with children 2 years old or younger will receive rations of wheat, protein and vitamin-fortified corn-soy-blend, and vegetable oil during the three driest months of the year. The hope: To build community and local government resources to the point where Save the Children no longer is needed in Liben and Filtu.

As part of Genale Pa, a women's pastoralist association in southern Ethiopia, women dairy farmers work together to make butter. They combine their profits in a savings account to pay for community projects, such as a new water pump.

Ashley Aakesson is a Mickey Leland International Hunger fellow, who worked on the Liben project of Save the Children Federation Inc. from July 2001 to June 2002.

Confront HIV/AIDS Head-on

The magnitude of the HIV/AIDS pandemic in Africa is clearly threatening current and future social and economic development. Already, significant numbers of families and individuals have been affected, either through illnesses or death of loved ones. Unfortunately, the disease is killing the youngest and most energetic people, inflicting immediate loss in productivity. Awareness campaigns about the disease, prevention of new infections and care of the sick need immediate attention.

So far, domestic political responses to the scourge have been far from satisfactory. Governments must acknowledge the seriousness of the threat posed by HIV/AIDS and declare national emergencies, mobilizing every resource needed to reduce its spread. Joint efforts by these governments and the international community, through the Global AIDS Fund, need more support and donations, scaling it up beyond the $2.1 billion, which is only one-fourth of what is needed to wage a credible fight against HIV/AIDS, tuberculosis and malaria.

Foster Good Governance and Peace

Peace and prosperity go together. National governments must establish a conducive legal, governance and institutional structure, as well as national and regional policies that provide incentives for peace, prosperity and development. Governments, nongovernmental organizations and private sectors then can work together to support communities' and farmers' development activities and help disadvantaged groups gain greater access to resources and markets. In addition, by improving transparency and accountability, governments will attract development partners and foreign investment. Promoting peace and democracy through dialogue and the rule of law will lay a stable foundation for social, political and economic development.

Conclusion

African agriculture and rural development face many constraints that must be reduced or removed to effect change and growth, especially in ways that will benefit poor and hungry people. A lot of these changes largely – though not exclusively – depend on work that Africans must do for themselves. Building trust, enacting just policies that benefit the poor, and investing in people, peace and development as a matter of priority are things that African governments and civil societies must do. But they cannot do everything alone. Other governments and development partners must lend support to strengthening African agriculture by increasing development assistance, deepening debt relief, reducing subsidies and opening markets to African trade, especially in agriculture.

Two farmers in Santiago, Cape Verde, grow cassava as part of a farmers' cooperative supported by ACDI/VOCA. Cassava is a staple food crop for many African countries.

Donors should engage with individual African countries' governments and civil societies, as well as regions, to identify specific priorities and development hurdles, and work out long-term, viable plans to transition countries toward self-reliance. Strategic partnerships and processes, such as the PRSP, can be forged in a way that allow local control and broad African participation in planning and implementation.

Long-term political and economic commitment by governments, donor agencies, countries, and regional and international organizations will be necessary to renew growth and development. The AGOA is an example of an initiative that can have important benefits for poor people if expanded to reduce trade barriers to poor peoples' agricultural products.

The promised increase of development assistance through the 2002 Bush-proposed Millennium Challenge Account and similar proposals by European governments, coupled with the commitment of African governments and G-8 countries to pursue the NEPAD vision and strive to fulfill the U.N. Millennium Development Goals – internationally agreed upon humanitarian goals, such as eradicating extreme poverty and hunger – are important steps forward. But to ensure Africa's future economic growth and self-reliance for Africa's poor and hungry people, African countries and the international community must recommit to its development of agricultural trade and rural development.

Daniel D. Karanja, Ph.D., is the international agriculture policy analyst at Bread for the World. **Melody R. Mc Neil** is a Mickey Leland International Hunger fellow at Bread for the World.

CHAPTER 5

Hunger
Hotspots 2003

By Margaret M. Zeigler

some 840 million people worldwide are undernourished, meaning they do not have access to the calories and nutrients they need to lead healthy lives. Poverty and lack of economic self-sufficiency are the primary causes of hunger, but extreme weather, HIV/AIDS and conflict also push vulnerable populations to the brink of survival. Without ways and means to cope with such disasters, hunger hotspots emerge, and these groups must rely on outside emergency assistance to survive.

Although it takes a couple of years to gather official international data, the number of undernourished people in the world likely increased in 2002. Recent progress against hunger has been slow, and the global economic downturn, combined with an upsurge in war-making and natural disasters – especially in parts of Africa – means that the number of people without enough food to eat probably has risen. Yet U.S. and European policymakers focused on the global war on terrorism and the impending war in Iraq, while reacting slowly to looming food emergencies across the globe. Now these crises threaten to overwhelm the humanitarian response system. Hunger hotspots have emerged in Central America, Central and East Asia, and Southern Africa, and only a Herculean effort will prevent millions of men, women and children from dying from famine in 2003.

Southern Africa Crisis

Southern Africa – comprising Lesotho, Malawi, Mozambique, Swaziland, Zambia and Zimbabwe – is the hunger hotspot where the most people are at risk. A total of 14.5 million people will need emergency food aid through April 1, 2003, and the crisis will continue into the year if the spring harvests fail again (see Figure 5.1).

The causes of this unusually severe famine present new challenges to the international humanitarian community. Usually a food-secure region, Southern Africa has had two years of drought in countries with populations made vulnerable by some of the highest HIV/AIDS rates in the world. Government corruption has only worsened this tragedy. In Malawi, corrupt government officials sold a major grain reserve. In Zimbabwe, a land reform program involving the forcible takeover of white-owned commercial farms has weakened investor confidence, disrupted food production and weakened the entire region's economies.

The role of HIV/AIDS in destabilizing populations cannot be underestimated. Millions of farmers cannot plant or harvest their crops because they are too sick to work. Parents are dying from the disease, leaving orphans to be cared for by grandparents. And relief foods packaged to satisfy hungry populations' nutrient and caloric needs are not sufficient for people suffering from HIV/AIDS, who require almost 50 percent more protein and foods

Volunteers in Malawi help distribute 50-pound bags of maize to people who are most vulnerable to the food shortage, such as this single mother.

richer in micronutrients. The food shortage in Southern Africa is the first-ever to hit a region where much of the population already suffers from HIV/AIDS.

Complicating the humanitarian response to the famine is the resistance of Southern African governments to accept food aid containing genetically modified (GM) corn, which is the primary relief food from the United States and other non-E.U. donor nations. Lesotho, Malawi, Mozambique, Swaziland and Zimbabwe are concerned about possible environmental effects of

Figure 5.1: Southern Africa Food Crisis

Populations in need Sept. 1, 2002 to March 31, 2003

Country	Number of Country Population in Need	Percent of Country Population in Need
Zimbabwe	6,700,000	49%
Malawi	3,300,000	29%
Zambia	2,900,000	26%
Lesotho	650,000	30%
Mozambique	590,000	3%
Swaziland	270,000	24%
Total	14,400,000	

Source: U.S. Agency for International Development, Office of U.S. Foreign Disaster Assistance Fact Sheet, Nov. 4, 2002.

The International Humanitarian Food Aid System Saves Lives

During the second half of the 20th century, famines with victims numbering more than several million were rare. The vast majority of famine deaths occurred during two major totalitarian regimes during the 20th century: Close to 15 million people died during Stalin's forced collectivization in the Ukraine and former Soviet Union, and nearly 30 million Chinese died during the communist revolution and Mao's Great Leap Forward in the 1950s. In countries where civil war or genocide were taking place, or where governments prevented humanitarian access, the numbers of famine deaths also were high, such as in Cambodia during the 1974-1979 Pol Pot era, the 1990 civil conflict in Somalia and the current crisis in North Korea.

Enhanced information about impending food shortages coupled with the development of a more sophisticated international emergency food aid response system in the 1980s and 1990s prevented full-blown famine. Farmers in North America and Europe were able to produce higher yields of food; efficient storage and transportation capacities enabled donor nations and humanitarian organizations to move food aid quickly into hunger zones to avoid millions of deaths.

In the 1990s, food donor nations, such as the United States, Canada, Japan and members of the European Union were able to provide significant contributions in either bulk grain or cash donations to the U.N. World Food Program (WFP) and nongovernmental relief agencies, such as Catholic Relief Services, Lutheran World Relief and World Vision.

Mortality in Major Famines: 19th & 20th Centuries

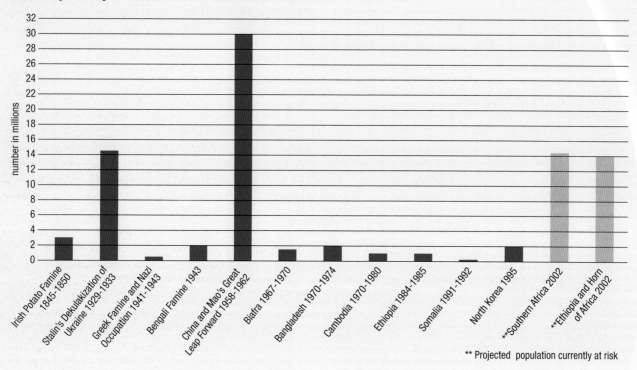

number in millions

Irish Potato Famine 1845-1850 · Stalin's Dekulakization of Ukraine 1929-1933 · Greek Famine and Nazi Occupation 1941-1943 · Bengali Famine 1943 · China and Mao's Great Leap Forward 1958-1962 · Biafra 1967-1970 · Bangladesh 1970-1974 · Cambodia 1970-1980 · Ethiopia 1984-1985 · Somalia 1991-1992 · North Korea 1995 · **Southern Africa 2002 · **Ethiopia and Horn of Africa 2002

** Projected population currently at risk

GM corn. They also are concerned about their future agricultural exports to Europe because some European consumers prefer food from non-GM countries. Some countries are accepting the corn if it is milled before distribution so their farmers cannot plant the GM corn. However, Zambia has refused to accept any GM food, milled or not, citing health concerns for its population and potential contamination of future crops. Meanwhile, the U.S. State Department is campaigning for international acceptance of GM crops and has shown no patience with these concerns.

The milling capacity in this region remains a significant impediment to timely food aid. Most corn was shipped in large ocean vessels months before the November 2002 decisions by the recipient governments to accept only milled corn. The Republic of South Africa is the region's only nation with the capacity to mill the vast quantities required in this crisis. The movement of grain from storage areas in Southern Africa to milling points and then back to countries for distribution presents a logistical nightmare for the humanitarian agencies trying to respond to the impending crisis.

Moreover, violence threatens to erupt over some governments' discriminatory distribution of the milled corn. In Zimbabwe, the government of Robert Mugabe has been accused of preventing distribution in districts that voted for the opposition party in the 2002 presidential election. In Zambia, the government prevented the delivery of food aid to Angolan refugees – who are fully dependent on such aid for survival – living in camps operated by the U.N. High Commission for Refugees.

Donor nations' response to the travesty in Southern Africa has been disheartening. At the end of 2002, the United States – the single largest donor – had donated 45 percent ($275 million in food aid and cash) of the region's request for food and other humanitarian aid ($611 million). If massive deaths are to be avoided in 2003, other donors must move rapidly to fulfill their part in a multilateral effort. Several E.U. nations, such as the United Kingdom and Denmark, have donated cash to purchase food in the region, and Canada has made significant contributions of grain and cash as well. But the gap is still large.

Republic of South Africa, Angola and Namibia

While the Republic of South Africa has avoided the severe hunger threatening its neighbors, it remains mired in poverty, malnutrition and a widespread HIV/AIDS epidemic.

Angola, a country emerging from 27 years of civil war that left nearly 1 million people dead and 4 million

It's Saturday, and school children in Zimbabwe have had nothing to eat for two days.

displaced, has just begun to address its extreme poverty. The February 2002 death of Jonas Savimbi left the National Union for the Total Independence of Angola (UNITA) forces without its charismatic leader, and the government of Angola declared victory. Angola's diamond and oil wealth could be harnessed for development, but progress in reintegrating former combatants and clearing Angola of the millions of landmines has been slow.

In neighboring Namibia, the same drought affecting other Southern African nations has damaged corn and millet crops in the northern Okavango region. In November 2002, reports of the first famine-related deaths in Okavango emerged. Of the country's 2 million people, the famine threatens to claim at least 350,000 lives. Although Namibia will be able to meet most of its emergency needs, it has requested $4 million to purchase emergency food supplies for vulnerable rural populations, such as the elderly, members of female-headed households and children.

West Africa

In 2002 West Africa experienced mixed progress in efforts to develop and reduce military conflict. Mali and Sierra Leone continued to improve their food security, while other countries suffered ongoing conflict.

Côte d'Ivoire normally is a food-secure country, but an attempted coup in September 2002 started a period of volatility. Rebel groups of exiled soldiers, former students and people from the ethnic groups of northern Côte d'Ivoire attempted to topple the government of President Laurent Gbagbo in the capitol city of Yamoussoukro. The rebels successfully sacked three of the largest cities in the North, which has led to a growing humanitarian crisis that may destabilize the entire West African region in 2003. To escape the violence, more than 200,000 Côte d'Ivoire residents have fled on foot to areas further south.

Next door in Liberia, large numbers of people continue to become internally displaced as they flee areas of conflict in their country. Some 200,000 people are receiving emergency food assistance because of Liberia's instability after its decade-long civil war.

Sierra Leone's civil war ended in 2001, and successful national elections were held in 2002. The small country continues to make progress as reconstruction and peace begin to take hold. With more than half its population displaced during the civil war and still suffering from some of the most brutal human rights violations ever, Sierra Leone's economic and psychosocial recovery still has a long way to go. Food aid is centered on maternal nutrition programs and school feeding for children throughout the country.

Diamond Industry Must Help Stop Trade of 'Blood' Diamonds

The illicit trade in diamonds from many West African and Central African countries has contributed to the purchase of arms used by brutal rebel groups in a number of conflicts throughout Africa in the past decade. A campaign launched in 2000 by human rights groups has clarified the role of so-called conflict diamonds. They enable rebels to buy weapons and inflict human rights violations.

The Kimberly Process, an international agreement requiring the diamond industry to regulate its production and marketing of diamonds, will succeed only if the diamond industry provides regulation and oversight of its activities and independent monitoring of compliance. The new system requires any rough diamond to have a certificate of origin in order to be transported, bought or sold within a country that is a signatory to the convention.

Mauritania has suffered greatly from a two-year drought, prompting an emergency operation in 2002 by the U.N. World Food Program to meet the needs of women and children in community feeding centers. World Food Program estimates that 700,000 of the country's 2.5 million people are food insecure. At the end of 2002, this emergency operation remained woefully underfunded.

Central Africa and the Great Lakes Region

The current conflict embroiling the countries of the Great Lakes region of Central Africa was sparked with the 1994 genocide of Rwandan Tutsi. Within months, Hutu extremists killed more than 800,000 Tutsi men, women and children and thousands of moderate Hutu. The international community's failure to halt this violence led to a mass exodus from Rwanda of the moderate Hutu, who moved into neighboring Burundi, Tanzania and Zaire (now known as the Democratic Republic of Congo). The presence of these Rwandan refugees in turn exacerbated long-standing conflicts within the Democratic Republic of Congo, leading to civil war. More than 2 million Congolese since have died from starvation, disease, murder and chronic poverty.

For the past three years, armies from six nations have become involved in the Congo conflict, also dubbed Africa's World War. Meanwhile, Rwanda and Burundi are encumbered in an ongoing conflict between Hutu and Tutsi political and ethnic groups. And Uganda, another one of the Great Lakes nations, has suffered from a 16-year civil conflict between the government of Uganda and a rebel group known as the Lord's Resistance Army (LRA). The LRA, led by a fundamentalist religious leader named Joseph Kony, has struck repeatedly in the country's north, displacing more than 800,000 Ugandans. These internally displaced people have taken refuge in camps where they survive on emergency humanitarian food assistance.

Sudan, Somalia

Several long-running conflicts in Africa showed signs of resolution during 2002. In both Sudan and Somalia, seeds of peace are beginning to take root despite outbreaks of fighting between various rebel forces and government troops. Food security has improved in both countries, and negotiations on long-term peace may prove fruitful in 2003.

In Sudan, a 19-year civil war between northern government troops and southern rebels has claimed nearly 2 million lives and displaced more than 4 million people within the country. In 2002 the rebel leaders of the Sudan People's Liberation Movement participated in peace talks with representatives of the government of Sudan. These talks were facilitated by a number of international mediators, including the U.S.- sponsored envoy to Sudan, former Sen. John Danforth.

In Somalia, signs of war weariness also have emerged. Warlords have wreaked havoc since 1990, and the fighting led to a famine killing 200,000 Somalis. In 2001 and 2002, talks between Somali warlords produced some peace in this fractured nation. Plentiful rain during the past two years also gave Somalia a small surplus in food production for the first time in a decade.

Ethiopia, Eritrea

The newest and perhaps most severe hunger hotspot emerging at the end of 2002 was found in the East African nations of Ethiopia and Eritrea. Historically a food-insecure region, Ethiopia and Eritrea – once a single country ruled by Ethiopian kings – continue to struggle with drought, poverty and a rapidly spreading HIV/AIDS epidemic that is weakening the population and increasing vulnerability to malnutrition and disease. Estimates of populations at risk of famine range between 12 million and 14 million people. A war between Eritrea and Ethiopia from 1998 to 2000 resulted in hundreds of thousands of deaths of men who were traditional pastoralists and farmers, leaving many widows struggling to raise families and grow food. A continuing drought that began in 2000 has destroyed two successive harvests. Moreover, tensions over scarce water resources have sparked violence between ethnic Afar and Isaa tribes in Ethiopia's Afar region.

To further complicate matters, the U.S. wheat harvest in 2002 was lower than normal because of a drought in the Midwest. Corn, sorghum and wheat are needed in

Figure 5.2: Central Asia Hunger Statistics, 2002

Country	Population	Number of Malnourished	Percent Malnourished	Number of Population Dependent on Emergency Feeding
Afghanistan	27,755,775	19,429,043	70%	7,000,000
Kazakhstan	16,731,519	1,338,522	8%	n/a
Kyrgyzstan	4,822,166	385,773	8%	n/a
Tajikistan	6,719,567	4,300,523	64%	734,000
Turkmenistan	4,688,963	375,117	8%	n/a
Uzbekistan	25,563,441	4,857,054	19%	n/a

Sources: CIA World Fact Book 2002; ReliefWeb; State of Food Insecurity 2002

Ethiopia and Eritrea, but the costs of food relief will be higher because of the lower supply.

The simultaneous food crises in Southern Africa and the Horn of Africa will challenge the logistical capacity of aid agencies to administer and distribute food aid. This hunger hotspot could become a crisis in 2003. Massive quantities of food aid must be mobilized immediately to avert millions of deaths.

Afghanistan and Central Asia

Since the terrorist attacks of Sept. 11, 2001, the U.S. military campaign in Afghanistan has received almost daily media coverage. Ameliorating the devastation in Afghanistan has become a higher priority for donor nations and many humanitarian relief agencies. The United States is the prime contributor to reconstruction in Afghanistan, where it has been joined by E.U. nations and Japan. The humanitarian community has worked hard to alleviate hardships faced by the Afghani people, whose condition stems from decades of discord and oppression, including the 1970s Soviet invasion, suppression by the Taliban, ongoing regional conflict between warlords and a recent severe four-year drought.

In 2002 donors supplied food, blankets, medical supplies, personnel and funds for reconstruction and development, but much aid remains in the capital city of Kabul, and sporadic distribution of aid and ongoing security concerns hamper reconstruction of outlying regions. The harsh winter of 2003 will make the situation worse as food insecurity and lack of employment opportunities leave 70 percent of Afghanistan's 25 million people malnourished (see Figure 5.2). Despite Afghanistan's high political profile, development assistance falls far short of the need.

Some former Soviet Union republics have experienced fates similar to Afghanistan's. The 1991 collapse of the Soviet Union gave birth to new sovereign republics in Central Asia. However, these new nations – Kyrgyztan, Tajikistan, Turkmenistan and Uzbekistan – have received little development assistance, either from their former parent state, Russia, or other developed areas like the European Union and United States. This neglect has allowed warlords, fundamentalist groups and dictators to dominate. Consequently, these nations-in-infancy now suffer from severe poverty and hunger. They also lack roads and other infrastructure, and have no agricultural programs or health care.

In Tajikistan, the poorest of the former Soviet republics, two-thirds of the population lives below the poverty level. This situation is worsened by landslides that kill many villagers, leave many others homeless and ravage productive soil. Accessibility to rural villages is difficult because of the mountainous terrain and lack of government funds for basic services. Children often suffer the most in this region; 46 percent of children younger than 5 experience chronic malnutrition.

North Africa, Middle East and Iraq

With attention focused during the second half of 2002 on the potential war in Iraq, the mainstream media paid less attention to the declining nutritional status of the Palestinian people. In August 2002, U.N. Secretary General Kofi Annan sent special envoy Catherine Bertini, an American and former head of the World Food Program, to Palestine to investigate the growing humanitarian crisis. Bertini documented the dire impact that the Israeli-Palestinian conflict has had on the population's nutrition and drew attention to vulnerable Palestinians' lack of access to humanitarian aid.

The U.S. Agency for International Development-funded nutritional survey found severe and moderate rates of malnutrition in children younger than 5 in Gaza Strip and West Bank (13.3 percent and 4.3 percent, respectively). Children in Palestine also suffer from anemia, decreased immunity from diseases and psychosocial trauma. The study pointed to a "distinct humanitarian emergency in regards to acute, moderate and severe malnutrition."

The World Food Program and International Committee of the Red Cross are providing food and vitamin supplementation for nearly 1.5 million Palestinian women and children, but economic development that would allow Palestinians to buy the food they need cannot begin without peace and security. Israel's restriction of access to and from Palestinian territories severely curtails both humanitarian and economic development assistance.

Since 1991, people in Iraq have suffered from the comprehensive sanctions imposed by the U.N. Security Council at the behest of the United States. The sanctions have contributed to a breakdown of public services, particularly water purification, preventive medicine, sanitation, electricity, transportation and supply of nutrition to children. Since the sanctions began, an estimated 500,000 Iraqi children younger than 5 have died, primarily as a result of diseases attributed to poor water quality. The Iraqi water purification system has collapsed because chlorine and other sanctioned items needed for the maintenance of pipe systems are in short supply. The sanctions have brought not only great suffering to the poorest Iraqis, but also have enriched Saddam Hussein and his inner circle, providing them with the opportunity to earn more than $2 billion dollars annually in illegal oil sales through Syria.[1]

Europe, Russia, Balkans, Caucasus

Europe includes the countries of the European Union, plus the Independent States of the Caucasus, Russia, Turkey and Ukraine. Despite the region's abundance of food and relatively high average incomes, it includes several hunger hotspots.

One of the largest pockets of poverty and hunger is in the former Soviet state of Georgia. Its population of 5 million hosts some 300,000 internally displaced people and refugees, mostly from nearby Armenia, Azerbaijan and Chechnya.

In Russia, the Caucasus region encompassing Chechnya and Ingushetia is a significant hunger hotspot. A century of conflict between Moscow and the independence movement in Chechnya has resulted in a civil war. In October 2002, Chechen rebels took over a theater in

Marty Lueders

Despite the European Union's overall wealth and abundance of food, several countries struggle with severe poverty and food insecurity.

Moscow and held some 700 people hostage for three days.[2] Russia has brutally cracked down on this breakaway region, and the capital of Grozny has been all but leveled. One-third of the 785,000 people living in Chechnya are desperate for food, shelter protection and security. The Russian army has occupied Chechnya for the past seven years, and political leaders on both sides are stalemated over the issue of Chechen independence.

Asia

Home to most of the world's chronically undernourished people, Asian countries have made some progress in the past decade in reducing hunger. China has made great strides against hunger since 1990. The number of undernourished people has declined by 74 million. During the past decade, the populations of Indonesia, South Korea, Taiwan, Thailand and Vietnam also have increased their earning's ability, enabling many people to move out of the ranks of the hungry poor.

In India and Pakistan, tensions have flared over the status of Kashmir, a disputed territory now within the borders of India. The countries, both of which possess and have threatened to use nuclear weapons, moved to the brink of war in 2002. India and Pakistan both contain millions of poor and hungry people. Humanitarian programs are difficult to implement in Pakistan because of anger toward the West resulting from its support of Israel and the war in Afghanistan. In India, hunger and poverty have diminished in the south, but persist in urban areas where destitute rural peasants come seeking food and work. Tribal areas in the northeast also remain hunger zones. Despite these regional challenges, the Indian government is making hunger reduction a higher priority.

A 19-year civil war in Sri Lanka ended in September 2002. With 64,000 people dead and more than 800,000 internally displaced, Sri Lanka requires significant food aid and reconstruction investment.

Asia's most dire hunger hotspot remains the Democratic People's Republic of Korea, which first appealed openly to the international community for emergency humanitarian food aid in 1995. Since then, the World Food Program and a small number of non-governmental organizations have been the conduit for food aid from the United States, European Union and Japan. They assist almost a third of the country's 23 million people. In 2002 Japan and the European Union reduced their support, so fewer North Koreans are getting food assistance. Lack of access and freedom of movement in North Korea for humanitarian agencies hamper their ability to supply and monitor the food aid they deliver. Larger political issues, such as tension over the North Korean government's possession of nuclear weapons, create a volatile situation in which millions of lives hang in the balance.

Central America and the Caribbean

In the Western Hemisphere, 2002 saw hunger hotspots flare in Central America and the Caribbean. Most of Central America suffered from a food crisis produced by a deadly combination of drought and a decline in worldwide coffee prices that had a deleterious impact on the coffee-exporting farmers of the region. According to the World Bank, some 600,000 coffee labor jobs have been lost in the past two years in Central America. Reduced income is contributing as much to food insecu-

Haiti remains the most intense hunger hotspot in the Western Hemisphere.

rity as the drought. Media focus on the war against terror and the impending war in Iraq has kept most people in the United States from learning about the severe food shortages among neighboring countries.

Two hurricanes in September and October 2002 battered western Cuba, forcing more than 600,000 people from their homes. While the United States provides some humanitarian relief to Cuba during natural disasters, it has maintained a trade embargo since the 1960s because it opposes President Fidel Castro's policies.

Haiti remains the most intense hunger hotspot in the Western Hemisphere. Ninety-five percent of the 9 million Haitians are desperately poor, and their plight has not improved in the decade since they were liberated from military dictatorship. Most Haitians (70 percent)

work in agriculture, and the prices and export sales of Haiti's main crops, such as coffee, sisal and cocoa, have plunged. Soil degradation also constrains agricultural production.

South America

When the U.S. economy is strong, South America's economies prosper from an increased demand for their exports. But the past two years have seen slow U.S. growth, and South America has seen exports decline. Low prices for commodities, such as sugar, coffee, cocoa and copper, have contributed to low incomes and job loss in the region. About one-third of the people in South America earn less than $2 per day.

The hunger hotspots in South America are in northeast Brazil, mountainous regions of Bolivia and Peru, and war-torn Colombia, and among indigenous populations scattered throughout the continent. In 2002 hunger also emerged in the relatively developed country of Argentina. Fiscal mismanagement, corruption and the near total collapse of the economy in December 2001 triggered increased food insecurity.

A 40-year war in Colombia has displaced more than 2 million people, causing mass migration to urban areas. Colombia is the main exporter of coca consumed as cocaine in the United States and Europe, but conflict over whether the United States should help control its production has intensified. The 2002 election of President Alvaro Uribe Perez promises to escalate the conflict further, as the United States increases its role in assisting government forces to destroy coca crops and fight the Revolutionary Armed Forces of Colombia. Aerial spraying of crops increased in 2002, not only killing vast numbers of coca plants, but also poisoning the soil and surface water, thereby posing a major health risk to children. Poor farmers plant coca because it provides the highest return for them as they strive to feed their families. Crop substitution programs are not in place, and most of the affected farmers are without income for the coming year and will experience hunger in 2003.

Indigenous peoples are scattered in rural villages and mountainous zones throughout South America. Providing them with land rights, agricultural assistance, and basic health and education services could reduce their high rates of hunger and disease.

Brazil elected Luiz Inacio da Silva as president in October 2002. He is promising to reduce hunger in the country. Brazil is characterized by a wide gap between income groups. In the poor northeast region of Brazil, some 12 million people face hunger.

Dr. Margaret M. Zeigler is deputy director of the Congressional Hunger Center in Washington, D.C.

CHAPTER 6

Improving Agriculture
for Poor, Hungry People

By James L. McDonald

he agricultural system today is not sustainable. It hurts small farmers and rural communities in developing countries and fails to adequately deal with hunger and increasing poverty in rural America. Instead of helping U.S. farmers, current agricultural protections appear to speed the process of farm consolidation at a high cost to taxpayers and poor people around the world.

Changing the global agriculture system will not be easy, but it is achievable. It will require the efforts of governments and civil societies in developed and developing countries, international financial institutions, and concerned men and women, regardless of whether they live in cities or rural areas.

Clearly, if long-term development is to succeed in developing countries and poor people are to win the fight against hunger, agricultural reform must occur. *Hunger 2003* shows that making the agricultural trading system more equitable is in the interest of everyone, rich and poor.

Improving Agriculture: Difficult, Complex

Rural areas are home to three-fourths of the world's poor people, most of whom rely primarily on agricultural activities for their incomes. Despite their involvement in farming, the rural poor also are the people most likely to go hungry. In China, rural villagers consume half as much food as their urban counterparts.[1]

This condition occurs because agriculture is not being supported and developed in many poor countries. As demonstrated in Chapter 1, agricultural growth almost always benefits poor people. Therefore, if progress against hunger and poverty is to be made, countries must commit to strengthening their agricultural productivity and building national – and potentially international – agricultural trade.

However, improving agriculture is difficult and complex. Even if a farmer has access to fertile soil and enough water and other inputs, such as seeds and fertilizer, to produce a high quality crop, she still needs access to transportation and a market where she will receive a price that allows her to cover her costs or even make a profit. This simple scenario does not mention myriad other obstacles facing farmers as they try to tap into the global economy.

The Project for Integrated Rural Development of the Northern Region of Nicaragua, which was sponsored by the International Fund for Agricultural Development between 1982 and 1992, named no less than nine factors needed to improve the lives of the 6,000 small-farmer families in the region: agricultural extension, training, agricultural credit, research, marketing services and construction of roads, sewers, schools and health centers.[2]

Marty Lueders

Even if a farmer has access to fertile soil, enough water, seeds and fertilizer, she still needs access to transportation and a market if she is to support herself and her family.

What Do Developing Country Farmers Need?

When pondering what developing country farmers need, one almost has to ask, Where to begin? For one thing, farmers need tools to increase their productivity, such as access to information and technology. For another, farmers need markets at which to sell their produce and labor so they can accommodate the cash they need for their households and reinvest in agriculture. They need to produce both food to consume and food to sell.[3]

Although most poor small farmers do not participate in international markets, other people and companies in their countries usually do. Because of this, the negative effects of industrialized country commodity dumping and market protections trickle down and cost small farmers food security. Take the Malian farmers Baro, Modibo and Nyemey from the Introduction. Because depressed cotton prices leave Modibo with too little money to buy Nyemey's peanuts, Nyemey has no cash to buy the food his family needs to make it through the rainy season and the next harvest.

Ultimately for small farmers to succeed, developed country agricultural protection must be curtailed. Industrialized countries already have agreed to phase out protective measures; now they must follow through on their promises.

To take advantage of a fairer agricultural trading system, small farmers must have access to their local and national markets. To do this, they need to tap a variety of resources, some of the most important of which are communication networks, grain and seed storage facilities, credit, and property rights. Appropriate research and technology also must be pursued and supported to enhance agricultural productivity, especially in sub-Saharan Africa. The availability of these agricultural necessities will play a large role in determining whether small farmers become self-reliant (see Figure 6.1).

What Must Be Done for These Changes to Occur?

Small farmers, rural communities and developing country governments must do their part and commit to sustainable agricultural development, but to succeed they will need help, especially from industrialized countries. For developing country governments to support agriculture and rural poor people in their countries, they need increased poverty-focused development assistance and for international lending institutions to place a higher priority on agricultural investment. They also need greater and fairer participation in the international trading system and for industrialized countries to remove unfair trade barriers to agricultural products.

More Development Assistance

Most reforms require investment, and most developing country budgets already are strained. Therefore, bilateral and multilateral financial aid can play an important role in development strategies (see Table 6.1).

U.S. development assistance contributed significantly to the Green Revolution in East and South Asia and to other agricultural advances. It also has helped build roads in rural areas so that poor small farmers can get their products to market. It aids in providing the knowledge and skills poor farmers need to improve productivity and understand the market for their products. For example, the Cooperative League of the U.S.A. (CLUSA) uses U.S. Agency for International Development money to improve the "functional" literacy of small farmers in northern Mozambique. By helping farmers organize into cooperatives, farmers can pool their resources and share risks. Before CLUSA came along, small farmers were nervous about trying new things and reluctant to work with each other because no system ensured that all farmers would benefit equally.

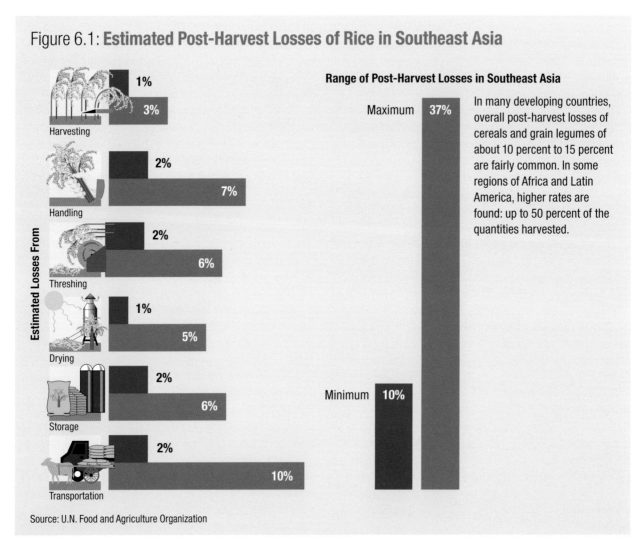

Figure 6.1: Estimated Post-Harvest Losses of Rice in Southeast Asia

Estimated Losses From

Harvesting — 1%, 3%
Handling — 2%, 7%
Threshing — 2%, 6%
Drying — 1%, 5%
Storage — 2%, 6%
Transportation — 2%, 10%

Range of Post-Harvest Losses in Southeast Asia

Maximum 37%

Minimum 10%

In many developing countries, overall post-harvest losses of cereals and grain legumes of about 10 percent to 15 percent are fairly common. In some regions of Africa and Latin America, higher rates are found: up to 50 percent of the quantities harvested.

Source: U.N. Food and Agriculture Organization

Table 6.1: U.S. Discretionary Spending on Foreign Economic Aid

U.S. foreign assistance amounts continue to decline both as a share of the U.S. budget and the economy, reaching some of the lowest levels since World War II.

	1980s Average	2003 under Administration's Budget	Comment on 2003 Figures
As a share of the budget	0.92%	0.55%	Tied for post-World War II low
As a share of the economy	0.20%	0.11%	Second lowest in post-World War II era
Inflation-adjusted level (in 2003 dollars)	$13.6 billion	$11.6 billion	Significantly below historical average

Source: Center on Budget and Policy Priorities

Improve International Monetary Fund, World Bank

Another crucial step in boosting agricultural development in poor countries is to improve international institutions, notably the International Monetary Fund (IMF) and the World Bank. The IMF and World Bank often have come under fire, but in recent years they have become more focused on poverty reduction and supportive of democratic participation in programs.

In 1999, responding to international pressure from nongovernmental organizations (NGOs) and others in the Jubilee Debt Campaign, the World Bank devised the Poverty Reduction Strategy process, which requires governments that receive its funds to draw up a comprehensive strategy to address poverty. While the process is far from perfect, it encourages strong citizen input and government accountability. Even more needs to be done to increase broad citizen participation in the development of Poverty Reduction Strategy Papers.

The World Bank also should put more emphasis on agriculture. World Bank lending for agriculture declined from $3.6 billion to $1.3 billion during the 1990s, dropping to only 9 percent of total lending.[4] This decline happened in part because of implementation difficulties in many agricultural and rural development projects, and partly because low commodity prices have made agricultural development less attractive economically. But given agriculture's importance to poverty reduction, a renewal of World Bank lending in this sector would make sense.

The IMF and World Bank also should be careful about insisting on deep, fast liberalization as a condition for financial assistance. In some cases, they have pushed for liberalization at a pace that proved damaging. In other cases, they extracted concessions that developing countries could have used in trade negotiations with industrialized countries. These practices should change.

Fairer Trade Rules

Although important, aid is only one part of the solution. Increased aid must be accompanied by reforms that allow developing countries to compete in export markets. Without market access, developing countries soon hit a ceiling beyond which they cannot grow.

Trade rules also must change if trade is to benefit poor countries (see Figure 6.2). Developed countries cannot be allowed to protect domestic producers while pushing liberalization abroad. Key changes include reducing tariffs on agricultural products, ending tariff escalation and tariff peaks, and eliminating both production-linked domestic and export subsidies.

Just as poor people face limited choices and lack of control over the forces that have a global impact on their

Although significant gains are being made in civic participation and democratization in many African countries, more needs to be done to ensure that poor people's voices are heard.

lives, poor countries are constrained in their ability to choose freely and negotiate on equal terms in the global trading system. Their lack of resources renders them nearly powerless. This reality must be recognized, addressed and corrected if trade is to become a tool that truly promotes development.

Reform WTO Rules

The place to begin correcting the inequalities of the trading system is with the WTO. Its rules govern 97 percent of world trade and greatly impact how the global food economy performs.

International trade rules should be true to the charter of the WTO and relevant for development. However, because the WTO is a member-driven forum with only a small secretariat, by itself, it can accomplish little. Any recommendations for WTO actions should be applied to member governments as well.

Essentially, developing countries need to use the WTO's rules-based system to protect their interests in the face of economic and political disparities. Initiatives like the Advisory Center on WTO law – an independent

organization established in 2001 to provide legal counseling services at reduced cost for "disadvantaged members of the multilateral trading system" that wish to bring cases before the dispute settlement board – need to be supported and expanded. Also, creative ways to increase the enforceability of rulings under the dispute settlement mechanism need to be found.

Better Acknowledge Differences

In addition, the WTO needs a better way to classify countries according to their measurable development, trade, food security and poverty. Although Kenya is among the most food insecure countries in the world, it is not classified as a least developed country and, therefore, is not eligible for related trade concessions under special and differential treatment. Qualifying for this special treatment exempts a developing country from certain requirements, such as reducing tariffs. This exemption could save a poor country the money it needs to pay for a school lunch program.

Bolivia, one of the poorest countries in the world, is classified as neither least developed nor net food import-

Figure 6.2: Industrialized Countries Move Slowly Toward Open Agricultural Markets

Industrialized countries are making some – albeit slow – progress in removing barriers to agricultural trade, but more needs to be done so that developing countries can compete on equal footing.

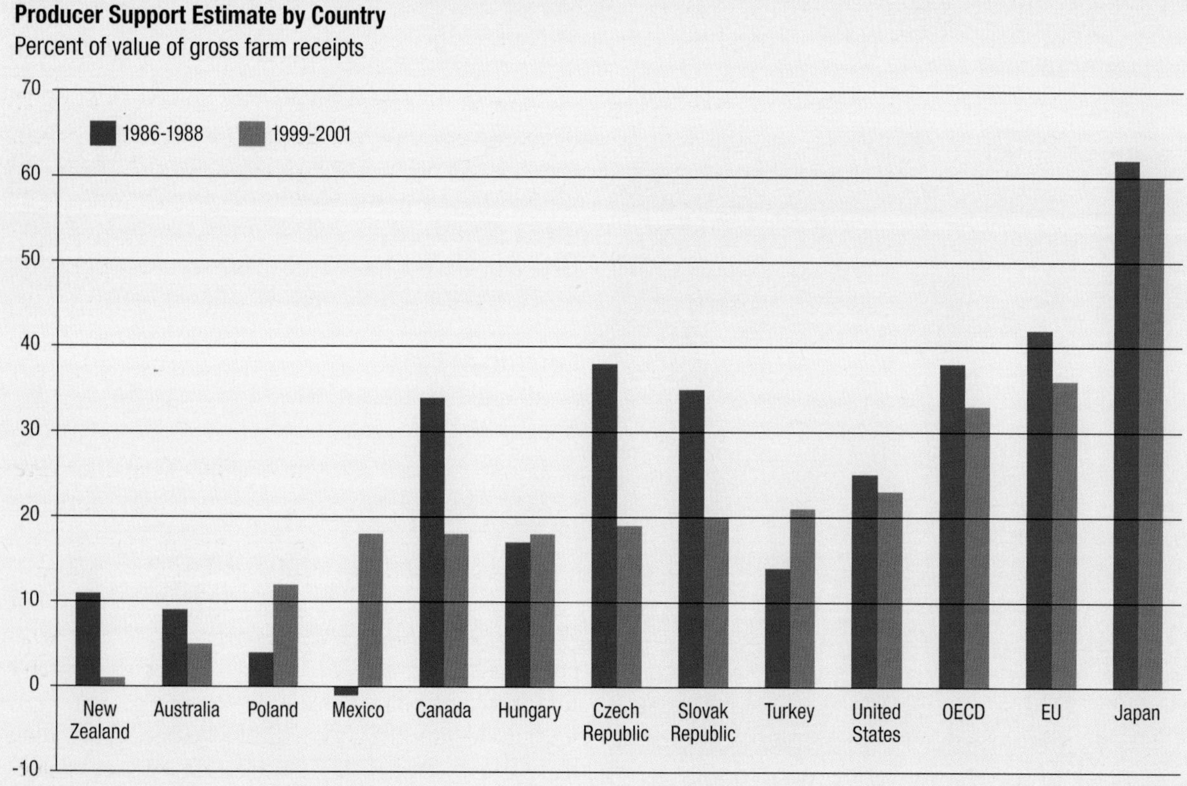

Producer Support Estimate by Country
Percent of value of gross farm receipts

Source: Agricultural Policies in OECD Countries, 2002.

ing. Consequently, it is neither exempt from certain agreements nor is it eligible to receive special assistance under the Marrakech Agreement, which pledges to remedy agricultural liberalization's negative effects on vulnerable countries. An International Food Policy Research Institute (IFPRI) analysis of food security data for 167 countries concludes, "There is a need for a better definition of food insecure countries, based on objective quantitative indicators."[5] Otherwise the special dispensations given poor countries to protect food security will not be effective.

As structured, WTO's exemption process, special and differential treatment, allows poorer countries more time to implement reforms or less-burdensome reform goals. No consideration is given to the fact that, without comprehensive development reform, many developing countries may not be able to satisfy reform requirements even 10 years down the road. Rather, agreements should be implemented based on so-called graduation criteria – measurable benchmarks – that gauge a country's ability to implement specific changes.

By establishing a means to better recognize and deal with social and economic differences among nations, countries can begin to address the trading inequities that result from power imbalances.

Strengthen Developing Countries' Negotiating Power

Developing countries also must gain negotiation expertise if they are to function effectively in the global trading system and participate actively in the formation of its rules.

First, developing country governments should make effective participation a priority, strengthening institutions and committing resources to the training and support of national trade officials. They could help defray some of these costs by forming agreements with other similarly interested countries so they can negotiate as a bloc.

Toward that end, the WTO and other organizations should sponsor training sessions targeted at trade officials from developing countries. These sessions should cover negotiation strategies as well as subject areas. The WTO and others should draw from the example of the Food and Agriculture Organization of the United Nations (FAO), which sponsors a technical assistance and education program to ensure that "developing countries are fully informed and equal partners in the current round of WTO multilateral trade negotiations."[6] In 1999 the FAO also launched the Umbrella Training Program on Uruguay Round Follow-up, a long-term resource for developing countries. WTO Director General Supachai Panitchpakdi – the first director general from a developing country (Thailand) – stresses the importance of these activities: "Enhanced technical assistance and capacity

The WTO needs a better way for recognizing and dealing with social and economic differences among nations so that countries can begin to address trading inequities that result from power imbalances.

building are essential if developing countries are to participate more fully in the multilateral trading system."[7]

The Doha Declaration, a document resulting from the agenda-setting meeting that launched the current round of WTO trade negotiations, mentions "technical cooperation and capacity building" eight times, including a specific section dedicated to the topic. These proposals must be backed up with concrete commitments, and capacity-building assistance must be explicit in the new agreement on agriculture.

Some allowances are being made. In December 2001, member nations pledged $20.2 million to a new Global Trust Fund to provide technical assistance to developing nations. Similarly, the World Bank and WTO in 2002 announced the establishment of a Standards and Trade Development Facility, a fund to help developing countries implement food-safety standards. However, more money is needed. Industrialized country members should help to finance such technical assistance.

Remove Trade Barriers

One of the largest steps in making global trade fairer for developing countries would be for industrialized countries to reduce their agricultural trade barriers. Simply adhering to promises made by industrialized countries at Doha and the March 2002 U.N. Summit on Financing for Development in Monterrey, Mexico, to pursue agricultural trade reform and support agricultural development in developing countries would improve today's global agricultural system tremendously and enhance the lives and food security of poor people worldwide.

But for this to happen, the United States, European Union and Japan must reform their agricultural systems and abandon trade-distorting policies, curtailing the massive subsidies offered to some of their farmers, and reducing tariff barriers to developing country products.

The IMF estimates that if all countries – developed and developing – moved toward agricultural reform, the world would gain $128 billion, with about three-fourths of that gain going to developed countries and a fourth benefiting developing countries.[8] This sum does not include other so-called dynamic gains that probably would result, such as countries' adopting new technologies, increasing investment and/or improving productivity – gains that could double or triple the $128 billion.

Although most countries and people stand to gain from increased agriculture liberalization, gains will be larger for some than others, and a handful of countries actually may lose.

The winners:

Among Industrialized Countries

- major agricultural producers like Australia, Canada and New Zealand, because they would receive higher prices and greater access to overseas markets;

- countries with higher agricultural protections that greatly alter food prices, such as members of the European Union, Japan, Korea, Norway and Switzerland, because domestic food prices probably would fall and consumers would pay lower prices; and

- the United States, although its gains would be more modest because its agricultural exports are not especially large as a portion of its economy and the prices paid by consumers are not as distorted by subsidies as in Europe and Japan.

Figure 6.3: More Than 1 in 4 Nations Classified As Low-Income Food-Deficit Countries

More than one in four nations worldwide are defined as low-income food-deficit countries, with more than half found in Africa. These countries are home to the vast majority of the world's 800 million chronically undernourished people in developing countries.

Many low-income food-deficit countries, particularly in Africa, do not grow enough food to meet their needs and lack sufficient foreign exchange to fill the gap by purchasing food on the global market.

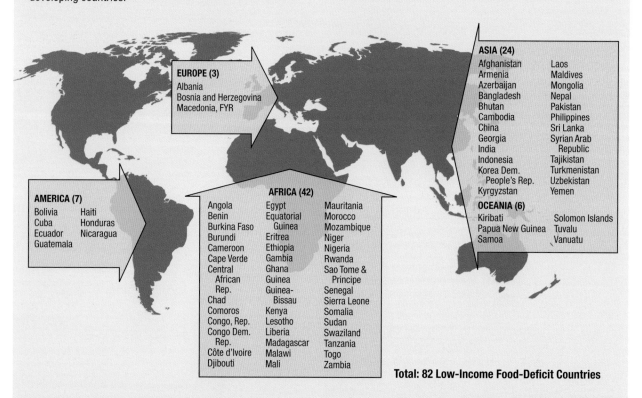

ASIA (24)

Afghanistan	Laos
Armenia	Maldives
Azerbaijan	Mongolia
Bangladesh	Nepal
Bhutan	Pakistan
Cambodia	Philippines
China	Sri Lanka
Georgia	Syrian Arab
India	Republic
Indonesia	Tajikistan
Korea Dem.	Turkmenistan
People's Rep.	Uzbekistan
Kyrgyzstan	Yemen

OCEANIA (6)

Kiribati	Solomon Islands
Papua New Guinea	Tuvalu
Samoa	Vanuatu

EUROPE (3)

Albania
Bosnia and Herzegovina
Macedonia, FYR

AMERICA (7)

Bolivia	Haiti
Cuba	Honduras
Ecuador	Nicaragua
Guatemala	

AFRICA (42)

Angola	Egypt	Mauritania
Benin	Equatorial	Morocco
Burkina Faso	Guinea	Mozambique
Burundi	Eritrea	Niger
Cameroon	Ethiopia	Nigeria
Cape Verde	Gambia	Rwanda
Central	Ghana	Sao Tome &
African	Guinea	Principe
Rep.	Guinea-	Senegal
Chad	Bissau	Sierra Leone
Comoros	Kenya	Somalia
Congo, Rep.	Lesotho	Sudan
Congo Dem.	Liberia	Swaziland
Rep.	Madagascar	Tanzania
Côte d'Ivoire	Malawi	Togo
Djibouti	Mali	Zambia

Total: 82 Low-Income Food-Deficit Countries

Source: U.S. Agency for International Development

Among Developing Countries

- major exporting regions, such as Latin America and sub-Saharan Africa because of tariff removals and higher world prices; and

- most other developing countries, although to a lesser degree.

Potential Losers

- large net food importers, such as North Africa, the Middle East and small island states, because of the potential increase in world food prices.

The losses would be small as compared to the gains agricultural liberalization would achieve, so winners could afford to compensate the losers. Agricultural liberalization should be accompanied by targeted aid to food-deficit countries, especially those that are low-income, as envisioned in the Marrakech Agreement (see Figure 6.3). Industrialized country governments presumably would phase out commodity subsidies gradually and, to some extent, replace them with other forms of assistance to rural areas.

Move to Action

Knowing the tools and actions needed to improve the lives of poor and hungry rural people is a first step, but not enough to ensure that these changes will happen. Governments, public and private institutions, and – most important – everyday people need to push for the necessary change.

One of the benefits of an increasingly integrated international society is that the world's players perform on a global stage. Governments, transnational corporations and civil society organizations all play their parts in international policy debates.

Global society also helps expose government corruption and injustice, while supporting good governance and efforts to encourage democracy. The international press tells the world about abuses, and civil society groups can share their insights with colleague groups in other countries via the Internet. The presence of foreign observers has become almost routine during elections in countries with nascent or weak democracies.

Good governance, which includes the rule of law, transparency, lack of corruption, conflict prevention and resolution, sound public administration, and respect and protection for human rights, is crucial to economic development, including agricultural development. And development is more likely to serve the needs of poor and marginalized people if they have a chance to participate in decision-making processes. Even in countries committed to improving agriculture, progress often is slow, delayed or manipulated by the power of vested interests.[9]

Therefore, the political empowerment of rural populations is an important aspect of agricultural and rural development.

Civil, Public Organizations

NGOs serve a crucial role in the society of developing countries by encouraging democracy and the participation of everyday people in development processes (see related story, p. 106). When facilitating greater participation in decision making or demanding greater accountability from governments and private sectors, NGOs serve their communities well. For example, World Vision has spent the past few years in Bangladesh working closely with local authorities, medical professionals, teachers, students, truck drivers, dock laborers, ship crews, rickshaw pullers and housewives to build awareness of HIV/AIDS. Although only 188 AIDS cases have been detected in Bangladesh so far, a UNAIDS/WHO estimate shows some 13,000 people are living with HIV.

Moreover, because Bangladesh is located near heavily infected neighbors – 40 million people in India, 75,000 in Pakistan, 34,000 in Nepal, and 8,500 in Sri Lanka have HIV – many experts believe Bangladesh is an HIV "time bomb" waiting to explode. In addition to creating awareness of the disease among Bangladeshis, World Vision works with local groups to provide counseling, medical assistance and education on safe-sex and condom use among the most vulnerable communities and high-risk groups. These efforts are proving successful in containing an HIV/AIDS outbreak in an especially vulnerable country.

Civil society also plays an important education role, which includes expanding research on the role of agribusiness and disseminating information on the activities of multinational corporations. For example, the U.S.-based Environmental Working Group maintained a database of farmers and landowners who received U.S. farm subsidies in 2001. Using this database, the group noted that the largest subsidy recipients are not smaller farmers but larger businesses, such as California-based Chevron Corp.,[10] which received more than $200,000 in farm subsidies per year from 1996 to 2000. Such information helped shape the public discussion on the 2002 farm bill.

One of the most promising changes in recent years has been that NGOs are becoming more strategic. The past 10 years have seen many organizations engage with governments and other institutions in new ways. In the United States, the umbrella organization InterAction, which includes humanitarian assistance, international development, and refugee and resettlement groups, campaigns to increase U.S. spending for international relief and development.

Agricultural Disaster Recovery Receives Boost from Seed Vouchers and Fairs

By Alisha Myers

Farmers near and far were attracted to the first seed voucher and fair in the southern Sudan town of Nimule. Some farmers traveled more than 20 miles on foot or bicycle under the hot sun. All were carrying an array of seed and root crops. They came out of curiosity; earning cash for seed was an opportunity not to be missed. It also was the first time they had heard the term "seed voucher and fair."

Catholic Relief Services (CRS) piloted the idea of a seed voucher and fair in southern Sudan in 2001-2002 as an alternative to the customary practice of distributing seeds and tools to farmers following emergency situations. In Sudan, a country ravaged by civil war for more than 20 years, farming communities are at risk of losing their crops both from displacement and drought. Studies and assessments have shown, however, that traditional seed systems in southern Sudan are both resilient and robust. Seed is an asset, the livelihood base for farmers, and as such farmers go to great measures to protect and preserve seed for the next planting season. The seed-voucher-and-fair methodology builds on the farmer seed system by recognizing that in most cases seeds are available in a community after an emergency.

The seed fair essentially is an agricultural market, organized on a specific day and at a specific location, where vulnerable households receive vouchers worth a specific cash value to purchase seed from registered farmers in the community. The seed-voucher-and-fair approach addresses seed unavailability following disasters, including when:

- Farmers have lost their crops as a result of conflict or natural disaster;
- Farmers are displaced during a conflict and not able to harvest their crops;
- An emergency-related disruption has interfered with planting;
- Seed stocks or food are stolen during a rebel attack; or
- Internally displaced persons or refugees are being resettled.

Among the many benefits of the seed-voucher-and-fair approach is that it promotes beneficiary and community cooperation, planning and implementation, and enables vulnerable farmers to access seeds that are locally available as well as meet their immediate needs.

Customary distribution of seeds and tools to farmers following a disaster, particularly displaced farmers, does not account for factors such as what seed might be locally available (in the case of southern Sudan, seeds usually are secured from a neighboring

These farmers gathered for the first seed fair in the southern Sudan town of Nimule.

Catholic Relief Services

The following steps are guidelines to implement a seed and voucher fair:

1. Assess the need	• Identify region/location of the disaster • Target beneficiaries • Assess the availability of seed
2. Plan	• Be sensitive to cultural issues • Encourage community participation • Prepare for implementation
3. Implement	• Register seed sellers • Distribute vouchers • Implement seed exchange, evaluation • Pay seed sellers
4. Evaluate	• During the seed voucher and fair • After the seed voucher and fair • Use qualitative and quantitative analysis • Monitor post seed voucher and fair outcomes

Reference: Tom Remington, Stephen Walsh, Edward Charles, Jeremiah Maroko, and Paul Omanga "Getting off the Seeds-and-Tools Treadmill with CRS Seed Vouchers and Fairs," *Disasters Journal*, 26.4 (2002): 316-328.

The seed fair encourages farmers in Sudan to use traditional seeds, which often are more resilient and robust than seeds from other countries.

country); a beneficiaries' knowledge about seeds and tools in that area; and/or the quantities and varieties of seed required by a farmer. The seed-voucher-and-fair methodology is an important innovation in expediting agricultural recovery for farming communities because:

- Seed vouchers and fairs empower disaster-affected communities to plant crops/varieties in the quantities of their choice;

- Farmers determine the quality of the seed they select;

- Seed vouchers and fairs are transparent and provide a more equitable distribution of resources;

- Communities are actively involved in the planning and implementation;

- Farmers are educated about alternative seed varieties and sources; and

- Seed vouchers and fairs promote linkages and knowledge-sharing among farmers.

To date, Catholic Relief Services has implemented seed vouchers and fairs in Burundi, Sierra Leone, Sudan, Tanzania and Uganda.

Alisha Myers is a Mickey Leland International Hunger fellow, who worked on the seed voucher and fair project with Catholic Relief Services.

Corporations' Role in Agricultural Development

The increasing integration of national economies has created opportunities, generated dilemmas and provoked controversy about the role of multinational corporations in development generally, and in agriculture particularly. The power of the corporate world's wealth, reach and capacity to enact change is impressive. Foreign direct investment increased an annual average of $0.6 billion from 1986 to 1990, to $3.7 billion from 1996 to 2000. Despite the general economic slowdown worldwide, in 2001 foreign direct investment rose slightly to $3.8 billion, although still lower than its peak in 1999 ($5.4 billion).[11]

Multinationals have contributed to development by building plants, roads and other infrastructure; creating jobs and investing in the local work force; lowering input costs for essential materials; transferring technology and best practices; collaborating with local scientists and engineers on research and development agenda; and reinvesting profits back in local communities. The very fact that multinationals "shop around" for appropriate places to invest their capital spurs developing country governments to adopt policies that they hope will create the conditions needed to attract foreign investment.

On the other hand, the question of where their profits go presents vexing questions. In an effort to increase the percentage of profits from multinational corporations that stay in the country, developing countries have adopted such policies as investment promotion, domestic content mandates, export-performance requirements, joint-venture requirements and technology-licensing mandates. But these requirements can work in ways counter to their intended purposes and reduce rather than increase the benefits to economic development. Moreover, the competition among developing countries to attract direct foreign investment not only can mean the diversion of resources from other, more productive, endeavors, but also a "race to the bottom" in terms of environmental and labor standards.[12]

Some argue that world food security cannot be addressed without also tackling the implications of corporate ownership, control and consolidation in global agriculture. Worldwide, the top 10 seed firms control 30 percent of the $24.4 billion commercial seed market, and the top 10 agro-chemical corporations control 84 percent of the $30 billion agro-chemical market.[13] Key elements of the global food system are in the hands of a small group of unaccountable, but powerful businesses whose overriding concern is maximizing profits.

The private sector within developing countries also can play a positive role in agricultural development. Private sectors within developing countries must be nurtured in ways that open opportunities, create access to

Africa and Bread for the World: A Steadfast Relationship

Bread for the World, a U.S. citizens' movement against hunger, has focused much of its lobbying power on African issues in recent years. Because Africa is the only part of the world where hunger is both pervasive and increasing, Bread for the World will focus its international work on Africa until these negative trends start to reverse.

Bread for the World's past work includes winning increases for poverty-focused assistance programs that benefit Africa and other developing regions, such as the 1980s child-survival programs that save thousands of children's lives every day. Bread for the World also helped win global attention to famine in the Horn of Africa in the mid-1980s. A 1990 campaign helped to shift the thrust of U.S. policy from Cold War manipulations to the Horn in support of peace, democracy and development. And as Congress slashed development assistance in the mid-1990s, Bread for the World members helped reduce these cuts to Africa.

Africa: Seeds of Hope

In 1998 Bread for the World developed and finally won approval for the Africa: Seeds of Hope Act. It helped to reverse the decline in U.S. funding for agricultural development in Africa. Bread for the World also has joined with Michigan State University and other organizations in the Partnership to Cut Hunger and Poverty in Africa, which has become a strong voice for increasing U.S. and African attention to agriculture and food security in Africa.

Africa Growth and Opportunity Act

In 2000 Congress approved the Africa Growth and Opportunity Act (AGOA), which opened some opportunities for U.S.-Africa trade. Bread for the World supported this step, but other groups, mainly African-American groups and the African ambassadors, played a larger role. Through AGOA, a handful of African countries have been able to expand apparel and textile production significantly. AGOA also mandated a series of high-level business consultations between government and business leaders in Africa and the United States.

Proclaim Jubilee

In 1999 and 2000, Bread for the World joined many other groups in the United States and worldwide in the Jubilee 2000 campaign for debt relief of the world's poorest countries, most of which are in Africa. Bread for the World helped win congressional approval for $2.5 billion in 1999 and 2000. Other countries contributed to the effort, and creditors allowed the relief because they knew that much of the poor-country debt was virtually worthless. Overall, poor countries have received some $40 billion in debt relief.

Bread for the World and other U.S. groups in the Jubilee campaign fought to ensure that the debt relief benefited poor people. The U.S. groups pushed to connect debt relief with intensified efforts to reduce poverty and for a process that would foster democratic participation. Uganda had developed a national poverty reduction strategy in connection with an early example of debt relief, and Bread for the World Institute suggested that this model be used for other countries. Through lobbying efforts, other religious groups convinced the U.S. government to pursue and develop this idea. Today, most of the world's poorest countries have developed Poverty Reduction Strategies, strategies that are the basis for World Bank and International Monetary Fund operations in those countries.

Church and other civil-society groups in many poor countries were part of the Jubilee campaign, and Bread for the World and other U.S. and European groups have been able to help their colleagues in poor countries push from below to make debt relief work for poor people. By all accounts, poor countries now have more children attending school and more rural clinics stocked with medicines because of debt relief. In at least a handful of countries, public consultations on debt relief have improved accountability, reduced corruption and strengthened democracy.

Africa: Hunger to Harvest

Since debt relief is a one-time event, in 2001 and 2002 Bread for the World focused on increasing U.S. funding for poverty-focused, effective development assistance – the kind of assistance that helps small farmers become more productive and allows all children to attend school. Bread for the World developed and won passage by Congress of the Hunger to Harvest: Decade

> Because Africa is the only part of the world where hunger is both pervasive and increasing, Bread for the World will focus its international work on Africa until these negative trends start to reverse.

of Support for Sub-Sahara Africa Resolution. This measure calls on President Bush to develop an international plan to reduce hunger and poverty in Africa and promises that Congress will approve funding for the U.S. share of the cost. In 2001 Congress approved some $400 million in increased funding for African development. In 2002 Congress passed only two of 13 appropriations bills, but a further increase in development assistance for Africa seems likely when Congress completes the appropriations process, which should wrap up in 2003.

Rise to the Challenge

In March 2002, President Bush proposed that the United States should increase its development assistance to poor countries by $5 billion. This increase – a doubling of the current level of U.S. poverty-focused development assistance – would take place in several annual steps. The new money would be channeled through a new Millennium Challenge Account and would go to poor countries with governments that demonstrate good governance, invest in their people and support free markets.

Bread for the World is mounting a new campaign, called *Rise to the Challenge: End World Hunger*. This campaign seeks to hold the president to his promise and to win approval from Congress on authorizing legislation that will make the Millennium Challenge Account an effective instrument for reducing hunger and poverty worldwide.

Because of international debt relief efforts, more children are in school and more rural clinics are receiving much-needed medication in 10 of the 15 poorest countries in the world.

capital and jobs, and develop growing middle classes. Appropriate local development activities could include domestic capital investment by local entrepreneurs; creating debt and equity markets that facilitate low-cost borrowing and mobilize savings of local citizens for investment in public companies; strengthening bank-lending capabilities so that credit flows to promising projects; and creating transparent accounting and governance procedures so that efficient, honest enterprises can flourish.

Whether global or domestic, the private sector must be encouraged to use its power well. Developing country governments not only must provide incentives for long-term corporate investment in agriculture, but craft regulations that protect the rights and interests of small farmers, the knowledge of indigenous peoples, and the health and safety of consumers.

Men and Women, Especially Women

Perhaps most crucial to the success of agricultural development efforts is the involvement of farmers, consumers, teachers and mothers.

The importance of involving farmers in devising agricultural development policies cannot be overstated. Farmers grow various crops in varied environments, and no single solution will meet everyone's needs.

Most farmers in poor, rural areas are women. Thus, women must be integral to any development discussion. Generally, women must gain legally recognized access to resources and decision making both in their homes and communities. Such gains would give them claim to social and legal rights that would increase their personal

and households' productivity and contribute directly to food security. Social and cultural institutions and practices prevent them from making appreciable or noticeable advances in many situations. So, conscious efforts must be made to include them in the process.

In rural households, women also play a central role in preventing the spread of infectious diseases, which are devastating many communities. As HIV/AIDS and its secondary infections claim more lives, women's resolve in coping with the crisis becomes critical. Rural areas are facing a historic moment – HIV/AIDS already has taken too many lives and devastated whole communities. Such a time calls for a concerted campaign that combines strong leadership, cooperation and careful policy applications, for treatment and prevention as well as helping families recover from the emotional and economic losses this bane entails.

United States' Leading Role

With its unrivaled political and economic clout, the United States plays the biggest role in shaping the international development framework. If the United States took the lead by adopting the policies on agricultural trade recommended in this report, countless poor people's lives would be improved.

Few people can deny the sway that U.S. leadership on agriculture reform would make. Look at how U.S. leadership was crucial in improving the debt cancellation program for poor countries. After being convinced by the Jubilee movement that some poor country debt should be written off, the Clinton administration persuaded the G-8, the IMF and World Bank to work together on a more ambitious international debt relief plan. In the wake of that debt relief, more children are in school and more rural clinics are receiving badly needed medication in 10 of the 15 poorest countries in the world.

As one of the countries that stands to gain from agricultural trade liberalization, the United States should take the lead in reducing its trade-distorting agricultural subsidies and in urging other countries to do the same. The agriculture negotiations underway as part of the Doha trade round provide an important opportunity in this regard. Meanwhile, the United States should increase development assistance to poor countries in Africa and other parts of the world, and work with other rich countries to improve the coordination of assistance. Effectively launching the proposed Millennium Challenge Account – and the parallel increase in development assistance that European governments have promised – is an important opportunity.

James L. McDonald is Bread for the World's vice president of program and policy.

CHAPTER 7

What You Can Do

Citizenship is a quality, through which a person can contribute to the progress and development of the society from where he receives nourishment for his body and soul.

N. Balasubramanian, India

We can act to make a difference in the fight against hunger by educating ourselves and teaching others about related issues, such as the importance of developing agriculture and rural economies for poor people around the world.

Every day lives are lost to hunger, but thankfully every day people can act to make a difference. If we want to see agriculture and trade change to benefit poor and hungry people everywhere, the time to act is now.

As global citizens, we are public actors who have rights and responsibilities to contribute to and create our public life. As U.S. citizens, we are blessed with ample opportunities to take such action. Yet for many, even the simplest privileges, like voting, have become mundane and often ignored chores.

Citizenship is about our participation in the decisions that shape our communities, our countries and our world. Narrowly, citizenship is about privilege and status. Broadly, it is about responsibility and identity. Citizenship is about human dignity and our sense of belonging and contributing to something larger than ourselves. N. Balasubramanian from India writes: "Citizenship is a quality, through which a person can contribute to the progress and development of the society from where he receives nourishment for his body and soul."[1]

Before people can participate fully and meaningfully in a global society, they must receive the nourishment of "body and soul." The good news is that progress in the fight against hunger has been made. During the past 25 years, the proportion of undernourished people in developing countries declined from about one-third to about one-fifth. But some 840 million people worldwide remain undernourished, and recent economic, political and environmental disasters probably have pushed these numbers higher.

People who are not being adequately nourished cannot fight the battle against hunger by themselves. Their efforts to feed their families must remain their primary activity. But we can add hope to their struggle by joining them in a citizens' movement to end hunger in our lifetimes.

By varying degrees, each of us has known hunger and remember how it can disrupt our lives. We've all skipped a meal or two during a day. We know that ache in the pit of the stomach and how it can interfere with thought. We have felt lightheadedness, dizziness and even passing nausea that can force us to stop what we are doing and momentarily close our eyes or drop our heads.

But for many people, hunger is not just an annoyance; it's a persistent gnawing. Imagine how as a parent you would sacrifice meals to ensure that your children did not share this sick feeling, and how it would break your heart to have to send them to bed without dinner even after making these sacrifices.

Hunger interferes with people's ability to work and be productive. Among children, hunger stunts their ability to learn and increases vulnerability to disease and death.

U.S. voters are concerned that people continue to go hungry both at home and abroad. According to a July 2002 telephone survey commissioned by the Alliance to End Hunger, 93 percent of Americans polled said that "fighting the hunger problem" was an important issue to them (see related story, p. 112).

Yet few politicians make the fight against hunger a campaign issue. According to Matthew Crenson and Benjamin Ginsberg, professors of political science at Johns Hopkins University, a consumer mindset is replacing the traditional value of citizenship among voters. "Increasingly, public officials regard us as 'customers' rather than citizens, and there are crucial differences between the two," Crenson and Ginsberg argue.[2] "Citizens own the government. Customers just receive services from it. Citizens belong to a political community with a collective existence and public purposes. Customers are individual purchasers seeking the best deal."

Consumerism permeates our society, and much good can be accomplished by being more aware of what you are buying and what your dollars support (see related story, p. 114). Though consumerism can help in the fight against hunger, political action in fact is a more direct and effective approach.

USDA Photo/Ken Hammond

Voters See Hunger as a Political Issue

By Linda Jucovy

Voters in this country are deeply concerned about hunger both here and in developing nations; they have strong opinions about how to address the issue, and they are more likely to vote for politicians who share their concerns and are willing to act.

Those were among the findings from a telephone survey of a random sample of 1,000 people, conducted in July 2002, that was commissioned by the Alliance to End Hunger. The nonpartisan Alliance is a recently formed group of 26 organizations that includes religious institutions, charities that assist poor and hungry people, businesses, labor unions, foundations, universities and civil rights organizations. Heifer International is a member of the Alliance.

Marco Grimaldo, the organizer for the Alliance, described it as, "a catalyst for bringing diverse organizations and institutions to the table to make real progress against hunger." He said the survey was "an important first step" toward making that progress. "We want to apply our learning from the survey to help political candidates do a better job of addressing the issue of hunger, especially during the next presidential election."

Bread for the World, a grassroots Christian organization, was a major force behind the development of the Alliance. Rev. David Beckmann, president of Bread for the World, said he was "surprised how strongly Americans support action to reduce hunger in the United States and around the world."

Ninety-three percent of those polled said that "fighting the hunger problem" was an important issue when they decided how to cast their vote for members of the House of Representatives and the U.S. Senate. And 4 percent – one of every 25 potential voters – said that it was the single most important issue in determining their vote. The survey, which has a margin of error of plus or minus three percentage points, also found that Republicans and Democrats hold similar views about the importance of reducing hunger and the best approaches for doing so.

One experience that contributed to the survey's strong findings was last year's terrorist attack on the United States. Seventy percent of respondents said the attack made them "more likely to want to reduce world hunger," while 68 percent said it made them "more interested in helping people in this country." The majority (59 percent) also said they wanted to fight hunger because it was "the moral thing to do," not because they believed it would help reduce the threat of terrorism or aid the U.S. economy.

"Because of Sept. 11, a lot of people have re-evaluated life a bit and they want to do what's right," Beckmann said. "The religious and moral arguments are what really move people. Everybody knows what it feels like to be hungry, and so they can empathize. They know it leads very quickly to dizziness and tiredness and grumpiness. They can see very quickly what happens to a family that's trapped in hunger."

To ensure the survey would not have a partisan slant, the Alliance brought together three men who most often find themselves on opposite sides of the political fence to do the polling and report on the results. One, Jim McLaughlin, worked for presiden-

In the United States, 13 million children experience hunger or are at risk of hunger.

USDA Photo/Ken Hammond

tial candidate Bob Dole and is a pollster for the National Republican Campaign Committee. The others, Bill Knapp and Tom Freedman, are Democrats. Knapp was a consultant to the presidential campaigns of Bill Clinton in 1996 and served Al Gore in 2000. Freedman served as a senior adviser to President Clinton.

Freedman said the survey "is part of the process of telling politicians what the American people want done." Its findings suggested that "we haven't done a good enough job of solving the problem of hunger, that the political system should have a more effective approach," Freedman said.

Some progress has been made in the fight against hunger during the past 25 years, as the proportion of undernourished people in developing countries has dropped from about one-third to about one-fifth of the population. But hunger continues to be widespread and deadly.

According to the most recent U.N. data, nearly 800 million people in the developing world are undernourished. The problem is most severe in Africa, where more than a third of the population does not have adequate food. And worldwide, more than 15,000 children die each day from hunger-related causes, including the effects of common diseases like diarrhea and malaria that destroy young people already weakened by a chronic lack of food.

While hunger in the United States is less widespread and deadly, the problem is still significant, affecting one of every 10 households in this country. About 33 million people, including 13 million children, experience hunger or the risk of hunger.

Of those, nearly 8.5 million, including 2.9 million children, frequently skip meals or eat too little, and sometimes go without food for an entire day. The others live in households that are "food insecure," a term the government uses to describe households that are struggling to put food on the table and are uncertain about whether they will have enough food.

One major effect of undernutrition is on children's performance in school. As a study conducted by the Center on Hunger and Poverty at Brandeis University suggests, a lack of adequate food stunts the ability of children to learn and develop to their full potential.

Beckmann is convinced that it is feasible to dramatically reduce hunger in the immediate future. The 1996 World Food Summit, held in Rome, set the goal of halving hunger in the world by 2015. "All of the organizations who are participating in the Alliance consider the goal to be realistic," Beckmann said. "They are also of one mind that U.S. leadership is pivotal. We're trying to move the hunger issue from the church basement to the White House."

Although fewer than half the people surveyed (49 percent) agreed with the statement that "hunger in the United States and throughout the world can be cut in half by 2015," they were more positive about what approaches to ending hunger would be most effective. Their response reflects the proverb: "Give a man a fish and he will eat for a day. Teach a man to fish and he will eat for a lifetime." More than 70 percent said that fighting hunger should include helping people who were chronically hungry obtain food and then helping them become self-reliant so they could buy or produce their own food.

And when respondents were asked more specifically, "When it comes to fighting world hunger, which [approach] do you think is most effective?," the most frequent response (37 percent) was "helping farmers in poor countries produce more food."

The survey also asked people who should take the lead in fighting hunger – government or charities – and they were evenly split in their response, at 46 percent for each. "People have a sophisticated knowledge that you need to combine the best" of public and private sectors, Beckmann said, "and they understand that the best way to reduce hunger is to help people provide for themselves. The survey finds a lot of good sense among the American public about what's going to work."

This article originally appeared in the Winter 2002 issue of *World Ark* and has been reprinted with permission from Heifer International.

Moreover, Americans prefer the most direct and effective approach to helping others. In the Alliance to End Hunger survey, nearly 40 percent of those polled said that the best way to fight world hunger would be to help farmers in poor countries produce more food. They also agree that the United States should support programs that promote economic development in poor countries – programs featured in this year's Hunger Report.

We know which road to take in the fight against hunger. We are armed with the knowledge, compassion for others and political opportunity to make a change. But Congress and the president need to hear the message. They need to know we care and that we expect them to take action to fight hunger and poverty.

Being a citizen means taking action, mindful that alone our efforts may seem invisible but as part of a whole they can shape our future. Margaret Mead said, "Never doubt that a small group of thoughtful, committed people can change the world. Indeed, it is the only thing that ever has."

Bread for the World/ Bread for the World Institute

The purpose of Bread for the World is to convey the anti-hunger message to Congress and the president to effect change. As a national Christian citizens' movement against hunger, its 46,000 members – including 2,000 churches – mobilize about 250,000 letters to Congress each year. In its nearly 30-year history, Bread for the World has won significant victories for poor and hungry people.

Rise to the Challenge: End World Hunger. Bread for the World's 2003 campaign, *Rise to the Challenge: End World Hunger*, will urge Congress to rise to the challenge of shaping the Millennium Challenge Account (MCA), extra funding for the purpose of helping poor countries reduce poverty and hunger.

President Bush has called for an additional $1.7 billion in 2004, $3.3 billion in 2005 and $5 billion in 2006 and each year thereafter, to fund the MCA. It would fund development programs in poor countries committed to helping hungry and poor people become self-reliant. When fully implemented, this historic proposal would double U.S. poverty-focused development.

This MCA has the potential to improve nutrition, health care, education, agriculture and drinking water for millions of people in developing countries. But these improvements can happen only if Congress approves the legislation and funding for the MCA.

To become involved in this campaign or participate in other ways at Bread for the World, you can:

● Become a member by visiting the Web site (*www.bread.org*) or call 1-800-82BREAD. As a mem-

Fair Trade Coffee: A Cup o' Joe Can Change Farmers' Lives

By Daniel Martin

Coffee is the drink of the friends of God, and of His servants who seek wisdom.

– Sheik Ansari Djezeri Hanball Abd-al-Kadir, 1587[1]

Millions of groggy, blurry-eyed Americans start their daily routine with a steaming cup o' Joe. In fact, consumers worldwide spent more than $50 billion on coffee in 2001.[2] While many need coffee as a jumpstart in the morning, millions of farmers in poor countries need it for a different reason – their livelihood.

However, making a living growing coffee has become difficult in recent years. As new countries enter the market, supply has dwarfed demand and coffee prices have plummeted, leaving small farmers struggling to make ends meet. One Nicaraguan coffee farmer described his life amid the coffee crisis this way: "We [have] no food. Instead, we go to the market and get some vegetables from the garbage. We take the best part and give it to the children."[3]

In 2001 coffee prices dropped as low as 44 cents per pound on the international market, (compared with prices consistently higher than $1 per pound in the late 1990s). Nicaraguan farmers need twice that just to cover production cost. The same year, more than 100,000 Mexican small farmers did not harvest, because to do so would have cost more than the market would pay.[4]

The effects have been devastating for rural communities. In Guatemala, 30,000 children are acutely malnourished with 6,900 of them at risk of dying.[5] The U.N. Children's Fund reports similar conditions in El Salvador, saying, "We've seen families abandon their children in their search for employment in the cities, while others have had to decide between buying food and paying for health care and education."[6]

In these regions, more than 25 million people are tied to coffee for their livelihood – from farmers to the peasants who work the fields to those who export the crop. The U.S. Agency for International Development estimates a loss of $1.5 billion in coffee revenue for Central America alone due to recent prices.[7] The crisis is so serious that some farmers who are in families that have grown coffee for generations are turning to growing coca, the main ingredient in cocaine, or marijuana because they can make up to 10 times more than growing coffee.[8]

Why Low Prices?

Since the early 1960s, coffee prices had been managed by the International Coffee Agreement (ICA), which used export quotas for producing countries and import quotas for consuming countries to keep prices between $1.20 and $1.40 per pound. In 1989, the quota provisions included in the agreement were allowed to expire. Without the quotas, stockpiled coffee flooded the market, and prices dropped quickly.

Prices were just beginning to recover when Vietnam embarked on a program of large-scale coffee production (made possible by government subsidies and donor encouragement). Within a few years, Vietnam's export of low-grade coffee to the United States had almost quadrupled, going from less than 4 million bags in 1995 to more than 15 million bags in 2001.[9] Such drastic increases in such a short period coupled with excess production in other countries has flooded the coffee market, driving prices down. Farmers in Central and South America were forced off their farms.

In May 2000, the (now-dissolved) Association of Coffee-Producing Countries agreed to withhold 20 percent of exports in order to lessen supply and drive up prices. After only six months, however, Vietnam released its holdings (about 150,000 tons) onto the market, depressing prices further.[10] Although it is cheaper to produce coffee in Vietnam, those farmers also are suffering from the market glut. Today, prices are still well below the production cost, and many farmers (and their families) in Latin America, Vietnam, Africa and elsewhere are going hungry.

A girl in Malawi is harvesting coffee beans to help supplement her family's income.

A partial solution to help small coffee farmers is available through U.S. grocery stores: Fair Trade coffee. Here's how it works. Regular coffee farmers, because they typically own small farms often in remote places, usually have access only to a middleman to buy their product. The middleman, because he has a captive market, can set the price low, with many farmers reportedly being paid a mere 24 cents per pound in 2001.[11] The middleman then takes the coffee to an exporter, who sells it to an importer, who finally sells it to a roaster.

In contrast, Fair Trade coffee is sold directly to roasters by democratically run cooperatives of small coffee farmers, thereby skipping the middlemen and ensuring that a greater share of profits go to the farmers. In addition, any company wishing to sell coffee under the Fair Trade label must pay the Fair Trade price, $1.26 or $0.05 above the market price (whichever is higher), per pound. Pricing, certification and licensing are done through the Fair Trade Labeling Organization, an independent, global umbrella group. Fair Trade coffee is so named because the farmers receive a fair price for their coffee, $1 per pound. Says Oxfam International, "The Fair Trade movement has clearly shown that producers can be paid double today's disastrously low prices without affecting the consumer's willingness to buy a good-quality product."[12]

The remaining 26 cents is funneled through the cooperatives. The cooperatives take the surplus money and reinvest it in communities where coffee farmers live, funding projects such as schools, scholarships, roads, health care, and other social service programs. One farmer from Costa Rica says: "With Fair Trade, we have fixed the roads and we have bus service. Our kids can go to school with the help of scholarships from the co-op's fund."[13] It should be noted, however, that Fair Trade coffee is not a solution for all coffee growers. As a niche market product, its impact will necessarily be limited. However, the more consumers demand Fair Trade products, the more farmers will be helped.

In addition to helping some farmers to earn a living, much of the Fair Trade coffee is grown in an environmentally friendly manner. Fair Trade coffee is often shade-grown, which means that farmers plant other trees, usually fruit trees, to provide shade for the coffee plants. When these other trees bear fruit, the farmer has either food for the family or extra income. Shade-grown coffee also encourages diverse species of migratory and local birds as well as other animals to live on the land. One environmentalist described shade-grown coffee as the "most environmentally benign and ecologically stable agroecosystem" in Latin America.[14] Much Fair Trade coffee also is certified organic, fetching an even higher market price.

With so many benefits, Fair Trade coffee is becoming more and more popular in the United States. In 1999 only 33 companies offered certified Fair Trade coffee, and by 2001 that number had jumped to 120, with overall Fair Trade sales tripling in the same time period.[15] Many specialty coffee shops, especially in larger cities, serve Fair Trade coffee, and most also sell it by the bag.

After much grassroots pressure, Starbucks began selling bags of Fair Trade coffee in their stores and via the Internet in 2001, and in May 2002, began serving it occasionally in their stores. Safeway, a major grocery chain, also has Fair Trade coffee available for purchase. On its Web site, *www.TransFairUSA.org,* TransFair USA, the American branch of the Fair Trade Labeling Organization, has a complete list of both coffeehouses and Web sites that sell Fair Trade coffee.

If your company or organization serves coffee, think about approaching management to see if it will switch to Fair Trade coffee. You could bring up the fact that in 2001, the U.S. House of Representatives successfully pressured some of the cafes and restaurants in its buildings to serve Fair Trade coffee. Many religious bodies have encouraged their congregations to serve Fair Trade coffee during fellowship times. Find out if your organization does so, and if not, encourage it to change as part of its outreach.

And last, but certainly not least, if you drink coffee at home, look for a way to switch to Fair Trade. Although it may cost a bit more per cup, for every bag of Fair Trade coffee sold, hundreds of farmers benefit. To paraphrase Sheik Abd-al-Kadir, Fair Trade coffee is the drink of the friends of God, and of His servants who seek justice.

Daniel Martin is a project assistant at Bread for the World Institute.

[1] Gregory Dicum and Nina Luttinger, *The Coffee Book*. (New York: The New Press) 1999.

[2] *White Paper: The Global Coffee Crisis*, submitted to U.S. House of Representatives Subcommittee on the Western Hemisphere, July 24, 2002, 10.

[3] David Gonzalez, "A Coffee Crisis' Devastating Domino Effect in Nicaragua," *The New York Times*, Aug. 29, 2002, p. A3.

[4] *White Paper*, 10.

[5] U.S. Agency for International Development, "Guatemala's Rural Crisis," March 21, 2002, http://www.usaid.gov/press/releases/2002/fs020321_2.html.

[6] CNN, "El Salvador Youth Face Malnutrition," October 22, 2002, http://www.cnn.com/2002/WORLD/americas/10/22/children.elsalvador.ap/index.html.

[7] U.S. Agency for International Development, "Central America in Crisis: USAID Response and Strategic Approach," May 24, 2002, http://www.usaid.gov/press/releases/2002/fs020523_4.html.

[8] Scott Wilson, "Coca Invades Colombia's Coffee Fields," *Washington Post*, Oct. 30, 2001, A17.

[9] *White Paper*, 8

[10] Gerard Greenfield, "Vietnam and the World Coffee Crisis: Local Coffee Riots in a Global Context," Focus on the Global South, Mar. 2002, http://www.focusweb.org/pubilcations/2002/Vietnam-and-the-world-coffee-crisis.html.

[11] Tim Weiner, "Low Prices Threaten Coffee Farmers' Livelihood, Report Says," *New York Times*, Sept. 19, 2002.

[12] Oxfam International, *Mugged: Poverty in Your Coffee Cup*, 2002: 40.

[13] Oxfam America and Transfair USA, "Fair Trade Coffee: The Time is Now," February 2002, 14.

[14] Dicum, 50.

[15] Oxfam America, 4.

ber, you will receive up-to-date information about how you can communicate with your government representatives and help shape hunger-related legislation. Your financial contributions also help to change policies that benefit hungry people worldwide.

- Involve your church. Each year, about 1,000 churches take up an "offering of letters" to Congress. Just as churches take up offerings of money to help people in need, these churches invite their members to consider writing to Congress on a Bread for the World issue.

- Become an activist. You can join or form a Bread for the World group in your church or community. Some groups meet just a few times a year to take specific action, such as visiting their Congress members or planning a workshop for local congregations. In most congressional districts, volunteers have organized telephone trees to mobilize action at key points in the legislative process.

Other Ways to Make a Difference

Many other groups – including most *Hunger 2003* sponsors – work to help small farmers and reduce poverty both internationally and in the United States. The following is a list of just a few such organizations where you can volunteer your time and/or support financially:

International Organizations:

DATA (Debt, Aid, Trade for Africa): DATA is a new organization that is being spearheaded by rock star Bono of the Irish group U2. DATA seeks to help Africa by pressuring developed country governments to cancel unpayable debt, fight HIV/AIDS and reduce trade barriers. Bono is using his status as a public figure to bring attention specifically to Africa and some of the major problems troubling the continent.

In addition to talking to developed countries, DATA also is encouraging African governments to practice democracy and be accountable to the poor in their respective countries. DATA hopes to help by "working to bring people and organizations from all around the United States and the world together to stop the spread of AIDS and extreme poverty in Africa."

DATA Inc.
1317 F St., NW
Washington, DC 20004
(202) 639-8010
E-mail: info@datadata.org
Web site: www.datadata.org

The Heifer Project: Begun in Spain in the 1930s, Heifer International is based on the idea that to become self-reliant, people need not a cup of milk but a whole cow. Since then, it has grown into a worldwide organization that seeks to help poor farmers by providing them with animals to raise in environmentally friendly ways. In return for the animals, families then pass on some of the offspring to other farmers nearby, thus making it a gift that keeps on giving.

Selected by *Worth* magazine as one of the 100 best charities in the United States, this organization gives tangible help to those in need all around the globe by connecting sponsors with farmers and their families.

Heifer International
P.O. Box 8058
Little Rock, AR 72203
Phone: (800) 422-0474
Web site: www.heifer.org

NETWORK: A Catholic social justice organization, NETWORK has been a persistent voice for economic justice on Capitol Hill for 30 years. Through lobbying and grassroots work, NETWORK encourages both Congress and the president to bring about a fairer and more equitable world. Its issues range from domestic concerns, such as welfare, housing and health care, to international concerns, such as sustained peace and international trade and investment. NETWORK draws from Catholic social teachings to influence the U.S. government to make just decisions.

NETWORK
801 Pennsylvania Ave. SE, Suite 460
Washington, DC 20003-2167
Phone: (202) 547-5556
Web site: www.networklobby.org

Oxfam's "Make Trade Fair" Campaign: Oxfam International has long been a leader in seeking justice for poor and oppressed people around the world. Through grassroots efforts and activities in more than 100 countries, Oxfam seeks to work with poor people and influence powerful people in order to bring about a better world.

Recently, Oxfam launched a Make Trade Fair campaign, which aims to give a "voice to the farmers, laborers and factory workers who are being cheated by the blatantly unfair rules of world trade." The campaign also provides you, the consumer, a voice in calling for fairer trade.

Oxfam America
26 West St.
Boston, MA 02111
Phone: (617) 728-2594
Web site: www.oxfamamerica.org or
www.maketradefair.com

UNICEF (U.N. Children's Fund): Begun in the aftermath of World War II, UNICEF is committed to helping children in developing and impoverished regions. Through working with governments and nongovernmental organizations, UNICEF strives to reduce hunger and malnutrition, promote education of girls and boys, decrease illness and child mortality, and protect children from the hardships of war and natural disaster.

The U.S. fund for UNICEF is one of 37 regional offices set up to support UNICEF through financial contributions, advocating for the world's children and raising awareness among the U.S. public.

U.S. Fund for UNICEF
333 East 38th St.
New York, NY 10016
Phone: (800) FOR-KIDS (367-5437)
Web site: www.unicefusa.org

Domestic Organizations:

Center for Rural Affairs: The Center for Rural Affairs is committed to policies that strengthen family farms and rural communities. Begun by two ex-VISTA volunteers in 1973, the Center for Rural Affairs is committed to building communities that stand for social justice, economic opportunity and environmental stewardship. It works on issues ranging from environmental conservation and problems facing rural schools to market access for farmers. In order to keep in touch with the rural communities it assists, the Center for Rural Affairs is located in Walthill, Neb., population 900.

Center for Rural Affairs
101 S. Tallman St.
P.O. Box 406
Walthill, NE 68067
Phone: (402) 846-5428
Fax: (402) 846-5420
Web site: www.cfra.org

The Community Food Security Coalition (CFSC): CFSC is "dedicated to building strong, sustainable, local and regional food systems that ensure access to affordable, nutritious and culturally appropriate food for all people at all times." CFSC helps develop self-reliance among all communities in obtaining their food by creating a system of growing, manufacturing, processing, marketing and selling food that is regionally based and grounded in the principles of justice, democracy and sustainability.

CFSC actively promotes local farmers' markets and local buying programs to help both local farmers sell their produce and low-income areas obtain fresh fruits and vegetables. They have more than 250 member organizations in the United States where members are active.

Community Food Security Coalition
P.O. Box 209
Venice, CA 90294
Phone: (310) 822-5410
Web site: www.foodsecurity.org

The Rural Advancement Foundation International – USA (RAFI-USA): Dedicated to community, equity and diversity in agriculture, RAFI-USA has been working for more than a decade to promote sustainable agriculture, strengthen family farms and rural communities, protect the diversity of plants and animals in agriculture, and ensure a responsible use of new technology. Based in North Carolina, they have been working on these issues both domestically and internationally. "RAFI-USA believes that farmers and consumers must be informed, involved with each other and active in protecting and directing the use of natural and human agricultural resources."

RAFI-USA
P.O. Box 640
Pittsboro, NC 27312
Phone: (919) 542-1396
Fax: (919) 542-0069
Web site: www.rafiusa.org

Rural Community Assistance Corporation (RCAC): RCAC is a nonprofit organization dedicated to assisting rural communities in achieving their goals and visions through training, technical assistance and access to resources. Begun in 1978 in California to help small towns implement housing programs, it has grown to a multimillion-dollar organization that continues to benefit the small communities of the rural West. In addition to providing loans to build housing, RCAC also provides loans and grants to rural health care facilities and works with agricultural workers to make sure basic needs are met. The U.S. Treasury has certified it as a Community Development Financial Institution.

Rural Community Assistance Corp.
3120 Freeboard Drive, Suite 201
West Sacramento, CA 95691
Phone: (916) 447-2854
Fax: (916) 447-2878
Web site: www.rcac.org

Endnotes

Introduction

1 Bharat Textiles, "Mali: U.S. Subsidies Create Cotton Glut That Hurts Foreign Cotton Farms." July 27, 2002. Available from http://ww.bharattextile.com/newsitems/1977990.

2 The people represented in this chapter are composites of real people interviewed in preparation for the report and through past personal experiences.

3 Food and Agriculture Organization of the United Nations, *State of Food Insecurity in the World 2001*. Available from http://www.fao.org/docrep/x8200e/x8200e00.htm; U.N. Children's Fund, *State of the World's Children 2001*. Available from http://www.unicef.org/pubsgen/sowc01.

4 Vandana Shiva, "The Real Reasons for Hunger." *The Observer*, June 23, 2002.

5 American's Second Harvest, "Who's Hungry: Hunger in Rural America." Available from http://www.secondharvest.org/whoshungry/whoshungry.html.

6 International Fund for Agricultural Development, *2001 Rural Poverty Report*. (New York: Oxford University Press Inc.) 2001.

7 Oxfam International, *Rigged Rules and Double Standards*. (Oxfam International) 2002, 101.

8 "Peanuts: The Moneymaker Crop for Georgia," *Return on Investment 2001*. A series of reports from the College of Agriculture and Environmental Sciences, University of Georgia. Available from http://www.ect.uga.edu/roi2001/files/peanuts.htm.

9 Leslie A. Whitener, Bruce A. Weber and Greg J. Duncan, *Rural Dimensions of Welfare Reform*. W.E. Upjohn Institute for Employment Research, May 2000.

10 International Monetary Fund, "World Economic Outlook, Trade and Finance." September 2002, 85. Available from http://www.imf.org/external/pubs/ft/weo/2002/02/index.htm.

Chapter 1

1 Food and Agriculture Organization of the United Nations (FAO), *State of Food Insecurity in the World 2001*. Available from http://www.fao.org/docrep/x8200e/x8200e00.htm.

2 FAO, *World Agriculture: Towards 2015/2030*. (Rome: FAO) 2002. Available from http://www.fao.org/docrep/004/y3557e/y3557e06.htm#TopOfPage.

3 U.S. Department of Health and Human Services, Centers for Disease Control and Prevention, "U.S. Obesity Trends 1985 to 2001." Available from http://www.cdc.gov/nccdphp/dnpa/obesity/trend/maps/.

4 Oxfam International, *Mugged: Poverty in Your Coffee Cup* (Oxfam International) September 2002, 10.

5 John Dixon, Aidan Gulliver, David Gibbon, et al, *Farming Systems and Poverty*. (Rome: FAO) 2001, 4. Available from http://www.fao.org/DOCREP/003/Y1860E/Y1860E00.HTM. The FAO defines the agricultural population as all persons who depend on agriculture, hunting, fishing or forestry for their livelihood. This estimate comprises all persons actively engaged in agriculture as well as their nonworking dependents.

6 International Fund for Agricultural Development, *2001 Rural Poverty Report*. (New York: Oxford University Press Inc.) 2001, 229.

7 FAO, "Mobilizing the Political Will and Resources to Banish World Hunger." Prepared for World Food Summit Plus Five, 2002, 63.

8 John Mellor, "Reducing Poverty, Buffering Economic Shocks – Agriculture and the Non-tradable Economy." Background Paper for Roles of Agriculture Project. (Rome: FAO) 2001, 2.

9 Roles of Agriculture Project, *Expert Meeting Summary Report*. (Rome: FAO) 2001, 14.

10 Colin Thirtle, Xavier Irz, Lin Lin, Victoria McKenzie-Hill and Steve Wiggins, "Relationship Between Changes in Agricultural Productivity and the Incidence of Poverty in Developing Countries." United Kingdom Department for International Development Report No.7946, Feb. 27, 2001, 2.

11 Ibid., 17.

12 Ibid., 21.

13 Berk Özler, Gaurav Datt and Martin Ravallion, "The India Poverty Project: Poverty and Growth in India, 1951-94." World Bank, 1996. Available from http://www.worldbank.org/poverty/data/indiapaper.htm.

14 FAO, "Mobilizing the Political Will and Resources to Banish World Hunger," 79.

15 Dario Fernandez-Morera, "Hernando De Soto." *ReasonOnline Magazine*. Available from http://www.reason.com/DeSoto.shtml.

16 Asian Development Bank, *Key Indicators of Developing Asian and Pacific Countries 2001*. (United States: Oxford University Press) 2001, 158.

17 Thirtle, 4.

18 Sophia Murphy, "Managing the Invisible Hand." Institute for Agriculture and Trade Policy, April 2002, 40.

19 U.S. Department of Agriculture (USDA), *Agricultural Factbook 2000*. (United States: USDA) November 2000, 10.

20 Ibid.

21 World Trade Organization (WTO), *International Trade Statistics 2001*. (France: WTO) 2001, 95.

22 Ibid., 102.

23 Murphy, 19.

24 Kazuhito Morimoto, speech given to The National Center of Young Farmers. June 8, 2002. Available from http://www.ifaorg/news/sp080600.htm.

25 WTO, "Agriculture: Fairer Markets for Farmers." Available from www.wto.org/english/thewto_e/whatis_e/tif_e/agrm3_e.htm.

26 Eugenio Diaz-Bonilla and Jonathan Tin, "That Was Then but This Is Now: Multifunctionality in Industry and Agriculture." Trade and Macroeconomics Division of the International Food Policy Research Institute Discussion Paper No. 94, May 2002, 18.

27 WTO, *International Trade Statistics 2001*, 99.

28 World Bank, *World Development Report, 2000/2001*. (New York: Oxford University Press) 2001, 180.

29 James Wolfensohn, "Chance for Rich Countries to Play Fair," *Daily Nation*, Sept. 26, 2002. Available from http://www.nationaudio.com/News/DailyNation/26092002/Comment/Comment12.html.

30 Bruce Gardner, "North American Agricultural Policies and Effects on Western Hemisphere Markets Since 1995, with a Focus on Grains and Oilseeds." Department of Agricultural and Resource Economics, University of Maryland, June 2002. Available from http://www.arec.umd.edu/Publications/papers/Working-Papers-PDF-files/02-12.pdf.

31 In many cases, low-income countries abandoned agricultural subsidies as part of the structural adjustments required for International Monetary Fund and World Bank loans.

32 WTO, "Agreement on Agriculture." Article 9. Available from http://www.jurisint.org/pub/06/en/doc/13.htm#13.009.

33 WTO, "Agriculture: Fairer Markets for Farmers."

34 Brent Borrell and Lionel Hubbard, "Global Economic Effects of the E.U. Common Agricultural Policy," *Economic Affairs Journal*, June 2000. Available from http://www.openrepublic.org/policyanalyses/Agriculture/IEA_REFORMING_THE_CAP/20000601_GLOBAL_EFFECTS_OF_CAP_IEA.pdf.

35 U.N. Conference on Trade and Development, *The Least Developed Country Report 2002*. (Geneva: United Nations) 2002, 7.

36 Ibid.

37 Mark Ritchie, Suzanne Wisniewski and Sophia Murphy, "Dumping as a Structural Feature of U.S. Agriculture: Can WTO Rules Solve the Problem?" Institute for Agriculture and Trade Policy, 4.

38 Ibid., 5.

39 Ibid.

40 Susan Sechler, "Starved for Attention." *The American Prospect*, (Vol. 13, Issue 1) January 2002. Available from http://www.prospect.org/print/V13/1/sechler-s.html.

41 FAO, "Mobilizing the Political Will and Resources to Banish World Hunger," 82.

42 Sechler.

43 Duncan Green and Matthew Griffith, "Dumping on the Poor." Catholic Agency for Overseas Development Policy Report, September 2002. Available from http://www.cafod.org.uk/policy/dumpingonthepoor200209.pdf 2002.

44 Ibid., 15.

Chapter 2

1 "Special Report: Voices of Idaho's Rural Residents." *The Idaho Statesman*, Summer 2001. Available from http://www.idahostatesman.com/news/ruralidaho/audio02.shtml.

2 Lyn Danninger, "Farmers Need to Reconnect, Prof Urges." *Honolulu Star Bulletin*, Oct. 25, 2002. Available from http://starbulletin.com/2002/10/25/business/story2.html.

3 R. D. Knutson, J. B. Penn and B. L. Flinchbaugh, *Agricultural and Food Policy*, Fourth Ed. (Prentice Hall) 1998.

4 U.S. Department of Agriculture (USDA), Economic Research Service (ERS), Resource Economics Division, *Agricultural Resources and Environmental Indicators*. Eds. William Anderson, Richard Magleby and Ralph Heimlich, September 2000, Chapter 5.1, 1.

5 USDA, ERS, "Food Marketing and Price Spreads: Current Trends." 2000. Available from http://www.ers.usda.gov/briefing/foodpricespreads/trends/.

6 USDA, ERS, "Food Marketing and Price Spreads: Farm-to-retail Price Spreads for Individual Food Items." 2000. Available from http://www.ers.usda.gov/briefing/foodpricespreads/spreads/.

7 Robert A. Hoppe, "Farming Operations and Households in Farming Areas: A Closer Look." USDA, ERS, AER-685, May 1994.

8 "Using Farm-sector Income as a Policy Benchmark." *Agricultural Outlook*, June/July 2001, 15.

9 These small farms include the following USDA categories: limited-resource, retirement, residential/lifestyle and farming occupation-low sales.

10 Ashok K. Mishra, Hisham S. El-Osta, Mitchell J. Morehart, et al, "Income, Wealth and the Economic Well-being of Farm Households." USDA, ERS, AER-812, July 2002, 26-32. Available from http://www.ers.usda.gov/publications/aer812/aer812.pdf.

11 "Assessing the Economic Well-being of Farm Households," *Agricultural Outlook*, August 2002, 31.

12 Cherly Anderson, "Her Story." Prairie Public Broadcasting. Available from http://www.prairiepublic.org/features/Farmwife/herstory.htm.

13 Mishra, 52.

14 U.S. Census of Agriculture, USDA, National Agricultural Statistical Service. Available from http://www.nass.usda.gov/census/.

15 Craig Gundersen, Mitchell Morehart, Leslie Whitener, et al, "A Safety Net for Farm Households." USDA, ERS, AER-788, Dec. 6, 2000, 17. Available from http://www.ers.usda.gov/publications/aer788/aer788.pdf.

16 "Higher Cropland Value from Farm Program Payments: Who Gains?" *Agricultural Outlook*, November 2001, 26.

17 Ibid.

18 Paul Sundell, "Agricultural Income & Finance Outlook." USDA, ERS, AIS-78, Feb. 26, 2002, 38. Available from http://www.ers.usda.gov/publications/ais78/ais7801.pdf.

19 Federal Reserve Board, "Survey of Consumer Finances." Available from http://www.federalreserve.gov/pubs/oss/oss2/scfindex.html. (These data stem from the 1998 survey, which is the most recent year available. Data from a 2001 survey are scheduled to be released in February 2003.)

20 U.S. Census of Agriculture.

21 USDA, *Food and Agricultural Policy*. 2001, Chapter 3, 48.

22 USDA, ERS, "Farm Income and Costs: Farm Balance Sheet – Debt." Available from http://www.ers.usda.gov/Briefing/FarmIncome/fbsdebt_txt.htm.

23 Jerome Stam, Daniel Milkove, Steven Koenig, et al, "Agricultural Income and Finance Annual Lender Issue." USDA, ERS, AIS-78, Feb. 26, 2002, 1. Available from http://jan.mannlib.cornell.edu/reports/erssor/economics/ais-bb/2002/ais78.pdf.

24 Ibid.

25 In 1996 and 1999, delinquency rates increased somewhat.

26 "Using Farm-sector Income as a Policy Benchmark," 18.

27 Daryll E. Ray, "Impacts of the 1996 Farm Bill Including Ad Hoc Additions." *Journal of Agricultural and Applied Economics*, (Vol. 33 No. 2) 2001, 245-60.

28 The three farm categories represent similar groupings as part of the USDA's Agricultural Resource Management Survey categories: rural-residence farms (small), intermediate farms (mid-size) and commercial farms (large).

29 "Understanding Rural America." USDA, ERS, AIB-710, 1995. Available from http://www.ers.usda.gov/publications/aib710/.

30 Leslie A. Whitener, Greg J. Duncan and Bruce A. Weber, "Reforming Welfare: What Does It Mean for Rural Areas?" USDA, Food Assistance and Nutrition Research Report Number 26-4, June 2002. Available from http://www.ers.usda.gov/publications/fanrr26-4/fanrr26-4.pdf.

31 American's Second Harvest, "Who's Hungry: Hunger in Rural America." Available from http://www.secondharvest.org/whoshungry/rural_hunger_stats.html.

32 A. Hamelin, J. Habicht, M. Beaudry, "Food Insecurity: Consequences of the Household and Broader Social Implications." *Journal of Nutrition*. (Vol. 129) 1999, 525-528. Available from http://www.nutrition.org/cgi/content/full/129/2/525S#SEC2.

33 Catholic Campaign for Human Development, "Poverty Pulse." January 2002. Available from http://www.usccb.org/cchd/povertyusa/povpulse.htm.

34 Jill L. Findeis, Mark Henry, Thomas A. Hirschl, et al, "Welfare Reform in Rural America: A Review of Current Research." Rural Policy Research Institute Policy Paper P2001-5, February 2001. Available from http://www.rupri.org/.

35 Center for Rural Affairs, "Trampled Dreams: The Neglected Economy of the Rural Great Plains." 2000; the six states include Iowa, Kansas, Nebraska, North Dakota and South Dakota. "Rural farm" is defined as having populations of less than 2,500.

36 Associated Press, "Central Nebraska Farmers Call on Politicians to Help with Drought." *Dodge City Daily Globe*, 2001. Available from http://www.dodgeglobe.com/stories/082602/nat_farmers.shtml.

37 U.S. Department of Labor, "Findings from the National Agricultural Workers Survey (NAWS) 1997-1998." Research Report No. 8, March 2000, 30.

38 Ibid., 31.

39 Tulare County is the second leading U.S. farm county, with 1999 farm sales of $3.1 billion.

40 "Napa's Homeless," CaliforniaConnected.Org. Produced by Angela Shelley. Researched by Autumn Doerr. 2002. Available from http://www.californiaconnected.org/segments/2002/08/22/segment2.html.

41 U.S. Department of Labor, 40-45.

42 USDA, *Family Economics and Nutrition Review*. (Vol. 12 Nos. 3 & 4) 1999, 93.

43 Dan Smalley, "Structural Change and Technology: The Policy Implications." Conference Paper, 2nd Annual National Symposium on the Future of American Agriculture, Aug. 10-11, 2000. Available from http://www.agecon.uga.edu/archive/agsym2000/smalley/Smalley.html.

44 The nation's 50 largest pork producers control the vast majority of U.S. pork production. The largest producer, Smithfield Foods, controls more than 24 percent, followed by Premium Standard Farms (7 percent), Seaboard Farms (6 percent), Prestage Farms (4 percent), The Pork Group / Tyson (4 percent), Cargill (4 percent), Iowa Select Farms (3 percent), Christensen Farms (3 percent) and Purina Mills (2 percent).

45 Richard J. Dove, "Testimony before Senate Committee on Government Affairs." March 13, 2002. Available from http://www.senate.gov/%7Egov_affairs/031302dove.htm#_ftnl.

46 Former Sen. Jean Carnahan, Press Release. Dec. 17, 2001. Accessed on Aug. 20, 2002 from http://carnahan.senate.gov/press/dec17c.htm.

47 C. Phillip Baumel, "How U.S. Grain Export Projections from Large Scale Agricultural Sector Models Compare with Reality." Institute for Agriculture and Trade Policy, May 2001. Available from http://www.iatorg/enviroObs/library/uploadedfiles/How_US_Grain_Export_Projections_from_Large_Sca.pdf.

48 Ray, 245-60.

Endnotes

49 Food and Agriculture Organization of the United Nations, "FAOStat Statistical Database." 2002. Available from http://apps.fao.org.

50 C. Phillip Baumel, Marty J. McVey and Robert Wisner, "An Assessment of Brazilian Soybean Production." *Doane's Agricultural Report*. (Vol. 63 No. 25) 2001, 5-6.

51 Paul C. Westcott, C. Edwin Young and J. Michael Price, "The 2002 Farm Act: Provisions and Implications for Commodity Markets." USDA, ERS, AIB-778, November 2002, 8. Available from http://www.ers.usda.gov/publications/aib778/aib778.pdf.

52 Sophia Murphy, "Farm Bill Outrage Goes Global" CommonDreams.org, May 29, 2002. Available from http://www.commondreams.org/views02/0529-07.htm.

53 USDA, Foreign Agriculture Service, "The U.S. WTO Agriculture Proposal." Available from http://www.fas.usda.gov/itp/wto/proposalhtm.

54 Ann M. Veneman, Speech to International Policy Council on Agriculture, Food and Trade, May 3. 2002. Available from http://www.usda.gov/news/releases/2002/05/0184.htm.

55 Jerry Skees, "The Potential Influence of Risk Management Programs on Cropping Decisions." Conference Paper, American Agricultural Economics Association, August 2000.

56 Ann M. Veneman, "Statement On the Introduction of the 2002 Farm Bill Legislation by Sen. Richard Lugar." USDA, Oct. 17, 2001. Available from http://www.usda.gov/news/releases/2001/10/0203.htm.

Chapter 3

1   Pitak Intrawityanunt, speech at World Food Summit Plus Five, June 10, 2002. Available from http://www.fao.org/worldfoodsummit/top/detail.asp?event_id=12727.

2   World Trade Organization (WTO), "Preamble to Agreement Establishing the WTO." April 1994.

3   Nancy Birdsall, "Asymmetric Globalization: Outcomes versus Opportunities." September 2001, 2. Available from http://www.bc.edu/bc_org/avp/cas/isp/inequality/Asymmetric_Globalization.pdf.

4   In the late 19th century, Great Britain undertook unilateral trade liberalization, but this act is almost unique in the history of international trade.

5   Eugenio Diaz-Bonilla and Sherman Robinson, "WTO Can Help World's Poor Farmers." *International Herald Tribune*, March 28, 2001.

6   WTO, "Agreement Establishing the World Trade Organization." April 1994, 9. Available from http://www.wto.org/english/docs_e/legal_e/04-wto.pdf.

7   Bread for the World Institute calculation; data from Food and Agriculture Organization's statistical database, FAOSTAT. Available from http://apps.fao.org.

8   Thomas C. Beierle, "From Uruguay to Doha: Agricultural Trade Negotiations at the World Trade Organization." Resources for the Future Discussion Paper 02-13, March 2002, ii.

9   Ibid., 21.

10 Some claim that with new payments under the 2002 farm bill, the United States has exceeded its amber box spending limit under the Agreement on Agriculture.

11 Beierle, 17.

12 U.N. Conference on Trade and Development (UNCTAD), *The Least Developed Country Report 2002*. (Geneva: United Nations) 2002, 117.

13 Not least a position under the U.S. Cold War security umbrella and authoritarian governments.

14 Eugenio Diaz-Bonilla, Sherman Robinson, Marcelle Thomas, et al, "WTO, Agriculture, and Developing Countries: A Survey of Issues." Trade and Macroeconomics Division of the International Food Policy Research Institute Discussion Paper No. 81, January 2002, 39.

15 Oxfam International, *Rigged Rules and Double Standards*. (Oxfam International), 2002.

16 As of Jan. 1, 2002.

17 Diaz-Bonilla et al, "WTO, Agriculture, and Developing Countries."

18 WTO, *International Trade Statistics 2001*. (France: WTO) 2001, 77.

19 Diana Tussie and Miguel F. Lengyel, "Developing Countries: Turning Participation into Influence." *Development, Trade, and the WTO: A Handbook*. (World Bank Group), 2002. 491.

20 Dani Rodrik, "The Global Governance of Trade as if Development Really Mattered." U.N. Development Program Background Paper, October 2001, 26. Available from http://www.undorg/mainundp/propoor/docs/pov_globalgovernancetrade_pub.pdf.

21 Tussie, 486.

22 T. Ademola Oyejide, "Interests and Options of Developing Countries and Least-developed Countries in a New Round of Multilateral Negotiations." UNCTAD Discussion Paper No. 2, May 2000, 25.

23 Ibid.

24 Richard W. Stevenson, "Seeking Trade, Africans Find Western Barriers." *The New York Times*, May 26, 2002.

25 Yoweri Museveni, speech at World Food Summit Plus Five, June 10, 2002. Available from http://www.fao.org/worldfoodsummit/top/detail.asp?event_id=12702.

26 Ahman Kabbah, speech at World Food Summit Plus Five, June 10, 2002. Available from http://www.fao.org/worldfoodsummit/top/detail.asp?event_id=12710.

27 WTO, "The Decision on Measures Concerning the Possible Negative Effects of the Reform Program on Least-Developed and Net Food-Importing Developing Countries." Feb. 4, 2002. Available from http://www.ictsd.org/issarea/africa/S&D/W77R1A1C1.pdf.

Chapter 4

1   The use of the word 'Africa' in this chapter is synonymous with 'sub-Saharan Africa.'

2   International Food Policy Research Institute (IFPRI), "Ending Hunger in Africa: Only the Small Farmer Can Do It." 2002, 2. Available from http://www.ifpri.org/pubs/ib/ib10.pdf.

3   United Nations Conference on Trade and Development, "From Adjustment to Poverty Reduction: What is New?" Economic Development in Africa, 2002, 6. Available from http://www.unctad.org/en/docs//pogdsafricad2.en.pdf.

4   World Bank, *Can Africa Claim the 21st Century?* (Washington, D.C.: The World Bank) 2000.

5   Nancy Birdsall, Stijn Claessens and Ishac Diwan, "Will HIPC Matter? The Debt Game and Donor Behavior in Africa." Conference Paper, WIDER Debt Relief Conference, Helsinki, Finland, Aug. 17-18, 2001, 5. Available from http://www.ceiorg/files/pdf/Hipc.pdf.

6   World Bank, "World Bank Says Trade Policies Hindering Debt Relief." Jan. 14, 2003. Available from http://web.worldbank.org/WBSITE/EXTERNAL/NEWS/0,,date:01-14-2003~menuPK:34461~pagePK:34392~piPK:34427~theSitePK:4607,00.html#Story2.

7   Structural Adjustment Participatory Review International Network, *The Policy Roots of Economic Crisis and Poverty: A Multi-Country Participatory Assessment of Structural Adjustment* (Structural Adjustment Participatory Review International Network) April 2002, 159. Available from http://www.saprin.org/SAPRI_Findings.pdf.

8   D. Booth, "PRSP Process in 8 Countries: Initial Impact and Potential for Institutionalization." Conference Paper, WIDER Development Conference on Debt Relief, Helsinki, Finland, Aug. 17-18, 2001. Available from http://www.wider.unu.edu/conference/conference-2001-2/parallel%20papers/1_2_booth.pdf.

9   International Fund for Agricultural Development, "Drylands: A Call to Action." 1998, 7. Available from http://www.ifad.org/pub/dryland/e/drylands.pdf.

10 The World Bank, "Fighting the Population/Agriculture/Population Nexus in Sub-Saharan Africa." *Findings*, (No. 28) December 1994. Available from http://www.worldbank.org/afr/findings/english/find28.htm.

11 Mark W. Rosegrant, Michael S. Paisner, Siet Meujer and Julie Witcover, *Global Food Projections to 2020: Emerging Trends and Alternative Futures*. (IFPRI) 2001, 5, 8. Available from http://www.ifpri.org.

[12] D. Byerlee, and Carl K. Eicher, eds., *An Emerging Maize Revolution in Africa*. (Boulder: Lynne Rienner Publishers) 1997.

[13] Rosegrant, 17-18.

[14] D. Karanja, "An Economic and Institutional Analysis of Maize Research in Kenya." Michigan State University International Development Working Paper No. 57, Michigan State University, Department of Agricultural Economics 1996. Available from http://www.aec.msu.edu/agecon/fs2/papers/idwp57.pdf.

[15] R. Mungai, "Female-Headed Households, Poverty and Welfare in Kenya." International Center for Research on Women, 2001, Draft.

[16] M. Buvinic and R. Mehra, "Women and Agricultural Development." *Agricultural Development in the Third World*, 2nd Ed. (Baltimore: Johns Hopkins University Press) 1990; R. M. Hassan, D. Karanja and H. Mulamula, "Availability and Effectiveness of Agricultural Extension Services for Maize Farmers in Kenya." *Maize Technology Development and Transfer: A GIS Application from Research Planning in Kenya*. (CABI Publishers) 1998.

[17] J. Govereh and T. S. Jayne, "Effect of Cash Crop Production on Food Crop Productivity on Zimbabwe: Synergies of Trade Offs." U.S. Agency for International Aid, Office of Sustainable Development Food Security II Cooperative Agreement Policy Synthesis No. 40, 1999.

[18] I. Husain and R. Faruqee, eds., *Adjustment in Africa: Lessons From Country Case Studies*. (Washington, D.C.: The World Bank) 1994; J. Govereh, A. Naseem and V. Kelly, "Macro Trends and Determinants of Fertilizer Use in Sub-Saharan Africa." Michigan State University International Development Working Paper No. 73, Michigan State University, Department of Agricultural Economics, 1999. Available from http://www.aec.msu.edu/agecon/fs2/papers/idwp73.pdf.

[19] NASFAM is an ACDI/VOCA project funded by the U.S. Agency for International Development as well as NASFAM members, shareholders and owner-controlled agribusiness associations.

[20] T. Reardon, E. W. Crawford, V. Kelly and B. Diagana, "Promoting Farm Investments for Sustainable Intensification of African Agriculture." U.S. Agency for International Aid, Office of Sustainable Development Food Security II Cooperative Agreement Policy Synthesis No. 3, 1996.

[21] The Microcredit Summit Campaign, "Microcredit in Tanzania, Tanzania Pride: Zainabu Saleh Msomoka." Press Information, 2001. Available from http://microcreditsummit.org/press/Pride.htm.

[22] Oxfam International, *Rigged Rules and Double Standards*. (Oxfam International) 2002.

[23] Joint United Nations Program on HIV/AIDS and World Health Organization, "AIDS Epidemic Update." December 2002. Available from http://www.unaids.org/worldaidsday/2002/press/Epiupdate.html.

[24] Mike Mathambo Mtika, "Social and Cultural Relations in Economic Action: The Embeddedness of Food Security in Rural Malawi Amidst the AIDS Epidemic." *Environment and Planning A* (Vol. 32 No. 2) February 2000, 345-60.

[25] World Bank, *Can Africa Claim the 21st Century?*.

[26] Ibid.

[27] J. Azam, A. Fosu and N.S. Ndung'u, "Explaining Slow Growth in Africa." *Africa Development Review* (Vol. 14, Issue 1) 2002, 177-220 (44). Available from http://www.blackwellpublishing.com/journalasp?ref=1017-6772.

[28] World Bank, *Can Africa Claim the 21st Century?*.

[29] IFPRI, "Ending Hunger in Africa: Only the Small Farmer Can Do It." 2002, 2. Available from http://www.ifpri.org/pubs/ib/ib10.pdf.

[30] Oxfam International.

[31] International Fund for Agricultural Development, *Rural Poverty Report: The Challenge of Ending Rural Poverty* (New York: Oxford University Press) 2001.

[32] World Bank, *Can Africa Claim the 21st Century?*.

Chapter 5

[1] Douglas Farah and Colum Lynch, "Hussein Said to Exploit Oil-for-Food." *The Washington Post*, Sept. 18, 2002.

[2] CNN.com, "Russian Troops Storm Moscow Theater." Oct. 26, 2002. Available from http://www.cnn.com/2002/WORLD/europe/10/25/moscow.siege/.

Chapter 6

[1] Oxfam Hong Kong, "Farthest Corner – Country Profiles." Available from http://www.oxfam.org.hk/english/cyberschool/world/031.htm.

[2] International Fund for Agricultural Development (IFAD), *Assessment of Rural Poverty: Latin America and the Caribbean* (Santiago: IFAD) 2001, 86.

[3] World Bank, *World Development Report 2003* (Washington DC: World Bank and Oxford University Press) 2003, 85.

[4] Food and Agriculture Organization of the United Nations (FAO), "Mobilizing the Political Will and Resources to Banish World Hunger." Prepared for World Food Summit Plus Five, 2002, 82.

[5] Eugenio Diaz-Bonilla, Marcelle Thomas and Sherman Robinson, "On Boxes, Contents, and Users: Food Security and the WTO Negotiations." International Food Policy Research Institute, Conference Paper, OECD/World Bank Global Forum on Agriculture Trade Reform, Adjustment and Poverty, May 2002, 12.

[6] FAO, "Trade in Agriculture, Fisheries and Forestry." Available from www.fao.org/ur.

[7] World Trade Organization, "World Bank Grant Kicks Off Bank-WTO Assistance on Standards." Sept. 27, 2002. Available from http://www.wto.org/english/news_e/pres02_e/pr314_e.htm.

[8] International Monetary Fund, *World Economic Outlook, Trade and Finance*. (Washington DC: International Monetary Fund) 2002, 85. Available from http://www.imf.org/external/pubs/ft/weo/2002/02/index.htm.

[9] IFAD, The Popular Coalition and United Nations Research Institute for Social Development, *Whose Land? Civil Society Perspectives on Land Reform and Rural Poverty Reduction* (Rome: IFAD) 2001, 3.

[10] Chevron Corp. merged with Texaco Corp. in 2001 and now is ChevronTexaco Corp.

[11] U.N. Conference on Trade and Development, "Overview: Foreign Direct Investment in Least Developed Countries." 2001, 1. Available from http://r0.unctad.org/en/subsites/dite/LDCs/pdfs/overview2002.pdf.

[12] Theodore H. Moran, *FDI and Development: The New Policy Agenda for Developing Countries and Economies in Transition*. (Institute for International Economics) 1998, 31-35.

[13] Action Group on Erosion, Technology and Concentration, "Globalization Inc. – Concentration in Corporate Power: The Unmentioned Agenda." Communique No. 71, July/August, 2001. Available from http://www.rafi.org/article.asp?newsid=154.

Chapter 7

[1] Saskia Rozemeijer and Rinato Mariani, "Final Report: Netforum International Conference on Education." U.N. Educational, Scientific and Cultural Organization, September 2001, 18. Available from http://www.ibe.unesco.org/International/ICE/46netforum/nfhomee.htm.

[2] Matthew A. Crenson and Benjamin Ginsberg, "From Citizens to Customers, Losing Our Collective Voice." *The Washington Post*, Nov. 3, 2002, B01.

Poorer Countries Would Gain from Open Agriculture Markets: A Technical Note

Xinshen Diao, Eugenio Diaz-Bonilla and Sherman Robinson of the International Food Policy Research Institute (IFPRI) use a world trade model to evaluate the impact of the elimination of subsidies and agriculture protection in industrialized countries on agricultural and food agroindustrial production in developing countries. Economic models are simplified representations of reality that typically begin with a set of assumptions. While not exact, they present a likely outcome based on past trends and known factors. Several models, including this model and the International Monetary Fund results cited elsewhere in this report, indicate that overall agricultural trade liberalization would lead to a net gain in income for developing countries.

For the study, IFPRI uses the Global Trade Analysis Project (GTAP) database, which includes 40 developing countries or country groups (see Annex 1, below).[1] The December 2002 results are aggregated into four groups: sub-Saharan Africa, Asia (developing economies), Latin America and the Caribbean, and the rest of developing and transition economies. The model finds that full agricultural trade liberalization of industrialized countries would increase developing countries' exports to $184.4 billion (see Table A.1).

According to the database, most developing countries' agricultural export markets are in the North. On average, 65 percent of developing countries' total agricultural exports are imported by northern countries, and mainly go to the three largest markets in the world – East Asia (represented by Japan and Korea), North America (mainly the United States) and the European Union.

There are 17 agricultural and processed food commodities or commodity groups in the model and the rest of the economy is aggregated in only one sector (see Table A.2 for all products used in the model). Except for rice, for which a few Asian countries' exports account for 70 percent of world rice trade, the North, especially the United States and Canada, dominates world grain exports. Exports of nongrain crops, such as fruits and vegetables, cotton, sugar and vegetable oil, largely are the domain of developing countries. Excluding intra-E.U. trade, developing countries account for 60 percent to 80 percent of world exports of these commodities, most of which are exported to the North. Due to such different export structures, agricultural exports of many developing countries generally do not compete directly with the exports of developed countries. However, exports of industrialized countries may compete with grain and animal products, in the domestic market of developing countries.

Although IFPRI's analysis includes a technological spillover variable, other additional dynamic effects have not been considered. It is likely that with greater incentives due to higher prices, developing countries could increase investment in agriculture and agroindustrial production, further expanding production, consumption and trade. On the other hand, observation suggests that technological spillovers can be uneven, and there are areas untouched by the global changes that have taken place. In particular, countries in South Asia and sub-Saharan Africa have a far lower share of the world's trade and capital inflows, and they remain among the poorest in the world.

---

[1] The GTAP project is coordinated by the Center for Global Trade Analysis, which is housed in the Department of Agricultural Economics, Purdue University.

ANNEX 1 Developing Regions/Countries

China	Hungary
Indonesia	Poland
Malaysia	Rest of Central Europe
Philippines	Associates
Thailand	Former Soviet Union
Vietnam	Turkey
Bangladesh	Rest of Middle East
India	Morocco
Sri Lanka	North Africa
Rest of South Asia	Botswana
Mexico	Rest of South African
Central America and the	Customs Union
Caribbean	Malawi
Colombia	Mozambique
Peru	Tanzania
Venezuela	Zambia
Rest of Andean Pact	Zimbabwe
Argentina	Other Southern Africa
Brazil	Uganda
Chile	Rest of Sub-Saharan Africa
Uruguay	Rest of World
Rest of South America	

Table A.1: Developing Country Agricultural Exports

	Trade in Billion Dollars					Percent Gain
		Agricultural Trade Liberalization of				
Developing Country Regions	1997 Trade Levels	United States only	European Union only	Japan, Korea only	All Industrialized Countries	All Industrialized Countries
Sub-Saharan Africa	$14.6	$15.3	$16.6	$14.9	$17.7	21.2%
Asia	$46.4	$49.4	$49.4	$49.7	$56.3	21.5%
Latin America and Caribbean	$59.1	$64.1	$66.9	$60.0	$73.7	24.8%
Other Developing Countries*	$27.1	$28.5	$34.3	$27.7	$36.7	35.4%
All Developing Countries	$147.2	$157.3	$167.2	$152.3	$184.4	25.3%

*Other developing and transition economies.

Table A.2: Effect of Trade Liberalization on Commodity Prices

Agricultural Liberalization Effect (Percent of Change) from

Commodities	United States	European Union	Japan, Korea	All Industrialized Countries
Paddy Rice	0.47%	0.74%	0.89%	2.27%
Wheat	3.42%	3.00%	0.25%	7.28%
Cereal Grains	1.36%	3.40%	0.19%	5.09%
Vegetables, Fruit, Nuts	−0.17%	0.49%	0.04%	0.34%
Oil Seeds	3.42%	4.95%	0.17%	9.42%
Plant-based Fibers	4.06%	0.13%	0.34%	4.46%
Other Crops	2.26%	0.14%	0.15%	2.41%
Bovine Cattle, Sheep and Goats, Horses	0.14%	3.65%	0.21%	4.05%
Other Animal Products	−0.08%	1.24%	0.46%	1.62%
Wool, Silk	0.03%	0.12%	0.45%	0.83%
Bovine Meat Products	−0.03%	1.68%	0.26%	1.91%
Other Meat Products	−0.08%	1.77%	1.67%	3.37%
Vegetable Oils and Fats	0.42%	1.57%	0.18%	2.26%
Dairy Products	0.18%	2.34%	0.26%	2.90%
Sugar	1.42%	3.41%	1.30%	6.14%
Other Food Products	0.24%	0.65%	0.11%	1.03%
Beverages and Tobacco Products	−0.01%	0.06%	0.05%	0.07%

Table 1: Global Hunger – Life and Death Indicators

	Population Total (millions) mid-2002	Projected (millions) 2025	Projected population change (%) 2002-2050	Total fertility rate 2000	% below age 15 2001	% urban 2000	Life expectancy at birth Male	Life expectancy at birth Female	Infant mortality rate (under 1) 2000	% of low birth weight infants 1995-2000[y]	% of 1-year-old children immunized (measles) 1999	Under-5 mortality rate per 1,000 live births 1960	Under-5 mortality rate per 1,000 live births 2000	Maternal mortality rate per 100,000 live births 1985-99[y]	Refugees as of Dec. 31, 2001 Country of origin	Refugees as of Dec. 31, 2001 Country of asylum
Developing Countries	..	..	..	3.1	..	40	..	..	63	14	69	216	91	440	..	..
Africa (sub-Saharan)	693.0	1,081.0	132	5.7	..	34	52	54	108	12[e]	51	261[e]	175[e]	1,100	..	..
Angola	12.7	28.2	319	7.2	48	34	44	47	172	..	46	345	295	..	445,000	12,000
Benin	6.6	12.0	173	5.9	46	42	53	56	98	15	82	300	154	500	..	5,000
Botswana	1.6	1.2	-27	4.2	42	50	39	40	74	11	86	170	101	330	..	4,000
Burkina Faso	12.6	21.6	172	6.9	49	19	46	47	105	18	53	315	198	480	..	..
Burundi	6.7	12.4	202	6.8	47	9	46	41	114	16[x]	75	255	190	..	375,000	28,000
Cameroon	16.2	24.7	114	4.9	43	49	54	56	95	10	62	255	154	430	..	32,000
Cape Verde	0.5	0.7	81	3.4	39	62	66	72	30	13	..	164	40	35	..	..
Central African Republic	3.6	4.9	75	5.1	43	41	42	46	115	13[x]	39	327	180	1,100	22,000	49,000
Chad	9.0	18.2	270	6.7	47	24	49	53	118	24	30	325	198	830	35,000	15,000
Comoros	0.6	1.1	199	5.2	43	33	54	59	61	18	..	265	82	..	..	..
Congo, Dem. Rep. of	55.2	106.0	229	6.7	49	30	47	51	128	15	15	302	207	..	355,000	305,000
Congo, Republic of	3.2	6.3	235	6.3	46	63	49	53	81	..	23	220	108	..	30,000	102,000
Côte d'Ivoire	16.8	25.6	112	4.9	42	46	44	47	102	17	62	300	173	600	..	103,000
Djibouti	0.7	0.8	64	6.0	43	83	42	44	102	..	21	289	146	..	1,000	22,000
Equatorial Guinea	0.5	0.9	185	5.9	44	48	49	53	103	..	24	316	156	..	..	..
Eritrea	4.5	8.3	198	5.5	44	19	53	58	73	14	88	250	114	1,000	305,000	2,000
Ethiopia	67.7	117.6	155	6.8	45	18	51	53	117	12	27	280	174	..	13,000	114,000
Gabon	1.2	1.4	47	5.4	40	81	49	51	60	..	55	287	90	520	..	20,000
Gambia	1.5	2.7	186	5.0	40	33	51	55	92	14	88	364	128	..	..	15,000
Ghana	20.2	26.5	58	4.4	40	38	56	59	58	9	73	215	102	210[x]	10,000	12,000
Guinea	8.4	14.1	147	6.1	44	33	47	48	112	10	52	380	175	530	5,000	190,000
Guinea-Bissau	1.3	2.2	161	6.0	44	24	43	46	132	20	70	336	215	910	1,500	7,000
Kenya	31.1	33.3	20	4.4	43	33	47	49	77	9	79	205	120	590	..	243,000
Lesotho	2.2	2.4	29	4.7	39	28	50	52	92	..	77	203	133	..	..	..
Liberia	3.3	6.0	204	6.8	42	45	49	52	157	..	..	288	235	..	215,000	60,000
Madagascar	16.9	30.8	178	5.9	45	30	53	57	86	15	55	364	139	490	..	..
Malawi	10.9	12.8	38	6.6	46	25	37	38	117	13[x]	83	361	188	1,100	..	6,000
Mali	11.3	21.6	221	7.0	46	30	46	48	142	16	57	517	233	580	..	9,000
Mauritania	2.6	5.1	175	6.0	44	58	53	55	120	..	62	310	183	550[x]	50,000	25,000
Mauritius	1.2	1.4	22	2.0	25	41	68	75	17	13	79	92	20	21	..	..
Mozambique	19.6	20.6	17	6.1	44	40	38	37	126	13	57	313	200	1,100	..	5,000
Namibia	1.8	2.0	35	5.1	44	31	44	41	56	15[x]	66	206	69	230	..	31,000
Niger	11.6	25.7	346	8.0	50	21	45	46	159	12	36	354	270	590	..	1,000
Nigeria	129.9	204.5	134	5.7	45	44	52	52	110	9	41	207	184	..	10,000	7,000
Rwanda	7.4	8.0	20	6.0	44	6	39	40	100	12[x]	87	210	187	..	60,000	35,000
Senegal	9.9	16.5	129	5.4	44	47	52	55	80	12	60	300	139	560	10,000	43,000
Sierra Leone	5.6	10.6	166	6.5	44	37	38	40	180	22	62	390	316	..	185,000	15,000
Somalia	7.8	14.9	229	7.3	48	28	45	48	133	..	26	294	225	..	300,000	..
South Africa	43.6	35.1	-25	3.0	34	50	50	52	55	..	82	130	70	..	..	22,000
Sudan	32.6	49.6	95	4.7	40	36	55	57	66	..	53	210	108	550	440,000	307,000
Swaziland	1.1	1.4	80	4.6	41	26	40	41	101	..	82	233	142	230	..	1,000
Tanzania	37.2	59.8	137	5.3	..	33	51	53	104	11	72	240	165	530	..	498,000
Togo	5.3	7.6	84	5.6	44	33	53	57	80	13	43	267	142	480	2,000	11,000
Uganda	24.7	48.0	241	7.1	49	14	42	44	81	13	53	224	127	510	20,000	174,000
Zambia	10.0	14.3	104	5.9	47	40	37	37	112	11	90	213	202	650	..	270,000
Zimbabwe	12.3	10.3	-18	4.8	45	35	39	36	73	10	79	159	117	700	..	9,000
South Asia	..	..	..	3.5	..	28	..	..	72	26	54	239	100	430	..	..
Afghanistan	27.8	45.9	142	6.9	43	22	46	44	165	..	40	360	257	..	4,500,000	..
Bangladesh	133.6	177.8	54	3.7	38	25	59	59	54	30	71	247	82	350	..	122,200
Bhutan	0.9	1.4	122	5.3	42	7	66	66	77	15	76	300	100	380	126,000	..
India	1,049.5	1,363.0	55	3.2	33	28	62	64	69	26	50	236	96	540	17,000	345,800
Maldives	0.3	0.5	137	5.6	43	26	67	66	59	12	86	300	80	350	..	..
Nepal	23.9	36.1	82	4.7	41	12	58	57	72	21	73	297	100	540	..	131,000
Pakistan	143.5	242.1	131	5.3	42	37	63	63	85	21[x]	54	226	110	..	10,000	2,018,000
Sri Lanka	18.9	22.1	20	2.1	26	24	70	74	17	17	95	133	19	60	144,000	..

Table 1: Global Hunger – Life and Death Indicators

| | Population | | | | | | Life expectancy at birth | | Infant mortality rate (under 1) 2000 | % of low birth weight infants 1995-2000y | % of 1-year-old children immunized (measles) 1999y | Under-5 mortality rate per 1,000 live births | | Maternal mortality rate per 100,000 live births 1985-99y | Refugees as of Dec. 31, 2001 | |
	Total (millions) mid-2002	Projected (millions) 2025	Projected population change (%) 2002-2050	Total fertility rate 2000	% below age 15 2001	% urban 2000	Male	Female				1960	2000		Country of origin	Country of asylum
East Asia and the Pacific	..	..	..	2.1	..	35	..	..	34	8	85	201ᶠ	44	140	..	..
Brunei	0.4	0.5	69	2.7	31	72	71	76	6	..	94	87	7	0	..	..
Cambodia	12.3	18.4	78	5.1	43	16	54	58	95	9	55	217	135	440	16,400	1,000
China	1,280.7	1,454.7	9	1.8	24	32	69	73	32	6	90	209	40	55	151,000	345,000
Hong Kongᶜ	6.8	8.4	10	..	16	..	77	82	..	..	..	..	..	..	..	..
Fiji	0.9	1.0	10	3.1	33	49	65	69	18	12ˣ	75	97	22	38	..	..
Indonesia	217.0	281.9	46	2.5	30	41	66	70	35	9	71	216	48	380	5,000	81,300
Korea, DPR (North)	23.2	25.7	14	2.1	26	60	62	67	23	..	34	120	30	110	50,000	..
Korea, Rep. of (South)	48.4	50.5	3	1.5	21	82	72	80	5	..	85	127	5	20	..	600
Laos, PDR	5.5	8.6	107	5.1	42	24	52	55	90	..	71	235	105	650	400	..
Malaysia	24.4	35.6	90	3.1	34	57	70	75	8	9	88	105	9	41	..	57,500
Mongolia	2.4	3.3	60	2.5	34	64	61	65	62	6	93	185	78	150	..	..
Myanmar (Burma)	49.0	60.2	40	3.1	33	28	54	59	78	16	85	252	110	230	450,000	..
Papua New Guinea	5.0	8.0	118	4.5	40	17	56	58	79	..	58	204	112	370	..	5,400
Philippines	80.0	115.5	82	3.4	37	59	65	71	30	18	79	110	40	170	57,000	200
Singapore	4.2	8.0	145	1.6	22	100	76	80	4	8	93	40	4	6	..	..
Solomon Islands	0.5	0.9	204	5.5	45	20	67	68	21	..	..	185	25	550ˣ	..	..
Thailand	62.6	72.1	15	2.1	26	22	70	75	25	7	96	148	29	44	..	277,000
Vietnam	79.7	104.1	47	2.4	33	20	67	70	30	9	93	219	39	95	295,000	16,000
Latin America and the Caribbean	531.0ᵈ	697ᵈ	53ᵈ	2.7	..	75	68ᵈ	74ᵈ	30	9ᵍ	92	154ᵍ	37ᵍ	190	..	..
Argentina	36.5	47.2	49	2.5	28	90	70	77	18	7	99	72	21	41	..	3,100
Belize	0.3	0.4	137	3.2	38	54	70	74	34	4	82	104	41	140	..	..
Bolivia	8.8	13.2	95	4.2	39	63	61	64	64	8	79	255	80	390	..	400
Brazil	173.8	219.0	42	2.3	28	81	65	73	32	9	99	177	38	160	..	4,050
Chile	15.6	19.5	43	2.4	28	86	73	79	10	5	96	138	12	23	..	550
Colombia	43.8	59.7	63	2.7	32	74	68	74	25	7	75	130	30	80	23,000	200
Costa Rica	3.9	5.2	49	2.8	32	48	75	79	10	6	88	112	12	29	..	10,600
Cuba	11.3	11.8	-1	1.6	21	75	74	78	7	6	96	54	9	33	1,100	1,000
Dominican Republic	8.8	12.1	70	2.8	33	65	67	71	42	13	96	149	48	230ˣ	..	500
Ecuador	13.0	18.5	76	3.0	33	65	68	73	25	16	99	180	32	160	..	4,300
El Salvador	6.6	9.3	89	3.1	35	47	67	73	34	13	99	210	40	120	217,000	..
Guatemala	12.1	19.8	125	4.7	43	40	63	69	44	12	83	202	59	190	129,000	700
Guyana	0.8	0.7	-34	2.4	30	38	59	67	55	14	87	126	74	110	..	..
Haiti	7.1	9.6	68	4.2	40	36	48	51	81	28ˣ	54	253	125	520	25,000	..
Honduras	6.7	9.6	81	4.0	41	53	64	68	32	6	98	204	40	110	..	..
Jamaica	2.6	3.3	46	2.5	31	56	73	77	17	11	96	76	20	95	..	..
Mexico	101.7	131.7	48	2.7	33	74	73	78	25	9	95	134	30	55	..	6,200
Nicaragua	5.4	8.6	117	4.1	42	56	66	71	37	13	99	193	45	150	3,100	..
Panama	2.9	3.8	46	2.5	31	56	72	77	20	10	90	104	26	70	..	1,500
Paraguay	6.0	10.1	149	4.0	39	56	69	73	27	9	92	90	31	190	..	50
Peru	26.7	35.7	60	2.8	33	73	66	71	40	10	93	234	50	270	750	750
Suriname	0.4	0.5	-11	2.2	30	74	68	74	27	11	85	98	33	110	..	..
Trinidad and Tobago	1.3	1.4	6	1.6	24	74	68	73	17	..	91	73	20	70	..	100
Uruguay	3.4	3.8	25	2.4	25	91	71	79	15	..	93	56	17	26	..	..
Venezuela	25.1	34.8	63	2.9	34	87	71	77	20	6	82	75	23	60	..	400
Middle East and North Africa	..	..	..	3.8	..	58	..	..	49	11ʰ	85	241ʰ	64	360	..	..
Algeria	31.4	43.0	63	3.1	34	60	68	71	50	7	83	255	65	220ˣ	10,000	85,000
Bahrain	0.7	1.7	328	2.5	28	92	73	75	13	10	94	203	16	46	..	..
Cyprus	0.9	1.0	9	2.0	23	57	75	80	6	..	..	36	7	0	..	1,300
Egypt	71.2	96.1	62	3.2	35	45	65	68	37	10	95	282	43	170	..	75,000
Iran	65.6	84.7	47	3.0	36	62	68	70	36	7	99	233	44	37	34,000	2,558,000
Iraq	23.6	41.2	154	5.1	41	77	56	59	105	23	63	171	130	..	300,000	128,100
Jordan	5.3	8.7	122	4.5	40	74	69	71	28	10	94	139	34	41	..	1,643,900
Kuwait	2.3	3.9	140	2.8	29	98	74	78	9	7	96	128	10	5	..	50,000
Lebanon	4.3	5.4	34	2.3	31	90	72	75	28	6	88	85	32	100	3,900	389,500

Table 1: Global Hunger – Life and Death Indicators

	Population Total (millions) mid-2002	Population Projected (millions) 2025	Projected population change (%) 2002-2050	Total fertility rate 2000	% below age 15 2001	% urban 2000	Life expectancy at birth Male	Life expectancy at birth Female	Infant mortality rate (under 1) 2000	% of low birth weight infants 1995-2000y	% of 1-year-old children immunized (measles) 1999y	Under-5 mortality rate per 1,000 live births 1960	Under-5 mortality rate per 1,000 live births 2000	Maternal mortality rate per 100,000 live births 1985-99y	Refugees Country of origin	Refugees Country of asylum
Libya	5.4	8.3	101	3.6	33	88	73	77	17	7ˣ	92	270	20	75	..	33,000
Morocco	29.7	40.5	63	3.2	34	56	67	71	41	9ˣ	90	220	46	230	..	..
Oman	2.6	5.1	189	5.7	44	84	72	75	12	8	99	280	14	14	..	..
Qatar	0.6	0.8	39	3.5	27	93	70	75	12	10	87	239	16	10	..	..
Saudi Arabia	24.0	40.9	152	5.9	43	86	71	73	24	3	94	292	29	..	..	128,500
Syria	17.2	26.5	101	3.9	40	55	70	70	24	6	97	201	29	110ˣ	100	397,600
Tunisia	9.8	11.6	24	2.2	29	66	70	74	22	5	84	254	28	70	..	..
Turkey	67.3	85.0	44	2.5	30	75	67	72	38	15	80	219	45	130ˣ	43,000	12,600
United Arab Emirates	3.5	4.5	47	3.1	25	86	72	77	8	..	95	223	9	3	..	..
West Bank and Gazaª	3.5	7.4	223	5.8	..	95	71	74	0	9	..	..	25	..	4,123,000	1,460,400
Yemen	18.6	39.6	282	7.6	50	25	57	61	85	26	74	340	117	350	..	69,500
Countries in Transitionᵇ	..	..	..	**1.6**	..	**67**	..	..	**30**	**9ⁱ**	**92ⁱ**	**101ⁱ**	**37ⁱ**	**55**	..	..
Albania	3.1	4.1	51	2.5	29	42	72	76	27	5	85	151	31	..	..	400
Armenia	3.8	3.7	-17	1.3	23	70	70	74	25	9	91	48	30	35	9,000	11,000
Azerbaijan	8.2	10.2	59	1.7	28	57	69	75	74	10	99	74	105	80	..	7,000
Belarus	9.9	9.4	-14	1.3	18	71	63	75	17	5	98	47	20	20	..	3,100
Bosnia and Herzegovina	3.4	3.6	-1	1.4	18	43	65	72	15	4	83	160	18	10	210,000	33,200
Bulgaria	7.8	6.6	-32	1.1	15	70	68	75	15	9	96	70	16	15	..	2,900
Croatia	4.3	4.1	-17	1.7	18	58	70	77	8	6	92	98	9	6	272,000	21,900
Czech Republic	10.3	10.3	-9	1.2	16	75	72	78	5	6	95	25	5	9	..	10,600
Estonia	1.4	1.2	-36	1.2	17	69	65	76	17	5	92	52	21	50	..	..
Georgia	4.4	3.6	-44	1.5	20	61	69	77	24	6	80	70	29	50	21,000	7,900
Hungary	10.1	9.2	-21	1.3	17	64	67	76	8	9	99	57	9	15	..	2,900
Kazakhstan	14.8	14.7	-5	2.1	26	56	60	71	60	6	99	74	75	65	100	19,500
Kyrgyzstan	5.0	6.5	51	2.6	33	33	65	72	53	6	97	180	63	65	..	9,700
Latvia	2.3	2.2	-25	1.1	17	69	65	76	17	5	97	44	21	45	..	..
Lithuania	3.5	3.5	-10	1.3	19	68	68	78	17	4	97	70	21	18	..	300
Macedonia, TFYR	2.0	2.2	3	1.7	22	33	70	75	22	6	98	177	26	7	23,000	3,600
Moldova	4.3	4.5	0	1.5	..	46	64	71	27	7	99	88	33	28	..	300
Poland	38.6	38.6	-12	1.4	18	66	70	78	9	6	97	70	10	8	..	1,800
Romania	22.4	20.6	-24	1.3	18	56	67	74	19	9	98	82	22	42	..	200
Russian Federation	143.5	129.1	-29	1.2	17	78	59	72	18	7	97	64	22	44	18,000	28,200
Slovakia	5.4	5.2	-12	1.4	19	57	69	77	8	7	99	40	9	9	..	3,100
Slovenia	2.0	2.0	-15	1.2	15	50	72	79	5	6	98	45	5	11	4,400	2,700
Tajikistan	6.3	7.8	35	3.3	38	28	66	71	54	13	79	140	73	65	55,000	4,600
Turkmenistan	5.6	7.2	42	3.4	37	45	63	70	52	5	97	150	70	65	..	14,000
Ukraine	48.2	45.1	-20	1.2	17	68	62	74	17	6	99	53	21	25	10,000	6,000
Uzbekistan	25.4	37.2	52	2.6	35	37	68	73	51	6	96	120	67	21	1,500	38,000
Yugoslavia, FR	10.7	10.7	-4	1.7	20	52	70	75	17	5	84	120	20	9	60,000	400,000
Industrial Countries	..	..	..	**1.7**	..	**79**	..	..	**6**	**7**	**89**	**37**	**6**	**12**	..	..
Australia	19.7	23.2	27	1.8	20	85	77	82	6	7	89	24	6	..	..	21,800
Austria	8.1	8.4	1	1.3	16	65	75	81	5	7	90	43	5	..	..	10,800
Belgium	10.3	10.8	6	1.5	17	97	75	82	6	8	83	35	6	..	..	41,000
Canada	31.3	36.0	17	1.6	19	77	76	81	6	6	96	33	6	..	..	70,000
Denmark	5.4	5.9	20	1.7	18	85	75	79	4	6	92	25	5	10	..	12,200
Finland	5.2	5.3	-8	1.7	18	67	74	81	4	6	96	28	5	6	..	2,100
France	59.5	64.2	9	1.8	19	76	74	83	4	6	84	34	5	10	..	12,400
Germany	82.4	78.1	-18	1.3	15	88	75	81	5	7	75	40	5	8	..	116,000
Greece	11.0	10.4	-12	1.3	15	60	76	81	5	7	88	64	6	1	..	6,500
Ireland	3.8	4.5	20	2.0	21	59	74	79	6	4ˣ	77	36	6	6	..	9,500
Israel	6.6	9.3	67	2.8	28	91	76	81	6	8	94	39	6	5	..	4,700
Italy	58.1	57.5	-10	1.2	14	67	77	83	6	6	70	50	6	7	..	9,600
Japan	127.4	121.1	-21	1.4	15	79	78	85	4	7ˣ	94	40	4	8	..	6,400
Luxembourg	0.5	0.6	32	1.8	19	92	75	81	5	4	91	41	5	0	..	..

Table 1: Global Hunger – Life and Death Indicators

| | Population | | | | | | Life expectancy at birth | | Infant mortality rate 2000 | % of low birth weight infants 1995-2000y | % of 1-year-old children immunized (measles) 1999y | Under-5 mortality rate per 1,000 live births | | Maternal mortality rate per 100,000 live births 1985-99y | Refugees as of Dec. 31, 2001 | |
	Total (millions) mid-2002	Projected (millions) 2025	Projected population change (%) 2002-2050	Total fertility rate 2000	% below age 15 2001	% urban 2000	Male	Female				1960	2000		Country of origin	Country of asylum
Netherlands	16.1	17.7	12	1.5	18	89	76	81	5	..	96	22	5	7	..	31,000
New Zealand	3.9	4.6	28	2.0	23	86	76	81	6	6	83	26	6	15	..	2,700
Norway	4.5	5.0	15	1.8	20	76	76	81	4	5	93	23	4	6	..	13,200
Portugal	10.4	9.7	-18	1.5	17	64	73	80	6	7	96	112	6	8	..	50
Spain	41.3	44.3	2	1.2	14	78	76	83	5	6	93	57	5	6	..	1,300
Sweden	8.9	9.5	10	1.4	18	83	77	82	3	4	96	20	4	5	..	18,500
Switzerland	7.3	7.6	1	1.5	16	68	77	83	3	6	81	27	4	5	..	57,900
United Kingdom	60.2	64.8	9	1.7	19	90	75	80	6	8	91	27	6	7	..	69,800
United States	287.4	346.0	44	2.0	22	77	74	80	7	8	92	30	8	8	..	492,500
World	**6,215.0**	**7,859.0**	**46**	**2.8**	**..**	**47**	**65**	**69**	**57**	**14**	**72**	**193**	**83**	**400**	**..**	**14,921,000z**

.. Data not available.

a Palestinian Territory.

b Central and Eastern Europe/ Commonwealth of Independent States (the newly independent states of the former Soviet Union).

c Special administrative region, data exclude China.

d Data include Antigua and Barbuda, Bahamas, Dominica, Grenada, Guadeloupe, Martinique, Netherlands Antilles, Puerto Rico, St. Kitts-Nevis, Saint Lucia, and St.Vincent and the Grenadines.

e Data include São Tomé and Principe and Seychelles. Data exclude Djibouti and Sudan.

f Data include Cook Islands, Kiribati, Marshall Islands, Micronesia, Nauru, Nieu, Palau, Samoa, Tonga, Tuvalu and Vanautu. Data exclude Hong Kong.

g Data include Antigua and Barbuda, Bahamas, Barbados, Dominica, Grenada, St. Kitts and Nevis, St. Lucia, and St. Vincent and the Grenadines.

h Data include Djibouti and Sudan. Data exclude Turkey and the West Bank and Gaza.

i Data include Turkey. Data exclude Slovenia.

x Data refer to a period other than the one specified in the column heading, differ from standard deviation, or refer to only part of a country.

y Data refer to most recent year available.

z Table does not include all countries represented in this total.

Table 2: Global Food, Nutrition and Education

| | Food supply | | Vitamin A supplementation coverage rate (6 to 59 months) 1999 | Adult literacy rate (% age 15 and above) 2000 | | | Total primary school (net)[hh] 1998 | Educational enrollment (% of relevant age group) | | | |
| | Per capita dietary energy supply (DES) (calories/day) 2000 | Food production per capita 2000 | | | | | | Primary school (net) 1995-99[i] | | Primary secondary, tertiary (gross %) 1999[c] | |
				Total	Female	Male		Female	Male	Female	Male
Developing Countries	**2,679**	..	**50**	**73.7**	..	..	..	**76**	**83**	..	..
Africa (sub-Saharan)	**2,226**	**98.4**[cc]	**70**[k]	**61.5**	..	..	..	**50**	**58**	..	..
Angola	1,903	103.8	94	..	..	..	57.0	..	..	21	25
Benin	2,558	123.1	100	37.4	23.6	52.1	46.0	50	75	34	57
Botswana	2,255	76.9	..	77.2	79.8	74.5	81.0	99	98	70	70
Burkina Faso	2,293	106.2	99	23.9	14.1	33.9	34.0	28	40	18	28
Burundi	1,605	82.2	92	48.0	40.4	56.2	38.0	37	38	16	21
Cameroon	2,255	100.4	100	75.8	69.5	82.4	..	71[x]	82[x]	39	47
Cape Verde	3,278	105.8	..	73.8	65.7	84.5	99.0	97	100	76	79
Central African Republic	1,946	107.2	100	46.7	34.9	59.7	53.0	27	51	20	29
Chad	2,046	94.7	92	42.6	34.0	51.6	55.0	39	65	20	42
Comoros	1,753	87.1	..	55.9	48.7	63.2	50.0	55	65	33	38
Congo, Dem. Rep	1,514	57.7	78	61.4	50.2	73.1	32.0	51	66	26	37
Congo, Republic of	2,223	92.6	74	80.7	74.4	87.5	..	93[x]	99[x]	56	69
Côte d'Ivoire	2,590	100.6	..	46.8	38.6	54.5	59.0	47	63	30	46
Djibouti	2,050	69.7	41	67.1	54.4	75.6	32.0	28	39	18	26
Equatorial Guinea	..	74.5	..	83.2	74.4	92.5	83.0	89	89	59	68
Eritrea	1,665	102.2	94	55.7	44.5	67.3	34.0	35	40	24	29
Ethiopia	2,023	102.5	86	39.1	30.9	47.2	35.0	28	43	19	34
Gabon	2,564	88.7	..	..	..	..	..	83	82	87	85
Gambia	2,474	104.1	..	36.6	29.4	44.0	61.0	55	64	37	53
Ghana	2,699	134.5	91	71.5	62.9	80.3	..	..	..	39	45
Guinea	2,353	119.0	100	..	..	..	46.0	30	49	20	37
Guinea-Bissau	2,333	111.3	77	38.5	23.3	54.4	..	32[x]	58[x]	27	47
Kenya	1,965	80.4	80	82.4	76.0	88.9	..	89[x]	92[x]	51	52
Lesotho	2,300	102.2	..	83.4	93.6	72.5	60.0	65	55	65	57
Liberia	2,076	92.9	93	..	..	..	..	31	43	..	..
Madagascar	2,007	76.7	94	66.5	59.7	73.6	63.0	69	67	43	46
Malawi	2,181	119.2	..	60.1	46.5	74.5	..	100[x]	100[x]	69	78
Mali	2,403	102.1	100	41.5	34.4	48.9	42.0	33	47	22	34
Mauritania	2,638	81.0	83	40.2	30.1	50.7	60.0	53	61	37	44
Mauritius	2,985	96.4	..	84.5	81.3	87.8	93.0	99	97	64	62
Mozambique	1,927	92.0	100	44.0	28.7	60.1	41.0	40	47	19	26
Namibia	2,649	88.5	83	82.0	81.2	82.8	86.0	88	84	80	77
Niger	2,089	101.1	100	15.9	8.4	23.8	26.0	19	30	12	20
Nigeria	2,850	115.4	23	63.9	55.7	72.4	..	33	38	41	49
Rwanda	2,077	91.2	93	66.8	60.2	73.7	91.0	68	67	39	41
Senegal	2,257	103.2	87	37.3	27.6	47.3	59.0	55	65	31	40
Sierra Leone	1,863	69.0	81	..	..	..	..	..	..	21	32
Somalia	1,628	81.7	63	..	..	..	..	7[x]	13[x]	..	..
South Africa	2,886	84.5	..	85.3	84.6	86.0	100.0	86	88	96	89
Sudan	2,348	128.7	79	57.8	46.3	69.5	46.0	37	43	31	36
Swaziland	2,620	69.2	..	79.6	78.6	80.8	77.0	100	100	70	74
Tanzania	1,906	76.8	21	75.1	66.5	83.9	48.0	57	56	32	33
Togo	2,329	100.3	100	57.1	42.5	72.4	88.0	61	85	49	76
Uganda	2,359	100.1	79	67.1	56.8	77.5	100.0	83	92	41	49
Zambia	1,912	82.3	75	78.1	71.5	85.2	73.0	86	85	46	52
Zimbabwe	2,117	92.4	..	88.7	84.7	92.8	..	87	87	63	67
South Asia	..	**105.4**[dd]	**35**	**55.6**	..	..	..	**66**	**78**	..	..
Afghanistan	1,539	..	78	..	..	..	..	15[x]	42[x]	..	..
Bangladesh	2,103	109.1	79	41.3	29.9	52.3	100.0	83	80	33	41
Bhutan	..	93.0	87	..	..	..	16.0	47	58	..	..
India	2,428	105.3	15	57.2	45.4	68.4	..	64	78	49	62
Maldives	2,592	93.4	..	96.7	96.8	96.6	..	92	93	77	77
Nepal	2,436	101.6	85	41.8	24.0	59.6	..	60	79	52	67
Pakistan	2,452	103.7	88	43.2	27.9	57.5	..	60	84	28	51
Sri Lanka	2,405	109.2	..	91.6	89.0	94.4	100.0	..	..	71	68

Table 2: Global Food, Nutrition and Education

	Food supply — Per capita dietary energy supply (DES) (calories/day) 2000	Food supply — Food production per capita 2000	Vitamin A supplementation coverage rate (6 to 59 months) 1999	Adult literacy rate (% age 15 and above) 2000 — Total	Adult literacy rate — Female	Adult literacy rate — Male	Total primary school (net)[hh] 1998	Educational enrollment — Primary school (net) 1995-99[i] — Female	Primary school (net) — Male	Primary secondary, tertiary (gross %) 1999[c] — Female	Primary secondary, tertiary — Male
East Asia and the Pacific	..	109.2[ee]	..	85.9[z]	..	..	..	96[h]	97[h]	..	..
Brunei	2,832	156.1	..	91.5	88.1	94.6	..	91[x]	90[x]	77	76
Cambodia	2,070	111.6	79	67.8	57.1	79.8	100.0	74	82	54	71
China	3,029	155.5	..	84.1	76.3	91.7	91.0	99	99	73	73
Hong Kong[a]	..	..	..	93.5	90.2	96.5	..	..	..	66	61
Fiji	2,861	87.0	..	92.9	90.8	94.9	100.0	100	99	83	84
Indonesia	2,902	99.3	64	86.9	82.0	91.8	..	93	97	61	68
Korea, DPR (North)	2,185	78.1	100	..	..	..	..	..	..	..	..
Korea, Rep. (South)	3,093	117.1	..	97.8	96.4	99.1[j]	97.0	98	97	85	95
Lao, PDR	2,266	127.3	80	48.7	33.2	64.1	76.0	72	80	52	65
Malaysia	2,919	103.8	..	87.5	83.4	91.4	98.0	96	95	67	64
Mongolia	1,981	89.4	87	98.9	98.8	99.1[j]	85.0	94	93	64	51
Myanmar (Burma)	2,842	142.6	42	84.7	80.5	89.0	..	..	..	55	55
Papua New Guinea	2,175	96.0	..	63.9	56.8	72.5	85.0	67[x]	79[x]	35	42
Philippines	2,379	105.8	78	95.3	95.1	95.5	..	93	98	84	80
Singapore	..	28.9	..	92.3	88.4	98.5	..	92[x]	93[x]	75	76
Solomon Islands	2,277	101.3	..	..	..	..	..	..	..	..	..
Thailand	2,506	105.5	..	95.5	93.9	97.1	77.0	79	82	61	60
Vietnam	2,583	137.6	55	93.4	91.4	95.5	97.0	94	95	64	69
Latin America and Caribbean	..	115.5[aa]	..	88.3	..	..	..	..	..	..	..
Argentina	3,181	121.9	..	96.8	96.8	96.8	100.0	96[x]	96[x]	86	80
Belize	2,888	141.4	..	93.2	93.2	93.3	99.0	86	90	72	73
Bolivia	2,218	112.5	85	85.5	79.3	92.0	97.0	87[x]	95[x]	67	73
Brazil	2,985	127.2	20	85.2	85.4	85.1	98.0	..	..	80	79
Chile	2,882	122.2	..	95.8	95.6	96.0	88.0	88	88	77	78
Colombia	2,597	92.6	..	91.7	91.7	91.7	87.0	..	..	73	73
Costa Rica	2,783	106.9	..	95.6	95.7	95.5	..	93	93	66	67
Cuba	2,564	58.8	..	96.7	96.6	96.8	97.0	95	94	77	76
Dominican Republic	2,325	93.9	53	83.6	83.6	83.6	87.0	85	84	75	69
Ecuador	2,693	125.7	42	91.6	90.0	93.3	97.0	91	90	74	80
El Salvador	2,503	84.6	..	78.7	76.1	81.6	81.0	78	78	64	63
Guatemala	2,171	99.6	..	68.6	61.2	76.1	83.0	75	81	45	53
Guyana	2,582	185.0	..	98.5	98.1	98.9	85.0	84	89	66	65
Haiti	2,056	81.5	..	49.8	47.8	52.0	80.0	66	66	51	53
Honduras	2,395	91.0	53	74.6	74.5	74.7	..	86	85	63	60
Jamaica	2,693	107.9	..	86.9	90.7	82.9	92.0	87	89	62	63
Mexico	3,165	112.2	..	91.4	89.5	93.4	100.0	100	100	70	71
Nicaragua	2,227	108.2	63	66.5	66.8	66.3	..	79	76	65	61
Panama	2,488	85.9	..	91.9	91.3	92.5	..	91[x]	91[x]	76	73
Paraguay	2,533	95.7	..	93.3	92.2	94.4	92.0	92	91	64	64
Peru	2,624	140.8	5	89.9	85.3	94.7	100.0	100	100	79	81
Suriname	2,652	73.8	..	..	..	..	..	100[x]	100[x]	86	80
Trinidad and Tobago	2,777	106.6	..	91.8	92.1	95.5	93.0	88	88	65	65
Uruguay	2,879	113.9	..	97.7	98.1	97.3	92.0	93	93	83	76
Venezuela	2,256	95.5	..	92.6	92.1	93.1	..	85	83	66	64
Middle East and North Africa	..	..	..	..	..	..	..	76[n]	85[n]	..	..
Algeria	2,944	110.9	..	66.7	57.1	76.2	94.0	91	94	69	75
Bahrain	..	104.1	..	87.6	82.6	90.9	97.0	98	96	83	77
Cyprus	3,259	111.1	..	97.1	95.4	98.7	81.0	96	96	70[n]	67[n]
Egypt	3,346	124.4	..	55.3	43.8	66.6	92.0	89	94	72	80
Iran	2,913	107.2	..	76.3	69.3	83.2	..	94	99	69	76
Iraq	2,197	49.4	..	..	..	..	..	88	98	..	..
Jordan	2,749	88.0	..	89.7	83.9	95.1	64.0	86	86	57	53
Kuwait	3,132	245.6	..	82.0	79.7	84.0	67.0	85	89	61	57
Lebanon	3,155	115.8	..	86.0	80.3	92.1	78.0	..	..	81	76
Libya	3,305	128.2	..	80.0	68.2	90.8	..	96[x]	97[x]	92	92

Table 2: Global Food, Nutrition and Education

	Food supply		Vitamin A supplementation coverage rate (6 to 59 months) 1999	Adult literacy rate (% age 15 and above) 2000			Total primary school (net)[hh] 1998	Educational enrollment (% of relevant age group)			
	Per capita dietary energy supply (DES) (calories/day) 2000	Food production per capita 2000						Primary school (net) 1995-99[i]		Primary secondary, tertiary (gross %) 1999[c]	
				Total	Female	Male		Female	Male	Female	Male
Morocco	2,964	85.3	..	48.9	36.1	61.8	79.0	64	77	46	58
Oman	..	107.3	..	71.7	61.6	80.1	66.0	86	86	56	59
Qatar	..	140.4	..	81.2	83.1	80.4	86.0	92	96	75	75
Saudi Arabia	2,875	61.6	..	76.3	66.9	83.1	59.0	73	81	60	62
Syria	3,038	115.8	..	74.4	60.5	88.3	93.0	92	96	61	65
Tunisia	3,299	707.8	..	71.0	60.6	81.4	98.0	94	97	72	75
Turkey	3,416	91.1	..	85.1	76.5	93.5	100.0	82	93	55	68
United Arab Emirates	3,192	220.0	..	76.3	79.3	75.0	83.0	98	98	71	65
Yemen	2,038	83.8	100	46.3	25.2	67.5	61.0	39	79	29	72
Countries in Transition[b]	..	..	..	..	..	..	..	**90**	**92**	..	..
Albania	2,864	139.5	..	84.7	77.0	92.1	..	100	100	71	71
Armenia	1,944	66.5	..	98.4	97.6	99.3[j]	..	..	..	77	82
Azerbaijan	2,468	66.1	..	..	..	..	96.0	90	89	72	70
Belarus	2,902	61.2	..	99.6	99.4[j]	99.7[j]	..	84[x]	87[x]	79	75
Bosnia and Herzegovina	2,661	63.4	..	..	..	..	..	100	100	..	..
Bulgaria	2,467	69.6	..	98.4	97.9	99.0	93.0	98	98	76	69
Croatia	2,483	65.8	..	98.3	97.3	99.3[j]	77.0	96	93	69	68
Czech Republic	3,104	79.4	..	..	..	..	90.0	87	87	70	69
Estonia	3,376	49.3	..	..	..	..	96.0	86	87	89	84
Georgia	2,412	72.0	..	..	..	..	..	95	95	71	69
Hungary	3,458	87.9	..	99.3	99.2[j]	99.5[j]	82.0	96	97	83	79
Kazakhstan	2,991	75.5	..	..	..	..	..	100	100	81	73
Kyrgyzstan	2,871	97.0	..	..	..	..	85.0	97	98	70	65
Latvia	2,855	46.7	..	99.8	99.8[j]	99.8[j]	94.0	92	88	83	80
Lithuania	3,040	56.0	..	99.6	99.5[j]	99.7[j]	94.0	..	..	83	77
Macedonia, FYR	3,006	83.4	..	..	..	..	96.0	96	97	70	70
Moldova	2,764	47.1	..	98.9	98.3	99.5[j]	..	..	..	75	70
Poland	3,376	84.8	..	99.7	99.7[j]	99.7[j]	96.0	94	95	86	83
Romania	3,274	102.4	..	98.1	97.3	99.0	94.0	91	92	70	68
Russian Federation	2,917	67.0	..	99.6	99.4[j]	99.7[j]	73.0	93[x]	93[x]	82	75
Slovakia	3,133	70.1	..	..	..	..	..	..	..	77	74
Slovenia	3,168	110.0	..	99.6	99.6[j]	99.7[j]	94.0	94	95	85	80
Tajikistan	1,720	42.4	..	99.2	98.8	99.6[j]	..	..	..	63	72
Turkmenistan	2,675	89.0	..	..	..	..	..	..	..	81	81
Ukraine	2,871	56.0	..	99.6	99.5[j]	99.7[j]	..	..	..	78	77
Uzbekistan	2,371	86.2	..	99.2	98.8	99.6[j]	..	89	87	74	79
Yugoslavia, FR	2,570	79.4	..	..	..	..	..	70[x]	69[x]	..	..
Industrial Countries	..	**103.8**[ff]	..	..	..	..	..	**96**[o]	**95**[o]	..	..
Australia	3,176	114.7	..	..	..	..	..	95	95	118[jj]	114[jj]
Austria	3,757	99.8	..	..	..	..	88.0	91	90	89	90
Belgium	3,701[y]	108.8[y]	..	..	..	..	100.0	98	99	111[jj]	107[jj]
Canada	3,174	105.4	..	..	..	..	96.0	94	96	98	96
Denmark	3,396	100.8	..	..	..	..	100.0	99	99	101[jj]	94
Finland	3,227	87.1	..	..	..	..	99.0	98	98	108[jj]	99
France	3,591	97.7	..	..	..	..	100.0	100	100	96	93
Germany	3,451	95.6	..	..	..	..	87.0	87	86	93	95
Greece	3,705	101.7	..	97.2	96.0	98.5	95.0	90	90	81	80
Ireland	3,613	103.4	..	..	..	..	100.0	100	100	93	89
Israel	3,562	81.7	..	94.6	95.4	96.8	95.0	..	..	84	82
Italy	3,661	101.2	..	98.4	98.0	98.9	100.0	100	100	87	81
Japan	2,762	88.8	..	..	..	..	100.0	100[x]	100[x]	81	83
Luxembourg	..	..	..	..	..	..	100.0	86[x]	84[x]	74[gg]	71[gg]
Netherlands	3,294	94.5	..	..	..	..	100.0	99	100	100	104[jj]

Table 2: Global Food, Nutrition and Education

	Food supply		Vitamin A supplementation coverage rate (6 to 59 months) 1999	Adult literacy rate (% age 15 and above) 2000			Total primary school (net)[hh] 1998	Educational enrollment (% of relevant age group)			
	Per capita dietary energy supply (DES) (calories/day) 2000	Food production per capita 2000						Primary school (net) 1995-99[i]		Primary secondary, tertiary (gross %) 1999[c]	
				Total	Female	Male		Female	Male	Female	Male
New Zealand	3,252	109.3	..	..	..	..	100.0	100	100	103[jj]	95
Norway	3,414	84.7	..	..	..	..	100.0	100	100	99	95
Portugal	3,716	98.9	..	92.2	89.9	94.7	100.0	100	100	99	94
Spain	3,352	113.9	..	97.6	96.8	98.6	100.0	100	100	99	91
Sweden	3,109	94.1	..	..	..	..	100.0	100	100	107[jj]	95
Switzerland	3,293	88.8	..	..	..	..	94.0	96	96	81	87
United Kingdom	3,334	86.2	..	..	..	..	100.0	98	97	112[jj]	100
United States	3,772	108.4	..	..	..	..	95.0	95	94	99	91
World	**2,805**	**106.2**	**50**	**..**	**..**	**..**	**..**	**78**	**85**	**..**	**..**

.. Data not available.

a Special Administrative Region, data exclude China.

b Central and Eastern European countries and newly independent states of the former Soviet Union.

c Preliminary UNESCO estimate and subject to further revision.

h Data exclude Hong Kong and Singapore.

i Refers to most recent year available during the period specified in the column heading.

j For purposes of calculating the GDI, a value of 99.0 percent was applied.

k Data include São Tomé and Principe and Seychelles. Data exclude Djibouti and Sudan.

n Data exclude Turkey.

o Data include Andorra, Holy See, Ireland, Liechtenstein, Malta, Monaco, San Marino and Slovenia.

x Data refer to a period other than specified in the column heading.

y Data include Luxembourg.

z Data exclude China, Hong Kong, Republic of Korea and Mongolia.

aa Data include Antigua and Barbuda, Bahamas, Barbados, British Virgin Islands, Cayman Islands, Dominica, Falkland Island, French Guina, Grenada, Guadeloupe, Martinique, Montserrat, Netherlands Antilles, Puerto Rico, St. Kitts and Nevis, St. Lucia, and St. Vincent and U.S. Virgin Islands.

cc Data include São Tomé and Principe. Data exclude South Africa.

dd Data exclude Afghanistan.

ee Data exclude China, Fiji, Papua New Guinea and Solomon Islands.

ff Data include Faeroe Islands, Liechtenstein, Malta and South Africa.

gg The ratio is an underestimate, because many students pursue studies in nearby countries.

hh Enrollment ratios based on the new International Standard Classification of Education and may not be strictly comparable to years before 1997.

jj For purposes of calculating the GDI, a value of 100.0 percent was applied.

The number '0' (zero) means zero or less than half the unit shown.

Table 3: Hunger, Malnutrition and Poverty

| | Undernourished population | | % under-5 (1995-2000p) suffering from: | | | | % Population using improved drinking water sources 2000 | | | Population in Poverty (%) | | | |
	Proportion of the population undernourished (%) 1998-2000	Number of undernourished people (millions) 1998-2000	Underweight Moderate & severe	Underweight Severe	Wasting Moderate & severe	Stunting Moderate & severe	Total	Urban	Rural	Below national poverty line 1984-2000p National	Below national poverty line 1984-2000p Urban	Below national poverty line 1984-2000p Rural	Below international poverty line $1 a day 1983-1999pq
Developing Countries	**17**	**798.8**	**28**	**10**	**9**	**32**	**78**	**92**	**69**	..	..	..	..
Africa (sub-Saharan)	**33**	**195.9**	**30[h]**	**9[h]**	**10[h]**	**41[h]**	**57**	**83**	**44**	..	..	..	..
Angola	50	6.3	..	..	..	..	38	34	40	..	..	..	..
Benin	13	0.8	29	7	14	25	63	74	55	33.0	..	..	..
Botswana	25	0.4	13	2	5	23	95	100	90	..	..	..	33.3
Burkina Faso	23	2.6	34	12	13	37	42	66	37	..	..	..	61.2
Burundi	69	4.3	45	13	8	57	78	91	77	36.2	..	..	..
Cameroon	25	3.6	21	4	5	35	58	78	39	40.0	44.4	32.4	33.4
Cape Verde	..	..	14[x]	2[x]	6[x]	16[x]	74	64	64	..	..	..	..
Central African Republic	44	1.6	24	6	9	39	70	89	57	..	..	..	66.6
Chad	32	2.5	28	10	12	28	27	31	26	64.0	63.0	67.0	..
Comoros	..	..	25	9	12	42	96	98	95	..	..	..	..
Congo, Dem. Rep.	73	36.4	34	10	10	45	45	89	26	..	..	..	..
Congo, Republic of	32	0.9	14	3	4	19	51	71	17	..	..	..	..
Côte d'Ivoire	15	2.3	21	4	10	22	81	92	72	36.8	..	..	12.3
Djibouti	..	..	18	6	13	26	100	100	100	..	..	..	..
Equatorial Guinea	..	..	..	..	..	..	44	45	42	..	..	..	..
Eritrea	58	2.0	44	17	16	38	46	63	42	53.0	..	..	..
Ethiopia	44	27.1	47	16	11	51	24	81	12	..	..	..	31.3
Gabon	8	0.1	..	..	..	..	86	95	47	..	..	..	..
Gambia	21	0.3	17	4	9	19	62	80	53	64.0	..	..	59.3
Ghana	12	2.2	25	5	10	26	73	91	62	31.4	26.7	34.3	44.8
Guinea	32	2.6	23	5	9	26	48	72	36	40.0	..	..	..
Guinea-Bissau	..	..	23	5	10	28	56	79	49	48.7	..	..	..
Kenya	44	13.2	23	7	6	37	57	88	42	42.0	29.3	46.4	26.5
Lesotho	26	0.5	16	4	5	44	78	88	74	49.2	27.8	53.9	43.1
Liberia	39	1.0	20[x]	..	3[x]	37[x]	..	..	..	..	..	..	..
Madagascar	40	6.2	33	11	14	49	47	85	31	70.0	47.0	77.0	49.1
Malawi	33	3.7	25	6	6	49	57	95	44	54.0	..	..	..
Mali	20	2.3	43	..	..	..	65	74	61	..	..	..	72.8
Mauritania	12	0.3	23	9	7	44	37	34	40	57.0	..	..	28.6
Mauritius	5	0.1	16	2	15	10	100	100	100	10.6	..	..	..
Mozambique	55	9.8	26	9	8	36	57	81	41	..	..	..	37.9
Namibia	9	0.2	26[x]	6[x]	9[x]	28[x]	77	100	67	..	..	..	34.9
Niger	36	3.8	40	14	14	40	59	70	56	63.0	52.0	66.0	61.4
Nigeria	7	7.3	27	11	12	46	62	78	49	34.1	30.4	36.4	70.2
Rwanda	40	2.8	29	7	7	43	41	60	40	51.2	..	..	35.7
Senegal	25	2.3	18	4	8	19	78	92	65	33.4	..	40.4	26.3
Sierra Leone	47	2.0	27	9	10	34	57	75	46	68.0	53.0	76.0	57.0
Somalia	71	6.0	26	7	17	23	..	..	..	..	..	..	..
South Africa	..	..	..	..	..	25[x]	86	99	73	..	..	..	11.5
Sudan	21	6.5	17	7	..	..	75	86	69	..	..	..	..
Swaziland	12	0.1	10[x]	..	1[x]	30[x]	..	..	..	40.0	..	..	..
Tanzania	47	16.2	29	7	5	44	68	90	57	41.6	24.4	49.7	19.9
Togo	23	1.0	25	7	12	22	54	85	38	32.3	..	..	..
Uganda	21	4.7	26	7	5	38	52	80	47	55.0	..	..	..
Zambia	50	5.1	25	..	4	59	64	88	48	86.0	46.0	88.0	63.7
Zimbabwe	38	4.7	13	2	6	27	83	100	73	25.5	10.0	31.0	36.0
South Asia	**24[y]**	**314.9[y]**	**46**	**16**	**15**	**45**	**85**	**94**	**80**	..	..	..	..
Afghanistan	70	14.9	48	..	25	52	13	19	11	..	..	..	..
Bangladesh	35	47.0	48	13	10	45	97	99	97	35.6	14.3	39.8	29.1
Bhutan	..	..	19	3	3	40	62	86	60	..	..	..	..
India	24	233.3	47	18	16	46	84	95	79	35.0	30.5	36.7	44.2
Maldives	..	..	43	10	17	27	100	100	100	..	..	..	..
Nepal	19	4.3	47	12	7	54	88	94	87	42.0	23.0	44.0	37.7
Pakistan	19	26.0	38	13	..	..	90	95	87	34.0	28.0	36.9	31.0
Sri Lanka	23	4.3	33	5	15	17	77	98	70	25.0	..	..	6.6

Table 3: Hunger, Malnutrition and Poverty

	Undernourished population		% under-5 (1995-2000p) suffering from:				% Population using improved drinking water sources 2000			Population in Poverty (%)			
	Proportion of the population undernourished (%) 1998-2000	Number of undernourished people (millions) 1998-2000	Underweight		Wasting	Stunting				Below national poverty line 1984-2000p			Below international poverty line $1 a day 1983-1999pq
			Moderate & severe	Severe	Moderate & severe	Moderate & severe	Total	Urban	Rural	National	Urban	Rural	
East Asia and the Pacific	..	..	17[i]	..	4[i]	21[i]	76[i]	93[i]	67[i]	..	..	..	..
Brunei	..	..	..	..	..	..	..	..	..	..	..	..	..
Cambodia	36	4.6	46	13	15	46	30	54	26	36.1	21.1	40.1	..
China	9	119.1	10	..	3	17	75	94	66	4.6	<2.0	4.6	18.8
Hong Kong[a]	..	0.1	..	..	..	..	..	..	..	..	..	..	..
Fiji	..	..	8[x]	1[x]	8[x]	3[x]	47	43	51	..	..	..	..
Indonesia	6	12.3	26	8	..	..	78	90	69	27.1	..	..	7.7
Korea, DPR (North)	34	7.5	60	..	19	60	100	100	100	..	..	..	..
Korea, Rep. (South)	..	0.7	..	..	..	..	92	97	71	..	..	..	<2.0
Lao, PDR	24	1.2	40	13	15	41	37	61	29	46.1	24.0	53.0	26.3
Malaysia	..	0.4	18	1	..	..	..	..	94	15.5	..	..	..
Mongolia	42	1.0	13	3	6	25	60	77	30	36.3	38.5	33.1	13.9
Myanmar (Burma)	6	3.1	36	9	10	37	72	89	66	..	..	..	..
Papua New Guinea	27	1.3	35[x]	..	..	..	42	88	32	..	..	..	..
Philippines	23	16.8	28	..	6	30	86	91	79	36.8	21.5	50.7	..
Singapore	..	..	14[x]	..	4[x]	11[x]	100	100	..	..	..	..	..
Solomon Islands	..	..	21[x]	4[x]	7[x]	27[x]	71	94	65	..	..	..	..
Thailand	18	11.5	19[x]	..	6[x]	16[x]	84	95	81	13.1	10.2	15.5	<2.0
Vietnam	18	13.7	33	6	6	36	77	95	72	50.9	25.9	57.2	..
Latin America and the Caribbean	11	54.8	8[j]	1	2[j]	16[j]	86[k]	94[k]	66[k]	..	..	..	..
Argentina	..	0.4	..	..	..	..	..	..	..	17.6	..	..	..
Belize	..	..	6[x]	1[x]	..	..	92	100	82	..	..	..	..
Bolivia	23	1.9	10	2	2	26	83	95	64	..	29.3	79.1	14.4
Brazil	10	16.7	6	1	2	11	87	95	53	17.4	13.1	32.6	11.6
Chile	4	0.6	1	..	0	2	93	99	58	21.2	..	..	<2.0
Colombia	13	5.6	7	1	1	14	91	99	70	17.7	8.0	31.2	19.7
Costa Rica	5	0.2	5	0	2	6	95	99	92	22.0	19.2	25.5	12.6
Cuba	13	1.5	4	0	2	5	91	95	77	..	..	..	..
Dominican Republic	26	2.1	5	1	2	6	86	90	78	20.6	10.9	29.8	3.2
Ecuador	5	0.7	15	2	..	27	85	90	75	35.0	25.0	47.0	20.2
El Salvador	14	0.8	12	1	1	23	77	91	64	48.3	43.1	55.7	21.0
Guatemala	25	2.8	24	5	3	46	92	98	88	57.9	33.7	71.9	10.0
Guyana	14	0.1	12	..	12	10	94	98	91	..	..	..	..
Haiti	50	4.0	28	8	8	32	46	49	45	65.0	..	66.0	..
Honduras	21	1.3	25	4	2	39	88	95	81	53.0	57.0	51.0	24.3
Jamaica	9	0.2	4	..	4	3	92	98	85	18.7	..	..	3.2
Mexico	5	5.2	8	1	2	18	88	95	69	10.1	..	..	15.9
Nicaragua	29	1.5	12	2	2	25	77	91	59	50.3	31.9	76.1	..
Panama	18	0.5	7	..	1	14	90	99	79	37.3	15.3	64.9	14.0
Paraguay	14	0.7	5	..	1	11	78	93	59	21.8	19.7	28.5	19.5
Peru	11	2.9	8	1	1	26	80	87	62	49.0	40.4	64.7	15.5
Suriname	11	0.0	..	..	..	..	82	93	50	..	..	..	..
Trinidad and Tobago	12	0.2	7[x]	..	4[x]	4[x]	90	..	..	21.0	24.0	20.0	12.4
Uruguay	3	0.1	5	1	1	8	98	98	93	..	..	..	<2.0
Venezuela	21	4.9	5	1	3	14	83	85	70	31.3	..	..	23.0
Middle East and North Africa	10[z]	40.0[z]	15[m]	4[m]	7[m]	23[m]	87[m]	95[m]	77[m]	..	..	..	..
Algeria	6	1.7	6	1	3	18	89	100	82	22.6	14.7	30.3	<2.0
Bahrain	..	..	9	2	5	10	..	..	..	..	..	..	..
Cyprus	..	..	..	..	..	..	100	100	100	..	..	..	..
Egypt	4	2.5	12	3	6	25	97	99	96	22.9	22.5	23.3	3.1
Iran	5	3.8	11	2	5	15	92	98	83	..	..	..	..
Iraq	27	5.9	16	..	..	22	85	96	48	..	..	..	..
Jordan	6	0.3	5	1	2	8	96	100	84	11.7	..	..	<2.0
Kuwait	4	0.1	10	3	11	24	..	..	..	..	..	..	..
Lebanon	3	0.1	3	0	3	12	100	100	100	..	..	..	..
Libya	..	0.0	5	1	3	15	72	72	68	..	..	..	..

Table 3: Hunger, Malnutrition and Poverty

| | Undernourished population | | % under-5 (1995-2000[p]) suffering from: | | | | % Population using improved drinking water sources 2000 | | | Population in Poverty (%) | | | |
| | Proportion of the population undernourished (%) 1998-2000 | Number of undernourished people (millions) 1998-2000 | Underweight | | Wasting | Stunting | | | | Below national poverty line 1984-2000[p] | | | Below international poverty line $1 a day 1983-1999[pq] |
			Moderate & severe	Severe	Moderate & severe	Moderate & severe	Total	Urban	Rural	National	Urban	Rural	
Morocco	7	2.0	9[x]	2[x]	2[x]	23[x]	80	98	56	19.0	12.0	27.2	<2.0
Oman	..	..	24	4	13	23	39	41	30	..	..	..	..
Qatar	..	..	6	..	2	8	..	..	..	..	..	..	..
Saudi Arabia	3	0.6	14	3	11	20	95	100	64	..	..	..	..
Syria	3	0.5	13	4	9	21	80	94	64	..	..	..	..
Tunisia	..	0.0	4	1	2	12	80	92	58	14.1	8.9	21.6	<2.0
Turkey	..	1.6	8	1	2	16	82	81	86	..	..	..	2.4
United Arab Emirates	..	0.1	14	3	15	17	..	..	..	..	..	..	..
Yemen	33	5.9	46	15	13	52	69	74	68	19.1	18.6	19.2	15.7
Countries in Transition[b]	**7**	**30.2**	**7[n]**	**2[n]**	**4[n]**	**16[n]**	**91**	**95**	**82**	**..**	**..**	**..**	**..**
Albania	8	0.3	14	4	11	32	97	99	95	..	15.0	28.9	..
Armenia	46	1.8	3	0	2	14	..	..	..	..	..	..	7.8
Azerbaijan	23	1.9	17	4	8	20	78	93	58	68.1	..	..	<2.0
Belarus	..	0.2	..	..	..	..	100	100	100	41.9	..	..	<2.0
Bosnia and Herzegovina	6	0.2	4	1	6	10	..	..	..	..	..	..	..
Bulgaria	15	1.2	..	..	..	..	100	100	100	..	..	..	<2.0
Croatia	18	0.8	1	..	1	1	..	..	..	..	..	..	<2.0
Czech Republic	..	0.2	1[x]	0[x]	2[x]	2[x]	..	..	..	..	..	..	<2.0
Estonia	..	0.0	..	..	..	..	..	..	..	8.9	6.8	14.7	<2.0
Georgia	16	0.9	3	0	2	12	79	90	61	11.1	12.1	9.9	<2.0
Hungary	..	0.1	2[x]	0[x]	2[x]	3[x]	99	100	98	8.6	..	..	<2.0
Kazakhstan	8	1.2	4	0	2	10	91	98	82	34.6	30.0	39.0	<2.0
Kyrgyzstan	8	0.4	11	2	3	25	77	98	66	51.0	28.5	64.5	..
Latvia	5	0.1	..	..	..	..	..	..	..	..	..	..	<2.0
Lithuania	3	0.1	..	..	..	..	..	..	..	..	..	..	<2.0
Macedonia, TFYR	4	0.1	6	1	4	7	..	..	..	..	..	..	..
Moldova	10	0.4	3	..	3	10	92	97	88	23.3	..	26.7	11.3
Poland	..	0.3	..	..	..	..	..	..	..	23.8	..	..	<2.0
Romania	..	0.3	6[x]	1[x]	3[x]	8[x]	58	91	16	21.5	20.4	27.9	2.8
Russia	5	7.2	3	1	4	13	99	100	96	30.9	..	..	7.1
Slovakia	..	0.1	..	..	..	..	100	100	100	..	..	..	<2.0
Slovenia	..	0.0	..	..	..	..	100	100	100	..	..	..	<2.0
Tajikistan	64	3.9	..	..	..	..	60	93	47	..	..	..	..
Turkmenistan	8	0.4	..	..	..	..	..	..	..	..	..	..	12.1
Ukraine	5	2.6	3	1	6	15	98	100	94	31.7	..	..	2.9
Uzbekistan	19	4.7	19	5	12	31	85	94	79	..	..	..	3.3
Yugoslavia	8	0.8	2	0	4	5	98	99	97	..	..	..	..
Industrial Countries	**..**	**..**	**..**	**..**	**..**	**..**	**100**	**100**	**100**	**..**	**..**	**..**	**..**
Australia	..	..	..	..	..	..	100	100	100	..	..	..	..
Austria	..	..	..	..	..	..	100	100	100	..	..	..	..
Belgium	..	..	..	..	..	..	..	..	..	..	..	..	..
Canada	..	..	..	..	..	..	100	100	99	..	..	..	..
Denmark	..	..	..	..	..	..	100	100	100	..	..	..	..
Finland	..	..	..	..	..	..	100	100	100	..	..	..	..
France	..	..	..	..	..	..	..	..	..	..	..	..	..
Germany	..	..	..	..	..	..	..	..	..	..	..	..	..
Greece	..	..	..	..	..	..	..	..	..	..	..	..	..
Ireland	..	..	..	..	..	..	..	..	..	..	..	..	..
Israel	..	..	..	..	..	..	..	..	..	..	..	..	..
Italy	..	..	..	..	..	..	..	..	..	..	..	..	..
Japan	..	..	..	..	..	..	..	..	..	..	..	..	*
Luxembourg	..	..	..	..	..	..	..	..	..	..	..	..	..
Netherlands	..	..	..	..	..	..	100	100	100	..	..	..	..

Table 3: Hunger, Malnutrition and Poverty

| | Undernourished population | | % under-5 (1995-2000p) suffering from: | | | | % Population using improved drinking water sources 2000 | | | Population in Poverty (%) | | | |
| | Proportion of the population undernourished (%) 1998-2000 | Number of undernourished people (millions) 1998-2000 | Underweight | | Wasting | Stunting | | | | Below national poverty line 1984-2000p | | | Below international poverty line $1 a day 1983-1999pq |
			Moderate & severe	Severe	Moderate & severe	Moderate & severe	Total	Urban	Rural	National	Urban	Rural	
New Zealand	..	..	..	..	..	..	..	100	..	..	..	..	..
Norway	..	..	..	..	..	..	100	100	100	..	..	..	..
Portugal	..	..	..	..	..	..	..	..	..	..	..	..	<2.0
Spain	..	..	..	..	..	..	..	..	..	..	..	..	..
Sweden	..	..	..	..	..	..	100	100	100	..	..	..	..
Switzerland	..	..	..	..	..	..	100	100	100	..	..	..	..
United Kingdom	..	..	..	..	..	..	100	100	100	..	..	..	..
United States	..	..	1^x	0^x	1^x	2^x	100	100	100	..	..	..	..
World	..	..	**27**	**10**	**8**	**32**	**82**	**95**	**71**	..	..	..	..

.. Data not available.

a   Special Administrative Region, data exclude China.

b   Central and Eastern European countries and the newly independent states of the former Soviet Union.

h   Data include São Tomé and Principe and Seychelles. Data exclude Djibouti and Sudan.

i   Data include the Cook Islands, Kiribati, Marshall Islands, Micronesia, Nauru, Nieu, Palau, Samoa, Tonga, Tuvalu and Vanuatu. Data exclude Hong Kong.

j   Data include Antigua and Barbuda, Bahamas, Barbados and Dominica.

k   Data include Bahamas, Barbados, Dominica, St. Kitts and Nevis, St. Lucia, and St. Vincent and the Grenadines.

m   Data include Djibouti and Sudan. Data exclude Turkey or West Bank and Gaza.

n   Data include Turkey.

p   Data refer to the most recent year available during the period specified in the column heading.

q   Measured in 1985 international prices and adjusted to local currency using purchasing power parities. Poverty rates comparable across countries, but revisions in PPP exchange rates prevents comparing this data to previous rates reported.

x   Indicates data that refer to years or periods other than those specified in the column heading, differ from the standard definition or refer to only part of a country.

y   Data exclude Afghanistan.

z   Data include Afghanistan.

The number '0' (zero) means zero or less than half the unit of measure.

Table 4: Economic and Development Indicators

| | GNP per capita | | GDP per capita | Human Development | Distribution of income or consumption by quintiles[k] 1983-2000[t] | | | | | | Total central government expenditure | Public education expenditure | Military expenditure | Per capita energy consumption | Average annual deforestation[m] |
	US$ 2000	Purchasing Power Parity (PPP) ($) 2000	% growth 1999-2000	Index (HDI) rank 2000	Lowest 20%	Second quintile	Third quintile	Fourth quintile	Highest 20%	Ratio of highest 20% to lowest 20%[e]	(% of GDP) 1999	(% of GNP) 1995-1997[t]	(% of GDP) 2000	(kg. of oil equivalent) 1999	(% of total forest) 1990-2000
Developing Countries	..	..	..	..	..	..	..	..	..	..	..	..	..	..	..
Africa (sub-Saharan)	**470[p]**	**1,600[p]**	**0.6**	..	..	..	..	..	..	..	**26.9**	..	..	**671[p]**	**0.8**
Angola	290	1,180[c]	-0.8	161	..	..	..	..	..	..	..	..	21.2[cc]	595	0.2
Benin	370	980	3.1	158	..	..	..	..	..	..	..	3.2	..	323	2.3
Botswana	3,300	7,170	2.5	126	..	..	..	..	..	..	..	8.6	3.7	..	0.9
Burkina Faso	210	970[c]	-0.4	169	4.6	7.2	10.8	17.1	60.4	13.13	..	3.6[x]	1.6	..	0.2
Burundi	110	580[c]	-1.6	171	5.1	10.3	15.1	21.5	48.0	9.41	26.1	4.0	5.4	..	9.0
Cameroon	580	1,590	2.0	135	4.6	8.3	13.1	20.9	53.1	11.54	15.9	..	1.3	419	0.9
Cape Verde	..	..	..	100	..	..	..	..	..	..	..	..	1.3	..	..
Central African Republic	280	1,160[c]	1.1	165	2.0	4.9	9.6	18.5	65.0	32.50	..	..	..	..	0.1
Chad	200	870[c]	-2.1	166	..	..	..	..	..	..	..	2.2	1.0[dd]	..	0.6
Comoros	..	..	..	137	..	..	..	..	..	..	..	..	..	..	..
Congo, Dem. Rep.	..	..	..	155	..	..	..	..	..	..	0.1	..	..	293	0.4
Congo, Republic of	570	570	4.9	136	..	..	..	..	..	..	32.8	6.1	..	245	0.1
Côte d'Ivoire	600	1,500	-4.9	156	7.1	11.2	15.6	21.9	44.3	6.24	22.4	5.0	..	388	3.1
Djibouti	..	..	..	149	..	..	..	..	..	..	..	..	4.4[dd]	..	..
Equatorial Guinea	..	..	..	111	..	..	..	..	..	..	..	1.7[x]	..	..	..
Eritrea	170	960	-10.6	157	..	..	..	..	..	..	..	1.8[w]	22.9[cc]	..	0.3
Ethiopia	100	660	3.0	168	7.1	10.9	14.5	19.8	47.7	6.72	..	4.0	9.4[cc]	290	0.8
Gabon	3,190	5,360	-0.6	117	..	..	..	..	..	..	..	2.9[w]	0.3[dd]	1,342	0.0
Gambia	340	1,620[c]	2.3	160	4.0	7.6	12.4	20.8	55.3	13.83	..	4.9	1.1	..	-1.0
Ghana	340	1,910[c]	1.3	129	5.6	10.0	15.1	22.6	46.7	8.34	..	4.2	1.0	377	1.7
Guinea	450	1,930	-0.3	159	6.4	10.4	14.8	21.2	47.2	7.38	21.2	1.9	1.5	..	0.5
Guinea-Bissau	180	710	5.2	167	2.1	6.5	12.0	20.6	58.9	28.05	..	..	1.3[dd]	..	0.9
Kenya	350	1,010	-2.5	134	5.6	9.3	13.6	20.3	51.2	9.14	26.0	6.5	1.8	499	0.5
Lesotho	580	2,590[c]	2.5	132	2.8	6.5	11.2	19.4	60.1	21.46	49.7	8.4	3.1[cc]	..	..
Liberia	..	..	..	..	..	..	..	..	..	..	..	..	..	..	2.0
Madagascar	250	820	1.6	147	6.4	10.7	15.6	22.5	44.9	7.02	17.4	1.9	1.2	..	0.9
Malawi	170	600	-0.4	163	..	..	..	..	..	..	..	5.4	0.8	..	2.4
Mali	240	780	2.1	164	4.6	8.0	11.9	19.3	56.2	12.22	..	2.2	2.5	..	0.7
Mauritania	370	1,630	1.7	152	6.4	11.2	16.0	22.4	44.1	6.89	..	5.1[v]	..	..	2.7
Mauritius	3,750	9,940	6.9	67	..	..	..	..	..	..	23.9	4.6	0.2	..	0.6
Mozambique	210	800[c]	-0.7	170	6.5	10.8	15.1	21.1	46.5	7.15	..	..	2.5	404	0.2
Namibia	2,030	6,410[c]	1.6	122	..	..	..	..	..	..	36.9	9.1	3.3	645	0.9
Niger	180	740[c]	-3.2	172	2.6	7.1	13.9	23.1	53.3	20.50	..	2.3[w]	1.4[cc]	..	3.7
Nigeria	260	800	1.3	148	4.4	8.2	12.5	19.3	55.7	12.66	..	0.7[y]	0.9	705	2.6
Rwanda	230	930	3.1	162	9.7	13.2	16.5	21.6	39.1	4.03	..	..	3.0	..	3.9
Senegal	490	1,480	2.9	154	6.4	10.3	14.5	20.6	48.2	7.53	..	3.7	1.4	318	0.7
Sierra Leone	130	480	4.9	173	1.1	2.0	9.8	23.7	63.4	57.64	20.9	..	1.4	..	2.9
Somalia	..	..	..	..	..	..	..	..	..	..	..	..	..	..	1.0
South Africa	3,020	9,160[c]	1.4	107	2.9	5.5	9.2	17.7	64.8	22.34	30.6	7.6	1.5	2,597	0.1
Sudan	310	1,520	6.4	139	..	..	..	..	..	..	9.0	1.4	3.0	503	1.4
Swaziland	1,390	4,600	0.0	125	2.7	5.8	10.0	17.1	64.4	23.85	34.2	5.7	1.6	..	-1.2
Tanzania	270	520	2.7	151	6.8	11.0	15.1	21.6	45.5	6.69	..	..	1.3[cc]	457	0.2
Togo	290	1,410	-3.7	141	..	..	..	..	..	..	..	4.5	..	313	3.4
Uganda	300	1,210[c]	0.8	150	7.1	11.1	15.4	21.5	44.9	6.32	16.6	2.6	1.8	..	2.0
Zambia	300	750	1.3	153	3.3	7.6	12.5	20.0	56.6	17.15	..	2.2	0.6	626	2.4
Zimbabwe	460	2,550	-6.7	128	4.7	8.0	12.3	19.4	55.7	11.85	35.7	7.1[x]	4.8	821	1.5
South Asia	**440**	**2,240**	**2.3**	..	..	..	..	..	..	..	**16.7**	..	..	**441**	**0.1**
Afghanistan	..	..	..	..	..	..	..	..	..	..	..	..	..	..	..
Bangladesh	370	1,590	4.1	145	8.7	12.0	15.7	20.8	42.8	4.92	12.7	2.2[v]	1.3	139	-1.3
Bhutan	..	..	..	140	..	..	..	..	..	..	..	4.1	..	..	..
India	450	2,340	2.0	124	8.1	11.6	15.0	19.3	46.1	5.69	15.9	3.2	2.4	482	-0.1
Maldives	..	..	..	84	..	..	..	..	..	..	..	6.4	..	..	..
Nepal	240	1,370	3.9	142	7.6	11.5	15.1	21.0	44.8	5.89	16.0	3.2	0.9	358	1.8
Pakistan	440	1,860	1.9	138	9.5	12.9	16.0	20.5	41.1	4.33	21.3	2.7	4.5	444	1.1
Sri Lanka	850	3,460	4.3	89	8.0	11.8	15.8	21.5	42.8	5.35	24.2	3.4	4.5	406	1.6

Table 4: Economic and Development Indicators

	GNP per capita		GDP per capita	Human Development	Distribution of income or consumption by quintiles[k] 1983-2000[t]						Total central government	Public education	Military	Per capita energy	Average annual
	US$ 2000	Purchasing Power Parity (PPP) ($) 2000	% growth 1999-2000	Index (HDI) rank 2000	Lowest 20%	Second quintile	Third quintile	Fourth quintile	Highest 20%	Ratio of highest 20% to lowest 20%[e]	expenditure (% of GDP) 1999	expenditure (% of GNP) 1995-1997[t]	expenditure (% of GDP) 2000	consumption (kg. of oil equivalent) 1999	deforestation[m] (% of total forest) 1990-2000
East Asia and the Pacific	**1,060**[q]	**4,130**[q]	**6.4**[q]	..	..	..	..	..	..	..	**15.0**	..	..	**920**[q]	**0.2**
Brunei	..	..	..	32	..	..	..	..	..	..	..	..	7.6[dd]	..	..
Cambodia	260	1,440	2.7	130	6.9	10.7	14.7	20.1	47.6	6.90	..	2.9	2.4	..	0.6
China	840	3,920	7.2	96	5.9	10.2	15.1	22.2	46.6	7.90	10.9	2.3	2.1	868	-1.2
Hong Kong[a]	25,920	25,590	9.2	23	4.4	8.0	12.2	18.3	57.1	12.98	..	2.9	..	2,661	..
Fiji	..	..	..	72	..	..	..	..	..	..	..	..	1.5[cc]	..	..
Indonesia	570	2,830	3.1	110	9.0	12.5	16.1	21.3	41.1	4.57	20.1	1.4[y]	1.1	658	1.2
Korea, DPR (North)	..	..	..	..	..	..	..	..	..	..	..	..	..	2,658	..
Korea, Rep. (South)	8,910	17,300	7.8	27	7.5	12.9	17.4	22.9	39.3	5.24	17.4	3.7	2.8	3,871	0.1
Lao, PDR	290	1,540[c]	3.3	143	7.6	11.4	15.3	20.8	45.0	5.92	..	2.1	..	..	0.4
Malaysia	3,380	8,330	5.7	59	4.4	8.1	12.9	20.3	54.3	12.34	19.7	4.9	1.9	1,878	1.2
Mongolia	390	1,760	0.3	113	7.3	12.2	16.6	23.0	40.9	5.60	25.2	5.7	2.5	..	0.5
Myanmar (Burma)	..	..	..	127	..	..	..	..	..	..	7.0	1.2[x,v]	1.7	273	1.4
Papua New Guinea	700[aa]	2,180[c]	-2.1	133	4.5	7.9	11.9	19.2	56.5	12.56	27.0	..	0.8	..	0.4
Philippines	1,040	4,220	2.1	77	5.4	8.8	13.2	20.3	52.3	9.69	19.7	3.4	1.2	549	1.4
Singapore	24,740	24,910	8.1	25	..	..	..	..	..	..	18.5	3.0	4.8	5,742	..
Solomon Islands	..	..	..	121	..	..	..	..	..	..	..	3.8[x]	..	..	..
Thailand	2,000	6,320	3.5	70	6.4	9.8	14.2	21.2	48.4	7.56	25.1	4.8	1.6	1,169	0.7
Vietnam	390	2,000	4.1	109	8.0	11.4	15.2	20.9	44.5	5.56	21.2	3.0	..	454	-0.5
Latin America and the Caribbean	**3,670**	**7,080**	**2.3**	..	..	..	..	..	..	..	**21.9**	..	..	**1,171**	**0.5**
Argentina	7,460	12,050	-1.7	34	..	..	..	..	..	..	17.0	3.5	1.3	1,727	0.8
Belize	..	..	..	58	..	..	..	..	..	..	..	5.0	..	..	..
Bolivia	990	2,360	0.0	114	4.0	9.2	14.8	22.9	49.1	12.28	23.1	4.9	1.5	562	0.3
Brazil	3,580	7,300	3.2	73	2.2	5.4	10.1	18.3	64.1	29.14	26.8	5.1	1.3	1,068	0.4
Chile	4,590	9,100	4.0	38	3.3	6.5	10.9	18.4	61.0	18.48	23.9	3.6	3.3	1,688	0.1
Colombia	2,020	6,060	1.0	68	3.0	6.6	11.1	18.4	60.9	20.30	19.1	4.1[v]	2.3	676	0.4
Costa Rica	3,810	7,980	-0.5	43	4.5	8.9	14.1	21.6	51.0	11.33	21.5	5.4	0.0	818	0.8
Cuba	..	..	..	55	..	..	..	..	..	..	..	6.7	..	1,117	-1.3
Dominican Republic	2,130	5,710	6.0	94	5.1	8.6	13.0	20.0	53.3	10.45	17.0	2.3	..	904	..
Ecuador	1,210	2,910	0.4	93	5.4	9.4	14.2	21.3	49.7	9.20	..	3.5	..	705	1.2
El Salvador	2,000	4,410	0.0	104	3.3	7.3	12.4	20.7	56.4	17.09	16.3	2.5	0.7	651	4.6
Guatemala	1,680	3,770	0.6	120	3.8	6.8	10.9	17.9	60.6	15.95	..	1.7[v]	0.8	548	1.7
Guyana	..	..	..	103	6.3	10.7	15.0	21.2	46.9	7.44	..	5.0	..	..	..
Haiti	510	1,470[c]	-0.9	146	..	..	..	..	..	..	11.5	..	..	265	5.7
Honduras	860	2,400	2.2	116	2.2	6.4	11.8	20.3	59.4	27.00	..	3.6	0.6[cc]	522	1.0
Jamaica	2,610	3,440	-0.9	86	6.7	10.7	15.0	21.8	46.0	6.87	39.1	7.5	..	1,597	1.5
Mexico	5,070	8,790	5.3	54	3.5	7.3	12.1	19.7	57.4	16.40	15.5	4.9	0.5	1,543	1.1
Nicaragua	400	2,080[c]	1.6	118	2.3	5.9	10.4	17.9	63.6	27.65	41.5	3.9[w]	1.1	539	3.0
Panama	3,260	5,680[c]	1.0	57	3.6	8.1	13.6	21.9	52.8	14.67	27.7	5.1	1.2[cc]	835	1.6
Paraguay	1,440	4,450[c]	-2.8	90	1.9	6.0	11.4	20.1	60.7	31.95	..	4.0[v]	1.0	773	0.5
Peru	2,080	4,660	1.4	82	4.4	9.1	14.1	21.3	51.2	11.64	19.6	2.9	..	519	0.4
Suriname	..	..	..	74	..	..	..	..	..	..	..	3.5[x]	..	..	..
Trinidad and Tobago	4,930	8,220	4.1	50	5.5	10.3	15.5	22.7	45.9	8.35	..	4.4[x]	..	6,205	0.8
Uruguay	6,000	8,880	-2.0	40	5.4	10.0	14.8	21.5	48.3	8.94	32.1	3.3	1.1	976	-5.0
Venezuela	4,310	5,740	1.2	69	3.0	8.2	13.8	21.8	53.2	17.73	19.4	5.2[x]	1.2	2,253	0.4
Middle East and North Africa	**2,090**[r]	**5,270**[r]	**2.0**[r]	..	..	..	..	..	..	..	..	..	..	**1,279**[r]	**-0.1**
Algeria	1,580	5,040[c]	0.9	106	7.0	11.6	16.1	22.7	42.6	6.09	30.4	5.1[w]	3.5	944	-1.3
Bahrain	..	..	..	39	..	..	..	..	..	..	..	4.4	4.0	..	..
Cyprus	..	..	..	26	..	..	..	..	..	..	..	4.5[bb]	3.2	..	..
Egypt	1,490	3,670	3.1	115	9.8	13.2	16.6	21.4	39.0	3.98	30.6	4.8	2.3	709	-3.4
Iran	1,680	5,910	3.9	98	..	..	..	..	..	..	25.6	4.0	3.8	1,651	..
Iraq	..	..	..	..	..	..	..	..	..	..	..	..	..	1,263	..
Jordan	1,710	3,950	0.8	99	7.6	11.4	15.5	21.1	44.4	5.84	31.5	7.9	9.5	1,028	..
Kuwait	18,030	18,690	-1.4	45	..	..	..	..	..	..	43.3	5.0	8.2	8,984	-5.2
Lebanon	4,010	4,550	-1.3	75	..	..	..	..	..	..	35.7	2.5[v]	3.6	1,280	0.3
Libya	..	..	..	64	..	..	..	..	..	..	..	..	..	2,370	-1.4

Table 4: Economic and Development Indicators

	GNP per capita		GDP per capita % growth 1999-2000	Human Development Index (HDI rank) 2000	Distribution of income or consumption by quintiles[k] 1983-2000[t]					Ratio of highest 20% to lowest 20%[e]	Total central government expenditure (% of GDP) 1999	Public education expenditure (% of GNP) 1995-1997[t]	Military expenditure (% of GDP) 2000	Per capita energy consumption (kg. of oil equivalent) 1999	Average annual deforestation[m] (% of total forest) 1990-2000
	US$ 2000	Purchasing Power Parity (PPP) ($) 2000			Lowest 20%	Second quintile	Third quintile	Fourth quintile	Highest 20%						
Morocco	1,180	3,450	-0.8	123	6.5	10.6	14.8	21.3	46.6	7.17	32.5	5.3[v]	4.2	352	0.0
Oman	..	..	..	78	..	..	..	..	..	..	31.6	4.5	9.7	3,607	..
Qatar	..	..	..	51	..	..	..	..	..	..	..	3.4[x]	..	..	..
Saudi Arabia	7,230	11,390	1.8	71	..	..	..	..	..	..	..	7.5	11.6	4,204	..
Syria	940	3,340	0.0	108	..	..	..	..	..	..	23.5	4.2	5.5	1,143	..
Tunisia	2,100	6,070	3.5	97	5.7	9.9	14.7	21.8	47.9	8.40	31.6	7.7	1.7	811	-0.2
Turkey	3,100	7,030	5.6	85	5.8	10.2	14.8	21.6	47.7	8.22	38.1	2.2	4.9	1,093	-0.2
United Arab Emirates	..	..	..	46	..	..	..	..	..	..	11.2	1.7	..	9,977	-2.8
Yemen	370	770	2.4	144	7.4	12.2	16.7	22.5	41.2	5.57	27.4	7.0	5.2	184	1.8
Countries in Transition[b]	..	..	..	..	..	..	..	..	..	..	..	..	..	..	..
Albania	1,120	3,600	6.9	92	..	..	..	..	..	..	29.8	..	1.2	311	0.8
Armenia	520	2,580	5.9	76	5.5	9.4	13.9	20.6	50.6	9.20	..	2.0	4.4	485	-1.3
Azerbaijan	600	2,740	10.2	88	6.9	11.5	16.1	22.3	43.3	6.28	22.7	3.0	2.7	1,575	-1.3
Belarus	2,870	7,550	6.1	56	11.4	15.2	18.2	21.9	33.3	2.92	30.9	5.9	1.3	2,381	-3.2
Bosnia and Herzegovina	1,230	..	3.1	..	..	..	..	..	..	..	..	..	..	518	..
Bulgaria	1,520	5,560	6.3	62	10.1	13.9	17.4	21.9	36.8	3.64	35.5	3.2	3.0	2,218	-0.6
Croatia	4,620	7,960	3.6	48	8.8	13.3	17.4	22.6	38.0	4.32	48.3	5.3	3.0	1,864	-0.1
Czech Republic	5,250	13,780	3.0	33	10.3	14.5	17.7	21.7	35.9	3.49	35.5	5.1	2.0	3,754	0.0
Estonia	3,580	9,340	7.8	42	7.0	11.0	15.3	21.6	45.1	6.44	35.6	7.2	1.6	3,286	-0.6
Georgia	630	2,680	1.9	81	6.1	11.4	16.3	22.7	43.6	7.15	15.0	5.2[x]	0.9	512	..
Hungary	4,710	11,990	5.6	35	10.0	14.7	18.3	22.7	34.4	3.44	43.4	4.6	1.5	2,512	-0.4
Kazakhstan	1,260	5,490	10.0	79	6.7	11.5	16.4	23.1	42.3	6.31	15.1	4.4	0.7	2,374	-2.2
Kyrgyzstan	270	2,540	3.9	102	7.6	11.7	16.1	22.1	42.5	5.59	19.7	5.3	1.9	504	-2.6
Latvia	2,920	7,070	8.3	53	7.6	12.9	17.1	22.1	40.3	5.30	35.4	6.5	1.0	1,586	-0.4
Lithuania	2,930	6,980	4.0	49	7.8	12.6	16.8	22.4	40.3	5.17	31.1	5.9	1.8	2,138	-0.2
Macedonia, FYR	1,820	5,020	3.6	65	..	..	..	..	..	..	..	5.1	2.1	..	..
Moldova	400	2,230	2.1	105	5.6	10.2	15.2	22.2	46.8	8.36	29.7	10.6	0.4	656	-0.2
Poland	4,190	9,000	4.0	37	7.8	12.8	17.1	22.6	39.7	5.09	35.2	7.5	1.9	2,416	-0.1
Romania	1,670	6,360	1.7	63	8.0	13.1	17.2	22.3	39.5	4.94	35.5	3.6	2.1	1,622	-0.2
Russian Federation	1,660	8,010	8.9	60	4.4	8.6	13.3	20.1	53.7	12.20	22.0	3.5	4.0	4,121	0.0
Slovakia	3,700	11,040	2.1	36	11.9	15.8	18.8	22.2	31.4	2.64	37.2	4.7	1.8	3,335	-0.3
Slovenia	10,050	17,310	4.5	29	9.1	13.4	17.3	22.5	37.7	4.14	40.5	5.7	1.2	3,277	-0.2
Tajikistan	180	1,090	8.1	112	8.0	12.9	17.0	22.1	40.0	5.00	12.4	2.2	1.2	543	-0.5
Turkmenistan	750[aa]	3,800	15.3	87	6.1	10.2	14.7	21.5	47.5	7.79	..	..	3.8	2,677	..
Ukraine	700	3,700	6.7	80	8.8	13.3	17.4	22.7	37.8	4.30	26.0	5.6	3.6	2,973	-0.3
Uzbekistan	360	2,360	2.5	95	4.0	9.5	15.0	22.4	49.1	12.28	..	7.7	1.7[cc]	2,024	-0.2
Yugoslavia, FR	940	..	4.9	..	..	..	..	..	..	..	..	..	..	1,258	0.0
Industrial Countries	..	..	..	..	..	..	..	..	..	..	..	..	..	..	..
Australia	20,240	24,970	0.8	5	5.9	12.0	17.2	23.6	41.3	7.00	23.4	5.5	1.7	5,690	..
Austria	25,220	26,330	2.7	15	6.9	13.2	18.1	23.9	38.0	5.51	40.3	5.4	0.8	3,513	-0.2
Belgium	24,540	27,470	3.8	4	8.3	13.9	18.0	22.6	37.3	4.49	45.7	3.1[u]	1.4	5,735	..
Canada	21,130	27170[c]	3.6	3	7.5	12.9	17.2	23.0	39.3	5.24	21.4	6.9[x]	1.2	7,929	..
Denmark	32,280	27,250	2.6	14	9.6	14.9	18.3	22.7	34.5	3.59	36.0	8.1	1.5	3,773	-0.2
Finland	25,130	24,570	5.5	10	10.0	14.2	17.6	22.3	35.8	3.58	33.4	7.5	1.3	6,461	0.0
France	24,090[z]	24,420	2.6	12	7.2	12.6	17.2	22.8	40.2	5.58	46.2	6.0	2.6	4,351	-0.4
Germany	25,120	24,920	2.9	17	8.2	13.2	17.5	22.7	38.5	4.70	32.6	4.8	1.5	4,108	..
Greece	11,960	16,860	4.1	24	7.5	12.4	16.9	22.8	40.3	5.37	30.9	3.1	4.9	2,552	-0.9
Ireland	22,660	25,520	10.3	18	6.7	11.6	16.4	22.4	42.9	6.40	33.0	6.0	0.7	3,726	-3.0
Israel	16,710	19,330	3.8	22	6.1	10.7	15.9	23.0	44.2	7.25	47.4	7.6[x]	8.0	3,029	-4.9
Italy	20,160	23,470	2.8	20	8.7	14.0	18.1	22.9	36.3	4.17	41.9	4.9	2.1	2,932	-0.3
Japan	35,620	27,080	2.2	9	10.6	14.2	17.6	22.0	35.7	3.37	..	3.6[x]	1.0	4,070	0.0
Luxembourg	..	..	..	16	9.4	13.8	17.7	22.6	36.5	3.88	..	4.0	0.7	..	..
Netherlands	24,970	25,850	2.8	8	7.3	12.7	17.2	22.8	40.1	5.49	45.9	5.1	1.6	4,686	-0.3

Table 4: Economic and Development Indicators

| | GNP per capita | | GDP per capita | Human Development Index | Distribution of income or consumption by quintiles[k] 1983-2000[t] | | | | | Ratio of highest 20% to lowest 20%[e] | Total central government expenditure (% of GDP) | Public education expenditure (% of GNP) | Military expenditure (% of GDP) | Per capita energy consumption (kg. of oil equivalent) | Average annual deforestation[m] (% of total forest) |
	US$ 2000	Purchasing Power Parity (PPP) ($) 2000	% growth 1999-2000	(HDI) rank 2000	Lowest 20%	Second quintile	Third quintile	Fourth quintile	Highest 20%		1999	1995-1997[t]	2000	1999	1990-2000
New Zealand	12,990	18,530	2.0	19	..	..	..	..	..	..	32.7	7.3	1.0	4,770	-0.5
Norway	34,530	29,630	1.6	1	9.7	14.3	17.9	22.2	35.8	3.69	37.0	7.7	1.8	5,965	-0.4
Portugal	11,120	16,990	3.1	28	7.3	11.6	15.9	21.8	43.4	5.95	38.8	5.8	2.1	2,365	-1.7
Spain	15,080	19,620	3.9	21	7.5	12.6	17.0	22.6	40.3	5.37	32.8	5.0	1.3	3,005	-0.6
Sweden	27,140	23,970	3.4	2	9.6	14.5	18.1	23.2	34.5	3.59	39.5	8.3	2.1	5,769	0.0
Switzerland	38,140	30,450	2.4	11	6.9	12.7	17.3	22.9	40.3	5.84	27.6	5.4	1.1	3,738	-0.4
United Kingdom	24,430	23,550	2.7	13	6.1	11.6	16.4	22.7	43.2	7.08	36.4	5.3	2.5	3,871	-0.8
United States	34,100	34,100	3.0	6	5.2	10.5	15.6	22.4	46.4	8.92	19.3	5.4[x]	3.1	8,159	-0.2
World	**5,170**	**7,410**	**2.5**	..	..	..	..	..	..	..	**25.2**	..	..	**1,671**	**0.2**

..   Data not available.

a   Special Administrative Region, data exclude China.

b   Central and Eastern European countries and the newly independent states of former Soviet Union.

c   Estimate based on regression; others are extrapolated from the latest International Comparison Program benchmark estimates.

e   Bread For the World Institute estimate.

k   Income shares by percentiles of population, ranked by per capita income, except as noted.

m   Positive data indicate loss of forest; negative data indicate gain in forest.

p   Data include São Tomé and Principe and Seychelles. Data exclude Djibouti.

q   Data exclude Hong Kong, Sinapore and Brunei.

r   Data include West Bank and Gaza. Data exclude Kuwait, Qatar, Turkey and United Arab Emirates.

t   Data refer to most recent year available during the period specified in the column heading.

u   Data refer to the Flemmish community only.

v   Data refer to expenditures by the ministry of education only.

w   Not including expenditure on tertiary education.

x   Data refer to a period other than specified in the column heading.

y   Data refer to the central government only.

z   Data include French Guiana, Guadeloupe, Martinique and Reunion.

aa   Included under lower-middle-income economies in calculating the aggregates based on earlier data.

cc   Data refer to 1999.

dd   Data refer to 1998.

The number '0' (zero) means zero or less than half the unit of measure.

Table 5: Economic Globalization

	Trade 2000						Investment 2000						Debt 2000	
	Exports of goods and services (% of GDP)		Manufactured exports (% of merchandise exports)	Food Trade		Imports of goods and services (% of GDP)	Gross capital formation (% of GDP)	Net private capital flows[c] ($ millions)	Foreign direct investment ($ millions)	Aid (% of gross capital formation)	Foreign direct investment (% of gross capital formation)	Foreign direct investment, gross (% of PPP GDP)	Total external debt (US $ millions)	Debt service (% of exports of goods and services)
				Food exports (% of merchandise exports)	Food imports (% of merchandise imports)									
	1990	2000												
Developing Countries	..	..	..	..	..	..	..	..	..	..	..	..	..	..
Africa (sub-Saharan)	**27**	**32**	**36**	**17**	**10**	**32**	**17**	**7,074**	**6,676**	**21.4**	**12.2**	**1.8**	**215,794**	**10.2**
Angola	39	90	..	..	..	74	28	1,206	1,698	12.3	68.1	39.9	10,146	15.1
Benin	14	15	3	15	25	29	20	30	30	55.9	7.0	2.8	1,598	12.6
Botswana	55	28	..	..	..	33	20	27	30	6.1	3.7	1.4	413	1.8
Burkina Faso	13	11	..	..	..	30	28	10	10	55.6	1.7	..	1,332	17.3
Burundi	8	9	0	91	23	24	9	12	12	150.2	19.0	1.7	1,100	37.2
Cameroon	20	31	5	23	19	27	16	-21	31	26.0	2.1	..	9,241	20.5
Cape Verde	..	..	..	..	..	..	..	..	..	..	..	..	..	..
Central African Republic	15	13	..	..	..	16	11	5	5	73.4	4.8	..	872	12.9
Chad	13	17	..	..	..	32	17	14	15	54.9	6.3	..	1,116	9.3
Comoros	..	..	..	..	..	..	..	..	..	..	..	..	..	..
Congo, Dem. Rep.	30	..	..	..	..	..	..	1	1	..	..	..	11,645	..
Congo, Republic of	54	79	..	..	..	42	24	14	14	4.2	1.8	..	4,887	1.6
Côte d'Ivoire	32	46	14	50	17	39	12	-47	106	30.4	9.2	2.5	12,138	22.4
Djibouti	..	..	..	..	..	..	..	..	..	..	..	..	..	..
Equatorial Guinea	..	..	..	..	..	..	..	..	..	..	..	..	..	..
Eritrea	20	16	..	..	..	86	38	35	35	76.2	15.2	..	311	1.1
Ethiopia	8	15	10	71	7	31	14	42	50	76.6	5.5	..	5,481	13.9
Gabon	46	37	..	..	..	35	26	142	150	0.9	11.6	14.5	3,995	15.0
Gambia	60	48	5	90	44	61	17	14	14	67.3	19.2	..	471	7.0
Ghana	17	49	15	48	13	70	24	71	110	49.5	8.9	2.1	6,657	19.3
Guinea	31	26	30	3	24	31	22	63	63	22.8	9.5	1.8	3,388	15.3
Guinea-Bissau	10	32	..	..	..	58	18	0	0	210.8	7.9	..	942	8.6
Kenya	26	26	21	59	14	36	13	53	111	39.0	8.4	1.1	6,295	17.3
Lesotho	17	28	..	..	..	88	40	111	118	11.4	32.5	12.9	716	12.1
Liberia	..	..	..	..	..	..	..	12	12	..	..	..	2,032	..
Madagascar	17	25	50	36	14	35	16	83	83	51.5	13.3	2.1	4,701	7.7
Malawi	25	26	..	..	20	38	13	45	45	200.5	20.3	..	2,716	11.7
Mali	17	25	..	..	..	40	23	76	76	69.3	14.6	..	2,956	12.1
Mauritania	46	41	..	..	..	57	30	3	5	75.3	1.8	0.0	2,500	25.9
Mauritius	65	64	81	18	14	67	26	-7	266	1.8	23.6	6.4	2,374	20.8
Mozambique	8	15	10	52	..	39	34	138	139	69.3	11.0	3.7	7,135	11.4
Namibia	47	49	..	..	..	56	24	..	..	18.3	..	3.6	..	..
Niger	15	15	2	29	39	23	11	13	15	108.8	7.7	..	1,638	9.4
Nigeria	43	52	0	0	20	41	23	908	1,082	2.0	11.6	2.9	34,134	4.3
Rwanda	6	8	..	..	..	24	15	14	14	118.1	5.2	0.8	1,271	24.7
Senegal	25	31	30	59	24	40	20	106	107	48.9	12.3	4.0	3,372	14.4
Sierra Leone	24	17	..	..	..	33	8	1	1	358.5	2.0	..	1,273	48.0
Somalia	10	..	..	..	..	..	..	0	0	..	..	..	2,561	..
South Africa	24	29	54[d]	9[d]	5[d]	26	15	2,736	961	2.6	5.1	1.2	24,861	10.0
Sudan	..	17	3	67	15	16	14	392	392	13.7	23.8	3.4	15,741	3.2
Swaziland	76	66	..	..	..	81	20	33	-44	4.6	-15.1	5.4	262	2.3
Tanzania	13	15[e]	15	70	16	23	18	182	193	65.3	12.1	2.1	7,445	16.2[e]
Togo	33	36	31	20	18	50	21	30	30	27.9	12.0	4.2	1,435	6.1
Uganda	7	10	6	67	14	26	18	231	220	73.0	19.6	3.5	3,408	23.7
Zambia	36	31	..	..	..	46	18	191	200	149.5	37.6	..	5,730	18.7
Zimbabwe	23	30	28	47	9	31	13	29	79	19.1	8.5	..	4,002	22.1
South Asia	**9**	**15**	**80**	**15**	**10**	**18**	**23**	**9,254**	**3,093**	**3.0**	**2.3**	**0.6**	**165,679**	**13.8**
Afghanistan	..	..	..	..	..	..	..	..	..	..	..	..	..	..
Bangladesh	6	14	91	7	15	19	23	269	280	10.8	2.6	0.6	15,609	9.1
Bhutan	..	..	..	..	..	..	..	..	..	..	..	..	..	..
India	7	14	79	14	7	17	24	8,771	2,315	1.4	2.1	0.6	100,367	12.8
Maldives	..	..	..	..	..	..	..	..	..	..	..	..	..	..
Nepal	11	24	77	21	17	32	24	-4	4	29.1	0.3	0.0	2,823	6.5
Pakistan	16	16	85	11	14	19	16	-53	308	7.3	3.2	0.5	32,091	26.8
Sri Lanka	29	40	75	21	15	51	28	262	173	6.1	3.8	1.1	9,065	9.6

Table 5: Economic Globalization

	Trade 2000						Investment 2000						Debt 2000	
	Exports of goods and services (% of GDP)		Manufactured exports (% of merchandise exports)	Food exports (% of merchandise exports)	Food imports (% of merchandise imports)	Imports of goods and services (% of GDP)	Gross capital formation (% of GDP)	Net private capital flows[c] ($ millions)	Foreign direct investment ($ millions)	Aid (% of gross capital formation)	Foreign direct investment (% of gross capital formation)	Foreign direct investment, gross (% of PPP GDP)	Total external debt (US $ millions)	Debt service (% of exports of goods and services)
	1990	2000												
East Asia and the Pacific	**26**[g]	**42**[g]	**83**[g]	**6**[g]	**5**[g]	**37**[g]	**30**[g]	**65,693**[g]	**52,130**[g]	**..**	**8.2**[g]	**3.9**[g]	**632,953**[g]	**10.8**[g]
Brunei	..	..	..	..	..	..	..	..	..	..	..	..	..	..
Cambodia	6	40	..	..	..	47	15	126	126	83.5	26.3	3.9	2,357	2.0
China	18	26	88	5	4	23	37	58,295	38,399	0.4	9.5	4.3	149,800	7.4
Hong Kong[a]	134	150	95	2	4	145	28	..	..	0.0	..	89.2	..	..
Fiji	..	..	..	..	..	..	..	..	..	..	..	..	..	..
Indonesia	25	39	57	9	10	31	18	-11,210	-4,550	6.3	-16.6	4.2	141,803	25.3
Korea, DPR (North)	..	..	..	..	..	..	..	..	..	..	..	..	..	..
Korea, Rep. (South)	29	45	91	2	5	42	29	13,215	9,283	-0.2	7.1	3.2	134,417	10.9
Lao, PDR	..	36	..	..	..	48	24	72	72	80.6	20.6	5.4	2,499	8.1
Malaysia	75	125	80	6	4	104	26	3,228	1,660	0.2	7.2	2.0	41,797	5.3
Mongolia	24	65	..	..	..	82	30	27	30	74.7	10.4	3.4	859	4.7
Myanmar (Burma)	3	0	..	..	..	1	13	188	255	..	..	..	6,046	4.7
Papua New Guinea	41	45	2	15	18	42	18	128	130	33.8	46.3	8.4	2,604	13.5
Philippines	28	56	92	5	8	50	18	2,459	2,029	4.3	15.2	2.8	50,063	13.6
Singapore	202	180	86	2	3	161	31	..	6,390	0.0	22.1	11.6	..	..
Solomon Islands	..	..	..	..	..	..	..	..	..	..	..	..	..	..
Thailand	34	67	76	14	4	59	23	-1,383	3,366	2.3	12.2	2.8	79,675	16.3
Vietnam	26	..	..	..	..	..	27	581	1,298	19.8	15.1	4.1	12,787	7.5
Latin America and the Caribbean	**14**	**17**	**48**	**21**	**8**	**18**	**20**	**97,305**	**75,088**	**1.0**	**19.1**	**4.5**	**774,419**	**38.7**
Argentina	10	11	32	44	5	11	16	16,620	11,665	0.2	25.7	4.5	146,172	71.3
Belize	..	..	..	..	..	..	..	..	..	..	..	..	..	..
Bolivia	23	18	29	30	14	25	18	923	733	31.6	48.6	8.9	5,762	39.1
Brazil	8	11	59	23	7	12	21	45,672	32,779	0.3	26.9	6.0	237,953	90.7
Chile	35	32	16	25	7	31	23	4,833	3,675	0.3	22.2	12.0	36,978	26.0
Colombia	21	22	34	19	12	20	12	3,130	2,376	1.9	23.9	4.5	34,081	28.6
Costa Rica	35	48	66	30	7	46	17	912	409	0.4	15.1	4.3	4,466	8.2
Cuba	..	16	..	..	..	18	10	..	..	..	..	..	..	..
Dominican Republic	34	30	..	..	..	39	24	1,142	953	1.3	20.4	5.2	4,598	4.8
Ecuador	33	42	10	37	9	31	17	904	710	6.4	31.1	5.3	13,281	17.3
El Salvador	19	28	48	42	16	43	17	338	185	8.0	8.3	1.5	4,023	6.7
Guatemala	21	20	32	56	12	28	17	178	230	8.3	7.2	10.1	4,622	9.4
Guyana	..	..	..	..	..	..	..	..	..	..	..	..	..	..
Haiti	16	12	..	..	..	27	11	13	13	48.1	3.0	0.3	1,169	8.0
Honduras	36	42	33	59	16	56	35	301	282	21.6	13.6	4.8	5,487	19.3
Jamaica	52	44	73	23	15	55	27	898	456	0.5	23.0	7.2	4,287	14.1
Mexico	19	31	83	5	5	33	23	11,537	13,286	0.0	9.9	2.3	150,288	30.2
Nicaragua	25	40	8	88	16	81	34	395	254	68.1	30.8	10.6	7,019	23.0
Panama	38	33	16	74	12	39	30	947	603	0.6	20.2	7.1	7,056	10.0
Paraguay	33	20	19	65	17	35	22	-16	82	4.9	4.9	1.7	3,091	10.4
Peru	16	16	20	30	12	18	20	1,553	680	3.7	6.3	1.3	28,560	42.8
Suriname	..	..	..	..	..	..	..	..	..	..	..	..	..	..
Trinidad and Tobago	45	65	29	6	8	52	19	673	650	-0.1	46.5	11.9	2,467	10.3
Uruguay	24	19	42	47	11	21	14	574	298	0.6	10.9	1.5	8,196	29.2
Venezuela	39	29	9	1	12	17	18	5,454	4,464	0.4	21.1	4.0	38,196	15.7
Middle East and North Africa	**33**[h]	**38**[h]	**14**[h]	**3**[h]	**18**[h]	**28**[h]	**20**[h]	**1,074**[h]	**1,209**[h]	**3.8**[h]	**2.7**[h]	**1.0**[h]	**203,785**[h]	**10.5**
Algeria	23	42	2	0	28	22	24	-1,212	10	1.3	0.1	..	25,002	19.6
Bahrain	..	..	..	..	..	..	..	..	..	..	..	..	..	..
Cyprus	..	..	..	..	..	..	..	..	..	..	..	..	..	..
Egypt	20	16	37	9	23	23	24	1,967	1,235	5.6	5.2	1.3	28,957	8.4
Iran	22	35	7	3	19	21	20	-610	39	0.6	0.2	0.0	7,953	11.4
Iraq	..	..	..	..	..	..	..	..	..	..	..	..	..	..
Jordan	62	42	69	16	21	69	20	455	558	32.7	33.0	2.0	8,226	11.4
Kuwait	45	57	20	0	17	31	11	..	16	0.1	0.4	0.7	..	..
Lebanon	18	13	..	..	..	38	18	2,028	298	6.6	10.0	..	10,311	..
Libya	..	..	..	..	..	..	..	..	..	..	..	..	..	..

Table 5: Economic Globalization

	Trade 2000						Investment 2000						Debt 2000	
	Exports of goods and services (% of GDP)		Manufactured exports (% of merchandise exports)	Food Trade		Imports of goods and services (% of GDP)	Gross capital formation (% of GDP)	Net private capital flows[c] ($ millions)	Foreign direct investment ($ millions)	Aid (% of gross capital formation)	Foreign direct investment (% of gross capital formation)	Foreign direct investment, gross (% of PPP GDP)	Total external debt (US $ millions)	Debt service (% of exports of goods and services)
				Food exports (% of merchandise exports)	Food imports (% of merchandise imports)									
	1990	2000												
Morocco	26	31	64	21	14	37	24	-293	10	5.2	0.1	0.8	17,944	25.9
Oman	53	..	12	4	22	..	..	56	23	..	..	0.7	6,267	7.3
Qatar	..	..	..	..	..	..	..	..	..	..	..	..	..	..
Saudi Arabia	46	50	7	1	18	26	16	..	..	0.1	..	1.1	..	..
Syria	28	38	8	9	19	35	21	107	111	4.5	3.2	1.6	21,657	4.8
Tunisia	44	44	77	9	8	48	27	966	752	4.2	14.1	3.9	10,610	20.2
Turkey	13	24	81	13	4	31	24	11,416	982	0.7	2.1	0.9	116,209	36.1
United Arab Emirates	65	..	..	..	..	..	..	..	..	..	..	..	..	..
Yemen	14	50	1	5	35	41	19	-201	-201	16.2	-12.3	3.3	5,615	3.8
Countries in Transition[b]	..	..	..	..	..	..	..	..	..	..	..	..	..	..
Albania	15	19	82	7	22	40	19	142	143	45.6	20.5	3.8	784	2.0
Armenia	35	23	43	14	25	51	19	159	140	58.9	38.2	6.6	898	7.6
Azerbaijan	..	41	8	3	19	38	26	175	130	10.3	9.6	2.5	1,184	8.0
Belarus	46	68	67	7	12	69	23	123	90	0.6	1.3	0.3	851	2.9
Bosnia and Herzegovina	..	27	..	..	..	58	20	4	0	82.0	0.0	..	2,828	..
Bulgaria	33	58	57	10	5	64	17	1,114	1,002	15.7	50.4	8.4	10,026	16.2
Croatia	78	45	73	9	8	51	22	2,451	926	1.6	22.1	5.5	12,120	25.5
Czech Republic	45	71	88	4	5	75	30	3,299	4,583	2.9	30.4	9.3	21,299	12.7
Estonia	60	84	73	8	10	88	26	485	387	5.0	30.2	10.2	3,280	8.7
Georgia	40	37	..	..	..	47	15	155	131	38.6	29.8	4.3	1,633	9.5
Hungary	31	63	86	7	3	67	31	1,721	1,692	1.8	12.1	5.0	29,415	24.4
Kazakhstan	74	59	20	7	9	47	14	1,900	1,250	7.4	49.2	7.8	6,664	16.8
Kyrgyzstan	29	43	20	16	14	55	16	-65	-2	102.9	-1.1	4.5	1,829	29.3
Latvia	48	46	56	6	12	54	27	583	407	4.7	21.0	5.8	3,379	15.8
Lithuania	52	45	60	12	10	52	21	799	379	4.2	16.2	3.4	4,855	17.1
Macedonia, FYR	26	45	66	19	15	62	17	187	176	42.2	29.4	4.9	1,465	9.3
Moldova	49	50	33	62	13	77	22	209	128	42.8	44.7	9.9	1,233	16.7
Poland	29	27	80	8	6	34	27	13,195	9,342	3.3	22.3	6.6	63,561	20.9
Romania	17	34	77	3	7	40	19	1,900	1,025	6.1	14.4	2.8	10,224	18.8
Russian Federation	18	46	22	1	15	25	17	2,200	2,714	3.6	6.3	2.4	160,300	10.1
Slovakia	27	74	85	4	7	76	30	2,185	2,052	2.0	35.7	12.2	9,462	18.0
Slovenia	84	59	90	4	6	63	28	..	176	1.2	3.5	1.3	..	..
Tajikistan	28	81	..	..	..	85	20	64	24	72.1	12.2	..	1,170	10.9
Turkmenistan	..	63	7	0	12	53	40	..	..	1.8	10.0	..	..	..
Ukraine	28	61	..	..	..	57	19	927	595	9.1	10.0	1.9	12,166	18.6
Uzbekistan	29	44	..	..	..	39	11	18	100	21.9	11.8	..	4,340	26.4
Yugoslavia, FR	..	32	..	..	..	50	14	0	0	93.6	0.0	..	11,960[f]	..
Industrial Countries	..	..	..	..	..	..	..	..	..	..	..	..	..	..
Australia	17	20	29	21	5	22	24	..	11,527	n/a	5.8	5.3	..	..
Austria	40	45	83	5	6	46	24	..	9,066	n/a	6.0	6.5	..	..
Belgium	71	88	78[j]	10[j]	9[j]	85	22	..	17,902[j]	n/a	36.7	26.6	..	..
Canada	26	44	64	6	5	41	20	..	62,758	n/a	19.7	16.1	..	..
Denmark	36	42	64	20	11	37	22	..	34,192	n/a	95.5	38.1	..	..
Finland	23	42	85	2	5	32	20	..	9,125	n/a	38.0	34.4	..	..
France	21	29	81	11	8	27	21	..	43,173	n/a	16.2	16.4	..	..
Germany	29	33	85	4	7	33	23	..	189,178	n/a	44.6	13.3	..	..
Greece	18	20	50	28	13	29	22	..	1,083	n/a	2.0	2.9	..	..
Ireland	57	88	86	8	6	74	23	..	22,778	n/a	85.4	49.2	..	..

Table 5: Economic Globalization

	Trade 2000						Investment 2000						Debt 2000	
	Exports of goods and services (% of GDP)		Manufactured exports (% of merchandise exports)	Food Trade		Imports of goods and services (% of GDP)	Gross capital formation (% of GDP)	Net private capital flows[c] ($ millions)	Foreign direct investment ($ millions)	Aid (% of gross capital formation)	Foreign direct investment (% of gross capital formation)	Foreign direct investment, gross (% of PPP GDP)	Total external debt (US $ millions)	Debt service (% of exports of goods and services)
	1990	2000		Food exports (% of merchandise exports)	Food imports (% of merchandise imports)									
Israel	35	40	94	3	5	47	19	..	4,392	3.7	20.6	6.7	..	..
Italy	20	28	88	6	9	27	20	..	13,175	n/a	6.0	2.4	..	..
Japan	10	10	94	0	13	8	26	..	8,227	n/a	1.1	0.9	..	..
Luxembourg	..	..	..	..	..	..	..	..	..	n/a	..	..	..	..
Netherlands	59	61	70	15	10	56	22	..	54,138	n/a	48.1	35.3	..	..
New Zealand	28	32	28	46	8	33	21	..	3,209	n/a	12.5	8.3	..	..
Norway	41	47	18	6	6	30	22	..	5,882	n/a	16.4	11.4	..	..
Portugal	33	31	85	7	11	43	28	..	6,227	n/a	21.1	15.9	..	..
Spain	16	30	78	14	9	32	26	..	36,023	n/a	24.9	16.5	..	..
Sweden	30	47	85	2	6	42	18	..	22,125	n/a	54.4	27.3	..	..
Switzerland	36	42	91	3	6	37	20	..	17,902	n/a	23.1	25.0	..	..
United Kingdom	24	27	82	5	8	29	18	..	133,974	n/a	52.9	38.7	..	..
United States	10	11	83	7	4	13	21	..	287,680	n/a	15.8	5.1	..	..
World	**20**	**23**	**78**	**7**	**7**	**23**	**22**	**..**	**1,167,987**	**..**	**14.0**	**8.8**	**..**	**..**

.. Data not available.

a   Special Administrative Region, data exclude China.

b   Central and Eastern European countries and the newly independent states of the former Soviet Union.

c   Net private capital flows consist of private debt flows (commercial bank lending, bonds and other private credits) and nondebt private flows (foreign direct investment and portfolio equity investment).

d   Data on export commodity shares refer to the South African Customs Union, which comprises Botswana, Lesotho, Namibia and South Africa.

e   Mainland Tanzania only.

f   World Bank estimate.

g   Data exclude Hong Kong and Singapore.

h   Data exclude Kuwait, Turkey and United Arab Emirates.

i   Data include Iceland. Data exclude Israel.

j   Data include Luxembourg.

The number '0' (zero) means zero or less than half the unit of measure.

n/a Not applicable.

Table 6: United States – National Hunger and Poverty Trends

	1970	1980	1990	1995	2000	2001
Total population (millions)	**205.1**	**227.8**	**249.4**	**262.9**	**281.4**	**284.8[d]**
Food insecurity prevalence estimates						
All U.S. households - food insecure (%)	..	..	..	10.3	10.5	10.7
Without hunger	..	..	..	6.4	7.3	7.4
With hunger	..	..	..	3.9	3.1	3.3
Adult members (total) - food insecure (%)	..	..	..	9.5	10.1	10.2
Without hunger	..	..	..	6.1	7.3	7.3
With hunger	..	..	..	3.4	2.8	3.0
Child members (total) - food insecure (%)	..	..	..	17.4	18.0	..
Without hunger	..	..	..	11.6	13.9	..
With hunger	..	..	..	5.8	4.1	..
Percent of federal budget spent on food assistance[a]	**0.5**	**2.4**	**1.9**	**2.48**	**1.83[e,f]**	**1.83[e,f]**
Total infant mortality rate (per 1,000 live births)	**20.0**	**12.6**	**9.1**	**7.6**	**6.9**	**6.9**
White	17.8	11.0	7.7	6.3	5.7	..
White, non-Hispanic	..	..	..	..	5.7[c]	..
African American	32.6	21.4	17.0	15.1	14.1	..
Hispanic	..	..	7.8	..	5.6[c]	..
American Indian	..	..	..	..	7.4[c]	..
Asian or Pacific Islander	..	..	..	..	4.1[c]	..
Total poverty rate (%)	**12.6**	**13.0**	**13.5**	**13.8**	**11.3**	**11.7**
Northeast	..	..	10.2	12.5	10.3	10.7
Midwest	..	..	11.9	11.0	9.5	9.4
South	..	..	15.9	15.7	12.5	13.5
West	..	..	11.6	14.9	11.9	12.1
White	9.9	10.2	10.7	11.2	9.4	9.9
non-Hispanic	..	..	..	..	7.5	7.8
African American	33.5	32.5	31.9	29.3	22.1	22.7
Hispanic	..	25.7	28.1	30.3	21.2	21.4
American Indian/Alaskan Native	..	..	..	..	..	..
Asian and Pacific Islander	..	..	..	..	10.8	10.2
Elderly (65 years and older)	24.6	15.7	12.2	10.5	10.2	10.1
Female-headed households	38.1	36.7	33.4	32.4	24.7	26.4
Total child poverty rate (%) (18 years and under)	**15.1**	**18.3**	**20.6**	**20.8**	**16.2**	**16.3**
White	..	13.9	15.9	16.2	13.0	13.4
non-Hispanic	..	..	..	..	9.4	9.5
African American	..	42.3	44.8	41.9	30.9	30.2
Hispanic	..	33.2	38.4	40.0	28.0	28.0
Asian and Pacific Islander	..	..	17.6	19.5	14.5	11.5
Unemployment rate (%)	**4.9**	**7.1**	**5.6**	**5.6**	**4.0**	**4.8**
White	4.5	6.3	4.8	4.9	3.5	4.2
African American	..	14.3	11.4	10.4	7.6	8.7
Hispanic	..	10.1	8.2	9.3	5.7	6.6

Table 6: United States – National Hunger and Poverty Trends

	1970	1980	1990	1995	2000	2001
Household income distribution (per quintile in %)						
All races						
Lowest 20 percent	4.1	4.2	3.9	3.7	3.6	3.5
Second quintile	10.8	10.2	9.6	9.1	8.9	8.7
Third quintile	17.4	16.8	15.9	15.2	14.8	14.6
Fourth quintile	24.5	24.8	24.0	23.3	23.0	23.0
Highest 20 percent	43.3	44.1	46.6	48.7	49.6	50.1
Ratio of highest 20 percent to lowest 20 percente	10.6	10.5	11.9	13.2	13.8	14.3
White						
Lowest 20 percent	4.2	4.4	4.2	4.0	3.7	3.7
Second quintile	11.1	10.5	10.0	9.3	9.0	8.9
Third quintile	17.5	17.0	16.0	15.3	14.9	14.7
Fourth quintile	24.3	24.6	23.9	23.3	22.9	22.9
Highest 20 percent	42.9	43.5	46.0	48.1	49.4	49.8
Ratio of highest 20 percent to lowest 20 percente	10.2	9.9	11.0	12.0	13.4	13.5
African American						
Lowest 20 percent	3.7	3.7	3.1	3.2	3.2	3.0
Second quintile	9.3	8.7	7.9	8.2	8.6	8.6
Third quintile	16.3	15.3	15.0	14.8	15.2	15.0
Fourth quintile	25.2	25.2	25.1	24.2	23.8	24.2
Highest 20 percent	45.5	47.1	49.0	49.6	49.3	49.2
Ratio of highest 20 percent to lowest 20 percente	12.3	12.7	15.8	15.5	15.4	16.4
Hispanic origin						
Lowest 20 percent	..	4.3	4.0	3.8	4.3	4.0
Second quintile	..	10.1	9.5	8.9	9.8	9.4
Third quintile	..	16.4	15.9	14.8	15.7	15.2
Fourth quintile	..	24.8	24.3	23.3	23.8	23.2
Highest 20 percent	..	44.5	46.3	49.3	46.4	48.3
Ratio of highest 20 percent to lowest 20 percente	..	10.3	11.6	13.0	10.8	12.1

.. Data not available.

a Data refer to fiscal year.

c Preliminary

d U.S. Census estimate

e Bread for the World Institute estimate.

f "Food Assistance" includes the following programs: Food stamp-related, Child nutrition, Supplemental food (including WIC), Food donations, Nutrition for the elderly, and Administrative costs.

Table 7: United States – State Hunger and Poverty Statistics

	Total population (millions) July 2001	Food insecure (% of households) 1999-2001	Food insecure with hunger (% of households) 1999-2001	Infant mortality rate (per 1,000 live births) 1998-2000			% population in poverty 2000-2001	Unemployment rate (%) 2001
				All races	White	African American		
Alabama	4.46	11.9	3.9	9.8	7.1	15.4	14.6	5.3
Alaska	0.63	11.1	4.3	6.3	5.1	..	8.1	6.3
Arizona	5.30	11.6	3.6	7.0	6.6	15.2	13.2	4.7
Arkansas	2.70	12.8	3.9	8.4	7.3	12.7	17.1	5.1
California	34.50	11.8	3.3	5.5	5.1	11.9	12.6	5.3
Colorado	4.42	8.6	2.5	6.5	6.1	14.7	9.2	3.7
Connecticut	3.43	6.8	2.6	6.5	5.6	13.6	7.5	3.3
Delaware	0.80	7.3	2.1	8.8	6.6	15.6	7.6	3.5
District of Columbia	0.57	9.8	2.9	13.5	5.7	16.9	16.7	6.5
Florida	16.40	12.2	4.0	7.2	5.6	12.5	11.9	4.8
Georgia	8.38	11.6	3.9	8.3	5.9	13.4	12.5	4.0
Hawaii	1.22	10.8	3.0	7.4	6.7	..	10.2	4.6
Idaho	1.32	13.0	4.5	7.2	7.0	..	12.0	5.0
Illinois	12.48	9.2	2.7	8.5	6.4	17.1	10.4	5.4
Indiana	6.11	8.5	2.5	7.8	6.9	15.4	8.5	4.4
Iowa	2.92	7.6	2.2	6.2	5.8	17.2	7.8	3.3
Kansas	2.69	11.3	3.2	7.0	6.8	10.5	9.1	4.3
Kentucky	4.07	10.1	3.0	7.4	6.8	12.6	12.6	5.5
Louisiana	4.47	13.2	3.0	9.1	6.1	13.5	16.7	6.0
Maine	1.29	9.4	3.1	5.4	5.5	..	10.2	4.0
Maryland	5.38	8.8	3.1	8.1	5.3	13.9	7.3	4.1
Massachusetts	6.38	6.7	2.0	5.0	4.5	9.9	9.4	3.7
Michigan	9.99	8.1	2.4	8.1	6.3	16.4	9.6	5.3
Minnesota	4.97	7.1	2.0	5.9	5.3	13.1	6.5	3.7
Mississippi	2.86	13.1	3.7	10.3	6.6	14.7	17.1	5.5
Missouri	5.63	8.6	2.3	7.5	6.1	16.0	9.4	4.7
Montana	0.90	13.2	4.0	6.8	6.2	..	13.7	4.6
Nebraska	1.71	9.9	2.9	7.0	6.3	16.0	9.0	3.1
Nevada	2.11	10.1	3.4	6.7	6.2	12.5	7.9	5.3
New Hampshire	1.26	6.5	1.9	5.4	5.3	..	5.5	3.5
New Jersey	8.48	7.8	2.4	6.4	4.9	13.3	7.7	4.2
New Mexico	1.83	14.6	4.2	6.9	6.7	..	17.7	4.8
New York	19.01	9.6	3.1	6.3	5.1	11.3	14.0	4.9
North Carolina	8.19	11.1	3.3	9.0	6.7	15.7	12.5	5.5
North Dakota	0.63	8.5	2.2	8.0	7.2	..	12.1	2.8
Ohio	11.37	9.1	2.8	7.9	6.8	14.5	10.3	4.3
Oklahoma	3.46	12.9	3.8	8.5	8.0	13.3	15.0	3.8
Oregon	3.47	13.7	5.8	5.6	5.5	8.7	11.3	6.3
Pennsylvania	12.29	8.4	2.2	7.2	5.9	15.5	9.1	4.7
Rhode Island	1.06	8.7	2.5	6.4	5.5	14.8	9.9	4.7
South Carolina	4.06	11.3	3.6	9.5	6.3	15.6	13.1	5.4
South Dakota	0.76	7.9	1.9	7.8	6.7	..	9.6	3.3
Tennessee	5.74	11.8	3.4	8.4	6.4	15.6	13.8	4.5
Texas	21.33	13.9	3.6	6.0	5.4	11.0	15.2	4.9
Utah	2.27	13.8	4.6	5.3	5.2	..	9.1	4.4
Vermont	0.61	9.1	1.8	6.3	6.2	..	9.9	3.6
Virginia	7.19	7.6	1.5	7.2	5.6	12.8	8.1	3.5
Washington	5.99	12.5	4.6	5.3	4.9	11.0	10.8	6.4
West Virginia	1.80	10.3	3.3	7.6	7.6	9.7	15.6	4.9
Wisconsin	5.40	8.4	2.9	6.9	5.8	16.7	8.6	4.6
Wyoming	0.49	9.9	3.2	7.0	6.9	..	9.7	3.9
Puerto Rico	..	..	..	10.2	10.2	9.8	..	11.4
United States	**284.80**	**10.4**	**3.1**	**7.0**	**5.8**	**13.8**	**11.5**	**4.8**

.. Data not available.

Table 8: United States – Nutrition and Assistance Programs

	Food Stamp Participation: Monthly Average by State						
	1995[e]	1996[e]	1997[e]	1998[e]	1999[e]	2000[e]	2001[e]
Alabama	524,522	509,214	469,268	426,819	405,273	396,057	411,292
Alaska	45,448	46,233	45,234	42,451	41,262	37,524	37,897
Arizona	480,195	427,481	363,779	295,703	257,362	259,006	291,372
Arkansas	272,174	273,900	265,854	255,710	252,957	246,572	256,441
California	3,174,651	3,143,390	2,814,761	2,259,069	2,027,089	1,831,697	1,668,351
Colorado	251,880	243,692	216,748	191,015	173,497	155,948	153,952
Connecticut	226,061	222,758	209,529	195,866	178,168	165,059	157,031
Delaware	57,090	57,836	53,655	45,581	38,571	32,218	31,886
District of Columbia	93,993	92,751	90,391	85,396	84,082	80,803	73,494
Florida	1,395,296	1,371,352	1,191,664	990,571	933,435	882,341	887,256
Georgia	815,920	792,502	698,323	631,720	616,600	559,468	573,537
Hawaii	124,575	130,344	126,901	122,027	125,155	118,041	108,313
Idaho	80,255	79,855	70,413	62,393	57,201	58,191	59,667
Illinois	1,151,035	1,105,160	1,019,600	922,927	820,034	779,420	825,295
Indiana	469,647	389,537	347,772	313,116	298,213	300,314	346,551
Iowa	184,025	177,283	161,184	141,067	128,790	123,322	126,494
Kansas	184,241	171,831	148,734	119,218	114,875	116,596	124,285
Kentucky	520,088	485,628	444,422	412,028	396,440	403,479	412,680
Louisiana	710,597	670,034	575,411	536,834	516,285	599,851	518,384
Maine	131,955	130,872	123,767	115,099	108,749	101,598	104,383
Maryland	398,727	374,512	354,436	322,653	264,393	219,180	208,426
Massachusetts	409,870	373,599	339,505	292,997	261,021	231,829	219,223
Michigan	970,760	935,416	838,917	771,580	682,680	602,857	641,269
Minnesota	308,206	294,825	260,476	219,744	208,062	196,050	197,727
Mississippi	479,934	457,106	399,062	329,058	288,057	275,856	297,805
Missouri	575,882	553,930	477,703	410,966	408,331	419,959	454,427
Montana	70,873	70,754	66,605	62,328	60,898	59,466	61,957
Nebraska	105,133	101,625	97,176	94,944	92,404	82,414	80,652
Nevada	98,538	96,712	82,419	71,531	61,673	60,905	69,396
New Hampshire	58,353	52,809	46,000	39,578	37,438	36,266	35,554
New Jersey	550,628	540,452	491,337	424,738	384,888	344,677	317,579
New Mexico	238,854	235,060	204,644	174,699	178,439	169,354	163,245
New York	2,183,101	2,098,561	1,913,548	1,627,170	1,540,784	1,438,568	1,353,542
North Carolina	613,502	631,061	586,415	527,790	505,410	488,247	493,672
North Dakota	41,401	39,825	37,688	33,801	33,442	31,895	37,755
Ohio	1,155,490	1,045,066	873,562	733,565	639,786	609,717	640,503
Oklahoma	374,893	353,790	321,894	287,577	271,351	523,287	271,001
Oregon	288,687	287,607	258,615	238,446	223,978	234,387	283,705
Pennsylvania	1,173,420	1,123,541	1,008,864	906,735	834,898	777,112	748,074
Rhode Island	93,434	90,873	84,627	72,301	76,394	74,256	71,272
South Carolina	363,822	358,341	349,137	333,017	308,570	295,335	315,718
South Dakota	50,158	48,843	46,901	45,173	44,065	42,962	44,594
Tennessee	662,014	637,773	585,889	538,467	510,828	496,031	521,510
Texas	2,557,693	2,371,958	2,033,750	1,636,175	1,400,526	1,332,785	1,360,642
Utah	118,836	110,011	98,338	91,764	88,163	81,945	79,716
Vermont	59,292	56,459	53,005	45,702	44,287	40,831	38,874
Virginia	545,829	537,531	476,088	396,581	361,581	336,080	332,312
Washington	476,019	476,391	444,800	364,418	306,654	295,061	308,589
West Virginia	308,505	299,719	287,035	269,140	247,249	226,897	221,361
Wisconsin	320,142	283,255	232,103	192,887	182,206	193,021	215,786
Wyoming	35,579	33,013	28,584	25,452	23,477	22,459	22,539
Guam	..	..	17,783	25,249	19,758	22,234	22,723
Puerto Rico	n/a	n/a	n/a	n/a	n/a	n/a	..
United States	**26,618,773**	**25,540,331**	**22,854,273**	**19,788,115**	**18,182,595**	**17,155,093**	**17,312,974**

Table 8: United States – Nutrition and Assistance Programs

	WIC[a] Annual Participation by State						
	1995[e]	1996[e]	1997[e]	1998[e]	1999[e]	2000[e]	2001[e]
Alabama	121,979	118,163	118,899	117,319	115,172	103,930	111,049
Alaska	19,235	22,410	23,537	23,829	26,131	24,395	23,628
Arizona	122,179	141,466	145,849	142,000	142,488	145,544	147,285
Arkansas	87,362	90,662	87,310	82,939	82,882	82,131	79,826
California	1,003,611	1,141,598	1,224,224	1,216,253	1,229,495	1,219,430	1,243,509
Colorado	70,617	70,523	75,068	74,679	74,801	71,967	72,124
Connecticut	63,625	62,520	59,368	60,267	58,299	50,867	49,252
Delaware	15,444	15,831	15,581	15,635	15,274	15,844	16,568
District of Columbia	17,368	16,116	16,747	16,593	16,406	15,060	15,204
Florida	317,095	332,130	354,971	345,150	337,559	296,298	316,758
Georgia	217,207	223,746	230,153	232,258	224,069	216,319	226,365
Hawaii	25,410	27,466	30,807	34,098	34,137	32,080	32,467
Idaho	31,120	31,085	31,475	31,678	31,543	31,286	32,641
Illinois	244,661	244,223	236,068	237,262	241,016	243,655	251,329
Indiana	132,621	132,532	132,700	131,099	128,269	120,648	117,880
Iowa	65,260	66,020	66,293	65,885	63,996	60,793	60,664
Kansas	55,890	54,377	54,754	52,896	52,345	52,773	53,260
Kentucky	118,198	119,457	122,948	122,910	122,056	112,182	111,004
Louisiana	133,992	139,603	139,223	136,866	135,430	130,042	125,916
Maine	26,905	26,300	26,663	25,786	24,646	22,073	20,962
Maryland	86,349	87,961	91,412	92,744	93,338	94,194	93,829
Massachusetts	113,605	115,942	118,818	117,681	115,042	113,842	112,623
Michigan	209,272	212,270	218,371	217,924	215,138	213,049	214,951
Minnesota	90,979	93,971	94,807	95,101	90,101	90,093	96,192
Mississippi	102,718	102,532	100,124	99,097	96,863	95,836	98,874
Missouri	127,005	129,245	131,638	128,176	126,640	123,738	125,144
Montana	20,889	22,155	21,679	21,428	21,346	21,288	21,413
Nebraska	35,715	36,101	33,041	31,770	33,047	32,793	34,427
Nevada	31,053	36,310	37,324	37,972	37,415	38,781	40,646
New Hampshire	19,423	19,342	19,179	18,678	18,100	17,049	16,507
New Jersey	141,962	137,988	141,514	140,732	129,603	127,013	128,577
New Mexico	53,816	56,131	54,040	56,183	56,494	57,802	59,464
New York	452,997	466,185	478,980	482,882	476,563	466,818	460,252
North Carolina	182,264	188,828	194,566	197,954	196,389	190,258	200,678
North Dakota	17,754	17,484	16,868	15,810	14,930	14,303	14,053
Ohio	259,121	258,400	254,668	250,815	245,994	242,921	247,092
Oklahoma	95,964	103,373	108,348	109,581	108,485	108,375	105,907
Oregon	82,212	86,048	89,299	31,341	92,831	86,061	93,246
Pennsylvania	260,544	262,111	257,018	246,337	235,526	230,914	226,434
Rhode Island	21,450	22,382	22,596	22,768	22,454	21,783	21,925
South Carolina	124,252	123,669	118,966	118,556	110,850	108,204	111,408
South Dakota	22,397	22,439	21,945	20,507	20,445	20,409	20,505
Tennessee	137,280	144,174	150,289	148,692	148,824	148,662	149,490
Texas	637,229	641,150	683,583	691,292	707,872	737,206	750,122
Utah	53,287	54,893	57,511	57,391	59,592	57,549	58,928
Vermont	16,140	16,061	16,133	16,308	16,051	16,401	15,966
Virginia	126,882	126,760	129,520	132,317	131,304	128,163	130,094
Washington	112,915	129,256	145,147	144,052	141,089	145,850	150,138
West Virginia	51,890	54,173	55,065	53,962	52,335	50,996	50,064
Wisconsin	109,151	109,712	108,886	108,352	104,041	100,574	100,128
Wyoming	11,745	11,965	12,447	11,789	11,583	10,907	11,103
Guam	..	..	..	..	..	..	..
Puerto Rico	182,795	204,717	211,454	206,968	205,228	214,651	219,620
United States	**6,894,413**	**7,187,831**	**7,406,866**	**7,367,397**	**7,311,206**	**7,192,604**	**7,305,577**

Table 8: United States – Nutrition and Assistance Programs

	TANF[b] Individual Recipients: Monthly Average by State[f]						
	1995	1996	1997	1998	1999	2000	2001[e]
Alabama	121,837	108,269	91,723	61,809	48,459	56,408	49,100
Alaska	37,264	35,432	36,189	31,689	26,883	23,838	16,997
Arizona	195,082	171,617	151,526	113,209	88,456	87,217	82,595
Arkansas	65,325	59,223	54,879	36,704	29,284	29,313	27,751
California	2,692,202	2,648,772	2,476,564	2,144,495	1,845,919	1,307,941	1,228,605
Colorado	110,742	99,739	87,434	55,352	40,799	28,837	27,132
Connecticut	170,719	161,736	155,701	138,666	88,304	66,407	59,566
Delaware	26,314	23,153	23,141	18,504	15,891	12,849	12,355
District of Columbia	72,330	70,082	67,871	56,128	52,957	46,893	43,425
Florida	657,313	575,553	478,329	320,886	220,216	152,709	124,586
Georgia	388,913	367,656	306,625	220,070	167,400	128,607	120,501
Hawaii	65,207	66,690	65,312	75,817	45,582	44,425	40,645
Idaho	24,050	23,547	19,812	4,446	3,061	2,309	2,246
Illinois	710,032	663,212	601,854	526,851	388,334	254,238	182,673
Indiana	197,225	147,083	121,974	95,665	105,069	99,073	115,519
Iowa	103,108	91,727	78,275	69,504	60,380	53,267	54,071
Kansas	81,504	70,758	57,528	38,462	33,376	31,620	32,967
Kentucky	193,722	176,601	162,730	132,388	102,370	88,747	81,750
Louisiana	258,180	239,247	206,582	118,404	115,791	74,888	65,504
Maine	60,973	56,319	51,178	41,265	36,812	28,191	26,134
Maryland	227,887	207,800	169,723	130,196	92,711	72,724	68,221
Massachusetts	286,175	242,572	214,014	181,729	131,139	101,452	95,057
Michigan	612,224	535,704	462,291	376,985	267,749	207,463	195,369
Minnesota	180,490	171,916	160,167	141,064	124,659	115,749	112,688
Mississippi	146,319	133,029	109,097	66,030	42,651	33,801	35,710
Missouri	259,595	238,052	208,132	162,950	136,782	124,773	121,364
Montana	34,313	32,557	28,138	20,137	16,152	14,249	15,401
Nebraska	42,038	38,653	36,535	38,090	35,057	24,037	23,802
Nevada	41,846	40,491	28,973	29,262	21,753	15,906	19,461
New Hampshire	28,671	24,519	20,627	15,947	15,130	14,035	13,501
New Jersey	321,151	293,833	256,064	217,320	164,815	130,317	113,481
New Mexico	105,114	102,648	89,814	64,759	80,828	72,343	56,105
New York	1,266,350	1,200,847	1,074,189	941,714	822,970	723,793	613,353
North Carolina	317,836	282,086	253,286	192,172	145,596	99,553	91,526
North Dakota	14,920	13,652	11,964	8,884	8,260	8,706	8,881
Ohio	629,719	552,304	518,595	386,239	311,872	245,085	199,352
Oklahoma	127,336	110,498	87,312	69,630	61,894	35,472	33,895
Oregon	107,610	92,182	66,919	48,561	44,219	41,889	41,976
Pennsylvania	611,215	553,148	484,321	395,107	313,821	239,125	215,175
Rhode Island	62,407	60,654	54,809	54,537	50,632	45,161	41,628
South Carolina	133,567	121,703	98,077	73,179	45,648	37,285	40,266
South Dakota	17,652	16,821	14,091	10,514	8,759	6,755	6,365
Tennessee	281,982	265,620	195,891	139,022	148,781	151,438	155,094
Texas	765,460	714,523	626,617	439,824	325,766	342,383	349,279
Utah	47,472	41,145	35,493	29,868	30,276	22,292	21,815
Vermont	27,716	25,865	236,570	21,013	18,324	16,119	15,060
Virginia	189,493	166,012	136,053	107,192	91,544	72,573	65,051
Washington	290,940	276,018	263,792	228,723	177,611	153,057	141,397
West Virginia	107,668	98,439	98,690	51,348	32,161	32,262	39,037
Wisconsin	214,404	184,209	132,383	44,630	47,336	38,056	40,030
Wyoming	15,434	13,531	10,322	2,903	1,886	1,183	987
Guam	..	..	..	..	..	9,914	9,729
Puerto Rico	171,932	156,805	145,749	130,283	111,361	92,299	75,114
United States	**13,930,953**	**12,876,661**	**11,423,007**	**9,131,716**	**7,455,297**	**5,962,218[h]**	**5,471,863[h]**

..   Data not available.

a   Special Supplemental Nutrition Program for Women, Infants and Children.

b   Temporary Assistance for Needy Families.

d   Preliminary data, subject to change.

e   Data refer to fiscal year.

f   Data refer to calendar year.

h   Data include U.S. Virgin Islands

n/a   Not Applicable.

Sources for Tables

Table 1: Global Hunger – Life and Death Indicators

Total population, projected population, projected growth rate, life expectancy: The Population Reference Bureau, *2002 World Population Data Sheet*, data posted at http://www.prb.org.

Population under age 15: Statistics and Population Division of the U.N. Secretariat, "Indicators of Youth and Elderly Populations," data posted at http://www.un.org/Depts/unsd/social/youth.htm.

Total fertility rate, urban population, infant mortality, low-birth weight infants, children immunized, under-5 mortality rate, maternal mortality rate: U.N. Children's Fund, *The State of the World's Children, 2002 (SWC)* (New York: UNICEF, 2002).

Refugees: U.S. Committee for Refugees, *World Refugees Survey, 2002* (Washington, DC: Immigration and Refugee Services of America, 2000) data posted at http://www.refugees.org.

Table 2: Global Food, Nutrition and Education

Per capita dietary energy supply, food production per capita: Food and Agriculture Organization of the United Nations (FAO), data posted at http://apps.fao.org/default.htm.

Vitamin A supplementation coverage, gender-related primary school enrollment: *SWC, 2002.*

Total adult literacy rate, gender-based adult literacy rate, total net primary school enrollment, combined educational enrollment: U.N. Development Program, *Human Development Report, 2002 (HDR)* (New York: Oxford University Press, 2002).

Table 3: Hunger, Malnutrition and Poverty

Undernourished population: FAO, *The State of Food Insecurity in the World, 2002* (Rome: FAO, 2000).

Underweight, wasting, stunting, safe water: *SWC, 2002.*

Population in poverty: World Bank, *World Development Indicators, 2002 (WDI).*

Table 4: Economic and Development Indicators

GNP data, PPP data, distribution of income or consumption, central government expenditures, per capita energy consumption, annual deforestation: *WDI, 2002.*

Human Development Indicators rank, public education expenditures, military expenditures: *HDR, 2002.*

Table 5: Economic Globalization

Exports, imports, net private capital flows, gross capital formation, investment, aid, debt: *WDI, 2002.*

Table 6: United States – National Hunger and Poverty Trends

Total population: U.S. Bureau of the Census, data posted at http://www.quickfacts.census.gov/qfd.

Food insecurity prevalence: U.S. Department of Agriculture (USDA), *Household Food Security in the United States, 2001.* Food Assistance and Research Nutrition Service, Report No. 29 (FANRR-29). Report posted at http://www.ers.usda.gov.

Infant mortality: Centers for Disease Control and Prevention, National Center for Health Statistics, *Births, Marriages, Divorces, and Deaths: Provisional Data for 2001*, data posted at http://www.cdc.gov/nchs/products/pubs/pubd/nvsr/50/50-16.htm.

Poverty by region: U.S. Bureau of the Census, data posted at http://www.census.gov/income/histpov/hstpov9.lst.

Other poverty: U.S. Bureau of the Census, *Historical Poverty Tables*, data posted at http://www.census.gov/hhes/poverty/histpov.

Income: U.S. Bureau of the Census, Historical Income Tables-Household, data posted at http://www.census.gov/hhes/income/histinc/h02.html.

Unemployment: U.S. Department of Labor, Bureau of Labor Statistics, data posted at http://www.bls.gov/cps/#charemp.

Table 7: United States – State Hunger and Poverty Statistics

Total population: U.S. Bureau of the Census, data posted at http://www.census.gov.

Food insecurity prevalence: USDA, *Household Food Security in the United States, 2001.* Food Assistance and Research Nutrition Service, Report No. 29 (FANRR-29). Report posted at http://www.ers.usda.gov.

Infant mortality: Centers for Disease Control and Prevention, National Center for Health Statistics, *Deaths: Final Data for 2000*, data posted at http://www.cdc.gov/nchs/products/pubs/pubd/nvsr/50/50-16.htm.

Poverty: U.S. Bureau of the Census, *Poverty in the United States: 2001*, data posted at http://www.census.gov/hhes/www/poverty01.html.

Unemployment: U.S. Department of Labor, Bureau of Labor Statistics, data posted at http://www.bls.gov/lau/staa_7000.prn.

Table 8: United States – Nutrition and Assistance Programs

Food stamp participation, Special Supplemental Nutrition Program for Women, Infants and Children (WIC) participation: USDA, Food and Nutrition Service Program, data found at http://www.fns.usda.gov/pd/.

Temporary Assistance for Needy Families (TANF): U.S. Department of Health and Human Services, Administration for Children and Families, data posted at http://www.acf.dhhs.gov/news/stats/recipientsL.htm.

Acronyms

AoA	Agreement on Agriculture
ARP	Acreage Reduction Program
CAFO	Concentrated Animal Feeding Operation
CAP	Common Agriculture Policy
CCC	Commodity Credit Corporation
CGIAR	Consultative Group on International Agricultural Research
CIS	Commonwealth of Independent States (former Soviet Union)
CLUSA	Cooperative League of the USA
CRP	Conservation Reserve Program
DAC	Development Assistance Committee of the OECD
FAIR Act	Federal Agricultural Improvement and Reform Act of 1996
FAO	Food and Agriculture Organization of the United Nations
G-8	Group of eight (United States, Great Britain, Germany, France, Canada, Japan, Italy and Russia)
GATT	General Agreement on Tariffs and Trade
GDP	Gross Domestic Product
GM	Genetically Modified
GNP	Gross National Product
HDI	Human Development Index
HIPC	Highly Indebted Poor Countries
IFAD	International Fund for Agricultural Development
IFPRI	International Food Policy Research Institute
IMF	International Monetary Fund
MCA	Millennium Challenge Account
MNC	Multinational Corporation

NASFAM	National Smallholder Farmers Association of Malawi
NEPAD	The New Partnership for Africa's Development
NGO	Nongovernmental Organization
ODA	Official Development Assistance
OECD	Organization for Economic Cooperation and Development
PRSP	Poverty Reduction Strategy Paper
SAP	Structural Adjustment Program
TRIP	Trade in Intellectual Property Rights
TRIM	Trade-Related Investment Measure
UNCTAD	U.N. Conference on Trade and Development
UNDP	U.N. Development Program
UNICEF	U.N. Children's Fund
UNITA	National Union for the Total Independence of Angola
USAID	U.S. Agency for International Development
USDA	U.S. Department of Agriculture
WFP	World Food Program
WHO	World Health Organization
WTO	World Trade Organization

Glossary

Acreage Reduction Program (ARP) – An annual voluntary land retirement system in which participating farmers idle a prescribed portion of their crop base acreage of wheat, feed grains, cotton or rice. Farmers were required to participate in the ARP to be eligible for benefits, such as Commodity Credit Corporation loans and deficiency payments. The 1996 farm bill repealed ARPs.

Base acreage (or Crop Base Acreage) – A farm's crop-specific acreage of wheat, feed grains, upland cotton, rice, oilseeds or peanuts eligible to participate in commodity programs under the 2002 farm bill.

Commodity Credit Corporation (CCC) – A federally owned and operated corporation within the U.S. Department of Agriculture (USDA) created to stabilize and support agricultural prices and farm income by making loans and payments to producers, purchasing commodities and various other operations. The CCC handles all money transactions for agricultural price- and income-support and related programs.

Commodity loan rate – The price per unit (pound, bushel or hundredweight) at which the CCC provides commodity-secured loans to farmers for a specified period of time.

Comparative advantage – Refers to the economic theory that in international trade it is more advantageous for a country to devote its resources, not to all lines of production in which it may have an advantage (usually a lower production cost), but to those in which its relative superiority is greatest.

Conservation Reserve Program (CRP) – A program created in the Food Security Act of 1985 to retire from production up to 45 million acres of highly erodible and environmentally sensitive farmland. Landowners sign contracts agreeing to keep retired lands in approved conservation uses for 10 years to 15 years. In exchange, landowners receive an annual rental payment, cost-share payments to establish permanent vegetative cover and technical assistance.

Counter-cyclical payment – A subsidy payment that adjusts automatically, increasing when commodity prices are low and decreasing when prices are high.

Covered commodities – Term used in the 2002 farm bill referring to those crops eligible for subsidy payments, including wheat, corn, barley, oats, upland cotton, rice, soybeans and other oilseeds.

Daily calorie requirement – The average number of calories needed to sustain normal levels of activity and health, taking into account age, sex, body weight and climate; on average, about 2,350 calories per person per day.

Debt relief – Measures to reduce the debt owed by developing country governments to either private lenders (commercial banks like Citibank), governments (like Germany or the United States) or international financial institutions (like the International Monetary Fund or World Bank).

Decoupled payments – Government program payments to farmers that are not linked to the current levels of production, prices or resource use. When payments are decoupled, farmers make production decisions based on expected market returns rather than expected government payments.

Deficiency payments – Direct government payments made to farmers who participated in the annual commodity programs prior to 1996. The crop-specific deficiency payment rate was based on the difference between the legislatively set target price and the lower national average market price during a specified time. The 1996 farm bill eliminated these payments and replaced them with production flexibility contract payments.

Developed countries – Also called industrialized countries or the North, these are high-income countries, which the World Bank defines as having a gross national income per capita of $9,266 or more in 1999. Most developed countries have an industrial economy, and most people living in these countries have a high economic standard of living (though significant populations also may live in poverty). Currently, about 50 countries in the world are considered high income, and their combined population is about 0.9 billion, less than one-sixth of the world's population.

Developing countries – Low- and middle-income countries in which most people have a lower standard of living and access to fewer goods and services than do most people in high-income countries. Also known as the Third World, the South and the less-developed countries. Currently, about 125 countries are considered developing and home to approximately 5 billion people.

Dumping – The practice of selling commodities in a foreign market at a lower price than in the domestic market.

Empowerment – Measures that expand poor people's ability and access to participate in, negotiate with, influence, control and hold accountable institutions that affect their lives. Broadly, it is the expansion of freedom of choice and action. It is a participatory process that places decision-making responsibility and the resources to act into the hands of those who will benefit.

Export subsidy – Special incentives, such as cash payments, extended by governments to encourage increased foreign sales; often used when a nation's domestic price for a food is artificially raised above the world market price.

Famine – An extreme collapse in local availability and access to food that causes a widespread rise in deaths from outright starvation or hunger-related illnesses.

Farmgate price – Price a farmer is paid for her or his goods.

Farm Security and Rural Investment Act of 2002 (farm bill) – The omnibus food and agriculture legislation signed into law on May 13, 2002, that provides a six-year policy framework (2002-2007) for the Secretary of Agriculture to administer various agricultural programs.

Food insecurity – A condition of uncertain availability of or ability to acquire safe, nutritious food in a socially acceptable way.

Food security – For every person, assured access – primarily by production or purchase – to enough nutritious food to sustain an active and healthy life with dignity. Includes food availability, food access and appropriate food use.

Food self-reliance – A strategy whereby countries boost yields, employing sustainable and efficient farming practices, and diversify their agricultural production, some for export and some for domestic consumption.

Food self-sufficiency – A strategy whereby countries, communities or regions rely exclusively on their own food production.

Foreign aid: See *Official Development Assistance.*

Free trade – An approach to trade that is based on the idea that market forces of supply and demand should determine prices and supply levels, without government intervention. In agricultural policy, free trade in its purest form would mean no government price- and income-support programs, supply management programs, export subsidies or other barriers to international trade.

Free trade agreements – Agreements between two countries (bilateral) or among several countries (multilateral) to move toward freer trade by eliminating or reducing government practices that distort trade. These practices may include tariffs (taxes on traded goods and services) and/or nontariff barriers, such as quotas (limits on the amount traded).

General Agreement on Tariffs and Trade (GATT) – An agreement established in 1948 providing the ground rules for multilateral trade policy by its member nations. Successive negotiating rounds of the GATT culminated in the Uruguay Round (1986 to 1994). In 1995, the GATT was replaced by the World Trade Organization.

Globalization – In economic terms, it is the process of increasing integration of national economies at the global level. In social terms, the increasing interconnectedness of peoples and cultures and the increasing exchange of ideas.

Green Revolution – Modification of agriculture in the 1960s and 1970s to improve agricultural production through the use of new technologies, including new machines, fertilizer, pesticides, irrigation and cultivation methods, and high-yielding varieties of grains, such as rice, wheat and corn. This revolution was meant to make India and other Asian countries self-sufficient in food production.

Gross domestic product (GDP) – The value of all goods and services produced within a nation during a specified period, usually a year.

Gross national product (GNP) – The value of all goods and services produced by a country's citizens, wherever they are located.

Heavily Indebted Poor Countries (HIPC) – Adopted in 1996 and enhanced in 1999, this comprehensive multilateral initiative provides a coordinated effort to reduce the external debt burdens of as many as 40 of the world's poorest countries, directing the savings toward poverty reduction.

Horizontal integration – The merger of two or more companies that are in the same line of business. For example, if supermarket group, Tesco, merged with rival, J. Sainsbury, that would be considered horizontal integration.

Human Development Index (HDI) – As used by the U.N. Development Program, a measure of well-being based on economic growth, educational attainment and health.

Human rights – The basic rights and freedoms afforded all human beings, including the right to food and other basic necessities, the right to life and liberty, freedom of thought and expression, and equality before the law. A summary list can be found in the U. N. Universal Declaration of Human Rights.

Hunger – A condition in which people do not get enough food to provide the nutrients (carbohydrate, fat, protein, vitamins, minerals and water) for fully productive, active and healthy lives.

Income-support payments – Direct payments to farmers that are intended to supplement their farm income without affecting market prices.

Infant mortality rate – The annual number of deaths of infants under 1 year of age per 1,000 live births.

Input – The resources that are used in farm production, such as chemicals, equipment, feed, seed and energy.

International Monetary Fund (IMF) – An international organization that makes loans to countries with short-term foreign exchange and monetary problems. These loans are conditioned upon the borrowing country's willingness to adopt IMF-approved economic policies.

Livelihood security – The ability of a household to meet its basic needs for food, shelter, water, sanitation, health care and education.

Glossary

Malnutrition – A condition resulting from inadequate consumption (undernutrition) or excessive consumption of a nutrient, which can impair physical and mental health, and can be the cause or result of infectious diseases.

Market access – The extent to which a country permits imports. A variety of tariff and nontariff trade barriers can be used to limit the entry of foreign products.

Market economy – An economy in which prices for goods and services are set primarily by private markets rather than by government planning or regulation.

Market liberalization – The degree to which a market is hampered by outside influence, such as tariffs or barriers. The less impediments, the more liberalized a market is said to be.

Microcredit – Small, short-term loans to low-income people, who are too poor to borrow from commercial banks, to help them start their own businesses, generate income and raise their standard of living.

Minimum caloric requirement: See *Daily calorie requirement*.

Multilateral trade negotiations – Trade negotiations between more than two countries, as distinct from bilateral trade negotiations, which take place between only two countries.

Nongovernmental organizations (NGOs) – Voluntary, nonprofit organizations that support community development, provide social services, protect the environment and promote the public interest.

Nontariff trade barrier – Any government action, other than tariffs, that may affect trade, such as informal agreements or quotas or nontrade policies that can impede trade, such as health, safety or labor standards.

North-South – Pertaining to relations between the rich countries of the North and the poor countries of the South.

Official development assistance (ODA) – The term used by the Organization for Economic Cooperation and Development for grants and loans to developing countries undertaken by governments to pursue economic development at concessional financial terms.

Organization for Economic Cooperation and Development (OECD) – A group of 30 industrialized countries that pursue economic development while fostering good governance in the public sector and in corporate activity. Members include: Australia, Austria, Belgium, Canada, Czech Republic, Denmark, Finland, France, Germany, Greece, Hungary, Iceland, Ireland, Italy, Japan, Korea, Luxembourg, Mexico, Netherlands, New Zealand, Norway, Poland, Portugal, Slovak Republic, Spain, Sweden, Switzerland, Turkey, United Kingdom and United States. The Commission of the European Communities also takes part in the OECD's work.

Parity price – A measurement of the purchasing power today of a particular commodity unit based on its purchasing power in 1910-1914. This price-support method was abandoned as part of the Food and Agriculture Act of 1965.

Payment limitation – The maximum amount of commodity program benefits a person can receive by law. "Persons," as defined by payment limitation regulations established by the Secretary of Agriculture, are individuals; members of joint operations; or entities, such as limited partnerships, corporations, associations, trusts and estates, that are actively engaged in farming.

Poverty line – An official measure of poverty defined by national governments. In the United States, it is calculated as three times the cost of the USDA's Thrifty Food Plan, which provides a less-than-adequate diet. In 2003 the poverty line is $15,260 annually for a family of three, $18,400 for a family of four.

Price-support payments – Payments to farmers that increase prices for certain commodities when supply exceeds demand and prices are unacceptably low.

Production flexibility contract payments – Fixed income-support payments to farmers, which were authorized under the 1996 farm bill and replaced deficiency payments.

Protectionism – Trade policy that protects domestic products or industries by limiting imports, as with tariffs or quotas.

Public policy advocacy – Citizen political action focused on the policies, programs and practices of governments, international financial institutions and corporations.

Trade bloc – A group of countries with similar interests who negotiate and bargain together, thereby increasing the strength of their collective voice.

Rule of law – Law by government that is fair and enforceable.

Safety nets – A policy that ensures a minimum income, consumption or wage level for everyone in a social group. It also may provide people or entities with protection against risks, such as lost income, limited access to credit or devastation from natural disaster.

Starvation – Suffering or death from extreme or prolonged lack of food.

Structural adjustment programs (SAPs) – Economic policy changes, often negotiated as a condition for loans, intended to stimulate economic growth. These measures generally involve reducing the role of government in the economy and increasing exports.

Stunting – Failure to grow to normal height caused by chronic undernutrition during the formative years of childhood.

Subsidy – A direct or indirect benefit granted by a government for the production or distribution (including export) of a good or to supplement other services.

Supply control programs – Programs designed to influence the supply of farm products on the market. Past and current programs have been both mandatory (farmers who produce in excess of assigned levels are penalized) and voluntary (farmers are encouraged to participate through financial incentives).

Sustainable agriculture – Agriculture that is grown in a way that does not deplete the earth of natural resources, does not harm the surrounding ecological equilibrium and allows for continued farming on the same land year after year.

Sustainable development – The reduction of hunger and poverty in environmentally sound ways. It includes: meeting basic human needs, expanding economic opportunities, protecting and enhancing the environment, and promoting pluralism and democratic participation.

Target prices – Support levels established by law prior to 1996 for wheat, corn, grain sorghum, barley, oats, rice and upland cotton. The 1996 farm bill did not reauthorize target prices. The 2002 farm bill reauthorized target prices for covered commodities to be used in calculating counter-cyclical payments.

Tariff – Tax or duty placed on imported, and sometimes exported, goods to protect domestic producers by keeping prices higher than world prices or to generate revenue for the government.

Trade deficit – The difference between the value of a country's imports and the value of its exports when the former is greater than the latter.

Transparency – The degree to which one can see the decision-making processes related to policies and spending priorities in a country or organization. A higher degree of transparency means more open management.

Under-5 mortality rate – The annual number of deaths of children younger than 5 years of age per 1,000 live births. A high rate correlates closely with hunger and malnutrition.

Undernutrition – A condition resulting from inadequate consumption of calories, protein and/or nutrients to meet the basic physical requirements for an active and healthy life.

Uruguay Round: See *General Agreement on Tariffs and Trade (GATT)*.

Vertical integration – The merger of two or more companies in the same supply chain. For example, if a supermarket group, Tesco, takes over a supplier (who might be the Hughes Farm, the local egg supplier), that counts as vertical integration.

Wasting – A condition in which a person is seriously below the normal weight for her or his height due to acute undernutrition or a medical condition.

Welfare – Financial and other assistance provided by government and private charitable organizations to people in need in the areas of nutrition, education, health care and employment.

World Bank – A multilateral economic development institution established in 1944 to extend loans and technical assistance for development projects in developing countries. It formally is referred to as the International Bank for Reconstruction and Development.

World Trade Organization (WTO) – An international organization, headquartered in Geneva, established in 1995 to enforce the Uruguay Round global trade agreement.

Acknowledgments

We are deeply grateful for the valuable insights provided by sponsors and colleagues who contributed to this report.

A special thanks to Eugenio Diaz-Bonilla, research fellow at the International Food Policy Research Institute, and Fred Kirschenmann, director of the Leopold Center for Sustainable Agriculture, who made presentations related to agriculture and trade at the June 2002 consultation for the report.

The following sponsors and colleagues participated in the expert consultation and/or reviewed a draft manuscript of the report.

Patricia Bonnard, Norm Braksick, Mark Malloch Brown, Henrich Brunke, Peter Carry, Winston Caroo, Stuart Clark, Marc Cohen, Gary Cook, Edward Cooney, John Coonrod, Elizabeth Drake, Christopher Dunford, John Flynn, Patricia Forner, Catherine Guirkinger, Chuck Hassebrook, Judy Heffernan, Barbara Hoffmann, Robbin Johnson, Michael Kuchinsky, Wallace Ryan Kuroiwa, Sandra LeBlanc, Sarah Lucas, Ronald Mathies, Anthony Matthews, Martin McLaughlin, Paul Montacute, Sophia Murphy, Lee Newberg, Heather Nolen, Douglas O'Brien, Bill O'Keefe, Tom Peterson, Don Reeves, Charles Riemenschneider, Joan Rosenhauer, Peter Rottach, Sue Schramm, Susan Sechler, Wallace Smith, Deon Stuthman, Daniel Sumner, Judith Symonds, Mary Kay Thatcher, Betty Voskuil, Barbara Wallace, Joshua Walton, Marceline White, Lisa Wright.

The following colleagues assisted with research trips to California, Minnesota and North Carolina and/or met with report staff to discuss issues related to U.S. farm policy and agricultural trade.

Betty Bailey, Mark Barwick, Ruth Campbell, Mary Clouse, Victor Contreras, Nancy Creamer, Jack Daniel, Jaime Duran, Bernie Evans, Jon Evert, Ralph Garcia, Kathryn Gilje, David Gist, Natalie Hampton, Chuck Hassebrook, Tom Mahr, Herman Hendrickson, W.R. "Bill" Jester, Robbin Johnson, Hans Kandel, Andy Kubiak, Rick Miller, Martha Mobley, David Orden, Doug Peterson, Paul Porter, Marty Primus, Bonnie Raquet, Jason Roehrig, Sherman Robinson, Jose Rodriguez, Deon Stuthman, Daniel Sumner, Dale Thorenson, Tammy Walhof, Kristin Wilson, Shoshana Zatz.

Thank you to the many farmers and Rural Life Outreach staff who shared their experiences with us over breakfast at the Frying Pan Restaurant in Moorhead, Minn., and the organic farmers who shared their thoughts with us as part of a test plot tour and dinner sponsored by the University of Minnesota, Agriculture Extension Services.

Sarah Farmer and Judy Siegel helped with the early research and editorial discussions of the report.

We also extend our gratitude to Bread for the World/Bread for the World Institute staff who provided comments, guidance and support in the research, writing and production of the report.

Sponsors

Patrons

Episcopal Relief & Development provides emergency assistance and rehabilitative support to people affected by natural disasters, war and civil strife. It also funds development projects around the world. Episcopal Relief and Development is the collective response of Episcopalians to help people in need in the United States and around the world. It strives to be the organized, tangible response to Christ's call to minister to the hungry and thirsty, the sick and those in prison, to clothe the naked and welcome the stranger. The Committee works with churches in the Anglican Communion as well as with other denominations, local organizations and partner agencies.

> 815 Second Avenue
> New York, NY 10017 USA
> Phone: (800) 334-7626
> Fax: (212) 983-6377
> Web site: www.er-d.org

Evangelical Lutheran Church in America World Hunger Program is a 26-year-old ministry that confronts hunger and poverty through emergency relief, long-term development, education, advocacy and stewardship of financial resources. Seventy-two percent of the program works internationally and 28 percent works within the United States. Lutheran World Relief (Baltimore) and Lutheran World Federation (Geneva) are key implementing partners in international relief and development throughout the world.

> 8765 West Higgins Road
> Chicago, IL 60631-4190 USA
> Phone: (800) 638-3522, ext. 2709
> Fax: (773) 380-2707

Christian Children's Fund (CCF) is a global force for children, helping the world's poorest and most vulnerable children survive and thrive to reach their full potential. One of the world's oldest and most respected international child development organizations, CCF works in 31 countries and assists approximately 4.6 million children and families worldwide, regardless of race, creed or origin.

CCF is a member of CCF International, a network of affiliated worldwide organizations, working for the well-being of children in 51 countries. CCF International supports locally led initiatives that strengthen families and communities, helping them overcome poverty and protect the rights of their children. CCF programs seek to be holistic and comprehensive, incorporating health, education, nutrition and livelihood interventions to protect, nurture and develop children in a sustainable way. CCF works in any environment where poverty, conflict and disaster threaten the well-being of children.

> 2821 Emerywood Parkway
> Richmond, VA 23294
> Phone: (800) 776-6767
> Web site: www.christianchildrensfund.org

The Community of Christ World Hunger Committee seeks to engage the church and others in a response to the needs of hungry people throughout the world. Its primary purpose is to support programs of food production, storage and distribution; fund projects to provide potable water; supply farm animals; instruct in food preparation and nutrition; and educate in marketing strategies for produce. It also seeks to advocate for the hungry and educate about the causes and alleviation of hunger in the world.

The majority of proposals reviewed by the committee originate with Outreach International and World Accord, agencies recognized by the church as engaged in participatory human development that is global in scope. Direct grants for community hunger projects, as well as disaster relief, also are considered.

> 1001 West Walnut
> Independence, MO 64050-3562 USA
> Phone: (816) 833-1000, ext. 3073
> Fax: (816) 521-3096
> Web site: www.CofChrist.org/hunger

Covenant World Relief is the relief and development arm of The Evangelical Covenant Church. Covenant World Relief was formed in response to the Covenant's historic commitment to being actively involved in Christ's mission to respond to the spiritual and physical needs of others.

> 5101 North Francisco Avenue
> Chicago, IL 60625-3611 USA
> Phone: (773) 784-3000
> Fax: (773) 784-4366
> E-mail: webster@covchurch.org
> Web site: www.covchurch.org

The Food and Agriculture Organization of the United Nations (FAO) was founded in 1945 with a mandate to raise levels of nutrition and standards of living, improve agricultural productivity and better the condition of rural populations.

Today, FAO is one of the largest specialized agencies in the United Nations and the lead agency for agriculture, forestry, fisheries and rural development. An intergovernmental organization, FAO has 183 member countries plus one member organization, the European Community. A specific FAO priority is encouraging sustainable agriculture and rural development, a long-term strategy for increasing food production and food security while conserving and managing natural resources.

> Viale delle Terme
> di Caracalla
> 00100 Rome, Italy
> Phone: (+39 06) 57051
> Fax: (+39 06) 570 53152
> E-mail: FAO-HQ@fao.org
> Web site: www.fao.org
>
> Liaison Office with
> North America (LOWA)
> 2175 K Street NW, Suite 300
> Washington, DC 20437-0001 USA
> Phone: (202) 653-2400
> Fax: (202) 653-5760

Sponsors

International Fund for Agricultural Development (IFAD) is an international financial institution and specialized agency of the United Nations headquartered in Rome. Established as a result of the 1974 World Food Conference, IFAD has an exclusive mission: to work with the poorest populations in rural areas of developing countries to eliminate hunger and poverty, enhance food security, raise productivity and incomes, and improve the quality of lives. IFAD adopts and advocates a targeted, community-based approach that emphasizes empowering rural poor people and promoting their access to productive resources.

Via del Serafico, 107
00142 Rome, Italy
Phone: 39 6 54591
Fax: 39 6 5043463
E-mail: ifad@ifad.org

1775 K Street NW, Suite 410
Washington, DC 20006 USA
Phone: (202) 331-9099
Fax: (202) 331-9366
Web site: www.ifad.org

The Lutheran Church–Missouri Synod World Relief/Human Care provides emergency relief and sustainable development funding for domestic and international projects. LCMS World Relief provides grants for Lutheran congregations and social ministry organizations in the United States as well as other groups with Lutheran involvement that are engaged in ministries of human care. Domestic support also is provided to Lutheran Disaster Response and Lutheran Immigration and Refugee Service. International relief and development assistance is channeled through the Synod's mission stations and partner churches as well as through Lutheran World Relief.

1333 South Kirkwood Road
St. Louis, MO 63122-7295 USA
Phone: (800) 248-1930
Fax: (314) 996-1128
E-mail: lcms.worldrelief@lcms.org

Lutheran World Relief (LWR) acts on behalf of U.S. Lutherans in response to natural disasters, humanitarian crises and chronic poverty in some 50 countries in Africa, Asia, Latin America and the Middle East. In partnership with local organizations, LWR supports more than 150 community projects to improve food production, health care, environment and employment, with special emphasis on training and gender equality. LWR monitors legislation on foreign aid and development, and advocates for public policies that address the root causes of hunger and poverty. LWR values the God-given gifts that each person can bring to the task of promoting peace, justice and human dignity. LWR began its work in 1945.

Lutheran World Relief
700 Light Street
Baltimore, MD 21230-3850 USA
Phone: (410) 230-2700
or (800) LWR-LWR-2
E-mail: lwr@lwr.org

LWR Office of Public Policy
122 C Street NW, Suite 125
Washington, DC 20001 USA
Phone: (202) 783-6887
Fax: (202) 783-5328
Web site: www.lwr.org

For more than 30 years, the **Presbyterian Hunger Program** has provided a channel for congregations to respond to hunger in the United States and around the world. With a commitment to the ecumenical sharing of human and financial resources, the program provides support for direct food relief efforts, sustainable development and public policy advocacy. A network of 100 Hunger Action Enablers leads the Presbyterian Church (USA) in the study of hunger issues, engagement with communities of need, advocacy for just public policies, and the movement toward simpler corporate and personal lifestyles.

100 Witherspoon Street
Louisville, KY 40202-1396 USA
Phone: (502) 569-5816
Fax: (502) 569-8963
Web site: www.pcusa.org/hunger

Share Our Strength (SOS) works toward ending hunger and poverty in the United States and abroad by supporting food assistance, treating malnutrition and other consequences of hunger, and promoting economic independence among people in need. SOS meets immediate demands for food while investing in long-term solutions to hunger and poverty by mobilizing both industry and individuals in such efforts as Operation Frontline, a food and nutrition education program that trains culinary professionals and financial planners who volunteer to teach six-week cooking, nutrition, food budgeting and financial planning classes to low-income individuals; Taste of the Nation, the nation's largest culinary benefit to fight hunger; and Writers Harvest: The National Reading, the nation's largest literary benefit.

733 15th Street NW, Suite 640
Washington, DC 20005 USA
Phone: (202) 393-2925
Fax: (202) 347-5868
E-mail: info@strength.org
Web site: www.strength.org

The U.N. Development Program (UNDP) is the United Nation's global development network, advocating for change and connecting countries to knowledge, experience and resources to help people build a better life. UNDP is on the ground in 166 countries, working with them on their own solutions to global and national development challenges. As they develop local capacity, they draw on the people of UNDP and its wide range of partners.

1 U.N. Plaza, 20th Floor
New York, NY 10017 USA
Web site: www.undp.org

The U.N. World Food Program (WFP) is the food-aid arm of the United Nations and the primary U.N. agency fighting to eradicate world hunger. WFP strives to provide "food for life" to sustain victims of man-made and natural disasters; "food for growth" aims to improve the nutrition and quality of life of the most vulnerable people at critical times in their lives; and "food for work" seeks to help build assets and promote the self-reliance of poor people and communities, particularly through labor-intensive work programs. WFP provides commodities to least developed and low-income food-deficit countries, with a focus on feeding the most vulnerable people: women, children and the elderly. WFP envisions a world in which every woman, man and child has access, at all times, to the food needed for an active and healthy life.

Via Cesare Giulio Viola, 68
Parco dei Medici
00148 Rome, Italy
Phone: (39-06) 6513-1
Fax: (39-06) 6590-632/637
Web site: www.wfp.org

The United Methodist Committee on Relief (UMCOR) was formed in 1940 in response to the suffering of people during World War II. It was a "voice of conscience" expressing the concern of the church for the disrupted and devastated lives churned out by the war. UMCOR has expanded its ministry to more than 70 countries by ministering with compassion to "persons in need, through programs and services which provide immediate relief and long-term attention to the root causes of their need." Focusing on refugee, hunger and disaster ministries, the work of UMCOR, a program department of the General Board of Global Ministries of the United Methodist Church, is carried out through direct services and a worldwide network of national and international church agencies that cooperate in the task of alleviating human suffering.

475 Riverside Drive, Room 330
New York, NY 10115 USA
Phone: (212) 870-3816
Hotline: (800) 841-1235
Fax: (212) 870-3624
E-mail: umcor@gbgm-umc.org

Benefactors

The Adventist Development and Relief Agency International (ADRA) is an independent humanitarian agency established in 1984 for the specific purpose of providing individual and community development and disaster relief. Committed to improving quality of human life, ADRA serves people in need without regard to their ethnic, political or religious association.

ADRA's development and relief work is divided among five core activities: food security, economic development, primary health, disaster preparedness and response, and basic education. In addition to feeding the hungry, ADRA works to prevent hunger through long-term development programs. Struggling families and individuals learn how to support and feed themselves by using agricultural methods that do not hurt the environment. ADRA also helps improve access to food and ensures equitable distribution of food among community members.

12501 Old Columbia Pike
Silver Spring, MD 20904 USA
Phone: (888) 237-2367
Web site: www.adra.org

America's Second Harvest is the nation's largest domestic hunger relief organization. Through a network of more than 200 food banks and food-rescue programs, America's Second Harvest provides emergency food assistance to more than 23 million hungry Americans each year, 8 million of whom are children. Last year, America's Second Harvest distributed 1.7 billion pounds of food to needy Americans, serving all 50 states and Puerto Rico. Its goal is to end hunger in America.

35 East Wacker Drive, Suite 2000
Chicago, IL 60601
Phone: (312) 263-2303
Fax: (312) 263-5626
E-mail: feedback@secondharvest.org
Web site: www.secondharvest.org

Baptist World Aid (BWAid) works through Baptist communities around the world, mitigating suffering and providing long-range help for persons in need, regardless of religion, nationality, tribe or class. BWAid also helps poor people avoid situations of famine and malnourishment and improves their capacity for self-help and wage earning.

405 North Washington Street
Falls Church, VA 22046 USA
Phone: (703) 790-8980
Fax: (703) 790-5719
E-mail: bwaid@bwanet.org
Web site: www.bwanet.org/bwaid

Brot für die Welt is an association of German Protestant churches that seeks to overcome poverty and hunger in developing countries, as an expression of their Christian faith and convictions, by funding programs of development, relief and advocacy. Founded in 1959, Brot für die Welt has funded more than 20,000 programs in more than 100 nations in Africa, Asia and Latin America. Its programs have shifted from relief efforts to development and empowerment. Brot für die Welt's education programs in Germany are intended to lead to greater understanding and lifestyle changes personally, and policy reform nationally, internationally and among European communities.

Stafflenbergstrasse 76; Postfach 10 11 42
D-70010 Stuttgart, Germany
Phone: 0049 711 2159 268
Fax: 011 49 7 11 2159 110
E-mail: bfdwinformation@brot-fuer-die-welt.org

Canadian Foodgrains Bank is a specialized food-program agency established in 1982 and now operated by 13 church-related relief and development organizations. It collects substantial amounts of food grain donations directly from Canadian farmers and more than 200 community groups that collectively grow crops for donation to the Canadian Foodgrains Bank. The approximately $3.9 million per year in grain and cash donations, combined with matching support from the Canadian International Development Agency, are used to provide food assistance and

Sponsors

food security support to food-deficit countries and communities around the world to meet immediate food needs and support the longer-term ability of communities and households to feed themselves. In addition, the Canadian Foodgrains Bank engages in focused public policy research and advocacy in the areas of agricultural trade policy, Canadian aid policy and the application of a human rights approach to reducing hunger.

> Box 767, 400-280 Smith Street
> Winnipeg, Manitoba
> Canada R3C 2L4
> Phone: (204) 944-1993
> Fax: (204) 943-2597
> E-mail: cfgb@foodgrainsbank.ca
> Web site: www.foodgrainsbank.ca

Catholic Relief Services (CRS) is the overseas relief and development agency of the U.S. Catholic community. Founded in 1943, CRS provides more than $300 million in development and relief assistance in more than 80 nations worldwide. Working in partnership with the Catholic church and other local institutions in each country, CRS works to alleviate poverty, hunger and suffering, and supports peace-building and reconciliation initiatives. Assistance is given solely on the basis of need. Even while responding to emergencies, CRS supports more than 2,000 development projects designed to build local self-sufficiency. CRS works in conjunction with Caritas Internationalis and CIDSE, worldwide associations of Catholic relief and development agencies. Together, these groups build the capacity of local nonprofit organizations to provide long-term solutions. In the United States, CRS seeks to educate and build awareness on issues of world poverty and hunger and serves as an advocate for public policy changes in the interest of poor people overseas.

> 209 West Fayette Street
> Baltimore, MD 21201-3443 USA
> Phone: (410) 625-2220
> Fax: (410) 685-1635
> E-mail: webmaster@catholicrelief.org
> Web site: www.catholicrelief.org

Church World Service (CWS) is a global relief, development and refugee-assistance ministry of the 35 Protestant and Orthodox communions that work together through the National Council of the Churches of Christ in the United States. Founded in 1946, CWS works in partnership with local church organizations in more than 80 countries worldwide, supporting sustainable self-help development of people that respects the environment, meets emergency needs and addresses root causes of poverty and powerlessness.

> 475 Riverside Drive, Suite 678
> New York, NY 10115-0050 USA
> Phone: (800) 297-1516
> Fax: (212) 870-3523
> Web site: www.churchworldservice.org

EuronAid, which began in 1980 to help deal with Europe's food surplus, is a specialized, operational network of European nongovernmental organizations active in food aid and food security for the purpose of eradicating poverty and alleviating the causes of hunger and food insecurity. EuronAid has 32 active members and has served more than 100 nongovernmental organizations worldwide.

> P.O. Box 12
> NL-2501 CA
> The Hague, The Netherlands
> Phone: 31 70 3305757
> Fax: 31 70 3641701
> E-mail: euronaid@euronaid.nl
> Web site: www.euronaid.nl

Foods Resource Bank is a Christian response to world hunger. Its goal is for hungry people to know the dignity and pride of feeding themselves by making it possible for them, through sustainable agricultural programs, to produce food for their families with extra to share, barter or sell. Foods Resource Bank endeavors to twin rural and urban communities in "Growing Projects" in the United States, allowing participants to give a gift only they can give. These volunteers grow crops, sell them in the United States, and the resulting money is used by implementing members (many of the mainline denominations) to establish food security programs abroad. Foods Resource Bank creates solidarity between America's bounty and the needs of the world's hungry.

> 2141 Parkview
> Kalamazoo, MI 49008 USA
> Phone: (269) 349-3467
> Web site: www.FoodsResourceBank.org

Future Harvest is a global initiative, incorporated in June 1998 as a charitable and educational organization to advance debate and catalyze action for a world with less poverty, a healthier human family and a better environment.

Future Harvest works to promote awareness and educate the general public and decision makers about the importance of food production and the role of agricultural science in meeting the human and environmental challenges of today and tomorrow, as well as build financial support for scientific research and charitable projects that bring the results of this research to rural communities, farmers and their families in developing countries.

> 2020 Pennsylvania Avenue NW, PMB 238
> Washington, DC 20006-1846 USA
> Phone: (202) 473-1142
> E-mail: info@futureharvest.org
> Web site: www.futureharvest.org

Heifer International is a nonprofit charitable organization working to end world hunger by giving cows, goats and 25 other kinds of livestock to impoverished, undernourished families around the globe. In turn, these people give their animals' offspring to others, multiplying the benefits of each donated animal. "Passing the gift" is fundamental to Heifer's approach to sustainable development. As people share their animals' offspring with others along with their knowledge and resources, an ever-expanding network of hope, dignity and self-reliance is created that expands the globe.

Since it began in 1944, Heifer has worked directly with more than 4 million families in 128 countries and 38 states in the United States, and has affected the lives of millions more through an average of six pass-on animals for each animal it provides. Each year Heifer's message of hope reaches millions of people through the media and through its own publications, such as its quarterly *World Ark* magazine. More than 40,000 people a year visit Heifer's three learning centers in Arkansas, California and Massachusetts where they participate in seminars, service learning projects and hunger immersion experiences.

1015 Louisiana Street
Little Rock, AR 72202 USA
Phone: (501) 907-2600
Fax: (501) 907-2602
Web site: www.heifer.org

MAZON: A Jewish Response to Hunger has granted more than $28 million since 1986 to nonprofit organizations confronting hunger in the United States and abroad. MAZON (the Hebrew word for "food") awards grants principally to programs working to pre- vent and alleviate hunger in the United States. Grantees include emergency and direct food assistance programs, food banks, multiservice organizations, anti-hunger advocacy/education and research projects, and international hunger relief and agricultural development programs in Israel and impoverished countries. Although responsive to organizations serving impoverished Jews, in keeping with the best of Jewish tradition, MAZON responds to all who are in need.

1990 South Bundy Drive, Suite 260
Los Angeles, CA 90025 USA
Phone: (310) 442-0020
Fax: (310) 442-0030
Web site: www.mazon.org

Mennonite Central Committee (MCC), founded in 1920 by the Mennonite and Brethren in Christ churches in North America, seeks to demonstrate God's love by working among people suffer- ing from poverty, conflict, oppression and natural disaster. MCC serves as a channel of interchange by building relationships that are mutually transformative. MCC strives for peace, justice and dignity of all people by sharing our experiences, resources and faith in Jesus Christ. MCC's priorities include disaster relief, capacity building (including Ten Thousand Villages), peace build- ing and connecting people.

21 South 12th Street, Box 500
Akron, PA 17501 USA
Phone: (717) 859-1151
Fax: (717) 859-2171
E-mail: mailbox@mcc.org
Web site: www.mcc.org

Oxfam America is dedicated to creating lasting solutions to global poverty and hunger by working in partnership with grass- roots organizations promoting sustainable development in Africa, Asia, the Caribbean and the Americas, including the United States.

Oxfam's grant awards and advocacy work aim to challenge the structural barriers that foster conflict and human suffering and limit people from gaining the skills, resources and power to become self-sufficient. Oxfam America envisions a world in which all people one day shall know freedom – freedom to achieve their fullest potential and to live secure from the dangers of hunger, deprivation and oppression – through the creation of a global movement of economic and social justice.

26 West Street
Boston, MA 02111 USA
Phone: (800) 77-OXFAM
Fax: (617) 728-2594
E-mail: oxfamusa@igc.apc.org
Web site: www.oxfamamerica.org

The mission of **Physicians Against World Hunger** is to alleviate chronic hunger by supporting programs that implement microlending and education to break the hunger cycle. As part of this educational service, beginning in 2003, Physicians Against World Hunger also will make available a speaker to societies and organizations that wish to know more about world hunger.

2 Stowe Road, Suite 13
Peekskill, NY 10566 USA
Phone: (914) 737-8570
Fax: (914) 737-6016
Web site: www.pawh.org

U.S. Fund for UNICEF works for the survival, protection and development of children worldwide through education, advocacy and fundraising. UNICEF works in more than 160 countries and territories providing needed assistance in the areas of health, nutrition, safe water and sanitation, education, child protection, and emergency relief.

333 East 38th Street, 6th Floor
New York, NY 10016 USA
Phone: (212) 686-5522
Fax: (212) 779-1679
E-mail: information@unicefusa.org
Web site: www.unicefusa.org

World Vision was founded in 1950 as a Christian humanitarian organization, serving the world's poorest children and families in nearly 100 countries. World Vision helps transform the lives of children and families in need around the world, without regard to religious beliefs, gender, race or ethnic background. Through sponsorship, World Vision assists children in struggling communi- ties in more than 100 countries with food, education, health care and vocational training, supported by monthly contributions from donors.

34834 Weyerhaeuser Way South
Federal Way, WA 98001 USA
Phone: (888) 511-6593
Web site: www.worldvision.org

Sponsors

Founded in 1961, the **Academy for Educational Development** (AED) is an independent, nonprofit organization committed to solving critical social problems. One of the world's foremost human and social development organizations, AED operates more than 200 programs to help individuals and communities improve their education, health, environment and economic opportunities in more than 130 countries and all 50 U.S. states.

> 1825 Connecticut Avenue NW
> Washington, DC 20009 USA
> Phone: (202) 884-8000
> Fax: (202) 884-8400
> E-mail: admin@aed.org
> Web site: www.aed.org

Reformed Church in America, founded in 1628, is the oldest Protestant denomination in North America. As part of its long history, the Reformed Church World Service (RCWS) is a program of mission services through which the church seeks to fulfill the biblical mandate to feed the hungry, give water to the thirsty, welcome the stranger and care for the sick. RCWS provides emergency relief to disaster victims and others in need of immediate assistance, participating in rehabilitation for people who have lost their homes and jobs, encouraging development of long-term solutions to overcome the problem of hunger and poverty, and seeking justice through advocacy on behalf of poor and needy people.

> 4500 60th Street SE
> Grand Rapids, MI 49512 USA
> Phone: (800) 968-3943
> Web site: www.rca.org

United Church of Christ (UCC): Justice and Witness Ministries; Wider Church Ministries is committed to sharing life in Christ and to an ecumenical global sharing of resources and prophetic vision of a just and peaceful world order, joining with God's concern for the poor and oppressed. Its missions extend to Africa, East Asia and the Pacific, Southern Asia, Latin America and the Caribbean. UCC Justice and Witness Ministries coordinates and stimulates all UCC hunger and hunger-related ministries, increases awareness and understanding of world hunger and related issues, and promotes, interprets and administers the UCC Hunger Action Fund.

> 700 Prospect Avenue
> Cleveland, OH 44115 USA
> Phone: (216) 736-3200
> Fax: (216) 736-3203
> E-mail: wcm@ucc.org
> Web site: www.ucc.org

World Hope International is a Christian relief and development organization seeking to transform lives through health care, education and enterprise. World Hope partners with individuals and organizations from around the world to promote justice, encourage self-sufficiency and inspire hope through programs, such as economic development, leadership and skill training, child sponsorship, and community health education. World Hope values grassroots, community-based development that is responsive to local initiatives. This approach affirms personal human dignity and enables people to create and act on their behalf and that of their community. World Hope also is committed to long-term sustainable development and the development and empowerment of local leaders. World Hope works in 30 countries around the world.

> P.O. Box 2815
> Springfield, VA 22152 USA
> Phone: (703) 922-9125
> Fax: (703) 923-9418
> E-mail: whi@worldhope.net
> Web site: www.WorldHope.org

Since 1944, **World Relief** has been helping churches to assist suffering people worldwide in the name of Jesus. As the humanitarian arm of the National Association of Evangelicals, World Relief equips churches to minister to hurting people's physical, emotional and spiritual needs. Working with local churches, World Relief serves in some of the poorest countries in the world. Its innovative ministries focus on microenterprise development, maternal and child health, HIV/AIDS, agricultural assistance, refugee care and emergency relief.

> 7 East Baltimore Street
> Baltimore, MD 21202 USA
> Phone: (443) 451-1900
> E-mail: worldrelief@wr.org
> Web site: www.worldrelief.org

Friends

ACDI/VOCA is a U.S.-based private nonprofit development organization that advances the pace of progress in emerging democracies and developing countries. Offering a comprehensive range of technical assistance services and strategies, ACDI/VOCA benefits small- and medium-scale enterprises, particularly agribusinesses, private and public associations, governmental agencies and others. ACDI/VOCA offers both long- and short-term assistance that focuses on economic growth at the grassroots level where long-lasting advancement begins and democratic traditions take hold. As appropriate, ACDI/VOCA provides a mix of volunteers and consultants, as well as methodologies honed through years of economic development success. This assistance is tailored to meet the unique needs of every ACDI/VOCA partner.

> 50 F Street NW, Suite 1075
> Washington, DC 20001 USA
> Phone: (202) 383-4961
> Fax: (202) 783-7204
> Web site: www.acdivoca.org

Action Against Hunger is an international humanitarian, non-governmental, nonreligious organization working to alleviate suffering of victims of hunger and malnutrition. It strives to address people's long-term food security needs, even while dealing with the short-term demands of acute food shortages, by implementing programs aimed at local self-sufficiency rather than merely providing temporary food aid.

Action Against Hunger was created in Paris in 1979 and since has developed within the framework of an interdependent international network, with headquarters in France (Paris), the United States (New York), the United Kingdom (London) and Spain (Madrid). Currently, its team of 4,400 international and national staff implements programs in 43 countries, collectively saving more than 4 million lives each year.

247 West 37th Street, Suite 1201
New York, NY 10018 USA
Phone: (212) 967-7800
Fax: (212) 967-5480
E-mail: aah@aah-usa.org
Web site: www.aah-usa.org

The Board of World Mission of the Moravian Church (BWM) represents the Moravian Church in America in overseas ministries. BWM nourishes formal mission partnerships with Moravian churches in Alaska, the eastern Caribbean, Guyana, Honduras, Labrador, Nicaragua and Tanzania, and with the Evangelical Church of the Dominican Republic. BWM supports medical clinics in Honduras and Nicaragua and has a long tradition of supporting educational efforts of all kinds. As a missionary-sending agency, BWM also is involved in evangelical witness among people who have had little opportunity to hear the gospel. Offices are in Bethlehem, Penn., and Winston-Salem, N.C.

1021 Center Street
Bethlehem, PA 18018 USA
Phone: (610) 868-1732
Fax: (610) 866-9223
E-mail: bwm@mcnp.org

Catholic Charities USA encourages people to help themselves by learning to advocate for their rights. By providing leadership, technical assistance, training and other resources, the national office enables local agencies to better devote resources to serving their communities. Catholic Charities promotes innovative strategies that address human needs and social injustices. The national office also advocates for social policies that aim to reduce poverty, improve the lives of children and families, and strengthen communities. In 2000 Catholic Charities provided food services to nearly 4 million people, clothing assistance to more than half a million people and provided temporary shelter to more than 100,000, in addition to helping nearly a million people with community-building services.

1731 King Street
Alexandria, VA 22314 USA
Phone: (703) 549-1390
Fax: (703) 549-1656
Web site: www.CatholicCharitiesUSA.org

Christian Reformed World Relief Committee (CRWRC) is the international relief and development agency of the Christian Reformed Church in North America. CRWRC carries out this ministry through a partnership with 170 churches and nongovernmental organizations in 30 countries around the world. Together, they: (1) respond to the needs of those in poverty through technical programs in agriculture, health, income generation and literacy; (2) develop strong Christian leadership at the community level; (3) emphasize evangelism and discipleship; (4) work for economic development and job creation; and (5) respond to disasters through emergency relief and long-term assistance. As a result, people and communities are able to overcome hunger and poverty in positive, permanent ways.

CRWRC – US
2850 Kalamazoo Avenue SE
Grand Rapids, MI 49560-0600 USA
Phone: (800) 552-7972
Fax: (616) 224-0806
E-mail: crwrc@crcna.org
Web site: www.crwrc.org

CRWRC – Canada
3475 Mainway
PO Box 5070 STN LCD 1
Burlington, ON L7R 3Y8
Canada
Phone: (800) 730-3490
Fax: (905) 336-8344

Christian Church (Disciples of Christ) has been spreading the gospel and exemplifying a passion for justice since 1832. With more than 3,700 churches in North America, the Christian Church (Disciples of Christ) is involved in many facets of justice work, from the environment to racial issues, from homelessness to hunger and nutrition programs, always with a focus on making a difference in the world by revealing the light of Christ.

130 East Washington Street
Indianapolis, IN 46204-3645 USA
Phone: (317) 635-3100
Web site: www.disciples.org

The Church of God, with national offices in Anderson, Ind., was founded in 1881. It has a long history of commitment to hunger relief and disaster aid and development. The Compassionate Ministries office of Church of God Ministries and its programs work in partnership with other domestic and international relief and assistance agencies to help feed and assist those in need.

1201 East 5th Street, Box 2420
Anderson, IN 46018-2420 USA
Phone: (765) 642-0256
Fax: (765) 648-2180
Web site: www.chog.org

Congressional Hunger Center (CHC) was formed in 1993 by Democratic and Republican members of Congress after the Select Committee on Hunger was eliminated. Now in its 10th year, CHC is training leaders at the community, national and international levels in solutions to hunger and poverty. Its leaders work in locations as varied as Native American reservations, urban Washington, D.C., and in Asia, Central America and Africa to gain experience with food security efforts at the grassroots level. Fellows then return to Washington, D.C., to help shape national

Sponsors

and international food security policy at a broad spectrum of host sites. Its two programs are the Bill Emerson National Hunger Fellows program, with a focus on domestic hunger, and the Mickey Leland International Hunger Fellows program, with a focus on global hunger. In addition, CHC administers a number of projects that educate members of Congress about hunger and poverty, and host occasional workshops and conferences covering food security and humanitarian issues.

> 229½ Pennsylvania Avenue, SE
> Washington, DC 20003 USA
> Phone: (202) 547-7022
> Fax: (202) 547-7575
> Web site: www.hungercenter.org

Food for the Hungry is an international organization that exists to fulfill a God-given mandate to help people overcome both physical and spiritual hungers. Efforts include integrated, child-focused development and relief programs in more than 25 countries in Africa, Asia and Latin America. Development efforts include programs that equip entire communities with the tools they need to pull themselves out of poverty. Additional relief efforts include responding to natural disasters, such as famines and earthquakes, and man-made disasters, such as war. Food for the Hungry also sends relief supplies to countries around the world.

> 7729 East Greenway Road
> Scottsdale, AZ 85260 USA
> Phone: (800) 2-HUNGER (800-248-6437)
> E-mail: hunger@fh.org
> Web site: www.fh.org

Founded in 1946, **Freedom from Hunger** fights chronic hunger with two of the most powerful and flexible resources ever created: money and information. Operating in rural regions of 13 developing nations, its Credit with Education programs build on the success of village banking by integrating basic health, nutrition, family planning and microenterprise management education into group meetings. Results from recent studies show beneficial impacts, not only on income and income-generating activities, but also on the health and nutrition of participants and their children. Freedom from Hunger's goal is to bring Credit with Education to 1.5 million women by the year 2005.

> 1644 DaVinci Court
> Davis, CA 95616 USA
> Phone: (800) 708-2555
> Fax: (530) 758-6241
> E-mail: info@freefromhunger.org

Islamic Society of North America (ISNA) is an association of Muslim organizations and individuals that serve the diverse needs of Muslims in North America. ISNA's mission is to provide a unified platform of expression for Islam; develop educational, outreach and social services that translate the teachings of the Quran and the Sunna into everyday living; and enhance Islamic identity within ISNA.

> Islamic Society of North America
> P.O. Box 38
> Plainfield, IN 46168 USA
> Phone: (317) 839-8157
> Fax: (317) 839-1840
> E-mail: membership@isna.net
> Web site: www.isna.net

Nazarene Compassionate Ministries International exists to incarnate the holistic ministry of Christ's compassion to the world, meeting physical, emotional, relational, intellectual and spiritual needs of people by providing resources to, empowering and enabling a network of individuals to touch their world in Jesus' name. Nazarene Compassionate Ministries is working in 143 areas worldwide, focusing on child development, disaster response and community development.

> 6401 The Paseo
> Kansas City, MO 64131-1231 USA
> Phone: (877) 626-4145
> Fax: (816) 333-2948
> E-mail: ncm@nazarene.org
> Web site: www.nazcompassion.org

Save the Children was founded in the United States in 1932 as a nonprofit child-assistance organization to make lasting positive change in the lives of children in need. Today, Save the Children works in 19 states in the United States and 47 other countries in the developing world to help children and families improve their health, education and economic opportunities. Save the Children helped 660,000 children and families rebuild their lives after war in the Balkans, an earthquake in Turkey and hurricanes in Nicaragua and Honduras, and has mobilized rapid life-support assistance for other children and families caught in the tragedies of natural and man-made disasters.

Save the Children is a member of the International Save the Children Alliance, an association of 26 independent organizations that provide child-oriented emergency response, development assistance and advocacy of children's rights in more than 100 countries.

> 54 Wilton Road
> Westport, CT 06880 USA
> Phone: (203) 221-4000 or (800) 728-3843
> Web site: www.savethechildren.org